Realisms Interlinked

Objects, Subjects, and Other Subjects

Also available from Bloomsbury

Comparative Philosophy without Borders,
edited by Arindam Chakrabarti and Ralph Weber
Imagination: Cross-Cultural Philosophical Analyses,
edited by Hans-Georg Moeller and Andrew Whitehead
Indian Epistemology and Metaphysics, edited by Joerg Tuske
Natural and Artifactual Objects in Contemporary Metaphysics,
edited by Richard Davies
Philosophy of Knowledge: A History, edited by Stephen Hetherington, Nicholas D. Smith, Henrik Lagerlund, Stephen Gaukroger, Markos Valaris
The Bloomsbury Research Handbook of Indian Aesthetics and the Philosophy of Art,
edited by Arindam Chakrabarti
The Bloomsbury Research Handbook of Indian Ethics, edited by Shyam Ranganathan

Realisms Interlinked

Objects, Subjects, and Other Subjects

Arindam Chakrabarti

BLOOMSBURY ACADEMIC
LONDON • NEW YORK • OXFORD • NEW DELHI • SYDNEY

BLOOMSBURY ACADEMIC
Bloomsbury Publishing Plc
50 Bedford Square, London, WC1B 3DP, UK
1385 Broadway, New York, NY 10018, USA
29 Earlsfort Terrace, Dublin 2, Ireland

BLOOMSBURY, BLOOMSBURY ACADEMIC and the Diana logo are trademarks of Bloomsbury Publishing Plc

First published in Great Britain 2020
Paperback edition published 2021

Cover design: Toby Way
Cover image: Still Life with Self Portrait (oil on canvas), Gertler, Mark (1891–1939) © Leeds Museums and Galleries (Leeds Art Gallery) U.K./Bridgeman Images

A catalogue record for this book is available from the British Library.

A catalog record for this book is available from the Library of Congress.

ISBN: HB: 978-1-3500-4446-3
PB: 978-1-3502-5007-9
ePDF: 978-1-3500-4447-0
eBook: 978-1-3500-4448-7

Typeset by Integra Software Services Pvt. Ltd

For Vrinda

Contents

List of Figures ix
Acknowledgments x

Part 1 Objects

Introduction: Do You See What I See? 3
1 I Touch What I Saw 9
2 Non-particular Individuals 21
3 On Perceiving Properties 35
4 Seeing Daffodils, Seeing as Daffodils, and Seeing Things Called "Daffodils" 45
5 Truth, Recognition of Truth, and Thoughtless Realism 51
6 Idealist Refutations of Idealism 65
7 Externality, Difference, and Inherence (*Samavāya*): Udayana's Refutation of Yogācāra Buddhist Pan-Mentalism 77
8 Is This a Dream? 91
9 The Object to a Verb: The Case of the Accusative 101

Part 2 Subjects

10 On Referring to the First Person 113
11 The Self at Other Times and in Other Bodies 127
12 Does Self-Awareness Turn the Self into an Object? 137
13 In Defense of an Inner Sense 145
14 Our Knowledge and Error about Our Own Cognitions 157
15 Fictionalism about the Mental 175
16 Nyāya Proofs for the Existence of the Self 185

Part 3 Other Subjects

17 Knowing You from the Bridge 197
18 The Grammar of Calling the Other 205
19 Knowing from the Words of Others 211
20 Can Another Person Teach Me What It Means? 225

21	Shadows of Ignorance	233
22	Concept Possession, Sense Experience, and Knowledge of a Language	247
23	On What There Will Be	255
24	Is There a World Out There? God Knows	273
25	Absence, Non-Existence, and Other Negative Things	285
	Notes	293
	Bibliography	316
	Index	327

List of Figures

1 El Greco—An Allegory with a Boy Lighting a Candle in the Company of an Ape and a Fool (Fábula). The Picture Art Collection/Alamy Stock Photo 4

2 The Müller-Lyer Illusion 168

3 Shadow of What? 234

Acknowledgments

The chapters of this book were written over a period of twenty-seven years, while I researched, taught, and delivered conference-papers or invited lectures on contemporary Anglo-American and classical Indian epistemology, metaphysics, philosophy of language, and philosophy of mind. I was able to teach in these areas using both Western and Indian analytical philosophies because I was taught by the best of teachers. Of them, the first four (Sir Peter Strawson, Sir Michael Dummett, Professor Bimal Krishna Matilal, and Pandit Vishvabandhu Tarkatirtha) are no more. In their absence, the last two (Professors Prabal Kumar Sen and D. Prahladachar) have been helping me understand the hardest texts of technical Indian philosophy for more than three decades now, setting up unreachable standards of clear exposition and selfless pedagogy.

At the Philosophy department of the University of Hawaii at Manoa, a three-year grant from John Templeton Foundation for research on Realism-links and Concepts of Omniscience enabled me to recruit my former graduate students Benjamin Zenk, Ian Nicolay, Amit Chaturvedi, Jane Allred, Adam Obrien, and Pavel Stankov as research assistants to help me in editing and retyping most of these chapters. Between 2010 and 2018, Dr. Ruth Lenney Kleinfeld's endowment for the Eastern Philosophy of Consciousness and the Humanities (EPOCH) program at UH Manoa enabled me to hire Emma Irwin as the most diligent and perceptive editor of my entire manuscript over the last three years. At the final stage, in 2019 Spring, I had editing help from Nicholas Raffel who I could recruit as a graduate assistant when I came to the department of Philosophy at Stony Brook University as the Nirmal and Augustina Mattoo Chair in Indic Humanities.

Finally, these realism-links could not have been forged without the persistent encouragement of the most thoroughgoing anti-realist Mark Siderits (to whom we all owe the phrase "fusion philosophy") who sustained me with friendship and philosophical disagreement over the last twenty-four years. Colleen Coalter, the exemplary commissioning editor at Bloomsbury, stood by me throughout this difficult period since offering me the book contract and getting the manuscript reviewed first by three and then two more anonymous referees, to whom I remain grateful.

Part One

Objects

Introduction: Do You See What I See?*

What is that thing a boy, a young man, and a monkey are intently looking at in El Greco's painting *An Allegory* (Figure 1)? It is something fiery from which the boy is trying to light a candle, by which all three faces are lit up. It is also the target of their joint attention. It is a thing, an object. One of the Sanskrit words for object "*artha*"—which happens to mean money too—is also the word for *purpose* and *meaning*. Even the English word "object" retains a connection with the concept of an end or purpose: the objective, as it is sometimes called. But meanings or purposes are never self-standing independent entities. They are always meanings of something or someone. A purpose or intended object is always someone's goal, intended by someone. Without someone consciously looking or aiming at it, it is not an object. Yet, an object, as we all understand it to be, has an opposite pull toward being a stand-alone *independent thing*, something which does not need anyone to look or aim at it for it to exist. If one is a realist about *objects*, taking external physical things that many of us perceive directly to be independent of our perceptions, then, this book argues, one is logically committed to being a realist about *subjects*, selves as enduring substances owning mental states. Buddhist or Humean phenomenalists, insofar as they embrace reductive anti-realism about persistent selves, thus, get logically committed to anti-realism about physical objects: ending up denying anything "permanent in perception" (to use the language of Kant's *Refutation of Idealism*)[1]. Similarly, if one is a realist about objects and subjects, one would be logically committed to realism about some universals or repeatable properties out there. A persistent self, over and above fleeting mental states which it owns, secures one kind of unity; and without that unity of a subject of experience, there is no objectivity of the object of experience which demands another kind of unity across different sensory modes of perception. With interconnected realisms about the self and the external object of perception in place, the chocolate candy my eyes see, my tongue and hands can claim to taste and touch, and you and I can correctly claim to touch the same thing on separate occasions. But universals such as tigerness and lotushood secure another kind of unity or property-identity across all the particular beasts we see as tigers, and all those flowers blooming

*We begin by taking a plunge into the most basic concept of an object which is succinctly articulated in realist terms by K. C. Bhattacharya: "By 'object' is meant a content that is other than the consciousness of it" see his *Studies in Kant*, Chapter 1 (Bhattacharyya, K. C., Edited by Bhattacharyya, Gopinath. (1983). *Studies in Philosophy* (2nd rev. ed.). Delhi: Motilal Banarsidass)

Figure 1 El Greco—An Allegory with a Boy Lighting a Candle in the Company of an Ape and a Fool (Fábula). The Picture Art Collection/Alamy Stock Photo.

in the water we call "lotus," arguably independently of the usage of the words for tigers and lotuses in any particular language. Besides such linking claims connecting metaphysical positions one can occupy in perennial debates concerning the world, the self, other selves, and common features that form natural kinds, this monograph also deals with classical Indian and modern Western refutations of idealism, the question of definition of truth and the status of truths unknown to anyone, and with the possibility or impossibility of non-conceptual perception and our knowledge of our own minds and of other minds.

The three parts of the book are divided according to the three basic concepts presupposed by the simple question: "*Do you see what I see?*" which one asks in order to check if one is seeing right. One does not need any special training in philosophy to understand that this question involves the concepts of an object, of myself, and of other subjects of experience. The reason why the concepts of objects, the self, and other selves deserve a fresh set of inquiry, even if my positive agenda of motivating interlinked realisms concerning them faces insuperable difficulties, is that each of these concepts comes already wrapped up in some cross-culturally shared sense of puzzlement.

Objects are *of* experience but not constituted by experience. They are mind-independent yet mind-intended things. The Sanskrit concepts of "*artha*" and "*viṣaya*" both bear the marks of this dual pull. In analyzing the concept of a material object (*rūpa*), an ancient Buddhist text (*The Path of Purification*[2]) states that the object of visual sensation puts up a resistance to ("objects to?") the eyes while coming within the range (*gocara*) of the eyes.[3] It claims to be both outside and given inside the content of perception. The object has to fit a cognition, but cannot be tucked inside the cognition in such a way as to be reduced to just an aspect of the cognition.

Besides this puzzle, there are other conceptual tussles at the heart of the concept of an object. Swarms of objects—including our own and non-human living bodies—constitute a common world in space and time that many of us at widely different moments and from widely different places can all be part of and observe. The world of events and processes that we suffer, enjoy, or simply undergo in which those objects participate gives rise to other puzzles of relation and constitution of facts and happenings. Then there are puzzles regarding objects and their properties permitting us to correctly or incorrectly arrange them into true and false propositions. Are we to regard those propositions as a distinct class of objects bearing truth-values as their properties? Such are the puzzles that the concept of an object comes wrapped up in.

The concept of the self as a subject of experience and the bearer of self-conscious thoughts brings with it its own share of puzzles. The singular term "I" which picks out nothing and none other than myself, without changing its sense, seems also to pick out distinct particular persons, one at a time, as the utterer changes. And yet, without flouting Frege, we cannot let a singular term with a single sense pick out distinct particulars as referents. Distinct senses but same reference are possible, as in the case of "The author of War and Peace" and "Leo Tolstoy"; but single sense determining many distinct references is not allowable except in case of a predicate expression such as "is a flower." (and even there the predicate refers to a single concept) Yet " … am an I" is not a legitimate predicate expression, although one twentieth-century Indian philosopher ended up saying that "I" is a common noun like the word "unique"! While each of us can understand "I"-sentences uttered by others, the full cognitive significance, the token mode of presentation through which each of us refers to herself or himself, is not entirely sharable. The meaning/sense of "I" seems to be at the same time public and private.

Finally, whichever addressee—another person—we may call by the commonest pronoun "you" in the singular, she is a self but not myself yet the very concept of a "second self other than myself" seems to smell of a contradiction. Our deepest concept of the self comes with a natural pull toward singleness which draws some philosophers toward a non-dualism of the purely subjective: the questioning of all otherness or difference as illusory. Yet it makes no sense to say that inner mental states, person-predicates such as "angry," "loves," or "is not feeling any pain" are only applicable to the single subject which is me, the speaker/writer of this token word "I." One cannot forget Strawson's mantra: "If only mine, then not even mine" which contraposed means that mental states are self-ascribable only if they are other-ascribable. Thus begins the puzzles surrounding the concept of a second person or other subjects.

Both in ancient Indian thought and in seventeenth-century and early twenty-first-century English thought, the concept of God has been invoked as a shock-absorber for these puzzles regarding objects, selves, and other selves. If we have to have the fundamental realist conception of how objects are in themselves, quite independently of how humans or birds or bats or worms find them to be, and yet preserve the connection between objectivity and availability to some (all-inclusive) perspective of a consciousness, then there must exist one Super-Consciousness, knownness to which constitutes objective reality and truth. But can an omniscient timeless spaceless consciousness have any perspective at all? Such a highly contentious claim about how God sees it all, if it could be defended, would connect all the above realisms with realism about God, at once taken to be the source of all objects, subjects, and other subjects. This transcendent yet immanent, bodiless yet personal, *Thou*, who may turn out to be identical with the soul, as it were, of the universe, generates its own puzzles. However riddled with contradictions this concept of God may seem, our examination of the interlinked realisms cannot afford to ignore Michael Dummett's claim that "the price of denying that God exists is to relinquish the idea that there is such a thing as how reality is in itself" (Dummett 2010, p. 44).[4]

Before we plunge into the actual battlefield of arguments back and forth between realists and anti-realists about physical objects, persons, and universal properties, let us examine perhaps the most general of all concepts that we use to make sense of the world and ourselves. This is the concept of "a thing." Let us see in how many distinct ways we can access the concept of "a thing," the blandest synonym of "an object."

An object is something, over which we can existentially quantify—it is what is denoted by a singular term. The most basic notion of an object, thus, makes it the semantic correlate of a *singular*, definitely identifying substantival linguistic expression—something P. F. Strawson would like to call a "basic particular."[5] To put it in only apparently paradoxical terms, whatever it is that a logical *subject*-term of a singular statement stands for is an *object.*

Then, in its most common use, a *thing* is a material body occupying a location in space with a more or less clear boundary. (But what about clouds? Rainbows? Shadows? Reflections in the mirror?) Such natural physical substances as a rock, a tree, a fruit, and such manmade artifacts as a table, a cell phone, a pencil-sharpener are all things. Second, a thing is the target of intentional attitude or awareness, and a common object of many people's perceptions or thoughts, something demonstrated as a "this" or "that." Even if what is pointed at with a deictic pronoun is an event or process, it can be loosely called "a thing." Third, in old German or English, (a Ding or thing) it is a meeting of different people, a cluster of human beings, a crowd. Fourth, it is a topic or subject of controversy, although it feels odd to say that an object is a subject-matter (is there a tension within this phrase "subject-matter" or is the tension all within the term "subject"?). Fifth, a thing is a personal style which is a distinguishing signature of an individual. For example: "It is Donald Trump's thing to repeat a word such as 'tremendous' or 'disaster.'" Sixth, a thing is something that exists (or existed) *independently of our perception, knowledge, or thought*. This sixth sense will occupy us in much of the first part of this monograph. Seventh, a thing is an object re-identifiable across different times, different perceivers, different sensory modalities of perception, and so on: a diachronically same-staying focus of interpersonal attention.

When we think of a thing, more narrowly, as an object, we find seven more negative criteria of what a thing/object is not. First, an object is not a thinking, feeling, and experiencing subject. I am not a thing, and I should not treat you or another person as a thing/object. A thing/object is usually not a predicated property, but a particular substance which is made the subject of a judgment. This criterion goes back to the "topic" sense of the fourth positive criterion: it is that about which we make a statement or judgment, not the predicate. A thing/object is not a concept, which harks back to

Frege's classic *object* (*Gegenstand*) versus *concept* (*Begriff*) distinction. A thing/object by itself is not a fact or what-is-the-case. (Could the object itself be a proposition? Could the proposition that Trump is psychologically unstable itself be the object of our consideration or conjecture or denial or even knowledge?)

A thing may be material, but the amorphous stuff or uncountable mass out of which things may be made cannot be called "a thing," just as the class of all dogs is not a dog. Thus, water or clay, iron or oxygen is matter but not a thing or object. A drop of water, a lump of clay, etc. can be an object/thing. An event or process is not a thing, although on certain occasions it can be spoken of as "a thing." It hardly seems apt to describe the First World War or the 2011 Earthquake in Japan as an object. Finally, a relation is not a thing, but what may subsist between things. Treating a relation itself as an object/thing tends to lead to a notorious vicious regress. (But can there be abstract objects? Non-particular individuals? Are subjects one kind of objects? When I think of myself, do I turn myself into an object of thought? Some of these questions will be discussed in the book later on).

Perhaps, instead of "thing," the concept of "reality" or "entity" should be taken to be the concept of the widest generality. It is surely more general than the concept of a substance or the concept of a particular. Everything that exists can be said to possess reality or be a real, or be an entity. But the concept of an object seems to be of even wider generality. Even an unreal, doubtfully real, or a non-existent thing is an object. The Cheshire Cat is one object, and Humpty Dumpty and Charlotte the altruistic spider are other objects, although how many unicorns there are may be an unanswerable question, each of them would have to count as a distinct object. According to some, the I, being a subject, is not an object—not because it does not exist or because its identity criterion is vague—but because it is never just an object of knowledge. Was that what the Buddha or Wittgenstein was getting at by proving that the I is not an entity in the world?

One way in which the concept of a thing, via the concept of our experience of a thing, leads to the concept of an experiencer or subject, is by the contrast between how a thing appears (in a certain lighting, from a certain distance, or through a certain medium or in a certain state of the mind and the body) and how it really is. There is no objectivity without the contrast between appearance and reality, and no appearance without someone to whom it appears.

When looking at a schematic line-drawing of a prism or cube, one seems to have a choice of thinking either that one is looking at those lines on paper, or that one is looking at how the lines come across to oneself, the appearance of those lines. But if appearances are mental, hence inner, then one should not be able to look at them—visually. Are mental states themselves objects? If they are directly accessible only to one single self, hence "logically private," can they be objects?

In grammar, an object is the accusative of a verb—what is intended by the verb. An object is that which bears the fruit of the action. I throw the ball and the effect of throwing affects the ball which then changes location. That which changes location by the throwing is the thrown object. I eat a slice of bread and it gets depleted as an effect of the action (eating) of which it is the object. In the cognitive case, an action is an act of awareness. But does my knowing or perceiving then make a difference to the object?

Raising such perennial questions, broadly speaking, this book is going to be about the world, one's own mind, and other minds, with forays into related fundamental questions of philosophy regarding truth, self, shadowy things, God, and absence. Apart from conceptual clarification and progress toward alternative solutions of substantial philosophical issues, these chapters demonstrate the advantages of doing philosophy in a cosmopolitan key, drawing equally from the wealth of arguments in Sanskrit, as well as Anglo-American and European sources, without slipping into woolly, difference-ignoring, "who-said-it first" sort of cultural comparisons. Its twenty-four chapters together give us a preview of future metaphysics, epistemology, and philosophy of mind without borders.

The chapters, beginning with an analysis of the concept of a thing, and ending with an analysis of the concepts of absence and nothing, together urge us—not so much to take sides in realism-versus-antirealism debates—but to excavate tunnels of interconnections between realisms with respect to different kinds of things.

1

I Touch What I Saw

Introduction: realism-links

The first realism-link I want to explore is between external-world realism and realism about the self. What I mean by realism about the self[1] will become clear as soon as I restate my point in clearer terms. Both realisms derive support from the plain fact of perceptual re-identification of objects across times and senses. In the face of that fact, realism about a persistent substantial self would turn out to be inconsistent with anti-realism about external physical objects. This will be the major contention of this opening chapter.

The Berkeleyan view that there is an abiding ego undergoing subjective states but no material objects for these states to focus on will be proved inconsistent. Equally incoherent, I shall argue, is the Parfitian[2] view that there are more or less persistent material objects plus experiences and thoughts about them but no stable owners of those states of consciousness. A reductive anti-realism about selves will logically commit us to a similar diffusion of material bodies into their secondary qualities, and of those, in turn, to subjective experiences and expectations. If we are afraid of such idealisms we should better not flirt with such "self"-lessness.

We are seemingly left with two alternatives: embrace dualism, that is, a full-fledged realism about substantial selves and material bodies, or adopt a radically reductive empiricism which yields nebulous aggregates of twilight qualities. Nyāya and Descartes took the first option. Buddhists and William James went for the second. Perhaps there are other more drastic revisionary alternative positions. The views I consider all accept the reality of thoughts or experiences—the common middle ground uncontroversial across the board for a dualist, idealist, no-soul-ist, radical empiricist, or even Lichtenberg[3]. Of course, one could deny even that, as fictionalism about consciousness does, and just consider matter to be real. In this chapter I cannot argue in detail against all eliminative or reductive views. But I don't want to end up in a Jaina vein with a disjunctive metaphysics.[4] It will be clear that the common-sense realistic package is more to my taste. I should like to argue that the

A version of Chapter 1 was read at the Sixth East West Philosophers' Conference at Hawaii in August 1989. I am thankful to the anonymous referees for suggesting improvements. Much of the research was done during my term (1988–1990) as a Jacobsen Fellow at University College London. First published in: *Philosophy and Phenomenological Research* LII, no. 1 (March 1992).

picture of us as ownerless objectless rivers of consciousness fails to account for re-identificatory experience. By eventually fudging the distinction between one person and another, such reductionism blurs the private-public and the subjective-objective divides. This results in the unintelligibility of linguistic communication. Plain facts evaporate; licenses to make one's own world are issued; and supposed world-makers themselves continue dividing, merging, re-emerging, and partially surviving. To the extent that we conceive of ourselves that way, cares would lessen, no doubt, but so would caring. Maybe this entails liberation from egoism. But whose liberation will it be anyway?

The method: good old Nyāya wine in a Fregean bottle

To build up my case, I shall consider realist arguments from both classical Indian and modern Western sources. Udayana—the eleventh-century precursor of the Indian "New Logic" (Navya-Nyāya)—saw the connection among realisms about physical objects, selves, and universals. He defended all three against the Buddhist reductionists who deemed all three to be grammatical fictions.[5] Frege, the father of contemporary analytic philosophy, felt the need to establish the self as a bearer of ideas in order to secure the objectivity of "thoughts" of which facts are a species.[6]

There are important differences between the Nyāya and the Fregean ontologies and concerns. But both seem to recognize the necessity and connectedness of subjective and objective unifiers of experience or, rather, the inter-dependent double need of mental states to be someone's and of something. By attempting, in my own way, a defense of a rather dated dualism of real selves and real objects, I hope incidentally to re-explode the myth that all Eastern Philosophy is idealistic, monistic, and mystical. Post-Parfitian Western philosophy will also, I hope, have more to learn from the East than mere mindlessness.

Although I shall chiefly deal with the basic insights and arguments, ignoring history and hermeneutic, I hope the exercise will illustrate the point that the reality of a philosophical problem is proved by its re-identification across centuries and cultures. The mapping of perceptual states onto the person and the external environment raises problems that I saw in Gautama's second-century aphorisms[7] and can now touch again in Colin McGinn's 1989 work on mental contents (which, however, upholds a different view of persons and objects).[8]

The Ego and the It

I will argue for the truth of a bi-conditional: Selves over and above experiences are real if and only if objects over and above experiences are real.

In this section I shall try to prove the "if" part of this claim: If we are realists about the external world, then we have to introduce substantial egos into our ontology. Now, to be a realist about material objects, let's say an apple, is at least to uphold the following two strict distinctions and two strict identities:

(A) The apple is distinct from just an experience or idea of an apple.
(B) The apple is distinct from just its red color, smooth texture, and sweet taste, and also from just a series or set of these qualities.
(C) The apple that I now touch (or bite or smell) is the same as the apple that I saw a while ago.
(D) The apple that I see is the same as the apple that you see.

We can tease out the existence of a self straightaway from A—the first distinction—because it implies the reality of both the items distinguished, viz., the apple and some experience of it. And experience cannot exist without an experiencer. The asymmetric individuation-dependence of experiences on relatively permanent subjects or owners of experience can be brought out at four different levels, viz., linguistic, epistemological, metaphysical, and conceptual.

> Linguistically, talk of perceptions presupposes prior reference to perceivers.
> Epistemologically, no sensations are knowable directly or indirectly without some sort of knowledge of the person who senses.
> Metaphysically, it seems ontically essential to a sensory state that it be unshareably borne by a conscious individual (like a dent needs a dentable surface).
> Conceptually, we cannot conceive of a token experience without having the concept of a bearer of that experience.

Notice that this fourfold identifiability-dependence is one-way on all accounts. For instance, take the epistemological dependence of mental states on the self. It might seem that conversely even a self cannot be known in isolation from a mental state. But a self's individuation-dependence is not on any particular token-experience but at most on some experience or other, whereas a particular token experience, if it has to be known, has to be known along with *that* particular subject to which alone it can be ascribed and not with some subject or other.

Some Buddhists insisted that the so-called self can be reduced[9] to the individual mental qualities with which it is constantly co-cognized. Whenever I encounter a green leaf, I am invariably acquainted also with my visual sensation of a green leaf. I cannot sense a hot cup of tea without being aware of my feeling of hotness. A mental/cognitive quality seems to be always co-accessed along with any object that I am aware of. But even if symmetric constant co-cognizability proved identity, one-sided knowability-dependence surely does not. To use Udayana's counter-example, a dark color cannot but be perceived along with some bright color (e.g., of sun rays or of light in general) yet they are quite distinct, because the bright color can be seen without the dark.

Could it be that although a single passing thought is not the thinker, a seamless series of experiences assumes that title of "self"? In order to be compatible with a realist view of objects as factorized above, such a series must be better integrated than a mere bundle of visual, tactile, olfactory, and similar sensations. The temperature cannot be an object of visual sensation and the color can never be an object of tactile sensation (except in special situations like synesthesia when it is assisted by memory of the very sort of trans-sensuous re-encounter which we are trying to explain). How then can the identity C—between what is seen and what is touched—be maintained? The ruling that all such claims of re-encountering the same object across times and senses are uniformly illusory will not do. Who commits the mistake? Can a visual experience imagine that it touched a cold surface? We cannot even credit the pair of sensations with the unitary conception of what it is for one object to have both color and temperature. The Jamesean picture of one thought dying away and the replacing thought finding it "warm" and greeting it as "mine" suffers from a number of conceptual flaws.[10] Would such unowned thoughts which "appropriated" the predecessors only in a rhetorical sense of "possessing" ever be able to form the notion of mind-independent objects bearing properties accessible to different senses? We shall come back to this question in a moment. Let us pause here and look harder into this notion of *owning* an experience.

While explicating the Buddha's doctrine of no-soul, Vasubandhu faces the same problem:

> How is this locution "Caitra remembers" possible? If there is no self whose is this memory? Why is the possessive case used here ("whose")? To express the relation of ownership, just as in "This is Caitra's cow." How is he the owner of the cow? Because the employment of the cow in carrying loads or milking etc. is under his control.
>
> Towards what end is a memory supposed to be employed so that we are looking for its owner? Of course, towards the object remembered ... But how exactly is the recollection to be "employed"? Is it by production or by movement? Since memory is incapable of movement it must be through production. So we conclude that the producer or the cause is the so-called owner and the effect produced is the owned possession.
>
> ... Hence whatever is the cause of memory is the owner of the memory.

Add to this the Buddhist[11] notion of a cause as a perishing predecessor, and you get the thesis that any immediate predecessor of a mental state is its owner. This version of the Stream-Conception is, in a way, directly opposed to the Jamesean version which holds that the successor thought calls its dying ancestor "mine" and "appropriates" it.[12] However, both doctrines are equally counter-intuitive. Strangely enough, upon one prevalent version of Buddhist epistemology, one aspect of the preceding mental state is also the object (the *ālambana*), the causal and intentional support of the succeeding mental state. So, here we seem to have a peculiar collapsing of the owner and the object of the cognitive state. That may not daunt the Buddhist idealist who professes the doctrine of reflexive self-awareness of individual perceptual states. But it is surely incompatible with realism about the object as spelt out by our initial fourfold list of distinctions and identities. Three of those claims (A, C, and D) entail the existence of mental states which need to be ascribed to something. C and D entail re-identification across times and senses which requires that the separate re-identifier endures in those times and runs across those sensations, because the sensations themselves do not, as it were, speak each other's language in order to even ask the question, "Have you grasped the same item as I have?" Even a single experience has the ascriptive demand which is strengthened by the integrative and retentive demands of synchronic and diachronic syntheses of such experiences. These are all demands for the same subject or substance. Suppose we ignore these demands and diagnose this adjectival understanding of mental events as a deep-rooted linguistic prejudice. I hope to show that the revised notion of the self as a heap or stream of mental events will then be inconsistent with distinction B, between properties of physical objects and the objects exemplifying those properties. Nothing short of a substantial self is thus implied by that crucial constituent of realism about physical objects.

Suppose, at any single cross-section of time it is a *heap* of perceptual, conceptual, dispositional, and hedonic properties dependent upon each other and on correlated bodily and cerebral events; and over a period of time, it is just a *stream* of such aggregates maintaining some sort of continuity and insulation. Can we go ahead with such a set and series (*rāśi-dhārā*)[13] notion of the self while retaining the notion of sweet red apples individuated in their environment?

If I am only a set of visual and gustatory sensations, what would the apple be for me? Since I shall not have the framework of predication or exemplification at my disposal (given that my self-knowledge is essentially additive), it will be at most a color plus taste or a color followed by a taste. But distinction B tells us that the apple is more than just a sum of its qualities. A bundle-self will look upon objects as similar bundles of properties severally accessible to its own members. Indeed, it is hardly intelligible how a "set-series" sort of self can even put together discrete sense-data as bundles. Temporal proximity will hardly do as a deciding factor. While looking at the ocean, one may smell a friend's cigarette-smoke and touch a beach towel. The resulting bundle of contemporaneous visual, olfactory, and cutaneous sense-data will yield no recognizably single physical object. Even if by some fluke the last bit of a time-slice of a subject-series succeeds to tie up the appropriate bundle, can it ascribe all the sensible qualities (or even one of them) as properties belonging to an external substance? Under the assumption that the subject of experience really is a series of mental states, one could imagine two alternative pictures. The first picture goes like this: the stream-self originally feels its own states in feature-placing forms like "Here comes a feel," "Now, there is a pinch of jealousy," or "Here comes a wish," rather than "I touch," "I am jealous," or "I wish." But the same subject feels external sensations in predicative forms like "The apple is red," "The water is cold," or "A stone rolled off." The second picture removes this incredible asymmetry. Both inner and outer experiences come through predicative judgments; yet, it insists, the subject-predicate model is mis-applied to the inner and correctly applied to the outer sensations. It should be obvious that both the pictures are equally bizarre. It is extremely arbitrary to hold that while the ascriptive model is never or never correctly applied to the inner realm, the additive model is never or never correctly applied to the outer. Experiences of the two realms come to us at the same time, often indistinguishably. Interpreting two aspects of them in two radically different styles leads to either false psychology or false metaphysics. Any such negation of a substantial person is thus incompatible with realism regarding objects. If there is an "It" beyond experiences and qualities, there must also be an "I" behind them.[14]

Finally, it can be shown that identity D of objects of two distinct owners of experience requires the existence of more than one self. Why can't "you" and "I"—in that part of the realist's claim—just mean rivers or clubs of unowned mental states? Now, rivers can branch off and clubs can exchange members or live intermittently. Such also are Parfitian persons.

But two such persons cannot talk of seeing the same physical object from unshareably distinct perspectives. Since such persons might have merged with one another and could have been teletransported or replicated at any point in their lives—sometimes sharing the same experiences and memories—checking against each other's memory for any two of them will be as powerless against mistake as the same person's remembering something twice (recall Wittgenstein's analogy of buying two copies of the morning paper).[15] So those many people whose ability to co-perceive the same object is part of the realist notion of the external world must be substantial selves rather than Parfitian[16] persons. A single Parfitian person does not remain strictly the same over time. Hence, two of them would not be strictly distinct. The publicness criterion of objectivity of physical items requires being the common target of many strictly distinct centers of experience.

Backtracking: someone in here entails something out there

I have tried to argue that a realist conception of material objects over and above their properties and independent of our experience of them compels us to believe in the existence of substantial selves, in more ways than one. The other side of the biconditional remains to be established. I am going to argue that if we are realists about selves, we have to be realists about the external world. First, I will raise and answer one possible objection. Can one even coherently talk about realism about the self? Can the mind be claimed to be mind-independent? Isn't that why no primary/secondary distinction has ever been drawn about the qualities of the mind? An object can be conceived to bear a quality, especially a primary quality without being recognized by anyone as having that quality.

There are two grounds for this objection. The first is a confusion between "mind" and "self." The mind cannot be independent of the mind but the self can. This sounds like a howler to the Western philosopher because not only is the distinction between inner sense—the faculty of introspection (which Indian philosophers call *manas* and which popularly, but misleadingly, translates as mind[17])—and the Ego or Self (which they call *ātman*) not made in the West (except, in a way, by Kant), but the notion of an objective self—a self which exists even during the gaps when it is not aware of itself—is nearly absent. The second ground for the objection is the widespread belief that mental states are self-intimating or rather necessarily recognized by the subject who bears them. The famous "knowledge implies knowledge of knowledge" thesis is a corollary of this.

But the Nyāya epistemologists rejected this doctrine of necessary self-awareness of all states of mind.[18] The self's normal stance is world-ward. Many of its own states may go unregistered if it does not pause to look within and perceive itself as undergoing claims of identity and distinction. Here are four principles concerning the reality of the self, more or less following Nyāya lines:

(E) The subject which ascribes to itself a set of cognitive, conative and affective states at t1 and the one which ascribes to itself another completely different set of such states to itself at t2 are strictly the same substance, even if the mental states have radically different contents, if the latter can remember the contents of the former set of mental states from an "inside point of view" as having been its own. (Notice that such memory is a sufficient but not necessary condition of such identity across times.)
(F) If a tactile sensation at a subsequent time t2 immediately arouses the perceptual judgment about a visual sensation at an antecedent time t1 remembered from inside—as both sensations of the same object—the subjects of these sensations must be the same.
(G) This subject is distinct from any particular visual or tactile experience which inheres in it (it is surely not just the organic feeling of breathing, as James once suggested).[19]
(H) It is also distinct from the entire set of sense-experiences, volitions, memories and organic feelings at one time or the series of such states across a stretch of time.

Notice that each of these identities and distinctions stands on the notion of disparate experiences that the self ascribes to itself and the contents of which it can compare, contrast, link up, and look back upon. Now, every experience, even an organic sensation of pain or pleasure, reaches outside itself to get at some physical item or other: a visual sensation individuates itself as of a color, a pain as inside the stomach, a thought as about a picture, and so on. Most of these experiences, especially those which we can self-consciously ascribe to ourselves, have a predicative content where something is felt to be of some sort. For example, my pen is seen to be blue and shiny. If all we had in our world were myself and my mental properties, then either all experienced properties will have to be ascribed to myself, resulting in unusual feelings like I am blue and shiny; or, alternatively, all our perceptual contents will be just aggregates of qualities conjoined in a heap or series. My experience of a heavy shell will then be reduced to an experience of which one part was the sensation of weight and the other part or the whole itself an idea of the shell. But, as Frege pointed out, what the experience claimed to grasp was not a shell which has weight as its part, but one which has weight as its property. A self which never really comes across an external world can hardly be imagined to have even the idea of objects unlike itself bearing properties unlike its own properties. Indeed, such a self cannot even distinguish between different mental states in terms of the objects they grasp, being deprived of the notion of such objects.

Can such a self still manage to persist across its objectless mental states (which somehow manage to differ phenomenologically!)? Here I borrow an argument from Strawson to show that we cannot think of such a self, or at least explain how it can ascribe differing experiences to itself. To make sense of our trans-temporal identity-claims about the self, we have to appeal to the idea of an objective time-order. Such an order of succession of events will have to be understood as a system of irreversible temporal relations independent of the self's subjective feelings. Since all that our self can feel are its own experiences, some of those experiences will have to be construed by the self as experiences of things outside the experiences. But there is only one way in which perceived things can provide us with the background of an objective time-order, namely, by enduring long enough to be re-encounterable in different perceptual experiences at distinct times.

Udayana anticipates the basic insight of this very argument when he argues from what I have called identity B to the object of perception being real, mind-independent, and irreducible to its qualities or to a set of them.

He enriches the argument further by bringing in the difference of sensory qualities along with the difference of times and by going into details about the relation of inherence which is testified to by our perceptual awareness of the color being in the object. In resisting the idealist pressure to reduce the perceived single object with many features into a mere collection of those features, he also anticipates Frege's point that if there are no objects outside my ideas then the logical distinction between properties and parts will vanish. Thus, it can be shown that a reductive anti-realism about the external world will lead to unavailability of the notion of a self which can re-identify itself across different successive experiential states.[20] Transpose this result and you get the conclusion of this section: realism about the self implies realism about objects outside the mind. A persistent self needs to discriminate between sensory states across which it has to ensure its own identity. Sensory states, to be discriminated, need to refer their contents to the external world. Nyāya, like contemporary externalists, holds that individuation of discreet co-personal mental states is to be done directly in terms of mind-independent objects and their equally mind-independent relations. There is no telling the difference between experience as of a blue pot and experience as of a red shirt unless there are blue and red pots and shirts at some time somewhere in the world (if not then and there). The conception of a subjective cognitive state becomes available to us only in the wake of error. Contentful experience spontaneously takes the form "This pen is red" and does not take the form "I am having a visual experience as of a red pen" or even "Here is an experience as of a red pen." It is only in the face of suspicion or detection of error that we curtail the claim and become aware of our beliefs. There is a certain cognitive bashfulness about confessions of a subjective state of belief which is appropriate only to a believer who fears a mistake. But the concept of error is patently parasitic on the concept of getting it right, and rightness can only be understood in terms of an order of things as they are independently of our beliefs, that is, of things which can be common persistent objects of many sensations of many people on many occasions.

Since there is no notion of belief without a notion of things about which belief can be wrong and right, there is no notion of a believer also without some notion of such outer topics of beliefs.

Conclusion: externalism without qualms

Our actual conception of a bit of experience with a structured content involves at least two types of items outside the experience, at its two opposite extremities, as it were. On the one hand, it requires a single experiencer capable of retaining its felt identity over a series of successive experiences. On the other hand, it depends upon an object with some features or a constellation of objects and features in terms of which its content is to be cashed. This dual individuation-dependence makes re-cognitive perceptual judgments at once evidences of the same I who touches and sees, as well as of the same object which is touched and seen. It also conceptually requires that we distinguish the I from the touching and seeing, as well as the object from the texture and color.

In case all of the above sounds like a rehash of the Kantian theme of the objective and subjective unities implied by the synthesis of experience, I wish to emphasize the vital difference. It is crucial for Kant that the I which thinks and unifies experience by applying concepts remains only a presupposition of knowledge and never becomes an object of knowledge. This unity of apperception is surely not the empirical self whose knowledge requires representation of something stable in space. This Kantian doctrine of the un-knowability of the real subject was fondly picked up by Indian Neo-Vedāntists early in this century. K. C. Bhattacharya remarked that if the self is what the word "I" expresses then "it is not meant or at best meant as unmeant and is accordingly above metaphysical dispute."[21] This opinion is by no means shared by the realist Nyāya philosophers whose chief "metaphysical dispute" with the Buddhists was about the self. Neither is this attitude shared by Frege who, though aware of the incommunicable residue of the "sense" of our individual uses of the pronoun "I," surely does not think that the self or the bearer of ideas is not known or not meant or referred to at all by words. Indeed Nyāya believes in the direct perceivability of the real self as much as it believes, once again unlike Kant, in the direct knowability of the real world of objects as they are in themselves.

An alleged Humean failure to perceive any self apart from fleeting experiences is symptomatic of the anti-realist. In response to a similar Buddhist argument from non-perception to non-existence, Udayana asks: "Is it only you alone who fails to find the self or everyone? You could never be sure about what all others do or do not perceive. As to your own non-perception that is no invariable sign of the self's nonbeing."[22]

What then is the positive evidence for the existence of the self? Udayana's answer is unambiguous: "Direct perception, to be sure."[23] For every conscious creature the judgment "I am" is self-evident. This judgment is pre-linguistic, so it could not be purely fictional or object-less: there is no question of our being merely duped by the pronoun. Since it is never challenged by any subsequent judgment, it is not doubtful also. It does not await our search for a premise or reason. Hence it is not inferential.[24] It could not always have been just a memory unless at some time it was presented as a datum. So it must be an indubitable perception. Even if we sometimes are mistaken about our own present mental states, a self-delusive judgment like "I am in pain" or "I see a snake," in order to be false, presupposes the existence of and my direct acquaintance with the self about whom it is false.

Just as a direct realist resists the Lockean move that we only directly perceive qualities of physical objects while the object itself remains unseen and unknown, Udayana resists the Humean move that introspection only reveals mental states. The internal sense organ, according to Nyāya, is in direct contact with the self (just as external senses reach out to touch tables and trees). Thus, I am acquainted with myself when I am acquainted with a pain or a wish or a cognitive state like my-acquaintance-with-the-table in me.

This is precisely what Frege argues using two subtle arguments.

First, consider my introspective judgment, "I am looking at the moon." A certain moonward gaze is surely one object of my knowledge. Is not *I*-the gazer another object? If we reduce this I to just another mental state or idea—to a Jamesean thought or a Yogācāra vijñāna (a momentary but continuous *ālaya vijñāna* or a perverted (*kliṣṭa*) psychosis—which incurably fancies itself to be permanent)—we face a vicious regress. This mental state or idea will need to be repeatedly present to "the same" consciousness. It must be my idea of myself in order to come alive. Part of this consciousness will again have to be the pretended, the feigned idea of the self, while the other part would have to do the feigning. Thus, "I should be boxed into myself in this way to infinity."[25]

Second: when I am introspectively aware of a lack of experience, the self makes a special claim as an independent object of perception. The content of negative introspective judgments of the common kind—like "I am not in pain"—cannot be reduced to just a particular perception of a mental event. Even the most ontologically austere analysis of outer perception of absence, for example, of a pen on a table, cannot get rid of the locus—the table—as a perceived object. Similarly, even if the missed feeling or its lack does not figure in our awareness of painlessness, as the locus of the absence the self has to be perceived if the absence has to be felt. This point was anticipated by K. C. Bhattacharya who, like Kant, was unwilling to objectify the self. He explained away such introspection of a want of feeling as my imagining a merely possible pain, or contrasting myself with a third person in pain. But confusing a clear perception of a non-suffering self with the mere non-perception of a suffering one seems to be a sheer mistake.

In Kant also we see a logical link between the self and material objects. But neither the ego nor the spatial permanent of his "Refutation of Idealism" is transcendentally real. They are both "made" by understanding. In Nyāya and Frege we have a real self knowing directly both itself and objects which are both independent of experiences and complete (unlike properties which are incomplete, i.e., parasitical on objects).

I want to end by reminding you of the fundamental differences between these two realistic schemes which I have more or less bracketed together against anti-realisms of various sorts. Frege's motivation for proving something real over and above subjective states was peculiar: once he had established a self, and then a plurality of selves and objects outside experience, the "way was clear" for recognizing mind-independent propositions as truth-bearers. These propositions he called "Thoughts" (*Gedanken*). A fact for him is just a true thought. Such thoughts are neither physical nor mental entities. Now, there is no place at all in Nyāya metaphysics for such a third realm. When many of us together perceive an apple to be red, apart from each of us and our unshareable sensations there is only one entity according to Nyāya—namely, a red apple out there. Both its substance and its qualities are equally physical. We can analyze the object into a substance, a quality, an action, a universal, a bonding relation of being in or exemplification. But on top of these there is no separate proposition or fact that the apple is red which I also apprehend. The Fregean tradition continues to speak of true and false thoughts as objective sharable contents of perceptual judgments and as meanings of sentences. Naiyāyikas would be anti-realists about such propositions. But that is another story.

As the above disagreement shows, it is still up for debate as to what further links can be drawn from the bi-conditional relation between realism about objects and realism about selves. In the next chapter, I will discuss the link between realism about external objects and realism about their properties. To be a realist about ordinary objects of perception is to hold that such objects exist as they often appear to us, whether we can know every detail about them or not. We identify and distinguish such objects by certain features that they may (or may not) objectively possess. These features may include particular qualities such as color, taste, and temperature, as well as non-particular properties such as the universal a certain object exemplifies. If propertied objects are mind-independently real, their properties must be mind-independently real as well. When we say this, are we talking just about the particular qualities objects possess or must we include their non-particular properties as well?

2

Non-particular Individuals

The plan

This chapter has five sections. In the *first*, I roughly characterize and indicate different varieties of non-particular individuals. In the *second*, I sketch two versions of an argument for the conditional conclusion that if one is a realist about middle-sized physical objects of outer perception then one is compelled to be a realist about *some* universals, that is, *some* non-particular individuals. In the *third* and the main section, I try to portray Strawson as a realist about universals given his original ways of assuaging neo-nominalistic qualms. In the *fourth*, I discuss Pranab Kumar Sen's[1] realistic theory of universals. In the *fifth* and final section, I contrast Strawson's position with the Nyāya ontology and epistemology of non-particular entities.

Nyāya and Strawson share the spirit of a descriptive metaphysician and thus also the pre-theoretical commitment to commonsense realism. Although Strawson's *persons* are not at all like Nyāya *selves*, Strawson's opposition to "No-ownership theories" of mental states strongly resembles the Nyāya attack against the Buddhist "No-self" view. It is not a historical accident that realisms concerning particular subjects and objects of experience, and realism regarding non-particular individuals, went hand in hand for both Nyāya and Strawson. I strongly suspect that they are conceptually interlinked.

Samples of sorts

Wisdom comes in handy as one *individual* topic of discourse which can be recognized—subject to correction—in some persons or some courses of action and yet as *not a particular* spatio-temporal item exhausted by its single occurrence. Another such non-particular individual would be the number twelve which months and apostles equally exemplify, yet which is one single number. If by a "particular" we understand

An earlier version of this chapter was read at a 1988 conference on "Realism–Non-Realism" at All Souls College, Oxford. I am grateful for comments from Professor B.K. Matilal, Dr. R.C. Walker, and Professor T.L.S. Sprigge.

The phrase "non-particular real" occurs in the following remark of Gopinath Bhattacharya: "The realist, as is well-known, postulates the existence of a distinctive non-particular real, viz. the Universal" in pp. 70–94 of his *Essays in Analytical Philosophy*, Kolkata, 1989.

an item which cannot exist in two different discontinuous places, wholly, at the same time, neither of the above-named items are particulars. Sanskrit is what both Gautama and Gadādhara wrote, though they were separated by nearly one thousand and five hundred years. To wit, non-particulars are indefinitely repeatable; particulars are not.

Some may baulk at my use of the word "individuals" for these general things. If it is just a linguistic discomfort, I could appeal to the use of the word "individuals" by a philosopher whose sensitivity to ordinary English usage is as famous as his philosophical work with that title. He remarks: "We have an endless variety of categories of *individuals other than particulars*" (my emphasis).[2] Of course, he does not consider these non-particular individuals to be the *paradigm* targets of genuine singular reference. But as he himself hastens to remind us, "paradigm cases are not the only cases."[3] Now, just as particulars are of innumerably different kinds, *kinds* are also of very many different sorts. There are many ways of classifying or grouping non-particular items. Types, kinds, properties could be distinguished as *different* sorts of non-particulars capable of having tokens, specimens, and instantiators, respectively. Some kinds are *natural* while others are *culturally constructed*.[4] Some of them come with general criteria of identity for things belonging to them and some do not (called "g-sorted" and "g-unsorted" by Strawson), and so on.[5]

We must pause here to notice what Strawson calls, with mock exasperation, "the untidy richness of the vernacular." What do we mean by a "kind" or a "sort"? Quine reduces them to classes. But neither Strawson nor Nyāya would approve of this move. Even if the Nyāya word for a genuine universal (*jāti*) *is* also used for a *caste or* a *species*, it is not the set of all birds or brahmins which is *a jāti*, but bird*ness* or brahmin*ness*. If being human, being silken, or being prudent is what we are talking about, it is what particulars can exhibit, instantiate, or possess, and not what they can be *members of* or *belong to.* (Perhaps we should draw a distinction between a kind and a kind-making property. It is the latter rather than the former that I shall concentrate on.)

Philosophers have countenanced non-particular items that are neither *kinds* nor *properties.* Philosophical issues (like *whether universals exist*) themselves are such. Answering to two distinguishable "whether"-clauses there are said to exist two distinct theoretical *problems.* If six people at different times and in different languages say the same thing, then regardless of whether they speak the truth or not, *what they say is* supposed to be a non-particular individual. Frege was a realist about these too. In his ontologically expansive moods, Strawson seems prepared to embrace such assertible contents as well into his world of individuals.

Interestingly, Nyāya does not have any place for such common bearers of truth and falsehood or contents of cognitive states. If six of us believed that Rahul Gandhi would win the election, then "being about Rahul Gandhi's winning the election" and "being affirmative" will capture the common properties of all six states or acts of belief, no doubt. But such about-ness is given a complicated relational account in Nyāya. Such properties would not count as *real* universals. Perhaps such contentual common features of either awareness-episodes or utterances will be regarded as *titular properties* like professorship, or, to use the classical example of an artificial kind—the property of being a cook. The so-called titular properties, however, do a lot of work. Although they do not belong to what Matilal calls the ontological inner circle,[6] they often provide the reason for our application of the same predicate, phrase, or "that"-clause to different particular or non-particular items. Take, for instance, the business of speaking classifyingly about properties themselves or of characteristics of genuine universals. For obvious metaphysical constraints, Nyāya does not admit that natural universals themselves can exemplify other *natural* universals. Is *g-sortedness* itself a universal exemplified by some but not all universals? Are there features like *being a criterion for classification of universals which* g-sortedness shares with other such criteria? Is cownessness something which cowness has? (Such a multiplication of "ness" after "ness" will be a rather nessy affair!) Recognizing the harmlessness of such a hierarchy at a conceptual level, but also the need for some restriction on what will qualify as a genuine objective—i.e., knowledge-independent—non-particular, Nyāya decided to call all but those *first-level* universals which pass some tests and inhere in unrepeatable particulars, "titular properties" (*upādhi*).

To one kind of multiply exemplifiable individuals I have not yet made any direct reference: relations. On the face of it *some* relations are just many-pronged particulars. Take *contacts*: the contact between this pen and this paper is quite distinct from the contact between these fingers and this pen. For one thing, they happen at different places of the pen and not always at the same time. Even if I touch the pen twice at the same place, there would be two distinct contacts. Contacts are thus seen to be relational particulars which may, of course, have a common feature, viz., *contacthood*, which is a property resident in relations but not a relation in itself. Some other relations, though repeatable, for example, marriage—I mean wedlock, not the wedding—are titular by the Nyāya criterion. The only genuine relation which seems to have the required feature of being a one-in-many—and hence universal—is the very relation which holds between a universal and any one of its particular exemplifiers. This tie is surely non-particular, but is it an individual? The Nyāya philosophers called it "inherence" and would *not* admit it to be an individual at all, for fear of a third man argument and also because it is a tie which is not *relational* in the sense in which a tie between two *particulars* is relational. Exemplification, too, is not a non-particular individual. Thus, it is difficult to find examples of genuine relation which hold between particulars and yet are not themselves particulars. The non-relational tie *exemplification*, or its converse *inherence*, forms a separate one-membered category in Nyāya.

But my own intuition at this point impels me to introduce *some* simple relations—even if I cannot be sure which ones—as universals exemplified by pairs and trios and quartets, thus enriching the Nyāya stock of objective non-particulars which could traditionally only be meanings of *one*-place predicates.

From one realism to another

In this section, I do *not* want to propose or endorse an argument from either our experience of similarity or our inescapable use of general terms, or from the dependence of causal laws upon repeatable features of things in favor of the mind-independent existence of universals. I shall only argue for the following conditional thesis:

> *If realism concerning ordinary external objects of perception is true then realism concerning non-particular individuals must be true.*[7]

Let me, first, characterize the antecedent of my claim, that is, explain what I take realism concerning ordinary external objects to involve. To be a realist about entities of type M is, at the minimum, to hold that items of type M exist, whether we know them or not. This crucial clause "whether we know them or not" could be strongly interpreted to mean: *whether we can know that such entities at all exist or not,* or it can be weakly interpreted as meaning: *whether* we *can know truths about them or not.* (Let us here remind ourselves that at least one such entity exists is *not* a truth about such entities, for otherwise that no such entity exists would also be a truth about such entities.) I wish to argue that a consistent realist must adopt the *weak* interpretation of this knowledge-independence clause. Realism about M-sort of things is *not* compatible with our necessary or actual complete ignorance or systematic error about even the existence of items of the sort M. To assert the existence of entities of a type is pragmatically to imply that the asserter *knows* that some things of that type exist and also *knows* what type he is referring to; that is, he knows what it takes to be a sample of that type even if he could make a mistake in identifying any individual sample or fail to recognize some samples altogether. It is therefore incoherent to add to the minimal existence-claim the strongly agnostic claim that *all* those recognition-transcendently existing things of type M might turn out to be—or might just *be,* without ever turning out to be—not of the type we know and refer to as M-type at all. From a globally realist point of view it might be shown to be logically possible or even necessary that there exist unknowable facts. Yet, it would be inconsistent to assert and thereby implicitly profess to know what sort of entities these unknowable facts involve.

This is why my robust realism about ordinary material objects of perception like chairs, bodies of other people, etc., holds that these chairs and other living human bodies exist in nature—*as* we occasionally see them—without always depending upon our finding them there. It is part of such realism that we can be occasionally, or even mostly, *mistaken* and *oblivious* about them. But such realism also insists that at least *some* of our perceptual judgments about them are correct, or capable of being correct, namely, at least those which would reveal the error in the others. To use the current idiom of statements and truth values: to be a realist about macroscopic objects of ordinary perception is to believe that our straightforward statements about externally perceived particulars are either true or false, whether in any individual case we can decide which truth-value they have.

Contemporary *semantic* characterizations of realism—especially those which are designed to prove its incoherence or inadequacy—have often perverted the claim of knowledge-independent bivalence to mean "being determinately true or determinately false *when it is in principle impossible to find out which.*" This could suggest a cognitive pessimism which is incompatible with what Wright calls the realist's "presumption." A real-life realist positively hopes "that our cognitive capacities can and do very often put us in position to know the truth."[8] It is when this bit is overlooked that the realist is pictured as a skeptic obsessed with the possibility of the actual nature of reality outrunning *all* our cognitive resources. If we think through the realist's claim of knowledge-independence of truth-values of statements of a particular kind we can see the implicitly *affirmative* force of a corresponding claim of the accessibility of the relevant type of entities (*about* which the statements of the given kind claim to be) always accompanying it.

Now, if ordinary perceived particulars have to exist *as* the physical objects we often know them to be whether or not we can apprehend them correctly in detail on every occasion, they must have (or lack) some *features* objectively; that is whether the ones we identify as wooden tables are actually so or not, woodenness and tableness must be actually exemplifiable. For a non-particular individual like tableness, exemplifiability is enough for existence. Hence, tableness has to exist independently of our awareness of it. Since bare or propertyless particulars would not be the macroscopic objects of ordinary perception, a world devoid of such actual features like cowness and treeness would not be a world where *cows* and *trees* can exist unperceived.

Ordinary perception is irreducibly *predicative* in structure. The myth of the pre-linguistic pre-conceptual acquaintance with featureless simples can yield all sorts of revisionary and reductive realisms and atomisms, but it surely does not yield realism about middle-sized perceived particulars which provide us that "massive central core" of conceptual agreement from where to conduct theoretical as well as quotidian talk.

One could here raise the objection that we actually find in Wittgenstein's *Tractatus* a realist ontology of particular objects which dispenses with universals altogether. To this interesting counter-thought, I have three immediate responses to make. First, it is not beyond dispute that Wittgenstein wished only bare particulars to be considered as nameable objects. Because his objects fit into one another like the links of a chain, and because there are passages both in the *Notebooks* and in the *Tractatus* hinting at some unanalyzable properties being themselves considered as objects, some interpreters have understood his "states of affairs" to be arising out of the plugging of particulars into non-particular individuals. After all, a property and a particular make a better match than one particular and another particular!

Second, even if we take the class of Tractarian *objects* to consist solely of particulars (as I am inclined to do), these objects could be atomic material points or sense data—neither of which would be ordinary objects of external perception. So Tractarian realism can hardly be looked upon as a non-reductive realism about macroscopic physical objects like chairs, walls, pillars, and people. *Its* non-commitment to universals would not affect *our* realism-link.

Third, even if we consider the Tractarian world where simple nameable particulars stand in non-nameable relations to form states of affairs which are pictured by mere juxtaposition of names of particulars, is that world quite free from repeatable items? What are the configurations or forms? Wittgenstein defines "forms" as possibilities of structure. Could not many different trios of objects share the same form, by virtue of different threesome structures realizing the same *possibility* of combination? Maybe these forms will only be showable. But that would not make them any less real. Indeed, unsayability of forms heightens their realistic status, making them in some ways "beyond words."

But perhaps my characterization of realism about perceived particulars as a kind of existence-claim will itself sound outdated and unattractive. So, let me give my second version of the same argument in terms of *statement*-realism rather than *entity*-realism. To be a realist about ordinarily perceived particulars, upon this formulation, is to hold that our perception-based statements about such objects as walls and pillars and people are either determinately true or determinately false of them, whether or not we can establish any one of them as either. Now, if statements of the sort "This is a table" have to be recognition-transcendently true or false, things like tableness must be capable of having or not having specific demonstrable particulars as their instances. For a statement to be true or false, just as we need an item for it to be true or false *of*, we also need an item which can be true or false of things. As we shall see in the fourth section, it is precisely the meanings of predicates which I am calling non-particular individuals. Without such general individuals our predicative statements about perceived objects would be incapable of being either true or false. The only way we could try to get around this is by analyzing the predicate "x is a table" as alluding to sets of possible particular sense data. It is doubtful if even then one could completely eschew non-particulars. In any case, realism about *tableness* seems more akin to commonsense than realism about possibilia or sets of sense data.

Strawson as a catholic realist

Although the above entailment struck me quite independently, I can now detect the seeds of this argument in Strawson's work.[9] Take the following passage, for example. Here, he is pointing out the inconsistency of conjoining realism about perceived particulars with the negation of realism about universals:

> Those philosophers who are suspicious of general properties, sorts, relations and types usually have no doubts about the reality of people, physical objects, datable events and tokens. This partiality of theirs has sometimes seemed paradoxical. For it has seemed unclear how they, or anyone else, could distinguish and identify the particular individuals they so readily accept unless they could distinguish and identify some at least, of the general sorts or kinds to which those individuals belong and some, at least, of the general features that characterize them. [10]

He then formulates what I call the realism-link between perceived particulars and non-particular individuals in the dictum: "practical recognition of particular things entails practical recognition of general things."[11] One should not read "practical recognition" here as designed to waive or withdraw the same claim about *theoretical* recognition. All he means is that we do in practice identify particulars on the basis of our ability to identify general features. To deny theoretical ontic status to the general features would therefore compel us to retract theoretical commitment from perceived particulars as well. This is exactly what I have been arguing. I shall not here go into the details of how Strawson opposes the narrow interpretation of Quine's slogan "No Entity without Identity"—which is often used to eliminate non-particulars, especially g-unsorted ones like character traits, literary styles, or gaits. About the selective permissiveness shown to classes and numbers but not to non-particular objects essential to grammar, literary criticism, or music, Strawson writes: "From such philistinism as this we can only avert our eyes."[12]

In admitting the real existence of universals of different sorts such as numbers, propositions, qualities, and relations, he has shown not only his commitment to realism but also his distaste for a scientistic or formalistic narrowness which might urge us to treat some non-particulars as more real than others. That is why I call him a *catholic realist.*

Now, although I am concerned here only with Strawson's realism concerning universals, I wish to defend generally my unapologetic use of the epithet "realist" at all about Strawson. Of course he is not an extreme "metaphysical realist." He does not entertain the possibility that even the most general structure of our actual thought and experience of the world could belie reality as it is. The epistemological masochism involved in the firm belief that things as they are in themselves are in principle unknowable by humans is a part of Kant that Strawson rightly jettisons. In this way, his realism is like that of Nyāya. At present lots of things exist unknown to many of us. But everything that exists *can*, in principle, be known and spoken of by us. It is this variety of "empirical realism" (in Kant's words) comparable to "human" or "internal" realism (in Putnam's sense), which Strawson attributes to Wittgenstein and Davidson, that I am attributing to Strawson.[13] Strawson strengthens his own realistic account of general individuals like musical notes and dance-steps with a perceptive diagnosis of the discriminatory anti-realism usually adopted about them. Here are some of his own answers to his fretful query: "Why the reductive tone?"

1. To be is to be the value of a variable. Spatio-temporal substantial particulars are our primary objects of reference, over which we can quantify. Unlike these earthy individuals, properties like prudence or architectural styles like Baroque do not have a common single criterion of re-identification, or principles of enumeration. That is why they are "bogus pretenders to the status of entities."[14]

To this, Strawson's reply is twofold. Even respectable particulars like a composite sound, a country, a historical event, or a lump of wax can lack g-sortedness, be mereologically vague or scattered, and be sliceable in indefinitely many ways. If that does not make us whittle away *their* reality-claim, why should universals suffer? Second, there are other criteria for counting as an individual, like being identifiable, predicate-worthy, or indeed definable, which properties like musical talent and types like melodic structures (called "*rāgas*" in Indian classical music) very easily satisfy.

2. Sometimes it is objected that non-particulars should not be recognized as real objects because they are not directly experienced like tables and teaspoons. Strawson does recognize this appeal to empiricism as *a bad* reason for baulking at universals. But he does not meet this worry head-on. He could have retorted—as Nyāya does—that in perceptually encountering and recognizing a particular to be an instance of a general kind we are directly acquainted with that general property which it exemplifies. Nyāya, of course, goes further: we could not have had the qualificative perception of the particular unless we had first a *bare* experience of just the generic feature which qualifies it.[15] Strawson concedes that we *cannot* perceive general features, and still maintains that in experiencing exemplifiers of them and discerning them as such we evince our grasp over the general *concepts* of such non-particular individuals. This

answer seems to preserve the Humean legacy of the absolute distinction between impressions and ideas which eventually leads to nominalism. To consider universals as unperceivable objects of mere thought is already to give in a little to nominalistic or conceptualistic pressure. Would it not be more natural to enrich our philosophical notion of perception so as to make it possible for us not only to hear some particular *playing* of a tune or a melody like the Blue Danube but also to hear the melody *itself* in that playing? Unheard melodies surely do exist and always will. But it is *too* romantic to think that *all* melodies are unheard. After all, we do not seem to be using "see" non-literally when we say, "I have seen that gait before." I suspect Strawson fears that to recognize direct experience of universals is to particularize them. But this fear is itself based on a sharp line between raw perception and conceptualized or word-tainted experience which Strawson comes very close to erasing.

3. Finally, universals fail the test of having a *common principle of identity for all things of a certain kind* which things of that kind must pass in order to qualify as genuine individuals. Strawson claims that universals do have principles of identity. We grasp these principles by grasping the sense of the predicates which introduce those universals. But unlike particulars which form kinds by sharing the same common principles of individuation, universals do not form kinds such that each property falling under a sub-type, for example, *wit* falling under the sub-type of intellectual qualities or *cowness* falling under the sub-type of animal essences, will necessarily satisfy the *same* criterion for each member *(any* intellectual quality or *every* animal essence) of that sub-type. Universals in this sense are more of *individuals* than particulars. They defy uniform grouping. "While one universal provides a criterion for identification of a whole range of similar particulars, similar universals do not always form a class with a common principle of identification for each member-universal." On the one hand, this resonates with the Nyāya insight that universals do not bear or exemplify other *universals* in themselves. We could still collect universals verbally into groups by such higher order predicative expressions as "being a style of painting" or "being a chemical property" or "being a character-trait." But these would only refer to titular universals like *knowability* (which is a property that all properties, including knowability itself, have). On the other hand, this shows why universals are bona fide individuals. They can be subjects of discourse and can be identified as such, because they themselves *are* the common criteria for identifying the whole bunch of particulars falling under them, and are too individualistic always to *have* further common criteria for identifying all or some of them as similar.

Those who would still insist on a narrow interpretation of the Quinean requirement of common criteria of identification would be basically repeating the dogma that only particulars are existent and universals will have to behave like particulars if they have to be real. It is such insistence that has driven friends of features to Platonism, the theory that features are themselves higher-level unobservable particulars with mysterious and perhaps inaccessible common criteria for identification. Strawson has no sympathy for such raving realism. Yet he respects abstract nouns. If we eliminate names of properties and all expressions referring to repeatable entities we shall not only cripple theoretical and even ordinary discourse, we shall be hypocrites, being "committed in thought to what we shun in speech."[16]

Pranab Sen's restricted realism

If Strawson's realism seems suspiciously catholic to us, Pranab Kumar Sen, a contemporary Indian philosopher, gives us a slightly more restricted and logically tightened version of realism which is, however, still heavily influenced by Strawson's theory of predication.[17] The cardinal proposition of Sen's theory is that a property is the *meaning* of a predicate when a predicate is the same as *an open sentence*. Sen carefully distinguishes his notion of *meaning* from the Fregean notion of *reference*. Fregean notions have a kind of "fatal attraction." If, bewitched by any one of them, you embrace it, you cannot resist most of the rest of the system. Thus, to accept properties as Fregean *referents* of predicates is to accept unsaturated entities (=concepts) in the realm of reference and thereby to accept truth-values as strange objects that whole sentences refer to. Universals, then, would be real all right, but not non-particular *individuals* as a Strawson or a Sen wants them to be. They would be functional entities, inaccessible to any reference except by broken parts of sentences. The divide between concepts and objects is sacrosanct in Frege. But Sen wants predicates to mean *objects*, for he clearly says that upon his account "a property is an *object*"—even a Fregean object.[18] Such a conception of meaning as a relation between the open sentence "x is wise" and the object *wisdom*, Sen observes, comes closer to Carnap's notion of "intension" and Mill's notion of "connotation," than to Frege's notion of "reference." Even Strawson rejects the doctrine of predicates standing for unsaturated concepts and with it the Fregean paradox that what is referred to by the name of the concept is not the concept at all. He too asserts emphatically that the "is" formula and the "has" formula of predication—which are, roughly, the Western and the Indian patterns respectively of copulation—introduce the same entity. While pointing out to Wiggins that once the copula is brought back into the scene there is no real need to maintain the distinction between the object denoted by the abstract noun and the concept "introduced" by the corresponding general term or predicative expression, Strawson compares the following two patterns of copulation and calls them *equivalent* as far as ontological commitment goes:

> The speaker said, of Socrates, {that he was wise}
> The speaker said, of Socrates, that he had {wisdom}.[19]

Now, if the bits within the braces are supposed to introduce the property there *does* seem to remain *one* difference between the two modes (the "is + general term"-mode and the "has + abstract noun"-mode). In the first property-introducing phrase, the variable ("he") indexed to Socrates stays as part of the general term so that even the word for property seems to involve reference in a general way to the particular under consideration. But in the second mode, that reference (what Sen likes to call non-singular reference) to a thing under consideration somehow *seems* to belong to the relation between the property and the particular, while the phrase introducing the property is expunged of all such anaphoric or general reference to any particular. This might well turn out to be a linguistic illusion. But it looks as if the first mode ascribes Socrates' *own* wisdom to Socrates, while the second mode ascribes wisdom as such to him—though Socrates' having it is said to be his *own* having. Sen quickly slides over this difficulty at the initial stage of his argument where he writes that "the-thing-under-consideration's being wise" and "being wise" must be equivalent, but comes back to the issue later in his paper.[20]

Without expending any more words on the above issue I wish to move on to pointing out where Sen's theory differs from Strawson's, and show what I think are definite Nyāya influences.

Faithfulness to common linguistic usage is undeniably the starting point for all realists and descriptive metaphysicians, so much so that Udayana, the eleventh-century Nyāya-Vaiśeṣika stalwart, writes, "If something is established in ordinary usage of words, it is as good as proved, how else can one ever hope to prove something?"[21] Yet, as Strawson memorably remarks, we must sometimes leave even our only sure guide. Thus, each and every abstract noun of ordinary language need not be assigned genuine universals as their meanings. This is why Nyāya came up with a list of six standard "impediments to genuine universalhood" and a few other tests which a putative property must pass before it can count as a genuine universal. I do not wish to discuss "universal-blockers" now. It is because of such a screening device that Nyāya realism has been aptly called "a rigorous descriptive metaphysics."[22] Without such a device, one's commitment to realism about universal looks shallow because it is too catholic. Sen introduces three such universal-blockers. Not every predicate means an objective universal. If it is analyzable, reducible or eliminable by definition, then the predicate does not connote any universal. If it is a contradictory predicate, like "x is a round square," it will automatically be non-simple and no properties should be assigned to it. If the predicate is paradox-generating, like "x is a property which is not predicable of itself," it cannot be assigned any property. Finally, Sen holds, once again like Nyāya, that if two simple properties F and G are such that their exemplification ranges are exactly the same, that is, some particular instantiates F, *if and only if* it also instantiates G, then these properties are the same; that is, the predicates which seem to mean them mean one and the same individual.[23]

I should mention at this point that the need for such universal-blockers has been felt also by Armstrong, who adds that disjunctive properties and negative properties should not be admitted as genuine universals.[24]

The second feature which Pranab Kumar Sen seems to have imbibed—somewhat tentatively—from Nyāya is attention to exemplar-specific attributes or what is best known in British philosophy as Stoutian particulars.

If we isolate the fact that he is wise as precisely the quality that is ascribed to Socrates, then Socrates' wisdom becomes something quite unrepeatable in Plato or anyone else. Of course, such "forms of facts," as Sen calls them, are not quite the same sort of items as the Nyāya particular qualities (and "facts" and "forms" are terms or notions not quite compatible with a Nyāya temperament). Colors, tastes, touches, and smells were treated by Nyāya as particular qualities which inhere in single substances and are quite unshareable. They are attributes and yet not repeatable non-particulars. The color (red) of this rose is distinct from the color (red) of that rose. Your pain is different than mine. Of course, in each of those particular colors there are non-particular color-universals. Both your pain and my pain exemplify a generic painness, which is a universal, resident not in a substance but in occurrent qualities. Sen almost embraces this doctrine by appealing to Strawson's occasional distinction between *John's anger* which is a quality belonging only to John but is itself an instance of *anger*—the non-particular individual. Strawson feels the need for distinguishing the two ties here, calling them "exemplification" (between John and anger) and "instantiation" (between John's anger and anger in general).[25] Nyāya finds the same non-relational tie "inherence" figuring at both the levels. The third aspect which is Nyāya-like in Sen's theory is the clearly articulated principle which Sen writes in italics: *To be is to be nameable.*

This is what makes him insist, against Frege, that the meaning of an open sentence and the reference of the corresponding abstraction are the same object. Meanings of at least some simple predicates are genuinely non-particular (unless Sen reduces *all* predication to ascription of particular Stoutian properties to other individuals which at some level, I think, will have to appeal to genuine generalities), and whatever is nameable can reasonably be called an individual. Sen thus believes in non-particular individuals too.

Contrasting Nyāya with Strawson

I have compared Nyāya and Strawson very often in this chapter. I wish to conclude by emphasizing how *unlike* in their details these two realisms are.

First, Strawson calls all qualities, including colors, mental states, etc., universals. Nyāya makes a strict distinction between non-universal qualities within which colors and mental states fall and genuinely sharable properties.

Second, both Strawson and Sen regard relations as universals. Sen is compelled to admit relations as objective universals because they have to be there as meanings of non-eliminable, many-place predicates. Russell had thought that the case for *relations* as universals is much stronger than that for attributes of the simple sort, because in order to eliminate the latter, the *relation* of resemblance has to be admitted as real and universal. But Nyāya does not admit relations in the inner circle of genuine mind-independent universals. As I have already remarked, I side with Sen and Strawson rather than with Nyāya, although I have tried above (in Section I) to hint at the sort of reason Nyāya might have for not finding *relations* in the class of *bona fide* non-particular individuals.

Third, Strawson admits propositions (or statements) as universals. Nyāya seems to avoid truth-bearers apart from *particular* pieces of personal cognitive episodes. Your falsely believing (or stating) that the earth is flat and my believing (or stating) the same thing are just two distinct mental (linguistic) events, both of which make reference to the same particular planet and the same non-particular shape-feature—flatness in a certain order of predication. Apart from these, there is no *universal* here introducible by a that-clause ("that the earth is flat") which would be the objective falsehood that we both believe (or state). Nyāya has many *reasons* to avoid these objective truths and falsehoods but also gets into deep *trouble* because of this avoidance. I think the reasons are worth the trouble.

Fourth, Strawson would classify *numbers* as first-rate samples of objective universals. Nyāya treats numerical properties not only as specific unshareable qualities of the particular counted clusters but also as having come into existence due to the counting. This is a confusing doctrine. Of course, once five pairs have all been found to be two in number, a universal twoness (or, to be literalistic, twonessness) is to be admitted as inhering in each of those five particular qualities of twoness—even according to Nyāya.

Fifth, Strawson believes that universals cannot be directly perceived or encountered in sense experience. As I have shown earlier, Nyāya rejects this narrow notion of experience and places our ability to be perceptually acquainted with some universals at the very heart of its doctrine of perception. Of course, not all universals are accessible to sense perception. Universals like *substancehood* are to be inferentially grasped, for not all substances themselves are perceptible. Besides, our *ordinary* perceptions never attach these theoretical categories of "being a substance" or "qualityhood," etc., to perceived objects. Substancehood is a philosophical universal, to be inferred as the property by virtue of which anything can be the inherence-hosting stuff-cause (*samavāyi kāraṇa)* of anything else. The doctrine of direct perceivability of some universals has always perplexed philosophers in the Platonic tradition. Perception of a particular as having an attribute may seem to presuppose perceptual knowledge of the attribute *as such*. But acquisition of the very concept of that attribute presupposes previous perception of particular instances of it: isn't there a *circularity* here? Unless you see flowerhood, allegedly, you cannot see particular flowers; but unless you see particular flowers first, you cannot begin to possess the concept of flowerhood. Which comes first?

An initial response will be to concede that perception of the instances is prior *in the order of acquisition*. But once dispositional grasp over the universal has been acquired, perceptual recognition of that universal in an instance is *logically prior to* the very concept of perception of the particular as an instance of that universal. The need for a bare perception of the universal property has often been recognized to be *a logical* or *conceptual* requirement rather than an actual introspectively detectable state preceding each perceptual experience. A deeper response could be as follows: direct perception of the universal (not *qua* a universal) presupposes prior familiarity with *some instances of it or others* (not with any specific instance). But a particular qualificative perception of, say, a material object such as a stone presupposes immediate perception of *that very* universal under which the object is identified on that occasion. The two dependencies are of distinct logical characters. The circularity is only apparent.

Sixth, Nyāya realism about universals is armed with a theory of blockers or disqualifiers of putative universals. Universalhood, for instance, is no universal. Strawson did not care to impose any such population control on his world of non-particulars. (Perhaps he thought that these do not take up any space after all.)

Seventh, Strawson's *predicates* necessarily stand for or introduce universals. They could never stand for particulars. (This would of course be inconsistent with recognizing John's anger as a particular.) Because of the "has"-model of predication, Nyāya insists that when I believe that Socrates has a beard, it is unnecessary multiplication of entities to hold that what he is believed to have is *the property of having a beard*. It is just the beard which is predicated of him. This gets rid of *beardedness* as a bogus universal.

Of course Socrates's beard and Plato's beard have a natural real universal *beardness* to share. But apart from that, Socrates and Plato do not share any extra feature of beardedness (*just as* they do not share a beard). Strawson could never reconcile himself with the claim that that mass of facial hair is exactly what is *predicated* of Socrates. He would suspect that the Nyāya epistemologist has been deluded by the copula "has."

Picture someone perceiving M. K. Gandhi as a wise man with a stick in his hand and with piercing eyes. Of course, having a stick in one's hand and having wisdom are different kinds of having, and each again is different from having piercing eyes. Even Nyāya recognizes that. That is taken care of by the exact relation or non-relational tie that the "has" stands for. It can be the "has" of possession, as in "Peter has a car;" or the "has" of a part-whole relationship, as in "Peter's car has a radio;" or the "has" of inherence, as in "The radio has a rectangular shape."

When either Sen or Strawson speaks of universals as real non-particular objects, they use the term "object" to mean what Dummett has recently called an *immanent object*.[26] Transcendent objects are self-standing particulars which (even in Nyāya) form the core of basic real entities which take up space or happen in time.

Does cowness, then, exist in *nature*? Strawson tends to say "No." Because cowness does not graze as cows do. It is *in* cows and cows are in nature. But its being *in* a cow, adds the Nyāya friend of Strawson, is *not* to be construed as a physical containment like that of a "berry in a bowl."

Insofar as Nyāya or Strawson never confers on *cowness* the kind of reality that particular cows have, neither of them has quite taken to "eating lotus with the Platonists."[27]

With the ontological link between ordinary objects of perception and universals established, I will now move to questions of epistemology. To be a realist about universals is to admit that we can know at least something about them. In what ways can we grasp such truths about universals? Universals, no doubt, play a role in our perceptual knowledge of particulars. Do we directly perceive these universals along with the objects they inhere in, or do we understand them only through abstract thought? If universals can be directly perceived, do they not have to have causal powers? If universals are timeless abstract entities, it seems ontologically awkward to claim that they can cause cognitive or brain states. How can we revise our picture of perception and its cognitive causation to accommodate sensory perception of universals? I will sketch such a revision in the next chapter.

3

On Perceiving Properties

Introduction

Unless universals take part in causation, and unless some of them are objects of ordinary sense-experience, insistence on the existence of universals would be vulnerable to a kind of fictionalism, as if the existence-claim were in need of the qualifier: "in a manner of speaking." Pranab Kumar Sen ends his essay "Strawson on Universals" with what I take to be a rhetorical question suggesting some serious disagreement with P. F. Strawson. He also whets our appetite for a more incisive treatment of this "sensitive" issue with a note that alludes to the work of Locke, Kant, Austin, and of the Nyāya epistemologists.

In this chapter I would like to take up Sen's bold suggestion—"if all our *present theories* of perception are incapable of accommodating the possibility of a perception of generalities, can't we think of revising our theories of perception themselves?"—and defend the thesis that universals can be perceived as directly as the particulars in which they reside. My method of defending this perceptualism about our knowledge of universals will be, first, to raise strong objections against that thesis, and then to answer them, working out, in the process, some required changes in our theory of perception.

I shall not argue against the nominalist claim that we can never see general properties because there aren't any. In the previous chapter, I have tried to prove the following conditional claim: *if realism concerning ordinary external objects of perception is true, then realism concerning some universals must be true.* Thus, if (even after being cautioned by physics and neuroscience) we claim to perceive the particular material objects that common sense undeniably feels that we do, then, insofar as our perception of these ordinary objects is irreducibly predicative in structure, we need to perceive the properties meant by those predicates as well. Even if we are often mistaken in ascribing the properties we seem to see in the external particulars, the detection of these mistakes presupposed that these mischaracterized particulars have real properties other than or incompatible with the ones we ascribe on those unlucky occasions. A normal nominalist is usually a believer in the mind-independent existence of particular objects (or particular insensible parts or causes of the objects) of perception. Such believers in the external world, I have tried to show in that chapter, would face an inconsistency if they denied the existence of language-independent and mind-independent universals.

But of course, it is possible to be an idealist or phenomenalist about the external world and to deny the existence of both ordinary material particulars and universals. That was the consistent but highly revisionary Yogācāra Buddhist (in effect Berkeleyan, minus God, minus self) package of wholesale anti-realism. In this chapter, I am not engaging with that position, although I shall address some arguments against the perceivability of universals put forward by the Yogācāra Buddhists. To clarify, I am not concerned here with a defense of realism about universals. But, assuming that there are mind-independent universals, I am concerned with the following questions. Can we only reason about them or can we also experience them? Can we encounter them with our sense-organs or can we access them only through thinking? Are they only conceived or, indeed, perceived as well?

I once asked a British music composer whether he thinks people actually *hear* the "musical work." He was unambiguous that the work itself is a universal that could be multiply exemplified in actual particular performances, during the long gaps between which it "is there" as a performable abstract entity, not to be equated with the scores, but merely represented by them. He said quite spontaneously that if the performance deviates too much from his original then it is *not his work* that people are hearing. Nonetheless, on a good day, in hearing an authentic performance of it, the audience, especially a well-trained audience, would most certainly *hear* the *work*, as well as hear that ephemeral sequence of sounds produced in the auditorium by the musicians on that occasion. That is why he said that when the critics write a review the next day they should make two separate sets of comments, one about the work and another about the particular rendition of it the night before. The distinction between these two targets of criticism would be clearer if the critic had heard more than one performance of the same musical composition. The discriminating critic's remarks are based on the experience of both, not on their *experience* of the performance(s) and their *thought* or imagination of the work. Against this intuitive theory that we perceive universals when we perceive one or more instances of them in the appropriate way, the following arguments could be given.

The first-sight argument

Only that sort of thing can be said to be genuinely perceived, an objector might say, which can be perceived in our very initial encounter with it through the relevant sense organ. But on the occasion of our sighting of the first particular exemplifier of a property we can never see the property it shares with other such particulars, because we have not yet seen those other particulars. Therefore, a property is never genuinely perceived by the senses unaided by abstract thinking. Even Russell (in *The Problems of Philosophy*), who believes that we can have direct acquaintance with universals, admits that whiteness or horseness can be seen only after several experiences of white patches or horses. We need to abstract the common property out of the instances, and thus, to use Russell's tell-tale phrase, "learn to be acquainted with" these properties. But a learnt acquaintance is no direct acquaintance, so goes this anti-perceptualist objection. Universals cannot be perceived on the untrained first sighting. It requires training to begin to see those particulars as falling under or manifesting the property with respect to which they resemble one another. Since the initial non-conceptual perception does not ever grasp a universal, a universal is not an object of pure sense perception. Concept-application, which is a non-sensory activity of thought, masquerades as perception when we *seem* to feel introspectively that we are *hearing* the common pitch across a regular interval between several strikes on the piano keyboard, or that, besides and along with the several ants, we are *seeing* the essence ant-hood.

A further argument is sometimes given to bolster this first-sight argument. A perception only grasps what is presented to the subject at the present moment of time. No one can claim to perceive the past or the future. The universal birdness is something that all past, present, and future birds have in common. The person who thinks he sees birdness must experience it as something belonging at least to all the birds that he had seen in the past and expects to see in the future. But to claim to see such a past- and future-involving entity is to mix up memory and expectation with what one is currently exposed to perceptually. Therefore, the so-called direct experience of the universal is never a perception proper.

There are many things wrong with the above line of argument. Most generally, the objection thrives on conflating "seeing" with "recognizing." Indeed, it is precisely those first encounters when an object goes unrecognized that count as cases of seeing, because otherwise any subsequent seeing would not count as seeing-again. First, it is not clear at all from where the first premise derives its strength. Even about particular concrete physical objects we cannot claim that we do not perceive them unless and until we attend to them in a naming-classifying manner the very first time they are presented to our senses. I am pretty sure that as a child, the first bird or ant I set my eyes on went unnoticed by me. A lot of tutoring, attention-drawing, and learning of the linguistic conventions regarding names and demonstratives might have been required before I started noticing birds and ants or telling them apart—and I am not even talking about noticing them *as* birds, *as* ants. The first-sight argument not only assumes that there is something like a pure non-conceptual perception of real particulars, it basically denies the status of proper perception to any subsequent experience which is due to trained attention, abstraction, comparison, and concept-application. Although this picture of real perception being untainted by concepts is popular among a certain stripe of philosophers—perception, they aver, is untouched by imagination, memory, concepts, and words like the baby's first experiences of the world—the average intelligent person takes the very first sighting of something to be a rather impoverished and vague experience of it. To see all aspects of it with care, to bring it under several classification schemes and to exclude it from some of those kinds or classes, to know what it is called and how it is described from different points of view is to get a *better* view of it, to enrich our perception of it, rather than to move away from genuine perception. Imagine a child saying "Where is it? I can't see it" after the first attempt at noticing something faint, distant, or easily confused with the background. "Try again," says the teacher, supplying some more clues and cues. "Ah! Now I *see* it," says the child. Such an assisted triumph of careful observation should not be discredited as just an intellectually adulterated non-sensory perception. The habit-honed experiences of an "experienced" perceiver are more, not less, genuinely experiential. Otherwise, the child ought to have said, "Ah! I now know what you are talking about, but since I have recognized it as falling under concepts meant by your words, alas, I no longer quite *see* it."

The very idea of pre-conceptual non-predicative perception is highly suspect. Even if we accept a variety of sense experience which is totally ineffable and free from any characterization of its own object, the vast majority of our adult perceptions are not like that, because we regularly tell each other what we saw and learn to see, hear, smell, and taste things better from what others tell us. To announce that only this first variety (what I have called elsewhere "immaculate perception"[1]) is genuinely sensory and all the rest is non-perceptual is intolerably hasty.

Let me rehearse here some five or six responses that Jayanta Bhaṭṭa (A ninth-century philosopher of the Nyāya school)[2] makes on behalf of the theory of real perceptible universals, after presenting the Buddhist Nominalist arguments against it.

i. Is it a "Royal Decree" that only the first awareness authentically touches the objects and is truly visual, whereas any subsequent ones are not so?
ii. Even if that first sight alone is the proof of something, how is one to ascertain that the unique specificity of a particular alone figures in such initial experience and not its shared properties as well? The duration of a non-conceptual perception, even if it happens in adult life before our experience gets structured into a judgment, is unobservably short. You (the nominalist) are saying that only the propertyless particular constitutes its content. We cannot decide who is right by mere swearing. So we must carefully analyze the content of the subsequent fully developed experience of particulars that we can talk about, and infer what must have been seen in that initial moment.
iii. The fact that upon our second and third encounters with the same sort of particular we recognize them to be of the same sort, shows that we must have seen the sort-making properties initially, though not as sort-making properties. If our first experience of a fruit would be totally innocent of any fruity character, then how and when suddenly out of the blue would our grasp of the fruit-universal arise through our subsequent experience? This point is worth pondering over.[3] It has been taken as uncontroversial that even if they actually possess general features those features could not be perceived at first. But once we start from this perception of the bare particular, our account of learning to acquaint ourselves with the shared properties or seeing similarities is never going to get off the ground. If the first sight shows only the propertyless particular, the second sight of another such particular is not a "second" sight of anything. And similarly the third sight of another instance of that as yet unperceived universal must fail to arouse any sense of resemblance or the feeling: "Ah! Another one of that kind," because one has never yet seen that kind, or that kind-making property, so that one could recall it. No amount of multiple encounters with individual dogs would then generate any sense of similarity or thought of shared property, because these allegedly pre-conceptual initial encounters would not be recognized as more than one encounter with the same object of perception, since the only object that can claim to be recognizably the same across them

would have to be the property which, on this account of concept-acquisition, is not perceived at all in these initial encounters. But we do see similarities and do experience individuals richly endowed with properties that we see that they share with other individuals experienced at other times and places. Therefore, this myth of the first encounter shorn of all properties must be dropped, and along with that the myth of imperceptibility of properties would be dropped too.

iv. You may say that generalities are mere imaginary constructions out of words (and their meanings) and do not owe their origin to any experience. "But that is not so. Even when the word for it is unknown, one sees the common form running through multiple instances, just as when a person from south India sees a convoy of camels for the first time." Similarly, when for the first time one's eyes fall on four fingers (this is Jayanta's example, but we now know from experimental studies of newborn's imitation behavior and other evidences that human children are born with basic face-recognition and body-part representation schemata), such visual perception already comes with a sense that those are four body parts of the same sort—even if four is not recognized as four, nor fingers as fingers. Here an extremely insightful remark made by Śālikanātha, an earlier philosopher of a distinct realist school (Prābhākara Mīmāṃsā), must be recalled: "What has been said (by the nominalist): individual cows (let's call them: 'the black-eyed-one,' 'the peaceful-one') are seen one at a time, but the universal cowness is not seen in any one of them, that is unproven. The universal is the form. Even when it is seen it need not be seen as a universal form. Until the other individuals are seen, recalled and compared, that the same form runs through them is not perceived. But the universal is what is actually uniformly seen and seen again among many particulars, not its uniform presence. Even when that characteristic of the universal—that it runs like a thread across many instances—is not grasped, that which possesses this characteristic, namely the universal itself, can be grasped."

v. Although, strictly speaking, a mere recalling of a past encounter with another instance of a universal would not be a perception, the seeing of a universal is not remembering but recognizing. Both remembering and recognizing depend on memory. The former takes the form: "That past *a* was *F*," whereas the latter takes the form: "This present *b* is the same *F* as that." The former is not a perception, but the latter is. Otherwise none of our perceptual recognitions of a familiar creature would count as perceptual. Because familiarity with a type invokes the memory traces of previously seen samples of the same kind. When I come back after a long absence to my own room, I may see it with nostalgia and warm hope. Does that show that I am not seeing my room as my old room but only thinking about the absent past and expected future?

vi. Finally, when we see a huge heap of tiny grains of the same natural kind, notice that here the compared particulars are co-present to the senses. It is only the common form shared by each individual grain which strikes the senses, not their unique individualities at all. It is nearly impossible for us to visually identify and re-identify the same grain in the same heap after a gap in looking. We are compelled to say that although the heap is seen generally as "a collection of some sesame seeds," the eyes must be seeing the particular grains as well, though not one by one as that very particular distinct from this other one. We are similarly compelled to say that even in the so-called first sight the universal is seen, though not as a recognized universal, because the question of recognizing it as running through many instances does not yet arise.

The cause-object argument

The second most important argument against my view that some universals can be seen in seeing their instances is given by Strawson, who is sympathetic to realism about universals but fails to understand how the ordinary talk about perceiving properties could be taken literally. Strawson's qualms can be formulated in the form of the following apparently valid argument:

A. If something has to be perceived, it must be the sort of thing that can *cause* an experience by interacting with our senses.
B. A universal, being an abstract entity, is not in time or space, hence it cannot cause an experience or interact with our senses.

Therefore, universals cannot be perceived.

Let us examine the premises of this argument. Śālikanātha anticipates this argument while critically defending the Prābhākara Mīmāṃsā claim that universals are accessible to sensory perception. He rebuts it by simply questioning the first premise. Every object of a perceptual experience need not be its cause. If x is known from the experience y, then x is the object revealed by y, he asserts, being committed to the rather peculiar view that all our awarenesses are correct and self-illuminating. Errors are explained in Prābhākara Mīmāṃsāas as failing to see the distinction between a correct perception and a correct memory, as cases of non-awareness rather than as instances of awareness gone astray. Thus, if an awareness certifies itself to be a visual awareness of a shared essence, then it must be so, because nothing can be a better judge of what exactly is the object of a cognition than the cognition itself. We need not take this infallibilist approach. But when I perceive the absence of my daughter at home, or see a big gap in the bookshelf, the absence or gap is surely something that somehow is registered by my senses. Yet, it sounds odd to say that the absence or gap—a negative entity—causes my perception in the same sense as a running dog would.

On a different note, this insistence on the object being the cause has always made way for the "scientific" rejection of direct realisms even about ordinary concrete macroscopic particulars. Yet, it seems initially plausible to hold that just as not all that causes a perception is its object (take the blood circulation or oxygen breathed in by the perceiver), similarly, not all that is its object is a cause. Under a certain interpretation of physics, what causes the optic nerves to carry the neural message that the brain processes as "seeing a dog" are some wave particles roughly in the area where the dog is seen to be. But it is the wave particles which are not seen but reasoned and thought about, whereas the dog, which is strictly speaking causally inefficacious, is undeniably the object of visual perception. If we deny perceivability to properties because of their causal inefficacy under a certain "scientific image," we also have to strip particular middle-sized concrete continuants of their intuitively obvious perceivability under that same image. Both will be reduced to "constructs of thought" under such a scientistic breaking down of real causal interaction. Under the "manifest image" both are equally objects of perception.

Even if we let **A** stand as a premise, **B** surely cannot be accepted so easily. True, the universal by itself is not there in space or time, because it is not there "by itself." We are not arguing here about the High Platonic universals which do not need their exemplifiers in order to exist and indeed are more real than them. We are talking about *seeing a universal as inherent in each one of its many instances*. If the instances are in space and time, then through them the Universal can be indirectly causally operative. Here we must remind ourselves that one of the most important philosophical grounds for postulating the existence of universals, at least in Nyāya-Vaiśeṣika, was their explanatory role as those generalities in virtue of which certain things and events cause other things and events ("limitors of cause-hood," to use the technical jargon of New Nyāya). Now just as the causal law that an A-type event causes a B-type event itself does not cause anything because it is not an event, similarly the property in virtue of which one event is a cause of another has a definite causal role to play, even if it is an abstract property present fully in many instances located in many different times and places. One way of thus rejecting the second premise of the cause-object argument would be to construe the causal role of a universal in the following fashion. The particular cat is supposed to be an object of the total perceptual (audio-visual) experience of "a grey cat jumping on the piano and the note C-sharp is heard" because unless that particular cat were there, that particular experience would not happen. Similarly the cat's grey color, as well as the catness of the cat must be objects of that experience because unless the cat was that shade of grey and unless it was a cat (unless, that is, it had catness), again, that specific experience would not have the content that it does. The general recognizable pitch-property of being C-sharp is also causally indispensable for the specific phenomenological content of that total experience. Thus, the visually accessible universal catness and the auditorily accessible universal C-sharpness are both causally necessary for the perceptual experience described above, and it is not correct that properties are causally idle.[4]

The reference argument

The last argument I shall consider has its roots in Frege's fear that to mention the meaning of a predicate with a name-like expression is to make a complete self-standing object out of it, when in reality it remains an unsaturated functional entity.

1. Whatever can be perceived must be an object of perception.
2. An object is something which can be the referent of a singular term.
3. But a property can never be the referent of a singular term.

Therefore, a property can never be perceived.

This argument has all the lure and all the weakness of a Kantian paralogism. Just as the paralogism of rational psychology skids over an ambiguity in the term "subject," this argument turns on an equivocation with the term "object." Whatever is the intentional accusative of a cognitive state is an object, in one sense. When I am reflecting on the shape called helix or on the moral virtue called honesty, that shape or that virtue is my object of imagination. But there is another sense of the term "object": a substance or thing. A stone is an object, but that the stone is rolling is not an object. In this sense, the shape helix is not an object, but something shaped that way would be. This latter sense, in which Frege draws the contrast between objects and concepts—that Michaelangelo's *David* is an object; that it is in Florence is a fact or true thought, and that the property by virtue of which filling up the blank in "_____ is made of a single piece of marble" with the name "David" yields a true sentence—is a concept. That property is not an object because, we could remark in Fregean vein, it is a function from objects to truth-values. But these two senses of the term "object" are totally distinct. Frege considered the realm of reference and the realm of sense to be utterly disjointed realms with no possible overlap. His objects, as against concepts, belong squarely to the realm of reference. But he routinely admits the possibility of making thoughts or senses of expressions the object (intentional accusative) of thinking or apprehension. The reference argument would succeed only if it could use the term "object" in **1** and **2** in exactly the same sense. But there is no non-question-begging way of establishing that only a substantial particular referent of a singular term could ever be the intentional object of perception. I just found out by touch that my computer monitor is colder than the surface of my palm. Must this fact be referred to by a name or singular term (formed with that prefixing device: "The fact that ... ") before I can claim that that is exactly what I have perceived? And if a non-commonsensical affirmative answer is insisted upon, then we can simply forget about the Fregean complications and reject premise **3.** Yes, a property can be the referent of a singular term. As Pranab Kumar Sen has ably demonstrated, we can cut through a lot of Fregean confusions, if we allow the meaning of the open sentence "x is wise," the intension of the predicate "... is wise," the property of being wise and the universal *wisdom* to be ontically all the same. Although he resolutely refuses to think of any complete or incomplete entity as a *referent* of a *predicate*, Sen has no problem assigning the object wisdom ("a property as an object") as the extension of the abstract name "wisdom." A property can be the referent of a singular term; it just cannot be a reference of a predicate, because a predicate expression does not do the job of referring according to Sen. So he rejects premise **3.** Notice his remarks (in response to Amita Chatterjee) which bring out the subtleties of his view:

> Going back to my favoured notion of a property, the possibility of translating a sentence with a predicate having a property as its intention into a sentence in which the predicate is replaced by a singular term having the same property as its reference—together, of course, with a two-place relational predicate like '.is possessed of ... '—unmistakably shows this. Although a property in this sense, i.e. *a property as an object*, is an 'intensional' entity, it can behave as an extensional entity in the context of the sentence which results from the translation. It does so for, first, in that sentence the singular term standing for the property would be interchangeable *salva veritate* with all other co-referential singular terms.

> Now, once this extensionality is established, there would be no difficulty in having a Tarski-type of truth theory for the so-called 'intensional' sentences. The development of the truth-theory would not be easy, but it would be possible.[5]

On tasting immanent universals

In a profound but somewhat puzzling passage in the *Posterior Analytics* (quoted as an epigraph for this essay), Aristotle had made a distinction between perception, memories generated by perceptions, and experience generated by consolidation of memories. But he also remarked rather mysteriously that perception is of the universal. For example, perception would be of man but not of Callias, the man. Of course, our initial perception of an arbitrarily chosen man would not clearly isolate the humanity inherent in him as a universal, distinct from his animality or dark-skinnedness. But the same humanity which must have been noticed by me in the very first instance later on is recognized in other specimens of humanity, since otherwise no amount of perceptions would make him "experienced" in what it is to be human.

But subsequent Western theories of perception have never faced this challenge of accommodating the fact that with our eyes and ears and skin and tongue we come across general properties with which we characterize, classify, distinguish, and cluster together our particular objects of experience. Of course, in one sense, we extract these empirical concepts—our recognitional capacities to detect universals as those very universals—from repeated perceptual encounters. But notice how we cannot ever acquire a concept by repeated encounter with bare particulars. While encountering many particulars, what we really need to *repeat* is our sensory encounter with the same attributes, ways, features, structures, patterns, relations, etc. Only a universal is repeatable, because it remains indivisibly the same while being found in many instances. Even if we manage to establish some a priori truths by reflecting upon, for example, the empirical concepts of sound and color, such as the truth that no sound has a color, our acquaintance with the property of being a sound, or with the property of being a color need not be a non-sensory acquaintance.

In Taber (2017)[6] we find a critical and comparative discussion of all the supportive arguments for Kumārila's Mīmāṃsā thesis that some universals must be immediately sense-perceived in order for linguistic communication and inference to function properly. Yet, Taber himself seems to side with the Western orthodoxy that our knowledge of universals must be intellectual or semantic—having to do with thinking and understanding—and therefore cannot be perceptual in the sensory sense.

"It remains very implausible that you can see, say, cowness," Taber remarks and goes on to justify his qualm by a quick argument: "What makes something a cow is a certain set of facts: it gives milk, it can moo, it chews the cud … that its DNA contains a certain sequence of genes. A collection of facts is not something one can see." Having thus expressed his serious disagreement with Kumārila, who staunchly believed in the direct perceptibility of universals, Taber goes on to compare Kurt Gödel's "perceptualist-realist" position about our epistemic access to abstract entities like "the objects of transfinite set-theory" to Kumārila's position about universals. Gödel, a typical Platonist, conceded that since abstract mathematical entities do not belong to the physical world, they cannot be objects of sensory perception, but insisted that we do have a direct "intuition" of them which is no less irresistibly forceful and reliable than veridical sense perception of physical objects.

Unfortunately, even Austin, who considered a couple of transcendental arguments in favor of the existence of universals and vindicated naïve-realism of a sort in a hostile atmosphere of phenomenalism and scientific realism, says dismissively: "The 'universal' is emphatically *not* anything we stumble across."[7] He also puts a strange and loose argument in the mouth of the realist about universals: "Since it is admitted that the things we sense are many or different, it follows that this 'universal,' which is single and identical, is *not sensed*." Actually, as we have seen before, this is a bad argument. As Jayanta[8] has pointed out, the things that we sense are known to be many and different, thanks to general properties which they are seen to share or not to share. Our theory of perception must make room for the appropriate complex of relations through which a universal (which is inherent in a particular material substance which, in its turn, is in contact with the sense organ) can link directly to the appropriate sense organ. As long as we understand how the operative link between the olfactory organ and the foul smell in the air is a logical product of the relation between the smelling inhalation and the air (contact) and between the particular whiff of air and its foul smell (inherence) and that smell quality and the general foulness which it shares with other distinct foul smells (inherence), there is no harm recognizing that we can smell (1) the general property of foulness as much as smell (2) the particular quality (odor) of that air as well as smell (3) the air. Such a detailed theory of distinct varieties of operative sense-object relations through which we perceive substances, tropes, events, event-universals resident in events, general properties of tropes, etc., is what Sen was gesturing toward when, in the last footnote to his paper "Strawson on Universals," he commented: "The Nyāya philosophers showed no hesitation in admitting the possibility of a perceptual access to universals, but rather tried to figure out what our perception has got to be to give us this access."[9]

I have a dispositional memory of the taste of a mango. My brain only remembers those tastes that my tongue has experienced once or more. I don't remember any particular mango or its specific taste. If I now eat an apple, I perceive that it does not have the taste of a mango. When I eat a particular mango, I clearly recognize that besides its own unique determinate taste—this one may be a bit tart with a sweet aftertaste—it does have a generic determinable mango taste. In that case, I must be tasting a universal in a particular too. Why not? Somehow, though, I expect that my two teachers Professor Strawson and Professor Sen would have had a philosophically juicy disagreement about this.

I have argued that it is both permissible and in line with our pre-philosophical intuitions to include universals along with the objects which exemplify them within the direct content of perception. Therefore, a realist about universals should be compelled to accept that perception is irreducibly predicative in its structure. With such an unconcealed rejection of non-conceptualism about perceptual content, we can now discuss the relationship between perception and speech. Many perceptions pass from our conscious awareness without being explicitly put into words. Yet, we can and do verbalize a good deal of our perceptions. Is the ability to be put into words an essential part of our possession of concepts usable in perceiving, or is there always a core of perception which is, in principle, unverbalizable?[10]

4

Seeing Daffodils, Seeing as Daffodils, and Seeing Things Called "Daffodils"

The question: Can we say what we see?

Do words or conceptual modes of presentation have a necessary role to play in awareness resulting from sense-object contact? This is a question which bothered Vātsyāyana, Diṅnāga, Udayana, Bhartṛhari, Frege, and Husserl and, more recently, Gareth Evans, Bimal Matilal, and Michael Dummett.[1]

The question concerns the exact content of a particular type of awareness which is called 'perception *(pratyakṣa)*. *And* it goes without saying that lots of such perceptions go without any *saying*. Yet, the only way to *talk* about their contents is to use names or descriptions of the items figuring as objects of the awareness to specify linguistically what structures the experience "bathes in" or what objects 'float in the perception.[2] To interpret the word "unverbalizable" *(avyapadeśya)* in Gautama's definition of perception, Vātsyāyana makes the following point: Concept-words may be needed to articulate the content of each perception *from outside* when we ascribe the perception to someone else. But that does not mean that the perceiver has *used* the concept or the word in identifying the object *from inside* the experience. The Sanskrit word *iti* (as) which he uses here to draw this distinction between seeing a color and seeing it as that color is also the quotational device. Imagine an Indian villager who has not read Wordsworth being presented with a bunch of daffodils. He will see a bunch of daffodils but not as a bunch of daffodils. We can use the word to describe what he has seen without implying that he has any inkling of the word or the concept it articulates. Just because words and classificatory notions are needed for perception-ascription *(abhilāpa)* it does not follow that they are submerged in or required *for perception.*

Since the time when I originally wrote this chapter, I have revised my views quite substantially on this issue. I now think that it is possible and natural to possess and apply conceptual modes of presentation without using or even knowing the words for them. So this "or" in the expression "words or conceptual modes of presentation" cannot be so glibly glossed over. My new understanding, which enables me to see Matilal's point in a more sympathetic light, is argued for in Chapter 22 of this book, which is a slightly revised version of "Sense-perception, Concept-possession and Knowledge of a Language." first published in: *Relativism, Suffering, and Beyond: Essays in Memory of Bimal K. Matilal.* P. Bilimoria, J. N. Mohanty, ed. Delhi; New York: Oxford University Press, 1997.

Buddhists like Diññāga would only consider pre-predicative pure wordless sensations to be proper perceptual knowledge. Any predication, conceptualization, or verbalization not only opens up the *possibility* of error, it necessarily distorts the pure individuality of the perceived particular. To identify is to classify, and for such arch-nominalists, to classify is to falsify.

So, strictly speaking, although inference and verbalized perception are admitted by the Buddhists as forms of knowledge on a pragmatic transactional level, knowledge in the absolute sense is confined to ineffable simple apprehension.

The argument for the omnipresence of words

In spite of his alleged Buddhist affiliations, Bhartṛhari (a philosopher of Grammar) went to the opposite extreme: no awareness is untouched by language. Implicitly or explicitly even infants or animals cannot have experience which is not at least potentially perforated with words. Two major arguments that the pan-linguist uses to prove his contention go like this[3]:

A1. No intentionality without linguistic structure.
A2. No consciousness without intentionality.

Therefore, no consciousness without linguistic structure. Furthermore,

B1. Every awareness illuminates something outside itself.
B2. Illumination consists in articulation of structure of the object.
B3. No articulation of structure is possible without a speech-like grid.
Therefore, awareness consists in use of speech (implicitly or explicitly).[4]

Notice that B1 will be right away rejected by subjective idealists like Diññāga. I also suspect that the Buddhist account of intentionality will have to be reductive such that to use Frege's example within the context of the idea of a heavy shell, the distinction between *parts* and *properties* will be smudged off. Heaviness is taken (by the realist) to be a property of the shell. But once the identities—heaviness = *mental image* of heaviness (or, difference from non-heavy things), shell = *idea* of shell—are established, the one mental entity becomes *part of* another and the exemplification relation is eliminated. If "aboutness" is construed in such intimately internalistic terms, the need for linguistic or predicative structure will melt away from the core of experience-episodes. As the object-ward arrow turns back reflexively to the inherent form of the awareness itself, awareness is liberated from all obligations to both language and world!

The Nyāya middle ground

Standard Nyāya epistemology stands somewhat in between Bhartṛhari and Diññāga on this issue. Unlike Buddhists, the Naiyāyika holds not only that perception most often *does* have predicative structure whether it is actually verbalized or not but also that proper knowledgehood attaches only to such predicative perception. The argument for this is straightforward:

> Nothing but *a true* awareness *can* be knowledge. An awareness is *true* just in case the predicated property actually belongs to the item which figures as the subject. So, truth presupposes predicative structure. Hence, perception can be *knowledge* only if it has a predicative structure.

To put the point a bit differently: only that which runs the risk of error can count as knowledge. This basic assumption of Nyāya—which Potter calls "fallibilism"—goes against the epistemologically over-ambitious Buddhist. Diṅnāga requires perception to be non-erroneous *(abhrānta)* and moreover regards only that piece of awareness as *knowledge* which *could not* be erroneous. Insofar as unmistakenness or "non-promiscuousness" *(avyabhicāritva)* is part of even the Nyāya definition of perception, we cannot *claim* to have seen something unless we have seen it correctly. But for the actual *truth* of the experience the external world must co-operate. Given such externalism, perception for Nyāya needs to be unmistaken but not unmistakable. As Socrates saw in the *Theaetetus,* if perception has a simple particular content, we either see it or do not see it, there is no possibility *of* seeing it *falsely.* It takes *two* to make room for error. Truth thus requires the duality of the subject and the predicate or of the object and the concept. Before it was given a taxonomic twist, the occurrence of the word "unverbalizable" (*avyapadeśya*) in that aphorism was interpreted by Vātsyāyana as applicable to *all* perceptions.[5]

Matilal underscores Vātsyāyana's ingenuity of interpretation as follows:

> In the sense-perception of a child (who has not yet learned the words to designate things) words do not play any significant role. When a person learns the name of a thing and perceives that thing, he says that it is called such-and-such. But as far as his awareness of that object is concerned it does not differ very much from the case of a child's perception. This shows that designation by name is not an essential factor in our perceptual process or cognitive act … the distinction, made for the first time, between conception and its phonological realization, may be attributed to Vātsyāyana … A child may be said to have concepts before he acquires the corresponding words.[6]

However, the matter is not so easily settled. After paying due tribute to Vātsyāyana, Matilal proceeds to develop points left unexplained. In his later work, *Perception,*[7] he formulates the problem in terms of the following principles:

> P1: For all x there is some f such that, if x is presented to awareness then x is presented under the qualifier f
> P2: For all x, and for all f, if x is presented under the qualifier f then *prior to such presentation,* f must first be presented separately

New Nyāya seems committed to both the principles. Notice that it is only a prior awareness of f which is presupposed and not a prior awareness *of* x on its own before "x as f" can be experienced. If I hear a certain utterance as qualified by a southern accent I must have a prior awareness of what it is for an accent to be southern, but I surely do not need to have *a prior* awareness of that particular pronunciation-token. Still, this sounds like a strange doctrine to many Western ears, for *particulars* have been often considered *intuited* or *given* prior to propositional awareness, whereas immediate bare acquaintance with universal features has rarely been proposed. We may find *PI* to be inconsistent with the received Nyāya wisdom that the form taken by pre-judgmental perception of an object is best verbally expressed as, for example, experience of cup *and* cupness. This would entail a *conjunctive* as against predicative piece of cognition. But isn't the cup—the bare object—identified once without any mode of presentation at all? Remember that even this-ness can serve as a mode of presentation. Nyāya has no qualms about indexical or even uniquely exemplifiable qualifiers, whereas perceiving an altogether unqualified particular is hardly ever admitted as possible. In being presented as an element of *cup-and-cupness* the cup does not *wear a* cloak. It is *with* its cloak.[8] If we take these two principles equally seriously, there seems to be a vicious regress. If perceiving any old x causally requires perceiving it under a mode *f* and if the mode has to be perceived *prior* to this predicative perception then, substituting *x* with f, even the mode needs to be perceived under a further mode g and so on.

Bhartṛhari's solution—which Matilal calls "Nativism"—was that f need not always be presented in experience because the basic word-concepts are beginninglessly and innately present in human consciousness. Even if I have not learnt the name "gold," the simple universal which is to be its meaning is entrenched in my consciousness such that even on the initial presentation of a sample piece of that metal I can apply the concept to it. Such a solution was not to a Naiyāyika's taste. The Naiyāyika lays down a further caveat to P2:

> When I know an ultimate simple universal (a natural kind or an unbreakable titular property), I *may* know it without any mode of presentation.

Doesn't this exception-clause look like just an *ad hoc* measure to stop the regress? Our understanding of speech is necessarily qualificative. Indeed, according to received Nyāya wisdom, it is *doubly* qualificative. Someone's statement "Bush is stubborn" can be understood only if the understander represents (committedly or otherwise) Bush under stubbornness, while stubbornness itself is brought under some mode of presentation like: *being a character-trait.* Thus, if simple universals are fit to be designated by words, they must be presented under a further mode of presentation. The exception-clause seems out of place!

Is there a non-conceptual part of all experience? A dilemma

At this point we seem to face a real dilemma: either we admit that the universal presented in a bare or unqualified way is ineffable or innate to consciousness so that each effable experience contains an unsayable element in it or we admit that even the qualifying universals can and may figure as meanings of "nessy" words (e.g., "goldness" or "stubbornness") and thus are presentable under further cloaks (when by "cloak" I mean a perceptual mode of presentation).This keeps open the possibility of a regress.

Finding a provisional solution between Matilal and Dummett

Dummett has always been interested in defending a variety of unverbalizable knowledge which is somewhere in between *propositional knowledge that* and *practical knowledge how*.[9] He thinks that our knowledge of a language is this kind of implicit knowledge and that is part of the reason why a truth-conditional theory cannot do full justice to what is known when a language is known. Now, as a realist, Frege is committed to *all* our knowledge having a thought content which, even if not actually put into a sentence, *can* be so expressed because *in the order of explanation* thoughts are nothing but meanings of sentences. Although we can never dig out any notion of a Fregean thought from a Nyāya theory of epistemic contents, there too one finds the same *realistic tendency* to assume that everything that is knowable is sayable. The Buddhist anti-realist, on the other hand, as we have already noted, typically considers the paradigm cases of knowledge to be beyond words.[10] Very recently[11] Dummett looks back at Husserl to excavate the source of what he calls Analytic Philosophy's Cardinal Priority thesis: viz., *language is prior to thought in the order of analysis.*

Dummett quotes a passage from Husserl which sounds like an outright denial of the possibility of non-qualitative perception. Husserl almost seems to repeat the Naiyāyika's Principle Pl—that whatever is experienced must be experienced as falling under a *type.* Dummett, then, locates in Frege the Nyāya-like principle that an object (reference) can be given to us only under this or that mode of presentation (=sense). But he thinks this principle eventually clashes with Frege's doctrine that grasping a thought denuded of *all* its verbal clothing *is a* logical possibility. Matilal notices a similar tension in Udayana. He thinks, on the one hand, that Udayana was so much influenced by Bhartṛhari that he had to admit that any experience worthy of being called knowledge (*pramā*) must be word-impregnated. Otherwise, it would not be subject to public epistemic appraisal. On the other hand, there was the principle of prior acquaintance with the qualifier which, to stop the regress, had to be admitted as non-predicative and pre-linguistic.

After unearthing this tension, Matilal comes close to suggesting that we forget about *nirvikalpaka*, or prior bare acquaintance with universals, when we are doing epistemology. His point is not to deny that such pre-predicative cognitive states exist or may even be necessary conditions of predicative perception, but rather that they are irrelevant to epistemology's project of distinguishing knowledge from error, because such non-conceptual sensation would be neither. Even the so-called inchoate wordless experience of an infant, he remarks, `may lack full-blown concepts. But this experience is only unconceptualized, not unconceptualizable.[12]

We may now wonder on what *basis* does Matilal settle the issue somewhat in favor of Bhartṛhari and Frege, and against the knowledgehood of prelinguistic perception? Doesn't he himself remind us that even Bhartṛhari has to soften his original pan-linguistic claim a little bit when he gives the example of the man running (barefoot) on grass having tactile sensations of the individual blades of grass without any remote possibility of verbalizing such sensory awareness? Just commenting that such *incom*municable experience could not be analyzable in epistemology *because* they are unverbalized does not convince us that they are not perceptions *at all.* Perhaps we should draw a distinction here between a full-fledged knowledge-episode which counts as a perception—a perceptual judgment—ready to be evaluated as "non-erroneous" and a perceptual experience like the tactile and proprioceptive feel of running barefoot on grass on a cold morning. True, we cannot *tell* what it is that we are aware of when we have such inchoate cognitions, as animals and infants cannot. But the unnameability of the object(s) does not entail the non-existence of any object. We cannot argue that inexpressible awareness is no awareness because it *lacks* object-directedness. Yet that is precisely what Matilal seems to conclude. The so-called bare sensory grasp of an infant, he decides, does not amount to awareness. Perhaps Matilal was trying to do justice to the explanatory priority of fully conceptualized predicative perception. In discussing the relation between thought and language, Dummett comments:

> Most unverbalized thought on the part of adult human beings is related to fully verbalized thought as a sketch to a finished picture; it can therefore be explained only in terms of that of which it is a sketch.[13]

Perhaps, further, Matilal is not totally *denying* that languageless experience can and does happen. He could be simply endorsing Udayana's downgrading it as non-knowledge. Bhartṛhari, of course, would have retorted that even the unsayable gets a place in his wordy world by being called "unsayable." After all, *avācya* ("unverbalizable") is a word, isn't it?

I have heard it occasionally suggested that Professor Matilal merely interpreted Indian philosophy but did not change it. I think the above recounting of his reasoning that Nyāya epistemology looks neater if we prune off non-qualificative awareness altogether shows that he *did* change philosophy in the same sense as a Raghunātha Śiromaṇi or a Russell did. And of course to that extent he ran the risk of refutation.

In order to be explicated as a specimen of knowledge, a particular perceptual awareness must be verbalizable despite its possession of an implicit non-verbal element. But how should this knowledge be described? Does a perceptual awareness grasp a timeless truth, or does truth arise from an awareness's specific relationship with its object? Nyāya upholds the thesis that everything which exists is knowable by us. It might seem contradictory to call everything knowable while still maintaining the realist intuition that there are some unknown truths. We cannot point out any specific unknown truth without thereby knowing it. But are unknown truths true propositions which are not grasped or even graspable by anyone, or can we consider them true awarenesses which have passed unrecognized by whoever had them? In the next chapter, I will articulate a definition of truth which allows us to take the latter, non-contradictory position.

5

Truth, Recognition of Truth, and Thoughtless Realism

Introductory remarks

In the West, Socrates initiated the practice of philosophy as a search for correct definitions of fundamental concepts such as Virtue, Beauty, Courage, Knowledge, and Friendship. But the search would often abort and seldom succeed. According to Donald Davidson, the only definitions that Plato finally found satisfactory were answers to the not-so-momentous questions: "Who is a sophist?" "What is a triangle?" and "What is mud?"[1]

In ancient India, the Nyāya Sūtras tried to construct systematic philosophy with the three avowed steps of enumerating, defining, and examining the definitions and defending the definienda against actual and imagined counterattacks. Unless you can *define* what perception or inference or knowledge or substance or a universal is, how can you go on to *prove* that such things exist, *and if you* cannot *prove* that such *things exist, how can you claim* that *they exist at* all? The sophists and skeptics showed how all definitions suffer from under-coverage, over-coverage, non-applicability, incoherence, circularity, or infinite regress. It was hard to withstand the devastating critique of all definitions and all alleged means of knowledge launched by Nāgārjuna, Jayarāśi, and Śrīharṣa. The business of proposing a "conclusive definition" of anything became difficult, complicated, and abetting for skeptical dialectics. But the classical Indian philosophers would not give up.

Witnessing the fate of the correspondence, coherence, pragmatist, and, most recently, deflationist or minimalist definitions of *truth*, Davidson has recently called the

The two philosophers Gaṅgeśa (thirteenth century) and Frege (late nineteenth, early twentieth century) had very similar insights about truth, although we shall explore how widely divergent their views were about the bearers of truth. Witness the following two remarks:

"Where something really is, apprehension of that there is true awareness; or, apprehension of an object through a certain predicate when, in fact, that object possesses that predicated feature (is *pramā* in the sense of true awareness)"—Gaṅgeśa, in *Tattvacintāmaṇi*, edited by Kamakhyanath Tarkaratna, Bibliotheca Indica, Calcutta 1884, Vol. 1, p. 401 and, "It is worthy of notice that the sentence 'I smell the scent of violets' has the same content as the sentence 'It is true that I smell the scent of violets'. So it seems, then, that nothing is added to the thought by my ascribing to it the property of truth"—Gottlob Frege, in "The Thought: A Logical Inquiry" in *Logical Investigations*, Oxford: Blackwell, 1977.

very drive to define truth a “folly” and an “ugly urge.”[2] He is not the first to be cynical about the matter. Before him both Kant and Frege argued that a general definition of truth is impossible. After a quick summary of their arguments, I shall go on to recount several reasons that Gaṅgeśa, the early fourteenth-century Indian epistemologist, gave for *not counting* truth as a genuine natural *universal*. Gaṅgeśa also rejected a naive correspondence theory of truth.

I shall try to show that in spite of defining truth as a (non-universal) feature of personal and ephemeral awareness-episodes—of *jñāna*—rather than as an eternal feature of impersonal objective propositions or thoughts, the Nyāya realists such as Gaṅgeśa could, with exemplary ontological parsimony, maintain that truth is independent of recognition of truth.[3] Their realism about external objects of perception as well as about universals managed to combine epistemic modesty (the view that not all that is true is known to be true by us) with epistemic optimism (the hope that everything that is reality—constitutively the case—can be directly or indirectly known by someone or other) as well as fallibilism (the view that all that we believe may not be true).

Thus, although both error and ignorance about objects *outside* our awareness are recognized as possible, we are not eternally doomed to be in error or ignorance. Nyāya realism never claimed that there are things-in-themselves or truths-in-themselves which are in principle unknowable. The Indian realists only claimed the existence of those things which they could also find accessible by some means of knowledge. Hence the famous thesis:

> Everything that we can talk about has existence and knowability (or its converse, “Everything that has existence has knowability and nameability”).

Even if, extensionally, all that exists is knowable and all that is knowable exists, the existence of each of these things does not *consist in* being known (or talked about). An object of knowledge, especially when the knowledge-episode is generated in part by that object, must be antecedent to that piece of knowledge and therefore could not be constituted by it. First the object exists, then it is registered in veridical awareness, and *then* it is spoken of by words. But the merely existent, the known existent, and the known and named existent are all one and the same entity. Hence the co-extensiveness of the three universal domains.

This joint insistence on the knowledge-independence and the universal knowability of objects has recently come under fire. Roy Perrett has shown, using an elegant proof in epistemic logic, that the universal knowability thesis is logically incompatible with the central realist tenet that certain things are true without our actually recognizing them to be true.[4] The bottom line of this proof is that if everything is knowable then everything is known! For those of us who wish to vindicate Nyāya's claim as a robust realism about a knowable but knowledge-independent external world of particulars and universals, such a proof would be bad news! Luckily, as I try to show in this chapter, the proof does not work.

After showing how the Nyāya definition of truth escapes Kant's and Frege's arguments against the very possibility of a definition of truth, I shall endeavor to explain why realism does not need non-mental atemporal truth-bearers (propositions) which are eternally and wholly true (or wholly false), and why knowledge-independence of truths and things can be shown without admitting the existence of unknowable things or truths. Realism about epistemically accessible objects can very well live with the fact that we cannot ever find one (currently) unknown truth.

The elusive nature of the false and the unknown

The seemingly innocent distinction between true and false beliefs is the source of unending trouble. It is akin to dividing fruits into apples and non-apples. While it is almost certain that some of my current beliefs are false, there is no coherent way in which I can get hold of any one of these errant beliefs while it remains my belief. This incapacity is not primarily due to my lacking a general criterion of truth. Even if I were wiser and had such a criterion, I could not locate a belief, call it mine, and diagnose it as false. For, to call it false would also mean that it is no longer my belief (unless I am confessing self-deception; but can self-deception be concurrently *confessed*?). Thus, although I know that its being true is not ensured by its being believed by me, I can ascribe falsity only to others' beliefs and to my own past beliefs. I simply cannot judge a present belief of mine to be false. The attempt to be epistemologically modest by adding "I believe" before a claim that *p* is unsuccessful. Just as the reverse qualification "It is true" fails to strengthen, this qualification fails to mitigate the assertion any further than the simple assertion that *p*.

We shall remark later on that, just like the untrue beliefs that I know are lurking somewhere in my web of beliefs, the unknown truths also pose a similar problem. Being known by me is a contingent and eminently dispensable property of things or truths. But I cannot produce a single object or proposition that is true and claim that I do not know *that* object or *that* proposition.[5] This does not entail that I know all things any more than the fact that I cannot find a currently held false belief of mine entails that all that I believe is true.

Redundancy of the qualification "It is true" may be the reason why philosophers have always been suspicious of truth as a property, just as they have been suspicious of existence as a property. It has proved tricky to point out what difference is made to a thing talked about by adding "and it exists" to the list of its predicates. That does not mean that any and every thing we seem to talk about must exist.

Similarly, it is not clear whether anything new is added to the content of her own belief by a person when she says about her belief that it is true. Also, it is far from obvious what sort of thing a belief has to be so that it can retain the same content no matter whether we affirm or deny the truth predicate of it. But from this suspected redundancy of the truth predicate one should not jump to the conclusion that all that a person believes is already true.

Frege was intrigued by the slippery nature of the adjective "true." He saw that even though endorsement and assertion (more accurately, reassertion) were done by the use of this adjective, it not only adds nothing to the sense of the original sentence, but it could not even add the assertive *force*, in case the original assertion lacked it. To say "If it is true that P then Q" instead of "If P then Q" is not to take away the unasserted character of the antecedent P. Yet, this adjective is surely not a piece of senseless gibberish. It *seems* to stand for a property that all true statements, beliefs, and judgments share. But because of this non-additive nature, Frege wondered: "May we not be dealing here with something which cannot, in the ordinary sense, be called a quality at all?"[6]

Frege argued that addition of "It is true that … " to a sentence does not enhance the content of the embedded sentence. He also maintained that each time anyone asserts a content, such a predication of truth is implied or understood. All predication involves predication of truth to a thought! Thus the truth-claim goes without saying and when said out loud goes without any communicative gain. But still the word "true" is neither unimportant nor meaningless. Indeed Frege remarked that it is because the word "true" is so transparent in content, that it "indicates the aim of logic."[7] In spite of giving the concept of truth so much weight, Frege was convinced that no general definition of truth can ever be given. He was particularly intolerant of the correspondence theory of truth which one would otherwise expect a realist like him to uphold.

In the next section, I will try to restate Kant's and Frege's reasons for avoiding attempts to define truth. I argue that they have failed to give any conclusive proof for the indefinability of truth. Socrates might not have successfully defined much else besides a "triangle" and "mud," but he kept trying. We too must continue looking for an adequate definition of truth. Even failed searches are of immense value to philosophy.

Kant and Frege on the indefinability of truth

In an uncharacteristically humorous passage, Kant compares the effort to answer the question "What is truth?" to milking a he-goat.[8] Also found in clearer terms in his *Logic*, the argument behind his indefinability thesis goes like this:

1. A general definition of truth for all cognitions would be a universal criterion of agreement of a cognition with its object.
2. A universal criterion applicable to all cognitions will have to abstract from the specific contents (matter, or reference to specific objects) of each of these cognitions.
3. But the (material) *truth* of every cognition concerns specifically this content, which varies from cognition to cognition.
4. So a general definition of truth will have to be at once unconcerned with the specific objects of different cognitions, because of its universality, and *concerned* with those specific objects because they are what determine the truth of each distinct cognition.
5. Since no definition could at the same time abstract from and be sensitive to the topics of the cognitions, the very idea of a general definition of truth is a contradictory idea.[9]

While there is much to heed in this argument, all that Kant has proved here is that there cannot be any universal recipe for determining the truth of all cognitions.

The conditions for the truth of different beliefs will vary as their content-structure varies. General definitions like "A cognition is true just in case it is an apprehension of reality" are rejected by Gaṅgeśa because all beliefs, including false ones, are apprehensions of reality insofar as there is nothing else to be apprehended. Strictly speaking, each belief that is true will have a distinct subject-matter-specific (homophonic) truth definition. But we could try to come up with a general rule for generating such specific truth-definitions for each structurally articulate cognition.[10] That is what I think Gaṅgeśa achieves by first denying that truth is a natural universal property and then generating a characterization which uses relative pronouns as if they were variables (*yat, tat*) to marks for qualificandum and qualifiers of cognitions. One of Gaṅgeśa's final definitions of true awareness is uncharacteristically nontechnical. To make an ungrammatical English translation for the sake of mirroring the logical structure of the original: "Awareness of *what* is *whereas* that being there is true awareness" (*yatra yad asti tatra tasya anubhavaḥ pramā*).[11] Gaṅgeśa anticipates Kant's concern[12]:

> The correlative pronouns "what" and "that" in the definition do not make the definition non-generalizable, because veridical awarenesses are not veridical with regard to all objects but only in restricted cases. Thus the question "Which awareness is true with respect to which place (= subjectmatter or object of awareness)?" will have different answers in case of different definienda. Hence it is in the fitness of things that the definition should be given in terms of open pronouns like "what" and "that".[13]

One definition of truth that Gaṅgeśa rejects outright is the pictorial version of correspondence theory. "Awareness of an object just as it actually is" is not a good characterization of veridical awareness. The phrase "as it is" (*yathā*) introduces the idea of resemblance. But an awareness of a cup has no resemblance with a cup. Whatever general resemblances there may be (e.g., that the cup is perishable, so is the awareness) are also there between a false awareness and its objects.

Frege too argues in great detail against the pictorial correspondence theory of truth. He fears that if the idea is said to be true in virtue of similarity with its object then a perfectly true idea will be identical with the object. Udayana expresses this concern when he brands the Nyāya position "externalism": "The alleged resemblance (similarity of form, *sārūpya*) between awareness and its object is not acceptable under externalism (*bāhyavāda*).[14] But Frege's chief argument against correspondence or any definition of truth is based upon one assumption which Nyāya realism emphatically denies.

Here is Frege's famous regress argument against the very possibility of defining truth:

1. Assume that "x is true" is defined by "x has feature F."
2. In order to see whether a particular thought S is true, by this definition, we shall have to check whether S has feature F.
3. But, to recognize the presence of a feature in a thing is to recognize the thought that that thing has that feature to be *true*.

4. So, in order to see whether S has F, we must first see whether the thought that S has F (call *this thought S2*) is true.
5. In order to see this, we must first see whether S2 has feature F.
6. Before we can judge S to be true we shall need to complete an interminable series of investigations under any definition of truth, whatever F might be.

Michael Dummett[15] and others have exposed the sophistry in this argument by showing how one can either block or neutralize the regress. It looks vicious only if one recognizes truth to be a substantial property but demands adherence to the indefinite reiterability of the "It is true that ... " operator without any change of sense.

The Nyāya will reject step 3 (truth predication is *not* involved in every other predication) and the dogma that all awarenesses reflexively ascribe truth to themselves. Ordinary human awarenesses are *not* self-aware, otherwise all looking or touching would be partly constituted by looking within or introspecting. Ascription of truth to an awareness is not the same cognitive act as that awareness or as registering the occurrence of that awareness.[16] It is the implicit assumption of this reflexive self-certification doctrine that has made Western theories of predicative perception so muddled and always at risk of losing touch with the causally operative external world of sensible things.

Gaṅgeśa agrees with Frege that "being true is not a material, perceptible property."[17] My smelling the scent of violets, even as *smell of violets*, is surely a case of smelling and its object must be a material perceptible property, namely the fragrance of violets. These two premises should have been enough to conclude that there is no recognition of any thought being true here. Whatever is cognized here is cognized entirely by the sense of smell. Yet, truth of thoughts cannot be smelled even by Sherlock Holmes.

Frege does not draw this conclusion. He draws the counterintuitive (and Kantian) conclusion that we cannot ever know that the violets are fragrant merely by our senses. That these *violets* are fragrant is a thought and we have to nonsensibly apprehend this thought in order to attain perceptual knowledge!

Frege gives a quick hint of a reductio argument against a purely sensory account of predicative perception. Such a thought-eschewing direct sensory account of concept-enriched perception is, by the way, the heart of Nyāya externalism. I am here referring to the view that senses grasp the same objects and properties that inferentially we think about or in language we publicly refer to and in action we engage with. Here is Frege's argument in favor of his view that perceptions, insofar as they are capable of being true or false, go beyond sensory acquaintance and involve apprehension of thoughts: "If I could know that the rose is fragrant simply by my olfactory sense, then I would have been able to also perceive by some sense that I do not smell anything at a certain moment! Since sensory perception of such a negative fact is impossible, sensory perception of violets as fragrant is also impossible."[18]

The Nyāya has two answers to this objection. First, my awareness that I am smelling or not smelling a rose is not on a par with the olfactory perception that the rose is fragrant (or of the fragrant rose). The former is an apperceptive awareness about my perceptual state rather than about the rose. Its instrument is the inner sense, not the olfactory sense organ. Second, there is nothing absurd about the claim that I do perceive by a sense organ that I am not smelling anything. The absence of smell is recognized by the olfactory sense organ, whereas the absence of any smell experience in me is recognized, albeit, perceptually, by the same inner sense which would have introspected that I am smelling something if I were. In the face of the Nyāya theory of perception of absences, Frege's argument from noticing lack of perception fails to add polemical support to his Kantian view of all perceptions as involving recognition of truth of thoughts.

Why truth is not a genuine natural kind

J. N. Mohanty, whose work on the Nyāya theory of truth is a classic in the field, shows discomfort with the explicit talk of veridicality "arising" or "being generated" in a cognition by some special excellences in its causal conditions. The cognition can be generated, but how can its truth be generated? Surely it is true that snow is white before and after somebody attends to the color of snow and has, according to Nyāya, an ephemeral episode of awareness that snow is white! I share his discomfort, but I do not think Gaṅgeśa's talk about "the origination of truth" is a result of sloppy use of words. Why is it so repugnant to think of the truth of a true awareness arising along with it? One reason could be a presumption that truth must be a universal property of all true cognitions. But Gaṅgeśa gives three good reasons why truth is not, technically, a natural universal (*jāti*). Hence it has no initial claim to eternity or timelessness.

As was discussed in Chapter 3, first a real universal residing in a perceptible particular must itself be perceptible, like the flowerness of a flower or the fishness of a fish. A piece of knowledge is a perceptible particular, because the knower can, through inner sense, perceive her own knowing. But the truth of that very piece of knowledge can never be perceived. It has to be always inferred from the pragmatic success that the awareness leads to. About the test of truth Nyāya is unambiguously pragmatist. Therefore, truth is not a real universal.

Second, a real universal, if it inheres in a particular, would permeate all of it. We cannot say that a fish is partly a fish. But truth can belong and can be ascribed to only a part of a complex awareness. Indeed, all false awarenesses are partly true (to be precise, they have to hit their subjects or qualificanda *correctly* in order to be false *of* them) according to Nyāya. Take the belief that Plato had a student called Aristotle whose Physics replaced Quantum Physics in AD 3000. Does not this have a good deal of truth in it? But it is not wholly true, at least not yet. So truth is not a real universal.[19]

Finally, real universals, in Nyāya Vaiśeṣika, have to pass a rather tough test. A universal property can be related to another universal property either by their respective extensions being totally disjoint or by their extensions being included into one another. Taxonomically, therefore, substancehood and qualityhood are two natural kinds because no substance is a quality (the extensions are disjoint). Substancehood and earthenness are also both natural universals because all earthen things are substances. But the extensions of two universals cannot partially overlap or intersect. That is a universal blocker called "intermixture." Truth belongs to direct perceptions, but not all direct perceptions are true. Truth also belongs to inferentially or testimonially gathered mediate knowledge, but not all such indirect awarenesses are true. The class of true awarenesses overlaps with, partially excludes, and is partially excluded by the class of perceptual awarenesses. Truth is blocked from being a genuine natural universal by the defect of intermixture.

If it is not an external universal property shared by all and by only true awarenesses, what is it? The technical Nyāya name for the category of characterizing general features which do not count as real universals is *upādhi*, which I translate as "titular property." The three distinct omnipresent properties, namely, existence, knowability, and nameability are also titular properties. A real universal cannot reside in another real universal. Knowability is in knowability because philosophers can know knowability. So, knowability is titular too.

Truth, as J. N. Mohanty has pointed out, is a "hybrid property." Unlike Fregean ontology, which has the true and the false hanging around eternally irrespective of human cognitions, Nyāya asserts that there would be no truth unless there were these object-directed non-self-cognizing episodes of awareness. The causal dependence is clear. Truth requires a match, not between proposition and fact, nor between belief and states of affairs, but between qualifiers figuring in awareness episodes and the objects which those cognitive episodes take as their qualificanda or chief topic. Since objects and properties become qualificanda and qualifiers only when awarenesses *arise* in individual knowers, truth also arises. Gaṅgeśa seems to extend the notion of non-locus-pervading properties to temporal parts.[20] He discusses this in the context of the suggestion that even a mutual otherness (*anyonyābhāva*) could be taken as non-locus-pervading. To quote:

> Therefore, about the pot which is baked red, the awareness "This (is, tenseless) black" would, of course, be veridical, because at some time blackness was in it. Surely, "It is black now" would be a false awareness. [Elsewhere he remarks:] "The black pot is (now) not black" is not contradictory because of distinctness of times. Experience thus shows that both an object and its otherness can stay in a single thing (at different parts).[21]

Paying attention to the time and occasion of a truth-claim is crucial for Nyāya. When Gaṅgeśa remarks that "a true cognition is not true everywhere, but only somewhere" (*na hi pramā sarvatra pramā kim tu kvacit*) by that "somewhere" *(kvacit)* he also means "at certain times only." This close connection between truth and time is difficult to understand from a classical Western realist standpoint where truth is often timeless.

Realism and the paradox of acknowledged ignorance

Udayana illustrates "self-awareness-contradicting" *(svajñānavirodhi)* with the statement "I do not know this (now)."[22] The demonstrative "this" claims that the utterer has immediate knowledge of the object, which the rest of the statement claims that the utterer has no knowledge of. Such an utterance would be pragmatically self-refuting even if it is not logically self-contradictory. Berkeley's master argument against externalism was basically an attempt to force the externalist into this sort of a self-refutation. The realist makes an innocent *general* claim: "There exist *some* objects that I do not know or know about." Berkeley challenges: "Is that so? Then show me one such object." Any fool who would try to meet this challenge directly will end up uttering what Udayana called a self-awareness-contradicting sentence: "Here is one object which I do not know." Russell thought he had made a great breakthrough when he got himself out of this impasse by means of his distinction between knowledge by description and knowledge by acquaintance. The realist claim may sound contradictory if plainly put: "We know that lots of things exist which we do not know!" But once we notice that the knowledge of their existence which is claimed and knowledge of them which is disowned are two distinct kinds of knowledge, we can then say, quite coherently, "We know, by description, generally, that lots of things exist which we do not know individually by acquaintance."[23]

Without using this distinction to support a scientific realism where material objects remain forever imperceptible, we can learn an important lesson from it: there are gaps in my knowledge and errors in my beliefs.[24] I know that only generally. I should not be tempted to give an individual instance of such an ignorance. For, the statement, "P and I do not know that P," is paradoxical. It is paradoxical because asserting P as the first conjunct pragmatically or conversationally implies that P is known by the asserter which is what the second conjunct denies. If "I" was replaced by my name or the present-tensed verb was replaced by "did not," it would no longer be paradoxical. "P but Arindam does not know that P" could be true. About all my new discoveries I could say, "P but I did not know that P." But just like "P is false but I believe that P," the present-tensed first-person acknowledgment of ignorance is self-refuting.

In his paper, "Is Whatever Exists Knowable and Nameable?" Roy Perrett has tried to refute the Nyāya thesis that everything that exists is knowable. He takes for granted the realistic commonsense thesis that there are some unknown truths. He then shows, using a *reductio* of the universal knowability thesis that the realist acknowledgment of some unknown truths, "p and it is not known that p" is inconsistent with the Nyāya insistence upon universal knowability.[25] "If p then it is knowable that p." The proof goes this way:

Initial assumptions:		
The universal knowability thesis:	$p \rightarrow$ it is possible that Kp	(T1)
The realist's avowal of non-omniscience:	$p \& {\sim}Kp$	(T2)
Knowledge, by definition, entails truth:	$Kp \rightarrow p$	(A1)
Knowledge distributes over conjunction:	$K(p \& q) \rightarrow Kp \& Kq$	(A2)
Now:		
(1) $p \& {\sim}Kp$		[T2]
(2) It is possible that $K(p \& {\sim}Kp)$	[Substituting 1 for p in T1]	
(3) It is possible that $(Kp \& K{\sim}Kp)$	[2, A2]	
(4) It is possible that $(Kp \& {\sim}Kp)$	[3, A1]	

We land in a contradiction because of the joint assumption of T1, T2, Al, A2. A realist would not like to give up T2, Al, or A2. The only way out is to give up T1. Therefore, the universal knowability thesis (T1) must go.

This looks unnerving at first for everyone who wants to hold on to the straightforwardly realist twin thesis that some truths are unknown yet all truths are in principle knowable.[26]

Perrett acknowledges that it is unfair to graft modal logic onto Nyāya because there simply is not any room for possible worlds in Nyāya thinking. He is well aware that Indian Logicians interpreted "Everything is knowable" as "Everything is actually known by God." But he guesses that the Nyāya would also hold on to a temporalized version of the claim of the universal knowability thesis: everything is actually known at some time or other by humans. The argument from liberation in support of this, however, is less than convincing: "If knowledge of the categories (*padārtha*) is supposed to be the means to such liberation, then Nyāya is committed to the possibility of such knowledge by humans."[27] The kind of liberating knowledge of all knowables, for example, does not amount to a detailed knowledge of each particular knowable object. Such detailed omniscience cannot be required as a means to a Nyāya style liberation, especially when it is explicitly said to consist in knowledge of the self as eternally distinct and free from its accidental qualities such as pleasure, pain, desire, and object-dependent cognitive states.

Now, the claim that humans *can* know all things can mean simply this: Everything is such that some human or other did, does, or will know all of them. This is a far cry from a claim of any single human being's guaranteed future omniscience. Since Nyāya rejects the reflexivity of cognitive states, it is possible for a person to have a piece of perception and immediately afterwards fall asleep. Since there will be no apperceptive awareness of that perception, it will never be known or remembered by him or by other humans. It is clear that the Nyāya Vaiśeṣika meant the following: so long as the human liberation-seeker knows what makes something a substance, a quality, a cause, an action, a universal, etc., and thereby attains self-knowledge with the proper moral preparation, he can hope to be liberated. Detailed omniscience of all things on heaven and earth was never a necessary or sufficient condition of Nyāya liberation. Perrett knows that the liberated human being, in Nyāya, knows nothing (rather than everything).[28] Being omni-temporally saddled with omniscience, God cannot ever afford to lose all awareness.

In any case, in view of the anachronism of modal operators in the context of Nyāya, Perrett gives a temporal ("Diodorean") version of the argument. He reads "S" as "at some time" and symbolizing "All truths are known at some time (by humans)" as:

$p \rightarrow SKp$,

calling this T3, the new proof proceeds:

1*. p & ~Kp
2*. SK (p & ~Kp) [From 1* and T3]
3*. S (Kp & K~Kp) [From 2* and A2]
4*. S (Kp & ~Kp) [From 3* and A1]

Now 4* is as much a contradiction as was 4.

Rescuing Nyāya from Perrett's proof

There are two kinds of problems with this second version. First, let us discuss the formal problems. In formulating the assumption T3, the letter "p" is used as a schematic letter standing for any arbitrarily chosen proposition. Basically T3 says: For all p, if p then there is a time at which p is humanly known. But in T2, "p" is not used in the same manner. What T2 says is: There is some p such that p and there is a time at which it is not known that p. Once we clarify that T3 uses universal quantification over propositions, $((\forall p)(p \rightarrow SKp))$ whereas T2 uses existential quantification over them, and also make explicit the existential quantification over times $((\exists t)(\exists p)(p \,\&\, {\sim}Ktp))$, the argument does not go through. Here are the first two steps re-stated fully:

1**. There is some p such that p and at some particular time it is not known that p. [Clarified T2]
2**. There is some time at which it is humanly known that there is some p such that p and at some particular time it is not known that p. [Replacing p by 1**, in Clarified T3]

Now the contradiction which was brewing at 2* which said that at some time it is known both that it is true that p as well as that p is unknown *totally vanishes* from 2**. There is no incoherence involved in admitting that at a certain time (let us say t1) it is humanly known that some true proposition (which is known to be true at t1) is such that at a certain time or other (let us say, t2) that proposition is humanly unknown. Every history of progress of human knowledge must assert many such claims!

To put it even more succinctly, once T2 is stated as an existentially quantified claim:

$$(\exists p)(p \,\&\, S{\sim}Kp)$$

the complex predicate "SK" would not simply distribute over both the conjuncts embedded inside the scope of the quantifier. Of course we can revise A2 now as follows:

$$K\,(\exists x)(Fx \,\&\, Gx) \rightarrow K\,(\exists x)(Fx) \,\&\, K\,(\exists x)(Gx)$$

which will give us, in the third step, at best:

$$SK\,(\exists p)(p) \,\&\, SK\,(\exists p)(S{\sim}Kp).$$

There is no possibility here of a conflict between the first and the second conjunct, simply because the "some time"(s) hidden under those similar-looking uses of the "S" operator could easily be two different times. Also, the second conjunct itself can simply be the truth that it is known at some time that for some (true) p, at some other times p was unknown!

What threat does this proof pose for Nyāya? We notice several problems. First, as Perrett himself apparently recognizes, it is not fair to represent the Nyāya claim about the universal knowability of *things* as the claim that all *truths* are knowable. It is not clear in the first place whether the very notion of "ALL TRUTHS" is coherent. The concept of the set of all truths may itself turn out to be a contradiction-generating concept. Besides, from a Nyāya perspective it is not clear what is meant by "knowing a truth." Does it mean knowing a proposition which is true (which should be synonymous with "knowledge") or does it mean knowing that one has known a truth (which is knowledge of knowledge)? They are very different things in Nyāya, for reasons discussed above. Thus, even if we forget the momentous matter of Nyāya's innocence of propositions (or Fregean thoughts), the thesis of knowability of all truths is not attributable to Nyāya on the basis of the fact that all that exists is said to be knowable. Truths are not the sort of things which exist in the Nyāya-Vaiśeṣika world.

Finally, we have seen that propositional truth works in a radically different way than truth of awareness episodes. If a proposition has one false conjunct the entire proposition is false. If an awareness has one true and one false part, it has truth, but only in part. We must be careful about assuming how the universal knowability of things or the actual unknownness of certain things is construed by Nyāya. If by "knowledge" we mean undetailed cognition of things as existing, then through the universal *reality* (*sattā jāti*) with which everything is somehow connected, even a certain non-ordinary perceptual connection (*sāmānyalakṣaṇā pratyāsatti*) with all that exists can be claimed by anyone who notices reality as the omnipresent universal in a single thing![29] In this sense Nyāya gives up the claim that there is a single totally unknown thing even for humans. How, then, can Nyāya maintain its *realism*?

Concluding remarks about knowledge-independence and knownness

I shall answer this question with the help of an idyllic (but by no means idealistic) analogy. Each and every flower in a certain garden may have a bee on top. It may be impossible to show, find, or describe a single bee-less blossom in that garden. But no one would dream of thinking of any one of those flowers as bee-dependent or bee-immanent. Similarly, each object in this world may be knowable, yet no object needs to be knowledge-dependent or knowledge-immanent. Knowledge-independence of objects need not be vindicated by showing or claiming the existence of unknown objects, let alone of unknowable ones. A flower is not made by a bee, nor is it inside a bee. In order for a flower to be there no bee needs to be on it.

We must draw, at this point, a distinction between two kinds of knowledge-dependence, namely, causal and *recognitional*. A state or object is causally knowledge-dependent if it could not exist or come into being without some knowledge or cognitive episode arising first. True pleasure, for instance, is causally knowledge-dependent. I cannot be truly pleased by something unless I first know it. But a state or object is *recognitionally knowledge-dependent* if it could not exist unless it is recognized as existing by a piece of knowledge of that object or state. A state of pleasure, according to Nyāya, is not recognitionally knowledge-dependent since it *can* exist without knowledge of that pleasure.[30] Similarly, truth of a particular awareness cannot exist without that awareness (remember that truth is not an eternal universal).

Since the only bearers of truth are awarenesses, truth is thus causally awareness-dependent. But a true awareness need not be assessed as true in order to *be* true. A separate piece of (inferential) awareness may certify the original awareness to have been true. Neither the original awareness nor its truth is dependent upon this separate recognition of truth. Truth is not recognitionally knowledge dependent.

Since Nyāya realism eschews non-mental truth-bearers, there is no place for causally knowledge-independent truth as a property (or referent!) of all true propositions.

Even for God, whose knowledge is coextensive with reality and truth, truth is not recognitionally knowledge-dependent. He knows all things because they are real; they are not real because he knows them. Knowability has been defined by Udayana as "the property of being related to some knowledge by the relation of causal *generatorship*."[31] X is knowable to the extent that X can or does causally generate knowledge (of X). This precludes the possibility of X's *consisting of* knowledge of X insofar as nothing causes itself. The constant co-cognition of existence and knownness is an inconclusive sign (*asat anaikantika hetu*) for the idealistic thesis. If all existing things were actually known, existence will still not consist in knownness. We do not need unknowability for demonstrating knowledge independence. Indeed knowledge-independence of the object is most clearly appreciated *when the object is known*.

The admission that all things are knowable can, if one does not take great care, lead to the idealist claim that any object of a particular awareness is identical with the awareness itself. We can escape this by admitting that although truth arises as a quality of mental awarenesses, the objects of our awarenesses—which alone make an awareness true or false—are still independent of our knowledge of them. Such awarenesses remain true whether we recognize them as so or not. This is not the only route one might take to affirm the reality of the world. There are certain (non-dualist absolute) idealists who are just as committed to saving the pragmatic reality of the external world as realists are. Such idealists believe that although external objects are distinct from and independent of mental states, both sorts of things are equally dependent (falsely projected) on a transcendent impersonal pure consciousness. Does this argument truly save the external world, or do these idealists paint a picture of the world that they would not ultimately accept?

6

Idealist Refutations of Idealism

Idealisms and idealisms

Idealism is a sticky doctrine. Each of us believes that there are lots of things existing and taking place beyond our actual or possible knowledge. No one seriously believes that whatever is unperceived or unimagined by oneself simply does not exist. Yet we have to live with the predicament that we cannot put our finger on any one such object without somehow touching it with our language and mind. Even our imagination seems to suffer from this incurable ambivalence between self-containment and self-transcendence.

Some famous refuters of idealism have, thus, themselves ended up with a profounder entanglement with idealism. Claims which establish the existence of material objects have been supported by metaphysics which relegate both the mental and the material world to mere appearance. Direct access to the external world has been ensured at the cost of reducing outer space to a subjective form.

This movement of philosophical thought has been illustrated not only in ancient India and modern Europe but also in contemporary analytic philosophy. Staunch supporters of realism who are out to explode the "myth of the subjective" or resist relativism are found to give up the notion of scheme-transcendent reality[1] or language-independent truth. Realisms become increasingly "internal,"[2] "reference … drops out,"[3] and coherence yields correspondence because the only available notion of reality is still grooved with our thought and our talk.[4] Whether we should call such double-aspect views "realisms" or "idealisms" is a largely nomenclatural question. It was once fashionable to add qualifications like "Objective," "Transcendental," "Critical," "Formal," "Absolute," etc., to idealism. Nowadays, "realism" is coupled with adjuncts like "Anti," "Quasi," "Reductive," "Internal," etc. Without entering into this jejune jungle of labels, I wish to re-evaluate two classical critiques of idealism which were launched from deeply idealistic points of view, namely those by Śaṅkara[5] in the East and Kant[6] in the West.

As we shall see, despite profound similarities, the subjective idealistic targets of both Śaṅkara's and Kant's attacks, as well as their own idealistic views, are very different. Moreover, the Eastern argument against a mentalistic reduction of the external world—although it anticipates some essential points of it—is structurally unlike the Western refutation of idealism. Yet if we ignore the inconsistencies, obscurities, and logical gaps in the details of these two sets of domestic disputes within idealism, we can derive the following three lines of thought:

1. They both rely on a conception of consciousness or subjectivity or self which has no bias toward the inner, the psychological, or the mind. Call the former pure consciousness "mind*" and the psychological individual mind "mind." The strategy is to make the world mind*-dependent but mind-independent.
2. Thus, they both try to achieve some sort of mind-independence without taking objects as metaphysically transcendent to consciousness.
3. They both embrace a picture of self-luminosity of awareness while rejecting the picture of reflexive self-awareness.

The Mind-only school of Buddhism

Although the Buddhist view, which Śaṅkara chose to attack, is sometimes termed the "Mind-only" school of thought, we must remember that the Buddhist subjective idealists did not believe in the existence of finite or infinite substantial minds or enduring selves. The position is somewhat like that of Berkeley[7] without God or souls.

Generally, but not necessarily, following Śaṅkara's own portrayal of his opponent, let us briefly rehearse the standard Buddhist arguments *for* idealism.

First, no consistent theory of a mind-independent material world is possible. The manifest middle-sized objects of our ordinary wakeful experience can either be admitted to be partless or infinitely divisible, or explained as collections of a countably finite number of atoms. The partlessness of atoms renders their size-increasing partial contact unintelligible. Complete all-round overlap of many atoms would never give us a larger aggregate. Yet if we do not believe in physical objects of unequal dimensions, their divisibility and the terminus of the process of division seem conceptually inevitable. The only way to escape such antinomies would be to give up our belief in physical bodies.

Second, the notion of a real object of awareness involves the twin concepts of being a cause of the cognition and being the intended topic (or phenomenological accusative) of it. But no external object can fulfill both roles. The atoms, which are said to constitute the pot, have the causal power to produce my perception, but my perceptual content does not reflect the atomic form. The gross pot, on the other hand, though it lends its form to my awareness, is not real enough to be its cause. If we confine ourselves to the inner flow of successive self—grasping perceptual states simultaneously caused and colored by their own objective aspects—we can manage to explain the construction of the so-called external world more parsimoniously and coherently.[8]

Third, awareness and its object are constantly co-cognized. We cannot think of an unsought object. The Berkeleyan flavor of this particular argument is unmistakable. Yet it is distinctive insofar as the constant correlation of an object and someone's apprehension of that object is tightened from both sides. An objectless cognition is shown to be as impossible as an uncognized object. If it is impossible to isolate them, then the object and the awareness must be the same.

Fourth, the standard argument from illusion. Our veridical wakeful awareness is phenomenologically indistinguishable from dream-awareness or other such illusory or hallucinatory awareness. Hence, they must be equally devoid of any outer support.

Śaṅkara's attack on the Mind-only school: a critical look

Following the classical Indian philosophical style, Śaṅkara starts with a mock-defense (of the above kind) of the subjective idealism to be demolished. His added zeal to counter those arguments is explained by the fact that his own Absolute Idealistic Monism, popularly expressed through calling the whole world mere Māyā (magical illusion), is likely to be confused with the idealistic doctrines sketched above. While refuting the Buddhist idealist, Śaṅkara's realistic emphasis makes it hardly credible that he himself holds the view that one undivided objectless, impersonal, transcendentally subjective consciousness is the sole reality. The intricate polemic starts with a head-on attack on the conclusion of the Buddhist arguments, namely that empirical awareness requires no object beyond itself.

1. This or that external object is lit up by every piece of awareness. The thrust of the submission is basically like Moore raising his hands to prove that there are physical objects. But Śaṅkara refines the reply by pointing out that the same awareness which testifies to itself and its object also testifies to the distinction between the two.

2. The idealist says that what is actually inner and mental appears as if it is outer and physical. But, if we have never actually encountered the physical and the external, how could we ever mistake things as such? If, as the first argument of the Buddhist tried to demonstrate, being a physical object is as incoherent as being a square-circle, how can anything appear like a physical object?[9]

3. The argument from constant co-cognition can be disposed of by pointing out that the alleged inseparability of knowledge and object only proves that if we have to deal with, talk about and refer to objects we have no access to them except through our cognition. But it does not show that the object is ontologically identical with awareness. Once again Śaṅkara plays a realist role in pointing out that the fact that the two are cognized together only proves that they are two rather than one.

4. Although awareness and object are inextricably presented together, they can be conceptually segregated. We can isolate our experience as the constant factor. Conversely, when we compare our perception of an object with the remembering or imagining of that object, it remains invariant while the cognitive states differ in quality. Thus, object and awareness can be isolated from one another. Here, once again, Śaṅkara anticipates Moore's central point against the idealist.

But how good is this argument from comparison and contrast? It surely brings out the non-identity of consciousness *simpliciter* with consciousness *of blue* because there is also consciousness of yellow. But does it show that blue and yellow could exist without anyone being conscious of them? Not all dance is a dance of Tango because there can be a dance of Waltz. But that does not prove that an undanced Waltz exists or is even possible.[10] Śaṅkara could of course balk at the analogy because there is no pure dance which is not a dance of Waltz, Tango, Fox-trot, or some such, whereas there is, according to him, pure objectless consciousness as our consciousness during deep dreamless sleep which we recall after waking up to have been devoid of any ordinary object.

5. Finally, the comparison with dreams, etc., is challenged by Śaṅkara on the basis of some essential qualitative disparity between veridical waking experience and dream or illusory experience. Subsequent cancellation and inner incoherence characterize dreams as detectably false, whereas the coherence and uncancelled nature of waking experiences testify to their truth. When we are ushered into a dream, there is no clear subversion of the previous waking life as we feel at our exit from dreams.

We must note here that Śaṅkara's realistic zeal strikes us as oddly hypocritical because elsewhere he himself makes the following kinds of subjective idealist remarks:

> The suggestion that there exists in reality something which is not known does not stand to reason. It is like saying that a visible form is seen but there is no eye to see it. This or that object apprehended may be absent but apprehension itself is never absent … It is incoherent to suppose that something really exists but is not known.[11]

Compare this idealistic passage with the same thinker's refutation of idealism:

"The objects which are apprehended in waking experience are never in any state of consciousness rejected as unreal."

Was he forgetting that according to himself the self-realized mystic's experience makes all external plurality melt away like a dream or a universal hallucination?

Clichés like "It's God's dream not mine" or "A dream that all of us dream together is not a dream" have their own problems. For a Monist like Śaṅkara, distinction between me and God, or between I and all of us, is not metaphysically available.

We can better locate the real contrast between Buddhist empirical idealism and Śaṅkara's transcendental idealism at the following points:

a. Śaṅkara's is a three-level theory of unreality: the unreality attached to unappearable non-entities; that which belongs to the content of individually subjective illusions, hallucinations, and, dreams; and that which belongs to the empirical world which is more real than the contents of a dream but less real than pure undifferentiated consciousness. If we call them the absurd, the illusory, and the phenomenal, respectively, Śaṅkara can be consistently interpreted as blaming the Buddhist for confusing the phenomenal with the illusory. Kant too blamed Berkeley for reducing bodies to mere illusions while he himself reduced them to phenomena.
b. Śaṅkara's own idealism can fall back upon the changeless transcendental self, which is the witness of all else while remaining unknown in itself, whereas the Buddhists have no consistent theory of re-identification of physical objects or of correct memory or of even apparent permanence of the knower because they insist on the momentariness of discrete unowned bits of sensation.
c. The consciousness which constitutes ultimate reality for Śaṅkara has no bias toward the mental or inner. Apparently, the Buddhist idealist also overthrows both the inner

spiritual ego and the outer material substance in one stroke. In fact, not only do the idealist Buddhists degrade bodies to mere illusion, they likewise reduce the ego. Yet, the remaining flow of self-grasping intentional states in Yogācāra Buddhism is still mental in nature. The view from inside is supposed to be truer than that from outside. Against this, an idealist refuter of idealism like Śaṅkara regards or disregards both inner and outer objects as equally objective, equally non-illusory, and equally non-real. According to Śaṅkara, we cannot assign any ontic status to our intentional cognitive states which we are not ready to assign also to their bona fide external objects because our psychological states are equally objects, equally rent with plurality, equally limited by temporal and even by spatial limitations. The real noumenal consciousness which witnesses all outer physical and mental phenomena is never made an accusative of any awareness not even available to introspection.

d. The subtlest distinction is between the two idealisms' notions of self-consciousness. The Buddhist idealist uses the self-luminous character of consciousness as a ground for concluding that awareness needs no external object. Śaṅkara rejects the lamp analogy and argues against himself that the perceptive awareness is not self-revealing. Fire does not burn itself, it requires fuel to burn. The lamp does not illuminate itself, it needs our eyes, or rather, our consciousness, to reveal the lamp.[12]

But without embracing some picture of self-revelation, how can Śaṅkara stop the feared infinite regress? Śaṅkara indeed characterizes the witness-consciousness to be self-intimating—not in the sense that it is its own object, but in the sense that it is pure subjectivity immediately presenting itself without being objectified or referred to.

A mentalistic idealism is abjured because it accepts one half of the immediately experienced world, viz. the grasping aspect, while rejecting the other half, viz. the grasped material objects. But a deeper metaphysical idealism is embraced because nothing but the never-negated pure consciousness is real. We must resist the temptation to call it the "Universal Mind," for it transcends the public/private distinction as well as the distinction between matter and mind.

I am not sure that the above four distinctions could be defended against all criticisms. Yet it is intriguing to notice that Kant too can distinguish his own idealism from that of his opponent only on similar grounds, namely (1) notion of an ever-unknown Self, (2) distinction between "appearance" and "illusion," (3) treatment of both the inner and the outer world as ontologically equidistant from things in themselves, and (4) distinction between empirical introspection and transcendental apperception.

Kant and his dogmatic idealist

The major dispute between the non-dualist Śaṅkara and his Buddhist subjective idealist opponent is with respect to the existence of the eternal self, which, at the ultimate level, is held to be identical with God. It is, of course, the heart of Buddhist idealism to deny the existence of any such eternal God or individual or universal self. Later on, in Kashmir Shaivism which borrows more openly and deeply from Yogācāra Buddhist idealism but regards the variety of objective public external world as a non-illusory "play" of dynamic self-consciousness, this disagreement with the Buddhist with respect to a permanent self (which is to be "recognized" as God) becomes even more stark. Buddhist anti-realism about the external world is repeatedly shown to be an inescapable and unpalatable logical consequence of the Buddhist denial of a permanent unitary center of consciousness. So, however confusing the alignments of the different shades of idealisms which refute each other may be, the patterns of their disputes corroborate our central claim: that realism concerning the external world requires realism concerning a persistent unitary self holding together the fleeting variegated manifold of mental states.

Unlike Śaṅkara, Kant never portrays the idealism he refutes clearly or faithfully, and it remains initially confusing that he regards Descartes (insofar as in the first *Meditation* he casts doubt on the very existence of external physical bodies) as a problematic idealist. There are three or more recognized versions of his attack on idealism. Sometimes he seems to be attacking the following position: there exists no external world beyond the world that we humans perceive and infer. This is done by insisting on the existence of things which we cannot directly know but without which there would be nothing to appear as the world. Kant's anti-idealism in this sense is extreme but the agnostic consequences too are as drastic as those of his own professed target of attack, viz. the problematic idealist. Sometimes he is attacking the position that the physical world in space is never as directly and certainly known as our inner mental states. This is done not by any reference to things in themselves but by appeal to the material bodies which are as much part of "Appearance" as the cognitive states are. Kant's realism here is secure but as "internal" as Putnam's these days. The two senses of the phrase "objects outside us"[13] that emerge are not only distinct but opposite. Things in themselves are metaphysically mind-independent but never known. Physical objects are in a broad sense mind-dependent but they are also objects of a direct perceptual knowledge.

Accordingly, one can get seriously confused by Kant's use of the label "Idealism." How does one become an idealist in the sense objectionable for Kant? By denying the existence or the direct knowability of extra-mental entities? In the *Prolegomena*,[14] Kant claims that although (like Berkeley) he has reduced all corporeal qualities to secondary ones, he is still a realist because he hasn't denied the existence of the knowledge-transcendent substrata. So, it would seem that it is the existence-denier who is the idealist to be refuted; whereas, he remarks explicitly in the *Critique*:

> The term "idealist" is not therefore to be understood as applying to those who deny the existence of external objects of the senses, but only to those who do not admit that their existence is known through immediate perception.[15]

Berkeley never denied that physical *objects* are immediately perceived. In fact, it is avowedly to restore the immediacy and certainty of our perception of material bodies that Berkeley proposed his theory. Hence Kant is sometimes charged of deliberately misconstruing Berkeley's position when he is attacking it. Once we forget about the noumenal things-in-themselves, about which Kant's arguments are historically shaky, and stick to the "outside in space" sense of "outside," we notice the following profound similarities between Kantian and Berkeleyan idealisms:

1. Both Kant and Berkeley set out to answer the skeptic and establish that we can know the existence of both ourselves and the external world with equal directness and certitude.
2. Both take space and objects in space as devoid of any absolutely experience-transcendent reality.
3. Both give some criterion for distinguishing mere subjective illusion from objective truth. It is quite false that Berkeley has no criterion of truth.[16] And indeed Kant's and Berkeley's methods of separating the real from the merely fanciful are similar.[17]
4. Was Kant then being simply dishonest or inconsistent in refuting idealism?[18] The passivity, clarity, vividness, and coherence with which normal veridical waking experience is received by us are taken equally seriously by Kant and Berkeley. Both locate the ultimate source of such experience outside the flow of ideas and outside our empirical egos.[19] But the real difference emerges in the two following points:

First, for Kant the cause *or* source of the subjective ideas is absolutely unknown and unknowable.[20] But for Berkeley, we can know if not by sense perception at least by intellectual notions our mind-independent source of objective ideas and know it to be spiritual in nature. Since Kant pleads ignorance he also can't assert that things-in-themselves are spiritual.

Second, Kant regards space as an a priori form of intuition presupposed by all experience. Berkeley considers the idea of space to be as empirical and derived from experience as any other. Recall Śaṅkara's objection: what sense can the idealist give to the universal mistake of considering inner objects to be outer, if there is no real encounter with the outer at some time? Berkeley but not Kant will be vulnerable to that objection. Kant provides rules for discriminating between correct and incorrect, objective and delusive applications of the a priori form of outsidedness in space. Indeed Kant seems almost to echo Śaṅkara when he remarks "in order even only to imagine something as outer, we must already have an outer sense."[21]

With the above preliminaries, let us now briefly recount the steps of Kant's much discussed refutation of idealism. In this "refutation" Kant's tone strikes us as over-realistic, especially when we consider its conclusion in the context of Kant's three main idealistic themes, viz. (a) the Copernican revolution, (b) the transcendental ideality of Space, and (c) the priority of the inner sense.[22]

I shall first go through the argument step by step and subsequently comment on each step.

The steps of the Kantian refutation: a scrutiny

A. I am aware of myself as changing through time.
B. This temporally conditioned experience of myself, like any other perception of change, presupposes something permanent in perception.
C. This permanent backdrop is not to be found within myself in the introspective world which is wholly in time and therefore only changeful.

D. So the presupposed permanent must lie outside me, in space.
E. So the objects in space, far from being inferred, invented or imagined on the basis of inner data, are actually logically presupposed by and epistemologically prior to even our experience of ourselves and our mental states.

If, therefore, inner experiences are indubitable, outer experiences in general must be equally, if not more, indubitable.

Now to come down to our detailed questions about each step:

Questions about step A:

Which is this "I" determined through time that is empirically known as ever-changing? Under the general Kantian framework, we could distinguish at least three distinct notions of self, manifested through three levels of self-awareness:

> First: the transcendental subject of apperception—the thought of whose presence as witness animates all our representations inner or outer. This is what makes my experience mine. But this "I" of "I think," like Śaṅkara's "self at the back" is clearly not an object of knowledge.
> Second: the inner temporal flux of mental states, which can be said to be the object of inner sense, e.g., the stream of cognitive and emotional states that I call mine.
> Third: the embodied myself which is experienced in some region of space as one moving and living body among others.

About this last item, Kant remarks in one of his later *Reflections*:

> First we are an object of outer sense to ourselves, for otherwise we should not perceive our place in the world.

Kant's doctrine of the inner sense is terribly murky. The inner sense does not have any manifold of its own. It occupies itself with the data of the outer sense only viewed from a different perspective and under the pure time-forms of succession and simultaneity. Apart from passing sensations, emotions, memories which ultimately refer to outer objects, there is no separate impression of the soul which inner sense furnishes us with.[23]

If the self-knowledge referred to in A cannot be of the third variety, we are left with the first two possibilities. But the experience of my body could hardly be in question because instead of presupposing or requiring some perceived outer object, it is itself an outer experience of a body in space. Again the first or apperceptive self-awareness does not even come up to the level of knowledge or experience. We are hard put to say which self-knowledge is in question in the very first premise of Kant's "Refutation."

Perhaps Kant could answer that since this is only a reductio-argument, it is enough if the *opponent* admits that the pure ego is empirically intuited, even if upon Kant's view no such self is available to perception.

Questions about step B:

When Kant says that experience of the self in time requires something permanent in perception, it is hopelessly unclear whether what is required is the experience of something permanent or the existence of something permanent, or both.[24]

For the purposes of the alleged proof, it is essential that it is the existence of the permanent which should be entailed. Otherwise, we would end up proving merely that in order to represent myself temporarily I must *represent* to myself a relatively stable material world. Kant warns us of this confusion and insists in the proof that:

> perception of this permanent is possible only through a thing outside me and not through a mere representation of a thing outside me.[25]

It is not clear that this stronger implication goes through. In order that I can see the clouds floating across the sky or the moon, all that is needed is that I see a blue sky or a moon as a relatively fixed backdrop—not that the fixed sky or the moon should be fixed.

Kant's answer to this would, perhaps, run as follows. Insofar as we entertain the possibility of the seeing of the permanent as mere seeming to see, we also cast doubts upon our perception of the floating clouds. Thus, if we have to trust our self-knowledge as the idealist does, we cannot treat our immediate outer experience as generally "untrustworthy inference."

Questions about step C:

This crucial step carries the least conviction. When Kant tells us in the First Analogy that all alterations are successions of states of some abiding substance, we understand him as saying that change must belong to the same entity which stays the same across the changing stages. If I find myself undergoing change, I must assume myself to be permanent enough to survive those changes. How can the permanence of something else help me make my own changes intelligible?[26]

Why can't I just notice myself as remaining the same across different changing moods, and other mental events? Kant could retort that no such permanent ego is actually available to inner sense, the unchanging unity of apperception remains a transcendental subject of thought only. Remember: Kant requires not only something permanent but something permanent in perception. The noumenal ego, if any, may be permanent, but it is not in perception.

Perhaps the outer object against which I am to piece together successive mental episodes is nothing other than my own body. But then shall I fail to identify two successive mental states at a long time-interval as belonging to my own mental history if my body too has undergone a big change in the meantime? Somehow Kant's story does not sound quite right.

Suppose that we cannot find the required "something permanent" within ourselves. What better hopes do we have of finding it without? The outer world is equally perceived through time and should therefore be equally changeful. If it is insisted that at least in space we can represent co-existence and material solidity, we need to be told further how the ascription of some fleeting states of mind to a single person can be helped by the representation of a permanent material object in space.

Questions about steps D, E, and the conclusion:

Even if we don't raise the above sorts of irksome questions or assume that Kant could have answered them satisfactorily, what does the "Refutation" prove? Taken in a weak sense, it establishes that the human mind is so constituted that without arranging its experience in a spatial way into a picture of an extra-mental physical world it cannot experience itself as someone having discrete psychological states. But this should not daunt any idealist! It matches perfectly the Buddhist idealists' diagnosis of our beginningless craving for the duality between the inner and the outer. This inability to look within without looking outside is what makes any ordinary awareness object-directed. An object-oriented piece of awareness could well be self-occasioned and self-grasping, or caused by just an earlier piece of awareness, or if we are Berkeleyans, by some divine activity—directly upon our minds.

Taken in the strong sense, Kant's proof has established that I could not have been conscious of any of my mental states as belonging to my empirical ego, unless there actually existed a directly perceived mind-independent material world. But wouldn't that be proving too much? Even Kant's transcendental idealism will fall a prey to this refutation.

How Kant and Śaṅkara are unlike each other

If I have given the impression that Kant's and Śaṅkara's own anti-idealistic idealisms come to the same position, let me dispel that by sketching out at least three fundamental dissimilarities between them.

Śaṅkara has a well worked-out theory of illusory super-imposition (e.g., of the snake on the rope) which he then applies to the case of the world-appearance. Hence, his notion of the original ignorance which covers up the one real and projects the plural objective world. Kant does not have such a notion of positive ignorance.

Second, while Kant emphatically denies (at least for humans) any definitive intuitive knowledge of the noumenal reality, Śaṅkara urges us to aspire after an immediate mystical insight into reality as it is.

Third, Śaṅkara is unwaveringly sure that the source of both sorts of appearance—mental and material, objects of outer and inner sense—is the same Absolute Self, which is identical with pure undifferentiated Impersonal Subjectivity. Kant, in keeping with his professed agnosticism about things in themselves, only throws a conjecture that:

> the something which underlies the outer appearances and which so affects our sense that it obtains the representations of space, matter, shaped, etc., may yet, when viewed as noumenon … be at the same time the subject of our thoughts.[27]

But he leaves the question open. Both, of course, develop these interesting notions of a consciousness transcending the empirical ego, an apperception distinct from the inner sense, a mind which is as far from or as close to the real subject of consciousness as is the physical world.

Whether these notions can be made fully intelligible will determine whether their idealistic refutations of idealism will succeed. If we call the transcendental consciousness "mind*" and the empirical object of inner sense "mind," the thesis of mind-dependence of the world is rejected and the thesis of its mind*-dependence is accepted.

Three options

Philosophers over the centuries and across cultures have felt that extreme epistemological ambition usually leads to total theoretical frustration. The obsessive lover of certitude ends up as a bitterly broken-hearted skeptic. The metaphysical realist's tendency to be satisfied by nothing short of a recognition-transcendent truth usually makes her reject all accessible notions of reality as mind-made. Complete mind-dependence of our experienced world is a natural corollary to the hope to find an absolutely consciousness-independent cause, core, or basis for it.

This suicidal movement of our thought about reality—classically illustrated by the four Buddhist schools sloping from Naïve-realism to Absolute Skepticism through Idealism—could be blocked at three alternative stages.

One can try, like some Indian realists[28] (about universals as well as about physical objects), to stop it at the very start by developing direct realist metaphysics and epistemology, and holding that everything that exists is knowable though not actually known by us.

Or, one can try embracing one kind of idealism while rejecting another. But this will require us to give sense to the notion of an impersonal subjectivity. Whether we do that by trying to participate in some Omniscient Interpreter's Mind or by searching for some unlimited One Absolute Self behind every bit of matter and mind remains an open choice.

Finally, we could give skepticism a very long rope letting it reign over all discursive thought, but try to reach reality through mystical insight.[29]

Here, as elsewhere, there is something to be said for the middle way. To review the other two options further, the subjective idealist argues that the inseparability of an awareness of an object and the awareness itself implies that the two are non-distinct, or at the very least, that they share the same mental nature. The anti-idealist idealists discussed in this chapter deny the claim that objects and awarenesses are non-distinct but agree that all things are permeated by an impersonal subjectivity. But does the inseparability of two things mean that they share a similar nature? We intuitively believe, for example, that parts and wholes are different despite the inseparability of the two. This particular distinction can be explained via inherence, a special relation which links a substance to its parts and properties. Would this crucial relation be possible if, as the idealist claims, all things are mental in nature? In the next chapter, I will argue that realism about a non-mental external world and realism about inherence can only be accepted together.

7

Externality, Difference, and Inherence (*Samavāya*): Udayana's Refutation of Yogācāra Buddhist Pan-Mentalism

The claim

Realism about the external world logically entails and crucially requires realism about inherence—that asymmetric relation which glues a whole to its parts and ties a universal, a quality, or a movement to its substratum (a particular substance). There is no '*out-there'nce* without some ontic '*in-here'nce*. Physical wholes and their parts, properties and their instances, qualities and their supporting substances cannot be *distinct in spite of their inseparability*, unless one is committed to the existence of a mind-independent external world. That is what this chapter will try to demonstrate, gleaning insights and arguments from Udayana's analytical *magnum opus: Discernment of the True Nature of the Self* (*Ātmatattvaviveka*), especially from its second and third parts, and from Frege's refutation of idealism in "The Thought: A Logical Inquiry (Der Gedanke)."[1]

The internalism of the Yogācāra Buddhist phenomenalist: "Objects are nothing but perceptions"

Let us use, with a measure of over-simplification, the word "phenomenalism" for the view that the ultimate constituents of the real world are ephemeral and reflexive awareness-episodes (*vijñāna*), each with a self-divisive intentional structure inherited from its causal ancestor. This is Yogācāra Buddhist pan-mentalism (a subjectivism without any substantive subject): *all that exist are inner mental phenomena.* Every momentary awareness is reflexively self-aware, dividing itself, as it were, into a grasped aspect and a grasper aspect. A series of such cognitions throws up two parallel illusions: the illusion of a stable cognizer-self created by the grasper aspect, which appears to be inside; and the illusion of an abiding external object projected by the grasped aspect as being outside. This is the *Awareness-Only*-Buddhists' diagnosis of our correlative errors of positing a world outside, and a self/ego/mind inside. Upon this account, the intuitive distinction between the process of knowing, the product of knowing (knowledge), and the object known turns out to be merely a distinction between different roles that the same awareness assumes. The process of sensing blue is the grasping form, the product is the sensation of blue, and the blue to be known/sensed is the grasped form internal and intrinsic to the sensory awareness. Knowing, knowledge, and the known are not separable from one another, and their distinction may well be a grammatical fiction ingrained in our concept-fractured imagination. Hearing the sound and the sound that is heard are identical. Their inseparability entails their identity. Differences that make us externalize our inner objects to a so-called public world are traces of a beginningless habit of duality-projection (*dvaya-vāsanā*[2]).

In the face of this formidable opponent, Udayana concludes his refutation of such anti-realism by affirming that the world out there is not an error—it is really just as it appears, "*tathyam*" (a word derived from "*tathā*," which means "just as it is")—and by showing that it is the Buddhist pan-illusionist Error-Theory of the World, which is actually a philosophical error.

To be out there is to be distinct

The Yogācāra Buddhist phenomenalism sketched above is the anti-realist opposition against which Nyāya (as well as Jaina and Mīmāṃsā) realists defend the common sense view that there exists a world of objects external to our minds. Externality is an ambiguous notion. "Outside"—like "left" or "front"—is perspective-dependent. There is an indexicality or ego-centricity about it. What is located outside depends upon who is calling it so and where they are standing. Your inside could be my outside. Another person's experiences and thoughts are *external* to me, even if they are private mental states and are thus *internal* in that sense. There is another sense of "external" which coincides with the physical, spatial, or extended. Even though my kidney is inside my body, it is external. In yet a third sense, externality simply consists in difference. The most radical denial of externality boils down to denial of difference of any sort: as long as one thing is outside—that is, *other than*—another, each of them is external with respect to the other. If honesty is something distinct from the actual honest individuals—they are many but honesty is one—then honesty is external to the very individuals in whom honesty is inherent. This is the ancient sense in which a realist (anti-nominalist) about universals is an externalist. When the same dog-hood inheres in countless distinct dogs, their dog-hood is out there, just like the dogs, distinct from, though inherent in, each of the individual canine bodies.[3]

Realists celebrate distinctions. But the dichotomy between objective physical entities/events and subjective mental states or ideas is neither clear nor distinct, even before one has muddied the waters with primary versus secondary qualities and perspective-dependence. Psychosomatic or phantom pains could be perceived as located in bodies yet be "in the mind" in an important sense. Also, it is possible for non-physical things to be external: honesty is non-physical, yet, for a realist about personal properties, it is "external." You do not become honest just by my thinking that you are, and you may be honest while no one knows that you are. So, knowledge-independence, physicality, and distinction are the three senses of externality. And this third sense of externality, distinction from particular instances, quickly leads to the first sense, knowledge-independence. If I *know* someone to be honest, her honesty would not depend upon my assessment. Her objective honesty would not be inside *my*—the judging person's—mind, even if it is a matter of the honest person's inner states and outer conduct. Other people's mental dispositions could be internal to them, but they would be external to me insofar as they are not my mental states. This is the sense in which it is possible to be a realist about other minds, without being a physicalist or a behaviorist. Indeed, behaviorists would be anti-realists about mental states. "External" or "outside" can simply mean "different," as in, "there is no Indian city outside of Kolkata which has trams." And difference is crucial to realism. Idealism or phenomenalism of all varieties erases or smudges some difference somewhere. To refute a phenomenalism is to rescue a real difference.

Different roles of difference

There exists a world of difference between the world and our awareness of it, not just when we are at variance with or in ignorance about it, but even on those occasions when we know it correctly, just as it really is. That thesis is the cornerstone of external world realism. It is precisely this difference that the pan-mentalist (*cittamātratāvādin*) denies, by insisting on a series of reductive "nothing but's": *that blue is nothing but some sensory awareness of blue; that a stone is nothing but someone's conceptual imagination of a stone; that the past event is nothing but my current memory or inference of it; that the substance that possesses qualities is nothing but the subjective bunching together of those qualities.* To refute the upholder of such mere mind theory, the realist need *not* go to the extreme of asserting that the two—world and mind, knives and occasional painful tactile sensation of knives, etc.—are absolutely *unrelated.* In order to be a realist about knives one does not have to say that they are really clusters of insensible untouchable atoms which are not objectively sharp and cutting, or that the really real is utterly unknowable. Indeed, a robust realist insists that the world has to be an object (or a collection of objects) of (sensory) consciousness—it has to really be just as most of us most of the time find it to be like—and that at least one sort of consciousness must be an element of, and in a way caused by, the world. The world we come to sense-perceive, think about, remember, and anticipate also happens to be really out there. Objects *outside* the mind can be objects *of* the mind. Correspondence and intentional targeting are consistent with distinction. Difference, after all, tolerates relatedness. It may even require it. Objects need not remain unknown, entirely unrelatable to, or concealed from consciousness in order to be independent of consciousness.

The phenomenalist challenge: show us one merely existing unperceived object!

When G. E. Moore holds up his hands[4] to prove the existence of the external world, he is not claiming that he is showing us two unperceived physical objects. He would be insane to invite us to see an unseen—let alone an invisible—noumenal hand. Indeed, centuries before Berkeley gave his Master Argument, which showed how an entirely unperceived tree cannot be coherently "imagined," Manorathanandin, a commentator on Dharmakīrti's magnum opus *Pramāṇavārttika*, succinctly anticipated the central insight of that phenomenalist argument:

> "What is it, then, that does not exist?" [The author, Dharmakīrti] answers: An external object such as blue, etc., does not exist 'unperceived, just-by-itself' (*kevalam*), since the sense-perception which would allegedly prove its existence is, ex hypothesi, incapable of proving such an only-object [since it is unperceived].[5]

It looks as if Manoratha were making the same point that was made by Jinendrabuddhi when he claimed, echoing the *Pramāṇavārttika* phrase "*yathānubhava*," that objects can be known to exist only as-they-are-experienced (*yathāsaṃvedanam*) and never as-they-are-in-themselves (*yathāsvabhāvam*). He thus treats "*yathā-svabhāvam*" and "*kevalam*" as interchangeable. And yet, the commonsense realist fails to understand why things could not be, in themselves, *just as we (correctly) see them to be*, without being *reducible to our seeing* them to be so. As far as Moore or the Nyāya school of thought is concerned, it is the very way in which the hand is perceived by everyone who looks at it which shows that there is a *relation* and hence a *distinction* between a hand and any one's perception of the hand. The pan-mentalist fails, albeit proudly, to give any coherent account of this intentional cognition-object relationship (this tiny but pivotal "of" in "perception *of* a patch of blue") without either making an identity-sign out of it, or simply sucking back the hand inside the perception. In the case of a perception of a brown hand, the phenomenalist smudges the distinction between the brown color and the physical substance (the hand), which has the color, by implying that the hand is made of consciousness. Against this, the realist insists that there is the hand out there and then there is someone's perception of the hand. If someone takes drugs and sees a blue hand[6] when looking at their own hand, the distinction between the two comes in handy to explain how the hand part is not illusory but the awareness of blue is. The flesh-and-bone body part is not just a "handy (perceptual) consciousness," any more than the gripping (i.e., absorbing) perceptual awareness of a hand is a body part that grips.

But, in order to oppose this pan-mentalist reductive or eliminative anti-realism, the Nyāya-Vaiśeṣika realist does not have to perform the impossible feat of demonstrating the existence of an unknown unseen hand in a world minus or preceding consciousness.

To demand such impossible demonstration out of the realist about the external world is to make a mockery of realism. Nyāya realists do not even fit in the strong Dummettian[7] template of taking truth (and falsehood) to be utterly independent of human recognition; truth, for a Naiyāyika, is a property of individual awareness-episodes and not of non-mental Fregean thoughts or propositions. Yet, no one can question the realistic spirit of Nyāya. Cognitions are mental (qualities of the soul). Truth is a property of cognitions. But truth is not mental.

In spite of his basic realism, Wittgenstein of the *Tractatus* unambiguously affirms that "the world is my world"—the "world as I found it." The only way in which such a subjectively findable, and morally negotiable, world can be "out there" and not "all in our head" is by being self-standing outside of it all, just as the viewer's eye must lie outside the visual field. Thus, the mind-independence of the external world, when analyzed, turns out to be, at bottom, the self's standing apart from the stream of its consciousness states, including those states which present the external world. The world of the Nyāya-Vaiśeṣika realists is also a world-for-the-self. It is a world which exists to enable selves to suffer and enjoy, although the self—especially a liberated self—stands entirely outside it. External objects or "bodies," as early modern Western philosophers would have called them, are primarily "knowables" (*prameya-s*), constituting a consumable world. Their world is not at all like the world of a twenty-first-century ultra-realist materialist, or even like the world of Cartesian dualists for whom immaterial selves cannot intelligibly move, interact with, or relate to their own physical bodies. Utterly unlike the world of imperceptible quarks and other subatomic particles and the *Tractatus* world (*Der Welt*) of atomic facts in logical space, the Nyāya world of substances, universals and particular qualities, basic individuators, events, relations, and absences is also a world of suffering and enjoyment that consists of property-possessing objects of someone's knowledge and someone else's error and ignorance. Physical objects are there to be lived through—enjoyed or suffered—by living souls. Even knowledge (at least for one version of the ancient Nyāya that Jayanta Bhaṭṭa reports on) is either embracing knowledge (*upādāna-buddhi*), abjuring knowledge (*hāna-buddhi*), or ignoring knowledge (upekṣā-*buddhi*). Knowledge is always pregnant with evaluation—negative, positive, or indifferent—and geared to action, which only an embodied self can undertake. The world to be known is not reality inertly lying out there out of reach. It is a consumable life-world whose "unseen" karmic causes of pleasantness and unpleasantness are made of the past desires and deliberate actions of selves. Above all, it is a world where to *be* is to *be knowable and speakable-about* (*astitva, prameyatva, and abhidheyatva* are co-extensive imposed properties). It is not the world of unknown and unknowable propertyless things-in-themselves. Even numbers in this world come into existence due to correct enumerating cognitions of conscious beings. Here, objectivity does not imply knowledge-transcendence in the strong sense of unknowability. It means knowledge-accessible, knowledge-independent status of everything that is real. To exist is to be knowable, but to be known or knowable necessarily means to be distinct from knowledge. Hence the corollary: no knowledge knows itself, no awareness is self-aware.

The world of objects is external only in relation to the self just as the self itself needs to be outside of its own series of cognitions or inner consciousness-episodes so that it can own the latter and call them "my" mental states Thus, an irreducible permanent self must exist "outside" the stream of cognitive states, in order for a set of property-possessing and event-undergoing physical substances to exist, and vice versa. This is the rationale of Udayana's provocative remark at the start of Book 2 of *ATV*: "If there is no external world, how can there be an '*atman*'—a self?"

In a more ambitious project, one could defend the thesis that the following four anti-reductionist realisms entail one another: realism about the external world, realism about the self, realism about universals and realism about the inherence-relation. Yogācāra Buddhism rejects all of them and comes up with a consistent package of pan-mentalism, no-self-theory, (exclusionist) nominalism and no-relation ontology.

To understand the refutation of idealism given by the Nyāya-Vaiśeṣika philosopher Udayana, we need to see how a defense of the permanent self as retaining its strict identity across times goes hand in hand with defense of objective wholes irreducible to parts, a rejection of exclusionist (*apoha*) nominalism, an adherence to realism about "inherence" or exemplification-relation, and a proof of an external world in space. This chapter is directly focused only on the last two prongs of his many-pronged realism. It spells out and examines the intricate arguments Udayana gives to resist the Buddhist denial of an external world of objects.

The argument from constant co-cognition (CCC) and its multiple rebuttals

First, Udayana organizes the numerous anti-external object argument strategies of the pan-mentalist opponent into three broad types of arguments, which are designed to prove that:

1. the grasper and the grasped are both ultimately real but numerically identical;
2. they are numerically distinct but of the same general nature or qualitatively identical;
3. the object or the grasped entity is simply a fiction, a nothing.

The idealist argument starts innocently with an appeal to the principle of identity of indiscernibles. If two items are invariably co-cognized, such that there is no way of telling them apart, then they must be the same. Where there is no (cognitional) separability, there is no (ontic) difference. We can regard X and Y to be distinct, only if X can be known in isolation from Y. A patch of blue and a patch of yellow are distinct because there is no rule that whenever you see a blue patch you must also see a yellow patch. But blue and awareness of blue are not discernible like that. Blue is constantly co-cognized with an awareness of blue; you cannot notice the patch of blue without noticing your being aware of blue also, especially if all awarenesses are self-noticing. Since they are inseparable, hence indiscernible, they must be identical or one and the same. The basic point is the same as Berkeley's challenge to the realist (which we talked about in section 5 above): *Show me one single tree which is not perceived or thought of by a mind*! Notice how, in Yogācāra Buddhism, the premise that awareness and its object are indeed *constantly co-cognized* (we can refer to this argument as the CCC argument) boils down to their epistemological doctrine of the necessary self-sensation (*sva-samvedana)* of all mental states. If a cognitive state makes a blue flower its object, then it must also make its own cognition of a blue flower its object. Since the flower and the cognition are inseparably registered in consciousness, the flower is nothing but—numerically identical with—the cognition.

A number of refutations of this argument came immediately from Nyāya, Mīmāṃsā, and Jaina realists about the external world. First, the conclusion that the blue flower is nothing but a mental cognitive state of consciousness flies against patent facts. An argument whose conclusion flies flatly against facts suffers from the fallacy "*bādha.*" If a sophisticated scientific reasoning is used to prove that a frozen lake in winter is hotter than an erupting volcano, the reasoning must be fallacious. Every bit of waking consciousness bears out the distinction between a state of consciousness and its object. The flower is blue, the perception is not. The dappled cow has sharply contrasting colors, black and white; our single perception of those colors has no color at all. Cognitions do not come colored. It is a cognition that is meant by the word "cognition of flower"; that word can never stand for a flower. The pillar is ten foot tall, not illuminating, and impenetrable; my consciousness of the pillar is transparent, illuminating, and without any height or solidity.

Second, the premise that the object and the cognition cannot be told apart is false. Not all distinctions are drawn by physical or temporal isolation. Dance and tango cannot be separated concretely. But we can isolate them by noting that not all dances are Tangos—there is the Foxtrot, and dance of Waltz, etc. Similarly, not everything about the Tango needs to be an actual dance. Consider the Rhythm of Tango and the Costume of Tango, which do not consist of dancing. Thus, blue and awareness of blue *can* be isolated by comparison and contrast, even if a bare blue or a bare awareness cannot be found. Not all awareness is awareness of blue, since there is awareness of red and yellow and awareness of bitter and sharp. And not all blue is connected to awareness. There can be a painting in blue, an expectation of blue, a remembrance of blue, or a conception of blue, none of which are a perceptual awareness of blue. Thus, the two are not even invariably co-cognized, let alone identical.

Finally, it seems that the argument ends up proving just the opposite of what it tries to prove. If the premise insists that a flower and the awareness of that flower are always observed "together," then it presupposes and implies that they are distinct. Only distinct things can be found "together." I cannot be "with" myself, and no one can claim to have seen Venus and the Evening Star or Mark Twain and Samuel Clemens "together," even once, let alone regularly. What togetherness proves is distinction, the opposite of identity.

Later, to make the idealist argument more attractive—and hence more fun to refute—a Nyāya logician Raghunātha tried to tighten the premise by dropping the term "together." What constant-co-cognition is meant to capture, he conjectured, is the fact that blue or a pot is never an object of a cognition of which the perception of blue or the awareness of the pot is also not an object. Technically, the relation between them can be that of non-distinction, because it is the relational property of "not being an object to any cognition which does not have *that* as its object" (*tad-aviṣayaka-jñāna-aviṣayatvam*), which is, after all, a relation everything bears with itself (so it is conducive to sameness).

Dr. Jekyll is the same person as Mr. Hyde, even if no one recognizes their identity, if and only if Dr. Jekyll cannot be an object of any cognition, which does not (actually) have Mr. Hyde as its object. Positively put, this means "being, as a rule, object(s) of one and the same awareness" (*niyamena eka-vitti-vedyatvam*), which is what the Buddhist claims is the relation that obtains between any awareness and its object.

This device helps stave off the damaging objection that the argument proves the opposite of what it wants to prove; but it still does not take care of counter-examples such as the left-side and the right-side of any surface. As long as a surface—however tiny—has any extension at all, it has two sides; to be aware of one is always to be aware of the other, because they are recognized relative to each other. But that shows them to be complementary and therefore not identical. Udayana starts a volley of objections against the CCC argument with a general threat: if the conclusion of the argument (i.e., that any x is identical with awareness of x) is true, then no arguments can be given for anything. All arguments will be fallacious, or worse—the distinction between fallacious and good reasoning will disappear, for all distinctions will disappear. For a valid and sound inference, the reason-property (e.g., smoke) must be distinct from the target property or probandum, which is to be proved in the site of the inference (e.g., fire). But the crucial enabling condition for a sound inference is knowledge of invariable, unconditional concomitance between the reason and the target properties. If the CCC argument flies, this knowledge would be identical with each of its two objects (the reason and the probandum). The reason and the target properties would become one and the same, which would make all arguments, including itself, useless. A distinguishing awareness between B and A will have to make both B and A its object. But the awareness is identical with B and also identical with A. As such, B and A will become identical.

This draws the debate into that troubled topic of awareness with variegated objects. Take, for example, our visual perception of a cloth, which is partly blue and partly yellow.

If blue and yellow are compared and contrasted by one and the same visual awareness, then, assuming the identity between the awareness and its object, the awareness is identical with both blue and yellow. In this case, blue would be identical with yellow, which is absurd.

A different *reductio as absurdum* charge against the same CCC argument goes as follows. On certain occasions, just as one feels that a pain is gone or that one is not seeing something, one is aware of a lack of awareness. If the CCC argument is sound, then on such an occasion, the absence of awareness would become identical with (its) awareness; but awareness and lack of awareness are incompatible. Thus, for CCC to be sound, incompatibles would have to be the same.

The external physical object riddled with contradictions: "Out" is out

The third line of phenomenalist attack proceeds by pointing out multiple incoherences in the very idea of any middle-sized physical substance (*sthūla dravya*) that can serve as the object of perception.

Even if common sense assumes that a perceptual cognition takes something outside itself as its object, actually the very idea of an outer object is incoherent at multiple levels. Since no cogent notion of a perceptible extended physical whole in space can be found, there is nothing outside cognition.

Vasubandhu—a fifth-century Yogācāra Buddhist stalwart—posed a mighty objection against any concept of an extended object divisible into partless atoms, which was the reigning notion of Buddhist and Vaiśeṣika realists of his time. This objection, which the realists had to wrestle with for centuries afterward, goes as follows. Let us call the further indivisible particle which one reaches at the terminus of a process of division an "atom." When such an atom is conjoined with six other atoms from four directions and top and bottom, the objection goes; do these six atoms touch the central atom at six different points of contact or at the same point? The first option cannot be acceptable because an atom is by definition partless and therefore cannot have six different sides or points on it. The second option would make increase of size unintelligible; the cluster of seven atoms would have the same size as a single atom, which is not acceptable either. Since there is no third option, the very idea of a bunch of partless atoms clustering together to make up a bigger extended whole is incoherent. Thus, no theory of external world of bodies in space can survive logical scrutiny.

Udayana meets this argument head-on by adopting two notably different stratagems. First, he throws back a mirror image of the same (mereological) argument against the Buddhist pan-mentalist's own preferred reality (an awareness-episode or cognition). Strong phenomenological evidence makes it undeniable that we often have a single perception of "mutually opposed" (e.g., blue and yellow) color patches. The perception itself is indivisible—it cannot be split up into first seeing blue, then seeing yellow. But then, does it intentionally relate wholly to blue content or wholly to yellow content or is it an entirely objectless cognition? Since the perception and the yellow are identical and the perception and the blue are identical, blue and yellow should be identical. Since that is impossible, the first alternative cannot be accepted. Upon the second alternative, either nothing is apprehended or the entire partless cognition is illusory. In this case, either the blue content or the yellow content is a false superimposition. But none of these sub-options under the second alternative are logically palatable. So, if the Buddhist jettisons the external physical objects on pain of these part-whole problems, then he has to jettison even consciousness or cognition due to the same sort of fear of incoherence.

The second stratagem of responding to Vasubandhu's six-atom counter-argument against external world-realism is an intricate logic of relations, which distinguishes the contact of ordinary divisible objects from the primordial fusion of ultimate simples. Normally, contact between a finger-tip and a cup requires that some parts of the finger-tip (maybe the nail on top, or the flesh inside) are not in contact with some parts of the cup (perhaps the bottom). Ordinary contact is indeed a "non-entirety-pervading" relation. But the contact between ultimate particles, somewhat like the concatenations of "Objects" (Gegenstande) in Wittgenstein's *Tractatus*, does not require the additional glue of a contact-relation (which, in Vaiśeṣika metaphysics, is strictly speaking a unary or one place quality). After two atoms get together thus "like the links of a chain" (without requiring a further connector), the second step of conjoining three dyads to form a triad-molecule can happen normally by local partitioning of the dyads from different faces. Udayana goes deep into the topology of such clustering of fundamental particles, exposing the "phoney" destructive dilemmas of the Buddhist pan-mentalist attacks against the very idea of a middle-sized physical object outside our awareness of it. The whole middle-sized object inheres in its constituent parts. The sense in which the atoms are "in" the cluster is not at all the sense in which the new substance generated by the clustering—"the whole" (parts-possesor) dyad is "in" the constitutive atoms because the space occupied by the ultimate atoms is not logically the space occupied by the middle-sized object. Early Buddhist atomism did not have the concept of inherence, which saves the Vaiśeṣika theory of physical objects from Vasubandhu's powerful critique. It is to inherence that we must now turn.

Inherence and objectivity: an interlude

"All [sorts of entities] would remain unapprehended, if the whole is not proved [to be *distinct* from and inhering in its parts]." So goes a crucial aphorism (2.1.34) in the second chapter of *Nyāyasūtra*. In his commentary on this aphorism, Vātsyāyana explicitly lists the six basic Vaiśeṣika categories: substance, quality, motion, universal, final individuators, and inherence; and announces that our perception of something like a pot as black, shaking, and earthen, and as an individual pot distinct from but inseparably in its parts, cannot be explained unless we establish the existence of the whole substance as distinct from the sum of its parts or particles.

The Vaiśeṣika realists have a clear-cut ontology of substances. A substance is the stuff that survives alteration of the qualities of something. B. K. Matilal[8] has detected all of the following five elements of the classical Western (Aristotelian) notion of substance in it: It is a locus of change, a substratum of qualities and actions, a subject of predicated properties and relations, a stuff or inherence-hosting cause of ephemeral attributes, and, except for ultimate simples, a concrete whole distinct from its constituent parts in which it inheres. Most generally, a substance is defined as a locus or possessor of particular qualities. A mango may have a particular shade of yellow, and a unique sour or sweet taste. It can fall from a tree and roll on the ground. Unlike the color, the taste, the falling, or the rolling, which themselves cannot have color or taste or undergo a falling or a rolling, the mango is a substance which can undergo change without going out of existence. For the mango to change is not for it to be replaced by another mango, but is for it to stay the same while assuming new qualities. When the mango changes from green to yellow, it is the substance which sustains the change. The substance is therefore the material or stuff-cause of the change or the inherence-hosting cause, as it is called in Vaiśeṣika. When a savory mango chutney is made out of this and other mangoes, the effect or product is a new substance which inheres in these material causes. The chutney inheres in the pulp from each of these mangoes, like a table inheres in its legs and top. This is the sense in which a constituent-substance can host an inhering new product-substance, making itself a part (but not a parcel) of the effect/product. To take a non-corporeal example, when a soul wills an action, the inhering state of willing is an effect which requires the soul as a causal condition to inhere in. So, the will is an inherent (inheror) effect arising in the inherence-hosting "stuff-cause"—the soul whose will it is. Although the soul, in dualistic Nyāya-Vaiśeṣika, is not a material or physical entity as a substance, it is still, in an Aristotelian sense, a "material cause."

From the perspective of contemporary mereology, some of the central disputes between the realist Nyāya Vaiśeṣika and the reductionist Buddhists are of great interest. The Buddhist wishes to resist positing any permanent entity other than its momentary phases, any core or essence of a substance other than its particular tropes, any abstract general property other than unrepeatable property-less particulars, and any existing substantial whole distinct from its parts. These four denials together make up the Mind-Only Buddhists' anti-realism.

We should remind ourselves of the ethico-soteriological context in which Gautama brings up this topic of the separate existence of a whole.[9] While the self is not the body, neither is the body to be reduced merely to its parts. It is only passionate identification with and possessive attachment to the whole body which is to be renounced, not the ontological commitment to its objective existence as something irreducible to its parts, all the way up to the dyads which are distinct substances, caused by, but not reducible to the single indivisible atoms that cluster together to cause them.[10]

Yet, our ontological commitment to wholes as distinct from its parts (taken individually or as a collection) seems to lead us into the following conundrum:

Suppose a certain substance W is composed of three parts A, B, and C. If I wish to maintain that W is distinct from A, B, and C, must I specify where W is located? As an object in space, if W exists, it must be some*where*. It could be in its parts or it could be outside of its parts. But surely the latter option is absurd. How can the table be located in a place other than where its parts are? We can't say that the threads which make a piece of cloth are in one part of space and the whole cloth is in another part of space. So, if the threads are in one spot, the whole cloth, as distinct from the threads, must be in the threads.

But if W is in A, B, and C, is it wholly in A, wholly in B, and wholly in C? That cannot be, because then there would be three distinct Ws, or a single material body will be wholly in three different sites, which is impossible. So, a part of W may be in A, another part in B, and yet another in C. But which part of W would be in A? Surely, if the whole table is partly in each of its four legs, then leg 1 cannot be located in leg 2. Well, then W is in A, with respect to part A, and so on. This amounts to saying that the part A is in part A, which violates the principle that nothing can be located in itself. A cannot be *in* A, because A *is* A.

Perhaps, then we should try the reverse. A, B, and C are in W, rather than W being in them. But again the question seems unanswerable as to whether A is in all of W or only in one part of it. Surely A cannot take up all of W because then B and C, which cannot occupy the same space, would be homeless. But if A takes up only part of W, it will have to be the part which is A itself, and we are back with the same difficulty of a thing residing in itself.

It is thus incoherent to suppose that W is a separate entity, whether or not we experience or feel the whole to be distinct from the parts. Just the apprehension or non-apprehension of an entity cannot decide whether it is there. A non-entity may be erroneously apprehended and real entities may remain unapprehended. These are serious worries about positing a whole as distinct from its parts.

The realist about wholes meets these worries with an ingenious move. The location of W in its parts is not at all like the location of a berry in a bowl. The relation between W and its parts, say A, B, and C is inherence (*samavāya*) - a unique inseparability relation which is also the cause of our sense of "X being irreversibly inseparably in Y." When we place a berry in a bowl, the relation between them is "contact" (*saṃyoga*), technically called an "occurrence exacting" asymmetric contact. But the berry can stay without the bowl and vice versa. W cannot stay without A, B, and C, although those parts can stay without W. This makes W an inseparable locatee of A, B, and C simultaneously, undivided into further fragments. Actually, W is an emergent effect, distinct from, but inhering in A, B, and C. The question "Is the cake in the flour or in the butter or in the sugar?" is not daunting to the Vaiśeṣika Beginningist,[11] because, insofar as the cake is a distinct new effect, its "being wholly in" the flour does not make it incapable of being wholly in the sugar and the butter. "Being wholly in" consists in "could not have been produced without" or "is inextricable from," which is quite the opposite of the in-location of a berry in a bowl, which could be always removed from the bowl.

Thus, the problem of the part and whole not only necessitates postulation of "inherence" as a unique relation which becomes the hallmark of Nyāya Vaiśeṣika realism about wholes, but also leads their epistemology of perception to a unique theory of seeing the whole object, even though the sense organ is in contact only with one side which is closer to the perceiver's body (the front), or with an exposed part of the surface of the object. The fully developed ontology of inherence—which besides connecting wholes with their parts, also connects qualities, motions to their substances, universals to their particulars, and basic individuating hacceities to their substantial individuals—becomes too complex to be handled in this chapter.

On parts and properties: Can a consciousness-only world contain real inherence?

Let us turn to Frege's refutation of idealism where also the part-whole relation crops up as the linch-pin. Frege gives an ingenious argument against the Idealistic reduction of all external objects into subjective ideas:

> Assume: Idealism, which boils down to anything being reducible to our idea or sensation of that thing, for example: The heavy shell = the idea or sensation of the heavy shell.

1. Weight (heaviness) is a *property* of the shell.
2. Weight is a property of the idea or sensation of the shell. (If X=Y then, for all F, if F is a property of X, F must be a property of Y).
3. But weight cannot be a property of any idea or sensation, since ideas or sensations could not be heavy or light.
4. Weight is and is not a property of the idea of heavy shell (conjoining 3 and 4).

Since Assumption 1 leads to a contradiction, namely that weight must be and cannot be a property of the heavy shell, it must be false. Therefore its negation must be true: the heavy shell is not identical with the idea or sensation of the heavy shell.

Generalizing from this example, no object is identical with the idea or perception of that object. *Esse* cannot be *Percipii* because the inherence relation between a property and the possessor of property is not available in a pan-mental world of nothing but ideas.

Suppose the Idealist pushes back by questioning premise 2, and says:

> It is not the weight which is a property of the idea of the shell. It is the *idea* of weight, since everything is an idea. When you substitute 'the shell' with 'the idea of the shell,' you must also substitute, uniformly, 'weight' with 'the idea of weight.' What is the problem in taking the idea of the weight to be a property of the idea of the shell?

To that, Frege has an answer which captures the basic flaw of any anti-realist reduction of external objects to subjective experiences or ideas or possibilities thereof: if, instead of weight, we consider the idea of weight, the relation between these two mental entities, idea of weight and idea of a heavy/weighty shell, would at best be the relation of part and whole. The more complex idea includes the simple idea as a part. But a part is not property in the relevant sense. The part-idea of weight does not inhere in the whole idea of the weighty thing.

It is here that we see most starkly the logic of inherence (samavāya) working against the idealist. If anything, the idea of the weighty substance is a complex whole which inheres in the idea of weight which is part of it. The part idea cannot be a property inhering in the whole idea, since inherence is an irreversible asymmetric relation and since the whole idea inheres in the part idea, if we insist on finding inherence in the world of mental content at all.

Frege remarks: "A part-idea is not a property of the whole idea anymore than Germany is a property of Europe."[12] In the entirely subjective realm, only part-whole relationships hold, if any relations hold at all. Udayana shows that if we take the full consequences of Buddhist pan-mentalistic reductionism, no relations—even causal connection, and part-whole relation—survive the reduction. There would be no room for genuine exemplification and substance-property relationship in a world of mere ideas. Externality of objects of cognition, thus, is closely connected to the generality (and instantiability) of properties and to the mind-independence of exemplification as a relation. You cannot be a realist about particular objects without being a realist about properties and the exemplification-relation.

A battle of banters: a rhetorical interlude on philosophical jokes at the expense of Yogācāra Buddhist eliminativism about the external world

When the idealist Buddhist says that it is logically impossible to think of an unperceived physical whole which can remain the same over time and is utterly distinct from its parts and its changing qualities, Udayana, in one place, compares him to a baby monkey which hears the story of Ramayana (where Hanuman flies across the ocean in one superhuman jump), tries to fly over the ocean and falls and announces, "The Ramayana is all untrue, this ocean is too vast to be flown across." The message, one presumes, is that the idealist has a rather limited logical imagination, using which she pronounces that an unperceived external object is impossible to imagine.

Ātmatattvaviveka is most probably an early work of Udayana. But instead of explaining away his dialectical banter as mere youthful rhetorical flourish, we are philosophically rewarded if we pay attention to the discursive work done by the sarcastic and jocular fables, analogies, and lampooning images that Udayana uses to strengthen his abstract epistemological arguments against the pan-mentalist Buddhist.

We have seen above how, if intentionality is claimed to be an identity-entailing relation, the Buddhist faces logical disaster with regard to visual sensation of a variegated patch of incompatible colors. Nothing can be at once yellow and blue all over. To avoid this repugnant consequence, the Buddhist supposedly takes a different tack—different, that is, from claiming that in every case, if x grasps y, x and y must be the same. Yellow and cognition of yellow must be the same because they both appear or are *manifest* to the same consciousness.

Udayana then asks: What on earth is this manifestedness? If it is the same identity-entailing "grasper-grasped relationship," which you have already given up, then by bringing it back under another name, you are "trying to keep the cow which has been sold off."[13] You have been shown how it cannot be a special kind of intimate intentionality relation that the grasped object bears, as a rule, with the subjective perception of it—as long as the perception and the object are claimed to be ultimately identical. For, all the proposed relations you have proved to be unobtainable between a cognition and a distinct outer object.

Now, the idealist counters: if, as the realist insists, a cognition, itself neutral and formless,[14] can relate objectually (to make up an English adverb corresponding to *grāhyatva* or *viṣayatā*) to an utterly unlike outer entity, then it should be possible for any cognition to manifest any object. If so, there would be total rule-less-ness with regard to which awareness grasps which object. In his tract "Establishment of the Internally Structured Character of Awareness," Jñānaśrī had laughed at the Naiyāyika's attempt at preserving the tight link between cognition and its specific object while denying the internal form or intrinsic objectual (self-aware) structure of each cognition. This attempt is likened to the gambit whereby a fool throws out the gold coin and ties a knot on the empty corner of his scarf. Udayana returns the scoff by comparing the idealist internalists who claim not to need any external object at all in order to explain the manifestness of the grasped object, with someone who does not even need any cloth-end but can tie a knot in a corner of the sky or a vacuum.

Conclusion

If an object is always found *together with* cognition, they must be distinct. Two things can be closely, even inextricably, connected, *and therefore* distinct. The "content-ness" (*viṣayatā*) *intentionality*-relation between an awareness and its object, and the inherence (*samavāya*) relation between a whole thing and its parts (between properties and property-bearers) are two ontologically intimate but difference-preserving relations, which have been contrasted and compared. Ontologically, a Nyāya realist is committed as much to the objectivity of inherence as a distinction-entailing inseparability-relation as to the perception-independence of the objects of perception. To highlight the link between these two realisms has been the major agenda of this chapter. The whole cannot exist without the parts, but is not reducible to them. Just so, the perceived object—though it can exist, but cannot be *perceived* without the perceptual cognition—is not to be reduced to the perception. Mereological inherence and cognitional objecthood are both intimate but irreversible difference-entailing relations. I cannot experience or imagine a tree unless it is made as an object of some kind of awareness, but there is as much difference between the tree and my awareness of the tree as there is between the tree and its roots and branches. Inseparability does not mean identity.

8

Is This a Dream?

The ineliminable possibility that the current experience is a dream

"What evidence could be appealed to, supposing we were asked at this very moment whether we are asleep or awake, dreaming or talking to one another in the waking state?"—Socrates asked Theaetetus. "Indeed, Socrates," answered Theaetetus "I do not see by what evidence it is to be proved; for the two conditions correspond in every circumstance like exact counterparts."[1] Theaetetus was a clever young man. Perhaps what he anticipated was the following difficulty. Even if one found a set of decisive criteria W consisting of, say, coherence, continuity, clearness, uncancelled contents, etc., which marks off waking life from dreaming, one could never be sure on any particular occasion of applying those criteria W, whether or not one was just dreaming that the current experience satisfies W.

Since then many stones have been kicked by the Dr. Johnsons, many hands have been raised and displayed by the G. E. Moores and many proofs of the external world have been offered by the Udayanācāryas and Vyāsatīrthas. But the dream-possibility keeps haunting philosophers. And when the fragility, absurdity, disjointness, and agonies of this world become unbearable, one cannot but hope to wake up one day from this nightmare of the so-called waking life. Texts such as Gauḍapāda's *Māṇḍūkyakārikā*, Vasubandhu's *Vijñaptimātratāsiddhi*, and the *Yogavāsiṣṭha* take this ineliminable skeptical possibility to its mystical idealistic culmination. More or less following the line of Gauḍapāda, the *Yogavāsiṣṭha* first shows that the conventional distinction between dreamt content and wakefully perceived content is drawn in forms of being inner *versus* being outer, between being enclosed or limited (*saṃvṛta*) within the sleepy mind of a single person *versus* being open to the public, being unstable *versus* being stable, being cancelled *versus* remaining uncancelled, etc. Generalizing from these hallmarks of a dream or a sustained illusion, Gauḍapāda formulates his favorite dictum: *ādau ante ca yat nāsti, vartamāne api tat tathā*.[2] That which was not there in the beginning and, will not be there at the end must be nonexistent even at present (when it appears to be existent). *Yogavāsiṣṭha* shakes our externalist realist conviction that the common world in which we think we are all awake is stable, uncancelled, continuous, un-enclosed, and safely re-indentifiable across times:

> That is said to be waking life which is connected by stable temporally continuous pieces of cognition. That kind of experience which is fickle and discontinuous is

> called a dream. But if one notices how ephemeral and momentary the objects of wakeful perceptions are, and if one can have the same or continuous dream even at other times, then waking life would become dream and dream life, because of its continuity would become waking.[3]

Thus, the impermanence thesis about the external world boils down to the dream thesis. There are further arguments which show dream and waking to be *counterparts* of one another, almost like mirror-images, except that there is no telling which one is the original and which one is the mirror-image. Elsewhere the *Vāsiṣṭha* puts this succinctly with a double-sun example:

> *yathā dvau sadṛśau sūryau yathā dvau sadṛśau narau/*
> *jāgratsvapnau tathaivaitau manāgapyatra nānyatā//105.18*[4]

Like two isomorphic suns or two exactly identical persons, waking and dream are copies of one another; there is not an iota of distinction between them. This claim is defended against Rāma's realist qualms regarding sublation (the over-riding cancellation of a previous state by a subsequent more real state): Doesn't waking up break or annul a dream, whereas nothing seems to annul waking life? Why should not this be the crucial dissimilarity between them? *Vāsiṣṭha* says:

> No, just as the span of the dream is enclosed by two periods of wakefulness, the span of each segment of waking life is flanked by two periods of sleep. If the dream person dies as he wakes up, the waking person also dies as he falls asleep. Dead here in a dream, he is said to be alive and woken up elsewhere, then dying there, he is back and born again in another dream—living thus from one dream to another. Both the periods—the sleep life and the waking life—have their own narrative histories equally convincing internal stories to tell, and thus they become analogues of one another.[5]

What is happening in *Yogavāsiṣṭha* is more than mere analytical or skeptical argumentation. A series of phenomenological analogies or points of resemblance between dreaming and waking are deepened through the literary and meditative devices of imaginary narratives. The stories are similar to the bizarre science fiction thought-experiments we find in contemporary Western philosophy. They craftily interweave multiple dreams and deaths within dreams and multiple waking-up experiences within a dream, until the possibility that one is passing from one dream to another when one seems to be waking up and the possibility that while falling asleep one is just waking up into another equally real—or, what is the same thing, equally ephemeral—world comes alive. Such vividly imagined possibilities open the way for an objectless non-intentional pure empty consciousness to shine forth without this flimsy ontological hierarchy of objective and subjective worlds.

This imaginative deepening of a logical possibility is a spiritual meditative exercise. Philosophical argumentation, vivified by imaginary identity-rupturing narratives, congeals into meditation. Spiritual experience is expected to dawn through simultaneously fictional, poetic, and analytically argumentative discourse in the *Yogavāsiṣṭha*. The underlying reasoning behind this spiritual exercise has been formulated in several classical Indian philosophical texts as follows:

Waking experiences are without external basis/object
Because they are experiences
Just as dream experiences are.[6]

To spell it out in the form of a set of initially plausible premises leading to an idealistic conclusion:

1. Dreams are devoid of real external objects.
2. The so-called veridical experiences of external objects during our waking life are phenomenologically indistinguishable from dreams. (From within the experience, the feeling of what it is like to experience the world in a dream is exactly the same as what it is like to experience the world while awake, at least for some vivid and cogent dreams.)
3. If two experiences are indistinguishable in their felt quality and their phenomenological internal content, then, if one of them is known surely to be false or devoid of external objects; the other must be so too.

Therefore, the so-called veridical experiences of waking life are also as false or as devoid of external objects as dreams.

The refuter of idealism—a Mīmāṃsāka, a Naiyāyika, or a Western realist such as Thomas Reid, or Moore, or Russell—has admirably attacked the argument by either questioning one or more of its premises or questioning the pan-illusionist philosopher's right to draw inferences at all, that is, pointing out a self-refutation in the idealist's claim to have proved anything at all during what he is telling us is his own dream. Accordingly, the refuter of idealism has all of the following four avenues of attack:

A. Premise 1 is false. Dreams *do have* external objects. As Kant puts it, no inner experience is possible without outer experience, and especially without a correct location of the perceiver's body in the objective spatio-temporal framework. If one explains illusory experiences in general and dream experiences in particular in terms of the *anyathākhyāti* (otherwise-presentation) theory of error then every individual bit of dream experience borrows its object from the external world given to waking life. After all, it is memories of waking life which get recombined and presented "otherwise" and in the wrong order in dreams. Insofar as dreams have physiological causes such as indigestion or stimulation of sensory centers in the brain during REM sleep—those physical causes of a dream could be called its objective supports (*ālambanas*) anyway.

When, after a rich and spicy dinner accompanied by heavy drinking at a restaurant, a philosopher dreams that he is having a conversation with a woman he has never seen before, he could politely tell this dream-lady the following: "Madam, it was nice meeting you, but I know you are nothing but that undigested piece of Tandoori chicken I ate last night." External objects support dream experiences, since the only objects available to us are external after all.

But the first premise may be questioned on a different ground as well. Why must we equate "external" with "real"? Adopting a strong realist line, Madhvāchārya challenges the equation of reality and externality. The dream objects are not unreal. It is only our judgment that they are external objects which would be false, because they are real but "internal" (single subject's mental) objects: "Even in dreams, a truly real world subsisting in the mind in the form of wishful-impressions is seen as if it is externally existing."[7] As far as the reality of the objects is concerned, dream objects are just as real as waking objects; it is only a mistake to take them as public external objects. In one sense therefore there is nothing inherently "false" about a dream.

B. Premise 2 is false. Dreams and waking experiences are *not* indistinguishable. This is the line of attack I want to flesh out in the next section using *Nyāyalīlavatī* of Vallabha.[8] But before that let me go outside Indian Analytical Philosophy and make a brief detour via twentieth-century Western Analytical Philosophy. There is a modern Western way of questioning this premise, which has no parallel in Indian Philosophy. Norman Malcolm holds that there are no dream-cognitions, properly so-called. If we are dreaming, then we are asleep. If we are asleep, then we cannot be thinking or judging. There cannot be any cognition, correct or erroneous, without thinking or judging. Therefore, there are no experiences or judgments in a dream to be contrasted or compared with waking experiences or waking judgments. All we have is a language game of talking about one's dreams *after one has woken up*, but that can be explained without assuming that some experiences were going on in the mind of the dreamer during the dream. Dream talk is just that: talking as if one had some experience without the support of any publicly verifiable experience one had while asleep. I shall not spend time on this provocative view on which there is a substantial amount of critical literature.[9]

C. Premise 3 is false or counterproductive. From inside the content of the experience, the visual experience of looking at a life-like statue may be exactly similar to the visual experience of looking at a man. But *ex hypothesi* the two experiences do not have the same kind of objective support. As Śaṅkarācārya has clinched the issue in his refutation of Vijñānavāda,[10] in spite or indeed because of the felt similarity with the awareness of things outside us, we say about dreams: *yad antarjñeya rūpam tat bahirvat avabhāsate* (That which is merely inside appears as if it is outside). Now, if any "outside" does not exist at all—if the very notion of things without the mind is as incoherent as the son of a barren woman—how can we even say "*bahir-vat*" when nothing can even appear to be *like* the son of a barren woman?

Finally, the tables could be turned against the idealist precisely on the basis of this premise: if the two experiences are exactly similar and waking experiences are known to have real external objects, then by the same logic, dream experiences also should have real external objects. This could also take the form of a counter-argument proving the opposite conclusion: dream experiences have external objects because they are experiences, just as waking experiences do!

D. The entire argument and, for that matter, any argument is unavailable to the idealist who believes that she is and we are constantly dreaming. One can get intellectual inspiration from dreams, but if a logical argument is given only during a dream then one has merely *dreamt* that the conclusion follows from the premises but has *not proved* that it actually does. The dream argument is operationally self-refuting because if it is valid and sound then it is as valueless as sleep-talk. Of course, there can be some controversy about whether a deductive inference drawn entirely within a dream can be claimed to be valid, but, for sure, the material (outside the dream) truth of a conclusion cannot be claimed from an allegedly sound inference entirely drawn within a dream!

Nyāyalīlavatī on dream and waking

Svapna or dreaming is listed as a case of "non-knowledge" (*avidyā*) in the standard Vaiśeṣika taxonomy along with doubt, error, and non-ascertainment. On behalf of a skeptical opponent, Vallabha asks: "But why is dream a case of non-knowledge, since it does not differ in nature at all from knowledge?"[11]

Suppose it is said that dreams are, after all, cancelled, broken, and superseded. The skeptic's response would be: "What does cancellation amount to here?" The experiential content or object is not taken away, neither is the effect of the dream on the person nullified, by the so-called annulment of the dream. If the dream was scary or rapturous, it remains so, even after it is "broken." All it amounts to is that there is another subsequent conflicting experience, which is true even of waking life, when it is followed and superseded by a dream. Your dream that you are swimming in an ocean "cancels and supersedes" your waking experience that you are in your bedroom, but your experience that you were on your bed in your own house was originally cancelled and superseded by your dream that you were swimming in the ocean! You cannot hope to establish that waking life is posterior and thus truer because one never knows how often, in a beginningless series, an apparently "final" waking-up period has been followed (hence "cancelled") by a subsequent dream period.

If we try to use some sort of a coherence criterion to distinguish the two states we would have to say something similar to what Udayana did at the end of his *Ātmatattvaviveka* chapter on the refutation of the idealist Buddhist. During the waking state, an internally coherent mutually corroborating set of experiences is the rule. Incongruence and mutual cancellation are the exception. During the dream state, incoherence seems to be the rule, and accidental consistency is the exception. When dreams corroborate each other that happens just by fluke. But this distinction between accidental and regular concordance is ultimately arbitrary. Even within the so-called fortuitous fitting together of the vivid, credible, and coherent experiences of a dream, the correct re-identification of an item encountered earlier is as common as in a waking experience. Within our waking life, on the other hand, the apparently coherent re-identification of the continuous flame of a candle as "the same" is rejected, upon scrutiny, as erroneous. Surely, the larger or fewer number of corroborating factors or the longer or shorter duration of the uncancelled experiences cannot be the deciding factors for the objectivity of one and the mistakenness of the other. As Socrates remarked against such a quantitative evaluation: "Well now, are we going to fix the limits of truth by the clock?"[12]

Vallabha's imaginary skeptic refers to the same counter-evidence here: "Not only is there occasional cancellation of our perceptions during the waking states. If we consider the 'waking world' of a madman it will most probably have a larger number and longer duration of mutually incongruous cancellable elements than many of our dream-worlds." So, larger numbers of incoherences or cancellations within their contents cannot demarcate dreams from wakeful states.

Let us now concentrate on *Nyāyalīlavatī*'s own examination of the skeptical no-distinction claim: the claim that dreaming and waking are indistinguishable. There are three senses in which dream and waking could be exactly on a par, as the skeptic above has claimed:

(i) Both of them are veridical experiences (*pramāṇatvena aviśeṣa*).
(ii) Both of them are erroneous (*apramāṇatvena aviśeṣa*).
(iii) Dream as dream and waking as waking are equivalent because dreamhood is the same as wakinghood (*svapnatva-jāgaratvābhyām*).

The first option is hopeless because the distinction between veridical and non-veridical experience is publicly established and is the very basis for the concepts of waking and dreaming. The idealist's thesis would lose its punch if dreams were taken to be as veridical as waking life. When I dream that I am swimming and experience soon after waking up that I am and was not swimming, both the verdicts cannot be equally true or veridical, since p and not-p cannot be true together. It is veridical wakeful experience which can be ascertained when one has actually woken up. And once the waking-up moment is ascertained, it is impossible to call the previous and the subsequent states equally veridical (unless one is ready to say that it is the same man who is a tribal chief in a jungle and a king in a palace in a faraway city).

The second option—that both dream-judgments and wakeful judgments are equally false—would lead to the rejection of the skeptic's or idealist's thesis. The pan-illusionist's contention that dreaming and waking are indistinguishable, insofar as it is a wakeful judgment, would also have to be false. Therefore its opposite must be true, and therefore, the two states must be actually distinguishable.

The third option is directly falsified by our immediate experience. Dreams have quite a different status, especially after they are exposed, from the status of waking. What if this immediate experience of ours that testifies to the distinction between the two states is itself false? What if, as philosophers, we need to correct or reject the common sense idea that dreaming is one thing and waking is another?

Here Vallabha makes the following move: What about this special philosophical corrective (revisionary) awareness, which tells us that our immediate experience of dream-reality distinction is false? Is that falsity-revealing awareness itself true or false? If it is itself false, then our natural commonsensical experience of the dream-waking distinction is correct and the distinction stands. If the corrective awareness is true, and waking and dreaming are non-distinct after all, then as a waking awareness it has to be non-distinct from all immediate experiences (i.e., have all the properties of both veridical and non-veridical experiences), and thus will have to be true and false at the same time.

Finally Vallabha says this:

> Even if we fail to offer watertight definitions of what it is to be awake and what it is to dream, the distinction between them is as patently evident as the distinction

> between pain and pleasure. Just as if someone, faced with some difficult cases where a painful experience is inextricably mixed with a pleasurable one, perversely claims that pain and pleasure are qualitatively the same feeling or that their distinction is not intelligible by analysis—we can only appeal back to our own experience—here too the general and radical distinction between dream and waking is to be accepted on the basis of direct experience.[13]

It is slightly ironic that Vallabha uses the parallel example of the antithetical couple pain and pleasure. In explaining why Uddyotakara lists *sukha* as one of the twenty-one kinds of *duḥkha*, Vācaspati says explicitly: "Even *sukha* is *duḥkha* because it is always connected with and indistinguishable from the latter."[14]

In their debate with the "All is suffering" Buddhist thesis, the Nyāya philosophers of life emerge with the following subtle stand. Pleasures do exist in human experience. Pleasures are distinct from but felt alongside pains. If one has to be liberated from all existential suffering, *one ought to look upon even those rare and unstable pleasures as pains*. What if one applies the same wisdom to the dream-waking distinction? Yes, there is a real distinction. We are not dreaming all the time. Sometimes we are genuinely awake and in touch with a real external world. But our so-called wakeful life is also so mixed up with errors and illusions and tiny bits of dreams and misjudgments that if one wants to attain "*tattvajñāna*" (knowledge of the true nature of things), one should *strategically* look upon even waking life as a kind of coherent protracted dream.

Now this is not what any classical Nyāya–Vaiṣeśika philosopher would come out and say. But Udayana's conjecture that the Advaita philosophers, in their urgency to get liberated, find this world to be of "little use" *(manda-prayojantvāt)* is perhaps a gesture toward a compromise like the above.

The alleged unintelligibility of objecthood

My own hunch is that the hidden insight of the pan-illusionist finds an underlying link between intentionality of any sort and "falsity." Of course, "falsity" here is given the technical sense of rational unintelligibility. Insofar as all our wakeful cognitive acts are directed toward an object other than themselves, they involve a mixture of dream-like conceptual linguistic imagination, and to that extent they are equivalent to dreams. Not only are our dreams, illusions, and false beliefs products of ignorance, but to perceive or cognize anything outside of consciousness itself, with the natural claim that what is perceived or accessed can and does exist unperceived or unknown, is to cognize an object of our ignorance.

An object of ignorance is what is seen as also partly unseen, what is known as knowledge-independent and partly unknown, what is grasped as escaping our grasp. That is why normal object-directed awarenesses are constituted by ignorance, just as our dreams are. Notice how the claim of falsity (or ignorance generatedness) is not based upon subjectivity (that our subjective mental states have constructed these contents) but is based precisely upon the claim of the objectivity of the content. This known-unknown nature is one of the incoherencies inherent in our notions of the world that manifests itself to our waking consciousness. We reject dreams as illusions because they are incoherent. We determine that although dreams are undeniably "presented" they must be "non-real" because they are subsequently annulled and superseded. The non-dualist idealists' point is that any object-directed cognitive state is incoherent in the same sense that dreams are: what appears in an object-directed cognitive state is undeniably presented, but it is equally vulnerable to subsequent annulment and is known as unknown.

Later Advaitins have examined many of the offered definitions or analyses of the relation between an awareness and its object—the relation broadly called cognitive intentionality in the West and *viṣayatā* or *viṣaya-viṣayī-bhava* in Indian epistemology. What is that relation or relational property in virtue of which something counts as an object of an awareness or cognition? If it can be shown that no coherent answer can be given to this question, then the very claim that a cognition latches on to something other than itself in the external world will be unintelligible. The world will thus be proved to be "false" or dream-like simply because it is presented to have such an incoherent property as "objecthood."

Nine such alternative definitions were considered by the dualist realist Vyāsatīrtha (of the Madhva lineage). They are as follows:

> Objecthood (of the cognition C) is:
> Def 1: The property of being the locus/bearer of the effect/outcome of cognition C (*jñāna-janya-phalādhāratvam*).
> Def 2: The property of being the target of attitudes of rejection, welcoming or indifference resulting from cognition C (*jñāna-janya-hānādi-buddhi-gocaratvam*).
> Def 3: The property of being the accusative of cognition C (*jñāna-kṛmatvam*).
> Def 4: Being that which endows its own form onto the cognition C (*jñānākārārpakatvam*).
> Def 5: Being that which, while appearing as such, endows its own form onto the cognition C (*dṛṣyamanatve sati jñānākārārpakatvam*).
> Def 6: Being fit to be mentioned by the use of linguistic expression immediately prompted by the cognition C (*jñāna-janya-vyavahāra-yogyatvam*).
> Def 7: Being that entity as a result of the cognitive instrument's proximity to which a cognition C of that very entity arises (*yat-sannikṛṣṭa-karnena yaj-jñānam utpadyate tatvam*).
> Def 8: The property of being illuminated by or reflected in the particular modification of cognition C (*saṃvidi bhāsamāntavam*).
> Def 9: Being that which demarcates cognition C from other cognitions without being dependent on any other relationship with the cognition (*saṃbandhāntaram antarā jñānavacchedakatvam*).

The details of the refutation of each of these definitions are mind-bogglingly difficult. None have gone unanswered by the opponent Mādhva defenders of objecthood as a perfectly intelligible feature of external entities of the real world. So we shall not consider the Advaita attack here in detail. But the general spirit of the attack against objecthood is well summarized by Madhusūdana himself:

> Objecthood belongs only the known object, intentionality or object-grasping character only belongs to the grasping awareness, yet the so-called "relationship" is supposed to subsist at the same time in both object and the awareness that it relates, since relations ought to be in both the relata. Yet no such two-place predicate of objecthood can be clearly formulated.[15]

Underneath this attack lies, I think, a general suspicion of all relations. In case of "being about" or intentionality, that general suspicion becomes most acute. Any other relation, say, between two ordinary objects such as cat and a mat, requires an understanding or a grasping mind to hold the two relata together. Thus, any two items, in order to bear a relation, must both be made objects of a consciousness. Now, when this objectification itself is the relation to be analyzed, consciousness and its object must both be the objects of consciousness. Apart from the immediate threat of self-objectification, and the usual regress of relation, such a C looking at O bristles with many other vague difficulties. Thus, it has proved difficult to spell out (*durṇirupyatvat ca)* without circularity. What makes my thought of a tree *of a tree*? What exactly is the link that connects someone's perception of a cup to that cup?

It is difficult, but not impossible. That is what a realist such as Udayana or Vyāsatīrtha would say. Just as each of the premises of the general dream-argument has been rebutted, the concept of objecthood has been intricately and sensitively analyzed by such great Nyāya stalwarts as Gadādhara Bhattacharya. The objectood property or relation has been construed as a self-linking relation (*svarūpa sambandha*) as reducible to the cognition itself, as reducible to the object itself, or as a third entity.

In the final analysis, the original remarks of Vyasatīrtha (in *Nyāyamṛta*) make sense:

Just because one cannot analytically articulate what constitutes "objecthood," it does not follow that objects are illusory or false. We cannot articulate what makes a grasping consciousness or cognition a cognition either (by the same token). Yet we cannot honestly or consistently deny that right now a cognition of something is occurring. If the reality of awarenesses remains undeniable even when intentional awareness cannot be defined easily, why should the reality of the grasped objects be denied because the definitions of objecthood are hard to defend?

Conclusion: disillusionment

There is one haunting problem with the alleged philosophical-mystical experience of waking up from the world-dream, or the process of correction of the world-error. How can the philosopher-mystic be certain, once having used the skeptical ladder to climb up to this anti-realist height, that this waking up is not itself another kind of dream awaiting a further disillusionment? What if our knowledge of Brahman as one non-dual subjective universal timeless consciousness itself is subject to further correction? The official Advaita answer to this worry is this: there is no content at all, no intentional object, of this dawning non-dual knowledge, which cancels and supersedes the world-illusion. Hence there is nothing left to be annulled. But that answer complicates matters. A normal waking experience, when it corrects a dream-experience, replaces it with another set of conflicting contents. Can a contentless "experience" even have the power to "break" or "cancel" a dream? Insofar as pure Brahman consciousness is not contradicted by anything, it seems impotent to even contradict anything!

Leaving aside such well-known problems, I want to end this chapter by drawing attention to one striking feature of the Advaita theory of correction of sustained error or disillusionment.

Sibajiban Bhattacharya has remarked: "Our awareness of appearance gets cancelled by subsequent knowledge. *This involves backward causation*. Here we have a cause with retrospective effect."[16]

Bhattacharya illustrates this with a poignant dialogue from Henrik Ibsen's famous play *A Doll's House*: When after a long married life, Nora expresses her "disillusionment" with her relationship with her husband, he (her husband) appeals to past good times and says: "How unreasonable and how ungrateful you are, Nora! Have you not been happy here?" Nora sticks to her guns, revises her own past opinion, and nullifies by a later act of interpretation the happening of all previous experience. She replies: "No, I have never been happy. I thought I was, but it has never been really so."

To the extent that backward causation is unintelligible or incoherent (of course, not every philosopher of time thinks so), the Advaita insistence on future spiritual awakening proving for us that our past and present life-experiences have been as insubstantial as a dream is also unintelligible. The best we could say would be that this external world causes me pain, so it is not of much use or interest to me anymore. But it would be existentially "ungrateful" for us to say that this world of externality, materiality, plurality, and pain was never actually seen or known by us. After all, it is from this very external world and its object-directed intentional awarenesses that we gleaned all the wisdom of our ancestors and revealed traditions. It is here that we learned the philosophical techniques that enabled us to question ultimate ontological value or worth. Like a broken relationship, even a broken world-dream cannot be nullified as "never having been there at all."

Disillusionment must be compatible with living amicably within and paying moral and social debts to the empirical world—just for old time's sake, as it were! K. C. Bhattacharya said in a creative reconstruction of the spiritual significance of Advaita that our experience of waking up from the world-error is as deeply liberating as a sense of half-incredulous repentance at a past misdeed of our own, in the feeling: "How could I have done that? Was that really me?"

The full phenomenological content of such profound disillusionment requires that I still recognize, even when enlightened, that I did indeed experience the world as external to myself and that the transactional world was all that I ever *knew*. I cannot afford to forget or deny my life of worldly vicissitudes and differences even when I have got the new eyes to see through change and beyond differences.

To dismiss hastily the external world altogether from a non-dualistic metaphysical high ground would be risky even for the non-dualists' enlightenment project, insofar as that requires good patient reasoning and proper moral conduct. Perhaps this is why Udayana felt that the Naiyāyika's project of proving the objective reality of the external world is perfectly compatible with the Advaitin's project of deconstructing the intentional relation of objecthood and uncovering the fundamental impersonal subjectivity and spirituality of all that there is.

9

The Object to a Verb: The Case of the Accusative

Introduction

This chapter tries to spell out the different aspects of the concept of an object to a verb. Not only cognition verbs such as "see" or "touch," "know" or "imagine" but even verbs like "cook," "kill," or "avoid" must have objects. I shall take a contemporary look at Bhartrhari's[1] analysis of what makes something an object to an action meant by a verb in the most general sense.

"Contemporary" is a slippery word. Whether in language or in thought, those who worship what is current tend to ignore the timeless universal structures of human experience, thinking, and speech. Bhartṛhari makes us aware of this in an avowedly non-partisan manner. When fashions of philosophizing and views of philosophers change rather fast, it becomes hard to figure out what is contemporary in philosophy of mind and language. Luckily, some philosophical topics never go out of fashion, in the East or in the West. Agency is one such topic. The problem of human freedom or agency of actions is a perennial philosophical issue. Here one can argue that Bhartṛhari's discussion of the meanings of the agent/subject-term in *Sādhana-Samuddeśa*[2] is relevant, if not to the solution, certainly to the articulation of the contemporary question: "When can someone X be said to be a free agent of an action?"

Bhartṛhari breaks this question of free agency down to seven distinct factors or sub-questions:

1. Did X start acting before deriving his/her/its power from anything else, such as the instruments?
2. Did X retain its predominance by subjugating all other contributors to the action to itself?
3. Are the operations of all other causal factors subject to the functioning of X?
4. If X wishes or stops functioning, do all the other conditions stop producing effects?
5. Is X irreplaceable or non-substitutable with another entity for this kind of action?
6. Even if any other action-condition (e.g., the ablative, the accusative, the instrumental, the locus) is lacking, does X have to be there for this action to be possible?
7. Does X get the action done, even if indirectly from a distance, through its influence over other more directly involved employed agents?[3]

Bhartṛhari's analysis of the concept of an other-employed agent can help us locate responsibility for violence even in such apparently "hired or other-appointed killers" whether in the sky of New York or in the communal atrocities of Gujarat! When such other-impelled doers try to pass the buck of responsibility to the *prayojaka-kartā*, the instigator, we could use Bhartṛhari's sharp formulation: "It is out of someone's own freedom that one assumes that subordinate role of an instrumental agent under someone else's deployment."[4]

This moral relevance of the theory of the nominative case is not a dramatic first discovery on my part. The grammatical notion of an agent as someone free or someone causing another free individual to do something has been exploited fully by Utpaladeva and Abhinavagupta. They call their Trika philosophy the "philosophy of freedom."[5] Also Raffaele Torella has already alluded to the same subtle point of Bhartṛhari's analysis of agency in the epistemological context of deciding whether the Māyā-induced experience has any share of creative responsibility in projecting the objects that are made to be manifested to it.[6] Indeed Torella traces the influence of Bhartṛhari's grammatical insight about the agency of the other-induced doer on Abhinavagupta's statement: *preryo'pi sa bhaved yasya śaktatā nāma vidyate*, "Only one who has the capability can be an impelled agent."[7] Thus, *the problem of agency* is a well-researched area of overlap between philosophy and grammar.

The concept of an agent finds its natural counterpart in the concept of an accusative, just as the concept of a subject has a natural counterpart in the concept of an object. If somebody does something, there usually is something or somebody else to which or whom he or she does it. Rāma bends and breaks the bow, Rāvaṇa abducts Sītā, America attacks Iraq. They cannot just bend, break, abduct, or attack without an object in each case.

I wish to take this other equally important "case study," in both the senses of that term, as a special case of Bhartṛhari's general relevance to the contemporary linguistic formulation of deeper moral, metaphysical, and epistemological issues, and as a study of the second important case or *kāraka*.[8] I shall discuss the notion of the accusative or object to a verb. This concept is at the heart of the problem of intentionality as it has been discussed by both early twentieth-century phenomenologists such as Husserl and late twentieth-century analytic philosophers such as Wittgenstein, John Searle, or Gareth Evans. The problem is expressed by this Wittgensteinian idiom: "What makes my perception, thought or expectation of something, the perception, thought or expectation *of* that thing? What makes the object of my knowledge or desire, the *object* of that thought or that desire?"

That the contemporary central philosophical issue about what makes something an object of awareness is best addressed via the different criteria of objecthood—*karmatva*—discussed in Sanskrit philosophical grammars, struck me first when I studied the nearly interminable arguments and counter-arguments between the dualist and non-dualist Vedāntins.[9] At one point[10] Vyāsatīrtha remarks that some *māyibhikṣavaḥ* (imposter-mendicants) have borrowed the following argument from the Yogācāra Buddhists in order to show that whatever is an object of awareness must be "false" in their technical sense.[11]

An object has to figure either as related to the awareness or as unrelated to it. It cannot figure as totally unrelated because then anything can be the object of any awareness, which is intolerable. But what relation does the intentional object have with the cognition? Here nine initial definitions of objecthood are tested and rejected by the imaginary non-dualist opponent. Intentionality or its converse: objecthood looks like a relational property but is not a two-term relation such as inherence or contact—hence it cannot be a relation.[12]

In his list of initially rejected definitions, Vyāsatīrtha first considers a cognitively adapted version of the grammatical definition of the accusative: "The Object is that which is the locus of the resultant effect of the cognition/action denoted by the verb."[13] The third definition in that list is more explicitly grammatical: "The Object is that which assumes the case-role of the accusative to a cognition." It is rejected because it suffers from under-coverage, failing to apply to objects of God's unlimited cognition, since such uncaused omniscience is not caused by any *kāraka* at all!

When I first struggled with these conjectures and refutations, it struck me that the problem of the adequacy conditions for something being an object of a mental state is a special case of the problem of the meaning of the accusative case as discussed by Bhartṛhari. I shall first summarize Bhartṛhari's discussion of the four kinds of criteria of objecthood and then apply those criteria to some vexed cases of intentionality to show how considerable clarity can be achieved by this cross-fertilization of classical Indian philosophical grammar and the contemporary analytic issue of what makes something an object of a cognitive or mental state.

Different kinds of objects to the verb

"What is most desired by the doer is the object"—this is the initial commonsensical definition of the accusative in the Aṣṭādhyāyī.[14] The category of the "desired" is itself subdivided by Bhartṛhari into three major kinds:

A1.1: what has to be brought about (*nirvartyam*)
A1.2: what has to be modified (*vikāryam*)
A1.3: the target (*prāpyam*)

A1.1 can again be conceived in two ways:

A1.11: When we say, " The potter (the clay-artisan) makes the pot," we may mean that the desired object was an absentee to a prior absence and is now brought about: a hitherto non-existent jar has begun to exist thanks to the effort of the potter (*asat jāyate*).

Or A1.12: When we say, "The speaker uttered the word," we may mean that the word was already there in the speaker's mind as an object of his wish-to-speak, and that this pre-existent word is only manifested by the noise produced at the *vaikharī* level. The pre-existent is manifested by its so called "birth." The difference here reflects the metaphysical difference between beginningism (in every causation, the effect begins to exist anew out of its own prior absence) and transformationism (in every causation, the effect lies dormant potentially in its own material cause).[15]

The second kind of desired object—that which is to be modified (A1.2)—admits of a division into two unlike sorts:

A1.21: When we say "Arjuna burnt the forest," the kind of modification that the doer makes the forest undergo is called "destruction." It would be disingenuous on Arjuna's part to plead, when accused, that he was merely trying to give the forest a different form!

A1.22: When about a goldsmith we say, "He is shaping the gold into an ear-ring," the gold is the object of desire as something "to be modified" which is not at all describable as "to be destroyed."

In English, the word "rice" refers to both the grains to be cooked and the cooked product. As such, the object, rice, mentioned in the sentence: "Ashok is cooking rice" could be both the to-be-brought-about and the to-be-modified kind of object. Ashok is trying to make steamed rice (*odanam = nirvartya*) by boiling rice grains (*taṇḍulam = vikārya*). In Sanskrit sometimes both the "what is brought about" and "what is changed" senses are present in a sentence with a verb with two objects. Take the first quarter of the famous invocation verse: *mūkam karoti vācālam*, "Makes the mute garrulous." English can disambiguate it by the use of the "out of": "Makes a garrulous person *out of the mute*." Here the *vikārya*—to be modified—character of the mute is made apparent by making the material-cause-ablative out of one of the objects. On the other hand, English can use "into" to mark the final product (*nirvartya*) sense of the desired object: "Changes the mute *into a garrulous person*." But the original has the flexibility of a reversal of meaning—the two kinds of accusatives are expressed by the same case-ending, especially since word-order is unimportant. Thus, *mūkaṃ karoti vācālam* can also mean "Makes the garrulous mute." To express this unambiguously, of course, we can use that elegant device called *abhūtatadbhāve cvi* and say *mūkīkaroti vācālam*!

A1.3: Now comes the third all-important category, the target or destination which does not get changed at all by the action described by the verb. By coming to a country I don't change or devastate it unless I am Ghengis Khan or Christopher Columbus, for whom the foreign country landed on is not a *prāpya* but a *vikārya*. So the object of coming or going or visiting is an accusative in this third non-causal sense. And if we are realists about the objects of thought, then thinking of is like visiting. Sanskrit uses the verb "to go" or "to get" or its prefixed versions (*avagacchati* or *upalabhate*) for knowing, understanding, and other cognitive acts. Thus, when I say "I get your point" or *bhavatāvivakṣitam artham avagacchāmi*, there is a specific claim that I have not made any change in the meaning that I grasped; that I have known it just as it was intended by you prior to my knowing. I do not mean that the speaker's meaning is a *vikārya*, and the interpreter's object of understanding is a subjective *nirvartya*. I have neither deconstructed your meaning like the burnt wood nor reconstructed it like the reshaped gold. I have simply got what you had put into words. Hence, it is a target-desirable, not a product or a modifiable:

kriyākṛtaviśeṣānāṃ siddhir yatra na gamyate,
darśanād anumānād vā tat prāpyam iti kathyate.[16]

Most objects of cognitive attitudes fall under this *prāpya* category. When I recall a past event or anticipate a future event, I don't expect my remembering or my expectation to actually bring about or modify the event. Of course, the Bhāṭṭa Mīmāṃsā are notorious for insisting that every act of cognition makes a difference to the object, by conferring on it the new property of cognizedness (*jñātatā*). Knowing, after all, is an action and its object must show some effect of the action, otherwise it would not be the object. For them, therefore, an object of knowledge will have some new attribute as a result of being known. There are deep implications of this much-refuted Bhāṭṭa theory of objecthood. It is intimately connected to the peculiar externalist doctrine that our awareness of our own awarenesses is inferential—we infer that we must have had knowledge from the sign that the object has this new property of knownness—not perceptual. It is also connected to the insistence that only that which is freshly known, and was not known before (at least by me) can be known by me. I cannot be said to have known something unless I have brought about the following change in it: that it was unknown before and now it is known! This Mīmāṃsā doctrine of the necessary freshness of the content of knowledge leads to the Advaita Vedānta theory that everything which we come to know is first concealed by a veil of positive ignorance. J. N. Mohanty has explored the Advaita doctrine that everything, either as known or as unknown, is an object of witness-consciousness. His insight into how something can be an object of ignorance or unknowing should count as extremely important contemporary work in the phenomenology of knowledge. We shall see shortly that the "undesired" must be an object if the desired is an object. Similarly, what I do not know must be an object of my witness within, if what I do know is its object!

Although Bhāṭṭas are realists, they have made it easier for the Advaita constructivists by talking about the object of knowledge as something to be changed by the act of knowing! Bhartṛhari mentions the view that there are no targets which are not changed by the verb with the example of snakes with poisonous sight that incinerated whatever they see. We could call such snakes "Rorty," since under the annihilating scrutiny of their relativistic vision, objects lose all their objective reality!

Besides these three kinds of desired objects there is a fourth mixed category (A4): undesired, ignored, otherwise unsaid, and shunted away from another case by a quirk of the verb form. Such objects are exemplified in uses like:

"He saw the thief." (Not because the thief was the most desired, unless of course "he" is a police-man and the thief was "wanted"!)
"He took poison." (The undesired.)
"She trampled the grass while walking." (To which the doer is indifferent.)
"He milks the cow." (When the ablative-ness of "gets milk from the cow" is somehow left unsaid)
"The boss upbraided the servant." (A yelling is usually given to or meant for a subordinate who takes the case-role of a dative, but in this case, because of the quirk of "upbraid" or *abhi-krudh* the servant becomes an object. A scolding is never a gift.)

Even "He fears the tiger" exemplifies an object of this sort, because it is surely undesired or unmentioned as a "source" of fear. In a subsequent verse, Bhartṛhari says that even the objectively undesirable can become a desired object when the doer, out of improper greed or rash yearning, seeks what is bad for him (*ahiteṣu yathālaulyāt kartur icchopajāyate*).[17] Helārāja quotes a releavent passage from Mahābhāṣya: "A man who has suffered much prefers to eat poison rather than take any more of those other torments that he has gone through."[18]

The last part of the section on the accusative is devoted to the so-called objectless verbs and to how even they can be given objects. What is the changeable object to a verb in a sentence like "The developer destroys the forest"? The forest can assume the role of a dummy subject or agent when, wishing to protect the developer from blame, we make the forest the nominative and use an objectless verb as in "The forest perishes." The object to the verb "see" can enjoy a certain "independence" and become a virtual nominative in the sentence "The duck-rabbit is seen." The accusative has its own "voice" as it were!

There is also an adverbial use of the accusative, where "Cooks a little" or "Worries a lot" does not mean that what is cooked or worried about is small or large in amount. The cooking is infrequent or the worrying intense.

The accusative as intentional object

This adverbial use of the object-role is the best place to start talking about the contemporary philosophical relevance of the theory of the accusative case. In the heyday of logical empiricist phenomenalism, the external object of perception was said to be simply a logical construction out of some adverbial modifications of the verbs for sensation. Thus, when one has a loud auditory experience, one would say "I heard a loud noise." But actually the object of the act of hearing was not a separate external entity called a loud sound, just as there is no particular *prāpya* target called "a little" (*stokam*) in "Cooks a little." A little is a manner or measure of cooking; analogously, a loud sound is a mode or intensity of volume of hearing. That was the theory which generated those famous "foundations of empirical knowledge" with indubitable first person statements like "I am appeared to redly and applishly" from which eventually "I see red apples" was supposedly logically constructed. This is like an early twentieth-century Carnapian-Yogācāra elimination of the external object of mind through adverbial analysis.

This particular use of the second case-ending is not taken as a proper occurrence of the accusative case by Bhartṛhari. Later grammarians such as Nāgeśa made effort to subsume it under the category of the accusative although even with an artificial "object" the verb remains objectless all the same. One immediate application that we can make of Bhartṛhari's discussion of what makes something an object is to recognize that there is no single way of defining objecthood. Objecthood seems to be a family resemblance concept.

Some objects of seeing such as some Escher drawings of impossible staircases simply strike our eyes as if they are the agents and we—the perceivers—are under their power. A word like *sadṛśa* is broken up to mean "that which looks similar" where the object itself works to look a certain way, leaving little freedom for the viewer. Bhartṛhari remarks: *sadṛśādiṣu yat karma kartṛtvaṃ pratipadyate.*[19] Take sentences like "The twins look similar" where grammatically "similar" in apposition to the nominative "twins" take up also a nominative role, although similarity is the object of perception. Here the object assumes the role of the agentive doer in the context of phrases such as "looks the same" or "appears similar." Yet in other cases, the object remains a simple target unaffected by the act of seeing. In yet another case—the object of imagination—the accusative is a product to be brought about. But the object of a complex mental act, such as exaggeration or understatement, is something to be changed by the mental act. Take the sentence: "The political campaign has hugely inflated the number of new jobs created by the minister." The number is the accusative to the verb "inflate." But which number? The actual number is an object as "something to be modified by exaggeration," although the exaggeration is only a mental act of will to deceive. Sometimes the target-object and the cooked object coincide. One later grammarian discusses the philosophically puzzling case of the second accusative in the sentence: "He takes sea-shell to be silver" (*śuktiṃ rajataṃ manyate*).[20]

Surely the illusory silver, though it is an accusative of "taking," cannot be a locus of the effect of action denoted by the verb, since no effect of the "(mis)taking" or the mis-perceiving act can actually reside in the silver as there is no silver. The silver is in one sense a *prāpya*, wished to be obtained, and, in another sense a *nirvartya*, to be cooked or made up. In another sense, it is neither. It has some affinity with the exaggerated number in the previous example, but it actually belongs to a unique class of "(imaginary) objects" by itself.

Wittgenstein raises the question: When one draws the picture of a person, is the picture or the person the object of the act of drawing?[21] This can be easily answered with the help of Bhartṛhari's multiple criteria for objecthood. The person is the target-object (*prāpya*), whereas the picture is the to-be-brought about or product (*nirvartya*) object! I draw you (without scratching your surface), by producing my drawing of you, and by changing the surface of the paper. You, the drawing, and the paper are each an accusative of drawing, as target, as producible, and as modifiable.

One might object that Bhartṛhari does want to unify all of these senses because he remarks: "Just as the same one ablative is explained in many different ways in the discursive texts, the same *karmatva* or accusativeness is shown through different means here."[22] The spirit of Bhartṛhari is different from that of the anti-reductionist anti-essentialist Wittgenstein who merely draws our attention to multiple uses of the objectual formulation and does not want to bring them under any unified sense. But this objection is rather superficial. After all, according to Bhartṛhari, the whole division of the different words (other than the verb) of the sentence into words standing for different action-enablers by the way of the agent, the instrument, the source, the locus, the receiver, the object, etc. is an artificial break-up that the speaker's intention imposes upon an undivided sentence-awareness unity. What analytic philosophers are trying to describe clearly is this language-imposed or use-determined structure, which breaks up the situation spoken of into different action-related roles. Even the action itself can thus be meant as its own object.[23] In English grammar, this is called a cognate object: "she walked a long walk," "he slept a disturbed sleep."

In spite of tantalizing similarities of concern, no one can claim that Wittgenstein is a linguistic non-dualist in the same way that Bhartṛhari is. But Bhartṛhari's analysis of the multiple criteria of objecthood can surely throw much light on the somewhat murky Wittgenstein-inspired contemporary attempts at spelling out the concept of an intentional object of a mental act. Still, we must remember that what one is looking for is not a definition but a set of criteria and an analysis. So the fact that the concept of an object is hidden within the notion of "what is desired" or "what is to be attained as it is" or "what is intended to be brought about" should not tempt us to bring the charge of circularity against such an analysis of objecthood. We have a robust pragmatic grasp over what it is to desire or not desire something and what it is to wish to modify or simply get or reach something. If we can explain the relation between awareness and its object in terms of these ordinary relationships, then that is more of a gain in conceptual clarity than being told, for instance, that a mental state is about an object if the concept or idea of that object constitutes its content. The latter blatantly invites a regress. The invited question "What makes the concept or idea, a concept or idea of that object?" renders this empiricist analysis regressive and redundant. Of course, analyzing the concept of an object in general into that which is most desired, undesired, attained, transformed, or produced is not entirely free from circularity. But it is still less immediately circular and more illuminating than the British empiricist answer.

I find the idea of "content" multiply ambiguous and rather cloudy. The so-called content of a cognition seems to be sometimes part of the cognition itself, and sometimes an object or a nexus of objects and relations intended by the cognition. Yet the concept of an accusative of a mental act seems to be clearer, even if it admits of many different sub-varieties. When I think of something, I sometimes think of it as desired or hated—in both cases I am acutely interested in it. Sometimes I think of it as what I have to take and transform physically or in imagination, and sometimes I think of it as barely to be registered and noted as it is. At other times I think of it as something I have to bring about for the first time. Bhartṛhari seems to have captured this entire loosely unified field of meanings of "object" by his nuanced discussion of the various actual uses of the accusative case in Sanskrit.

What philosophy must learn from grammar

But what is gained philosophically when all these distinctions are drawn and confusions are clarified? Let me answer this popular and plaintive question with the help of a story inspired by Kierkegaard. A man who has gathered a lot of dirty linen rushes into a sleek shop that has a sign in its window saying WASHING DONE HERE. The man takes it to mean that some objects such as dirty clothes are washed there. But, a very suave shopkeeper approaches him and explains: "Sorry, we do not wash clothes. Washing is not done here." This reminds me of the use that Helārāja—the commentator on Bhartṛhari– discusses in the context of verbs becoming objectless because the speaker does not wish to mention any object: "Cooking is not done here" (*neha pacyate*). But then the customer yelled, "Why does the sign say that you do?" The answer was: "We are a shop that sells those signs."[24]

I have not told you what makes something a *viṣaya*—an object—of knowledge, desire, ignorance, or an imaginative awareness.[25] But I hope I have been able to sell the sign that Bhartṛhari's analysis of the accusative case is a useful guide for finding an answer or a set of answers to that sort of a question. To quote Wittgenstein, I have tried to show that Bhartṛhari's discussion on accusative case is "A whole cloud of philosophy condensed into a drop of grammar."[26] As it is growing arid rather fast, contemporary analytic philosophy can use some rain from that cloud.

Recall the simple question with which we introduced the three major topics of this monograph: "Do you see what I see?" In this first part, the object seen by multiple perceivers has been discussed from different angles. Grammatically, the object of perception is the accusative to my act of seeing and I am the agent of seeing. Do I change or merely access the object when I know or perceive it? We have also discussed the concept of the self as the subject of particular awarenesses. But these are both to be distinguished from the concept of "I" as the grammatical first person. The first person does not always refer to the autonomous agent behind an action, even when used to describe perceptual experiences. What, if anything, does the pronoun "I" refer to? The next chapter, which initiates the second part of this book, will explore this endlessly fascinating hard question.

Part Two

Subjects

10

On Referring to the First Person

A unique pronoun

In our childhood we were entertained by the story of a pompous scholar who was tricked by a Bengali village schoolmaster who asked him to translate the English sentence, "I don't know" into Bengali. His reply, "*āmi jāni nā*," brought ridicule upon him. The villagers thought that he was confessing his own lack of knowledge. What could he have said to avoid this misunderstanding? Should he have said in Bengali that *that English sentence means that the speaker of that sentence does not know*? That would *not* have been a correct translation of the given sentence. The original does not mention the English language or a speaker, so why should its translation? The difficulty is not in going from one language to another, but in switching from a context-neutral sentence *type* to a statement made in a certain context by the utterance of a sentence-*token*. Of course, a further clarification of what precisely one does not know would have made the situation even more confusing. One's own ignorance of any specific object of knowledge is an epistemologically puzzling thing to confess, but the major source of trickery in that sentence lies in the ego-centric token-reflexive first person singular pronoun, which will be the philosophical focus for this chapter.

Any sentence-type starting with "I" as a subject term of course can become philosophically embroiled into two distinct issues: how the subject—a person—can become an object of reference and how the reference of "I," if any, can keep changing as the user of that sentence for making a statement changes. The metaphysical question of whether the self exists or not seems to merge with the grammatical and semantic question of how the first person singular pronoun manages to have the same sense but distinct references.

I start by refuting Wittgenstein and Anscombe who argued that "I" does not refer to anything at all. The central Wittgensteinian argument goes as follows: if reference cannot misfire on occasions, then it is not genuine reference. This *immunity to error through misidentification,* which is supposed to damage the claim of the indexical "I" as a referring expression, I shall show, needs to be re-examined. I then go on to discuss Frege's view that the sense (*sinn*) or mode of presentation by which every speaker picks out himself or herself by the use of that word is partially private and incommunicable. Thus, upon hearing "I feel pain in my back"! I do not *fully* understand the thought expressed. This is a tempting but troublesome view, since a Fregean *thought* is defined as exactly the same content that is fully understood by all competent speaker-listeners as the sense of the sentence uttered in a public language!! Everybody has to admit that the meaning of that word "I" is, in some sense, the same for everyone, and yet the reference varies from speaker to speaker. Perhaps Kaplan's distinction between character and content would help us here. I compare these insights with what Gadādhara says in his seventeenth-century monograph *Śaktivāda* about meaning of the terms "I" and "You" (*asmat* and *yusmat śabdārtha*), especially in reported speech, where the simple rule that "I" refers to the utterer of the sentence-token breaks down. Next, I allude to Madhusūdana Saravastī's view that *aham* (the Sanskrit equivalent of "I") does not refer to the self at all, but to a non-self—a confused entity which is a knot between consciousness and the particular felt but material body—*cit-jada-granthi*—which is more precisely called *ahaṃkāra (the ego-maker)*. In the context of the insightful infightings of the contemporary Western philosophers of language and the medieval Indian thinkers, I put forward my own conclusion about the meaning and reference of "I." I end the chapter with a speculative hint of my current attraction to Abhinavagupta's view that the unlimited I-ness or full subjectivity (*pūrṇāhamtā)* of consciousness includes all subjectivity—which is personal but not private—felt even in the live bodies of other "I"-users, such that "you" also means "another I." In intimate friendship, in moral reasoning and in aesthetic communion, the subjective but inter-substitutible "I" offers the possibility of becoming a "you" to another self. That is why we can and need to imagine what it would be like if I were you. Eventually, the singularity and flexibility of reference of the first person pronoun—its sharable unsharability, so to speak—may well be a sign that there is a single I of all consciousness, that the first meaning of the first person is the *uttamaḥ puruṣaḥ*—the Supreme Person (*puruṣottama)*.

Wittgenstein's argument for the no-self view

A dominant strand of common sense takes it to be obvious that by using the first person pronoun in the singular one refers to oneself, that there is nothing essentially incommunicable or private about each individual's use of that most frequently used monosyllable. Before complicating matters by asking what this word refers to, especially when this word seems to allow us to express or think such thoughts as "I might have been someone else," we must first address Wittgenstein's clear rejection of this view that "I" refers to myself.

In typical autobiographical statements like "I am feeling thirsty" or "I am depressed" the term "I," according to Wittgenstein, *does not stand for anything at all.* Although there could be independent reasons to think that Wittgenstein had a proto-Buddhist account of the self (some sentences of the *Tractatus* beckon us in that direction), this particular argument by which he shows that "I" does not refer to anything has nothing to do with a Humean or Buddhist no-self theory. Wittgenstein is not arguing that there is no self to refer to because introspection yields only passing states, nor is he saying that "I" does not refer to anything at all because it isn't sufficiently simple. Rather, his argument in *The Blue and the Brown Books*[1] starts from the necessary conditions of genuine reference:

1. One cannot be said to refer to an object with a linguistic or ostensive device unless one is picking out one among many possible objects of reference. If one is really referring, one can claim to have got the right object—the very object the speaker wishes to speak of or point out.
2. The choice of the right referent presupposes that there is a possibility of getting it wrong, of mistaking one object of identification for another.
3. But, when we use the word "I," the possibility of mistaking some other object for its referent simply does not exist.[2]
4. Therefore, one cannot make genuine reference with the normal introspective use of the "I."

The heart of this argument has been standardized by Shoemaker's elegant phrase: Immunity to Error due to Misidentification (IEM). IEM disqualifies the referential claims of the first person singular pronoun unless one is using it simply to refer to externally observable states of one's body, to the self as a mere object. Wittgenstein would have admitted that one could make an identificatory error in a gruesome battlefield where one could say, "(When I looked at the mirror) I thought I had a broken arm but it was a fellow soldier next to me who had a broken arm, not I." But such error regarding who it is that one is referring to is impossible in case of the incorporeal Cartesian *cogito*. The very immunity to mistake which Descartes thought made the *cogito* proof of the existence of the disembodied first person, according to Wittgenstein, shows that the introspection-supported "I" is a non-referring expression creating only a grammatical illusion of a pure subject of experience. Elizabeth Anscombe conveys the punch of the argument:

> Getting hold of the wrong object *is* excluded, and that makes us think that getting hold of the right object is guaranteed. But the reason is that there is no getting hold of an object at all.[3]

Anscombe strengthens this argument by adding more general considerations about self-consciousness, including bodily self-awareness. She imagines that if she ever suffers temporary loss of sensory-motor awareness of her own body, she can still have the thought: "I shall never let this happen again." The very fact that "I" is still guaranteed a reference, according to Anscombe, shows that the "I" could not refer to the embodied somatic self. She then constructs an argument parallel to the private language argument. "Refer," like "follow a rule," is a success verb. Genuine reference requires a gap between a speaker merely thinking that she is referring to some object and her really referring to it. But since the only legitimate thing "I" can stand for is a Cartesian thinking ego, there is no distinction between appearance and actuality, and therefore no genuine referring can take place. Notice that Anscombe's version of the argument entirely depends on the conditional premise regarding the Cartesian self. This assumption is what Strawson taught us how to reject.

Wittgenstein did not stop with exposing the error of our privileged access to a first person. He also gave a diagnosis of the grammatical illusion. Unlike statements about other people's feelings, statements describing one's own feelings are not descriptions at all and hence do not require a specified subject. The child's expression of, for example, pain is replaced in adult life by a pseudo-statement like "I am in pain." Just as one does not look for a subject or a predicate in cheering or groaning, one should not treat "I" as having the role of a private name. There is no reference involved in first person avowals of psychological states and no chance of reference failure, because an avowal is an expression, not an assertion of feelings.

But the above anti-referential argument of Wittgenstein has been much questioned. We may grant him the first premise that in order for us to refer to something it must be one amid a number of distinguishable things and a bodiless self will not be a possible object of discriminated reference in a spatio-temporal framework. That does not preclude the possibility of referring to a Strawsonian person[4]—a self in space which has both p-predicates and m-predicates. A self which feels nostalgic standing in a certain place could easily be spatio-temporally identifiable enough to be picked out by "I." In case of such a first person, our act of identification would be without any risk of reference failure. But, if the argument turns on the idea of getting hold of the right object—which requires vulnerability to error—we must recognize that one can re-identify correctly only what one has identified in the first place. When I think of myself as a subject, I am thinking of the same thing which *you* can rightly or wrongly get hold of as a second person. My talking about myself as a publicly available object would not have been possible unless I could refer, albeit unmistakably, to myself first in my own self-thoughts. Susceptibility to error may ultimately be a necessary feature of predicate-ascription, whereas in token-reflexive identification with tokens which are genuinely empty of all descriptive content, the bare reference may indeed be unmediated. But, to quote Strawson, "the inference from 'unmediated' to 'non-referential' is disallowed."[5] The immunity to error that my own self-reference enjoys would have disqualified my claim to refer only if I had mystifyingly held on to the elusiveness of the self which only I can refer to. Our incorrigible perception of our own current pains and pleasures is unmediated by any criteria—*sākṣi-pratyakṣa* (immediate witness-perception) of pleasure and pain being paradigmatically intrinsically correct—but those same mental states are ascribed on the basis of external criteria by others to us. Yet the p-predicates thereby ascribed with or without behavioral criteria retain their conceptual identity across first-person and second-person ascription. Exactly analogously, first-person reflexive auto-reference, though immune to identificatory error, can maintain sameness of target with second-and third-person reference through mistake-susceptible other-identification, as long as we do not insist that only I can refer to my inner self, but others can refer only to my body. If the located living being that others refer to as Arindam is the same as what I refer to as myself, then the immediacy and invulnerability of my own self-reference should not count against the genuineness of the referring function of "I" because of its co-referentiality with the mediate and vulnerable use of "Arindam" by others.

One also finds counterexamples to the Wittgensteinian claim that the self is immune to error through misidentification. Consider the following story:

> Paul used to be an over-confident heroic male. He used to never acknowledge that he ever felt fear. He undergoes psychotherapy and learns to recognize that when he is angry in a certain way, two things may happen: he may actually be not angry

> but afraid, and he may totally identify with his daughter. Once after this, he finds himself feeling that kind of mind-fogging anger. As a result of his inductively acute self-assessment he naturally has a clear feeling that either he or his daughter is now afraid. Over-correcting himself, he introspects that it is he himself who is afraid. But he gets it wrong. It is his daughter who is afraid. He commits what is in effect an identificatory error with regard to who it is that he subjectively feels the anger of. (Hogan and Martin, 2001)

There may be something counter-intuitive about this example, but the Wittgenstein-Anscombe thesis is more counter-intuitive. The price you pay if you accept Wittgenstein's conclusion is that self-ascriptions of inner states tell us nothing about what other people are saying about themselves. First- and third-person reports of mental states would never express the same propositions, for the first would not express any proposition at all! To buy Wittgenstein's argument is to concede that the very idea of knowing or being aware of oneself is nonsensical. That is not a price but a penalty I am not ready to receive. I would like to keep self-knowledge and self-reference intelligible, even if difficult.

Frege on the incommunicable sense of "I"

Gottlob Frege never doubted that with the word "I" each speaker refers to his or her self. Indeed, for his epistemology and metaphysics, the self—as a distinct bearer of ideas and mental states—is an extremely important object of thought and experience. Against Hume or any Yogācāra Buddhist style phenomenalist, Frege says:

> I am not my own idea and if I assert something about myself, e.g. that I do not feel any pain at this moment, then my judgment concerns something which is not a content of my consciousness, is not my idea, that is me myself.[6]

So making reference to a non-Parfitian self with "I" must be possible for Frege. But, applying his influential distinction between sense and reference to the case of the demonstrative "I," Frege had to face a serious problem. Let me formulate the problem in the following way, after John Perry, with a change of the example-individual.

Suppose Karl Marx says to himself "I wrote the *Capital*." Now, the thought he would express by these words would not be the thought expressed by someone else—or even Marx himself—by the sentence "Karl Marx wrote the *Capital*," for the singular terms "I" and "Karl Marx" have different senses while they have the same reference. But could someone else, Stalin for example, apprehend or have the thought expressed by the first autobiographical sentence? If so, it would be a false thought. They will not be the same thought. Thus, no one can ever have that thought except Karl Marx. Yet, it is part of Frege's basic theory of the nature of objective thoughts that thoughts, unlike tones or associated images, are completely communicable. Even if the name "Aristotle" is used with different associated criteria of identification or modes of presentation by different people, each of those modes of presentation is sharable, objective, sense-content which belongs to the non-private realm of thought. Yet, in a notoriously puzzling passage, Frege says:

> Now, everyone is presented to himself in a particular and primitive way, in which he is presented to no one else. So, when Dr. Lauben thinks that he has been wounded, he will probably take as a basis this primitive way in which he is presented to himself. And only Dr. Lauben himself can grasp thoughts determined in this way. But now he may want to communicate with others. He cannot communicate a thought which he alone can grasp. Therefore, if he now says, 'I have been wounded', he must use the "I" in a sense of "he who is speaking to you at this moment," by doing which he makes the associated conditions of his utterance serve for the expression of his thought.[7]

Thus, Frege seems to hold on to the following inconsistent set of claims:

1. When a speaker uses the "I" of soliloquy, as against the "I" which is just a shorthand for "the current speaker," the thought one expresses cannot be grasped by anyone other than the thinker to whom that token of "I" refers.
2. Every thought is objective and independent of the thinker.
3. The thought containing the exclusively first-personal sense or mode of presentation would not have existed unless that particular thinker existed and entertained that token thought, because it makes essentially indexical reference to the thinker and the context of utterance (in case of "I am wounded now" etc.).

Over the last fifty-five years, David Kaplan, John Perry, and others have been working on this problem. Just the sense-reference distinction would not do. Finer distinctions between cognitive contents, characters, type-modes of presentation, and token-modes of presentations have been drawn by Kaplan and others to grapple with the fact that Strawson had first drawn attention to: that even though the lexical meaning of the sentence may remain the same across different people making different uses of the same sentence such as "I am bored," the statements made by them may widely differ, in context-sensitive truth-value-bearing ways. Do we learn to use two kinds of "I," one for our private thoughts and one for public communication? But given that every bit of my vocabulary is learnt from others, how could my elders or peers ever teach me how to use this "I" of soliloquy? And when my friend tells me "I am depressed," am I doomed to understanding only one part of what she means, namely that the utterer of that sentence, whoever that is, is depressed? That does not sound right. If I care, I surely try to understand more than that, and occasionally I even understand exactly the way she herself—not just anyone like her, let alone any utterer of that sound token "I"—feels depressed.

Nearly three centuries before Frege, Gadādhara handles the same issues regarding contextual reference, learnable rule of use, and reason for application of the term *aham*.[8]

Gadādhara on the meaning/reference of "I"

Gadādhara starts by rejecting the simple view that the word "I" refers to just any self (*ātma-mātra*). Had "I" stood for any single self, we should have been able to report the knowledge or suffering of another person by saying "I know." It could be suggested, instead, that the general property of being an utterer of some word serves as a contingent indicator leading us on an occasion of its use, for example, by Chaitra, to the actual reason for application, namely, being the self of Chaitra, which then enables us to fix the reference as the self of Chaitra on that occasion. But that criterion is also too loose because Chaitra's use of "I" may then be taken as referring to Maitra's self as well, if on that occasion Maitra also was an utterer of any other word, or of another token of "I."[9]

We may tighten the meaning-rule to prevent this over-coverage. A particular token-utterance of the word "I" makes reference to that self, which has the property of being the self of the utterer of that very token of the word "I." This may become too stringent, for we must not look for a new referential power for every new occasion of use, as long as it is used by the same speaker. The specification of that particular token utterance surely could not be built into the meaning-rule for the word "I" since we do not have to re-learn or work out anew the referent of the first-person pronoun each time when the same speaker uses it multiple times. Gadādhara's objection can be reformulated in the following form. If "utterer of this particular sentence" were contingently synonymous with each use of "I," then the statement "I am the utterer of this particular sentence" would be reducible to the tautology: "The utterer of this particular sentence is the utterer of this particular sentence." But the statement is contingently true, not tautologous. Hence, the meaning-rule cannot be given like that. Ultimately, Gadādhara clarifies the role of "this self-same token-word" (*svapada*) in the self-referential specification of the general meaning-rule in such a fashion that it only helps us capture the context-and speaker-specific *character* of that utterance, rather than each individual token utterance (*tattatpadavyaktitvena na padānām viṣyatā; api tu tattatpadatvādi rūpānupūrvīviśeṣaprakāreṇa*), thus yielding the right reference-conditions for "I," "me," "my," etc., used by the same speaker.

But then he reminds us that even this rule will fail to give us the right referent in the context of reported or repeated speech. In *Durgāsaptaśatī* a sage tells a king the following: "In no time, when I kill you, the gods will roar right here in celebration, so said the Goddess (to Mahiṣāsura)."

Now, the utterer of that entire sentence is the sage Medhas and its addressee is the king. Yet, surely, the word "I" does not refer to Medhas; it refers to the Goddess, and it would be unfortunate to interpret the sentence as saying that the sage Medhas (who is the utterer of the whole sentence) is about to kill his listener, the king. Gadādhara's solution to this has been elegantly translated by Jonardon Ganeri:

> The explanation is that the above rule concerning the use of the first person pronoun is applicable only to an *independent utterance*, that is, an utterance not depending upon another person's self-referential utterance. In the above example the sage's utterance is not of such a sort, since it depends upon the Goddess's utterance as the route to denoting its referent. So the sage is not denoted by the first person pronoun.[10]

By the qualifier "independent utterance" only a very special kind of dependence is excluded. Otherwise, even the speaker of statements such as "I am going" would not be referred to by the use of "I" when the utterance is made, depending on the context. Many of our I-statements are dependent upon the context and are contingent upon preceding statements uttered by others. It is only when the utterance is dependent upon another person's self-reference-involving utterance that one is only reporting or repeating that we have to have this extra caution. In such cases alone, the speaker of the embedding dependent sentence is not meant by the "I" of the agent (of speech) mentioned in that reporting sentence. The Goddess is mentioned as the agent of speaking (*devī uvāca*—the Goddess said) in the dependent report, hence she, not the speaker of the dependent utterance, would be meant by the "I" of her speech, even if that particular token is not uttered by her but by the verbatim reporter.

What if the dependent reporting statement is not about what another person utters, but what he thinks? Can't an "I" refer to a non-utterer when such a person is reported to have a first-person thought? In Sanskrit you could say things like: "Though silent, that man believes 'I am very erudite'" (*ayam maunī puruṣaḥ aham pandita iti jānāti*).

Gadādhara also explains how upon hearing "Chaitra is more handsome than others," Chaitra grasps the sentence meaning directly as "According to this person *I am* more handsome than others."

Advaita Vedānta: "I" refers to the ego-maker, not to the unmeanable transcendental subject/self

These examples should remind us that the use of the first-person pronoun is indicative of egotism and pride. That is why the word for pride is *aham-kāra*—literally: utterance of the word *aham*. Frequent use of the word "I" is an unmistakable mark of conceit. But the word *ahaṃkāra* also has a technical sense. It is the material ego-making principle which evolves out of the three affective strands of pleasure, pain, and torpor and is responsible for an individual soul assuming all the suffering-causing involvement with psycho-physical characteristics. In all Vedāntic ontology, there is a sharp distinction between this quasi-material ego-maker *ahaṃkāra* and the real immaterial consciousness or self. In his *Advaitasiddhi*, Madhusūdana vigorously combats his dualist realist opponent Vyāsatīrtha on the topic: what is the direct referent of the first-person singular pronoun *aham*? Vyāsatīrtha emphatically says it is the self. No, Madhusūdana protests, it is the knot of materiality and consciousness which is technically known as *ahaṃkāra*. One inference that he proposes sounds almost circular:

The meaning of the term "I" is not-self
Because it is something meant by the word "I"
Just as the meaning of the word *ahaṃkāra* is.

Another argument is this:

Whatever is meant by the word "I" is other than the self
Because it is an object of the sense of ego
Just like the body is.

The underlying assumptions, of course, are these:

1. While the real self, identical with pure consciousness, is perpetually self-luminous, the object meant by the personal pronoun is temporarily unavailable even to the self at the time of deep sleep. Hence whatever is meant by that word must be other than the self, and something that is not necessarily self-luminous.
2. It is not the self, but this quasi-material principle of ego-making that assumes agency and doer-ship of all the mental acts that are superimposed on the self by the internal organ and other psychological accessories. Thus, even when the thread of the personal consciousness is picked up by the woken-up person who not only remembers that he is the same person as the one who fell asleep, but also remembers having lost all sense, including the awareness of being this particular individual during sleep, it is not the self but this egotistic claimant of memory "I am the one who remember my previous experience" etc. who is picked out by the pronoun "I."
3. Finally, the self cannot be an object of any identification. But the whole point of the use of the word "I" is demarcating oneself from other objects, and thereby count the ego as one object amidst many other conscious and unconscious objects. Hence it is this clot of object-pretending-to-be-a-conscious-center that is the direct meaning of *aham*. That is why in ecstatic Upaniṣadic utterances like "*yaḥ asau asau puruṣaḥ saḥ aham asmi*" (That, that Supreme Person I am), the word *aham* has to be taken obliquely and secondarily signifying the Self, for the self is never the directly spoken-of designatum (*vācyārtha*) of any word. It cannot be the object of reference because it cannot be an object.

The dualist Vedāntins reject these assumptions and arguments. Followers of Vyāsatīrtha refute the Advaita conclusion that the word "I" does not refer to the self, in defense of the common sense that it does.

Āryadeva's ingenious Buddhist argument for the semantic emptiness of "I"

The plainest and dearest word of ordinary language users, the word "I" has always held a logical mystery for philosophers. It is neither a singular referring expression like a proper name, nor a general or descriptive concept-word. One of the earliest recognitions of its role as a proudly singular designator picking out no one single fixed entity is to be found in Āryadeva, a direct disciple of Nāgārjuna, who uses the paradoxical semantics of "I" as an argument against the existence of the self.

Āryadeva's argument goes as follows:

> This is also why the self essentially does not exist. Had the self been essentially real, then just as it is the basis/support of one person's ego-usage (*ahaṃkāra*) it would have been also the basis/support of everyone's. Since in this world, hotness is the essential

> nature of fire, we do not find some fires which are not hot (but cold). Just like that, if the self essentially existed, then it would be the self for all, and would be the target of everyone's use of "I" (the object of everyone's ego-usage). But it is not so, hence it is said: What is your self is my non-self (for me it is an other/not-self), therefore this self is not necessarily (universally, as a rule) a self. Isn't it simply an imaginary superimposition of titles (such as "I," "the self," "person," etc.) on impermanent entities?

A semantic version of this can be formulated as the following formally valid argument:

> AS1. If a certain word "W" really meant a thing in a public language, then every user of that language would have meant that same thing by it, just as the word *agni* always refers to fire, in Sanskrit, no matter who uses it.
>
> AS2. But, every user of the word "I" does not mean the same thing by it, each user means a different person.
>
> Conclusion 1. Therefore, the word "I" does not really mean anything, which is equivalent to conclusion 2.
>
> Conclusion 2. The so-called self which each of our uses of "I" is supposed to mean is an imaginary (non-existent) conceptual construction.

Now, what is denied by AS2—"Everyone means the same thing by the use of 'I'" (U)—can mean either:

> U1: For all *x*, if *x* uses the word "I" there exists some (the same) *y*, such that whenever *x* uses that word, *x* means *y* (and *y* happens to be identical with *x*).

Or

> U2: There exists some (the same) *y*, such that, for all *x*, whenever *x* uses the word "I" *x* mean *y*.

Clearly these are utterly different claims. In U1 the universal quantifier governs the existential quantifier, whereas in U2 the existential quantifier governs the universal.

It seems uncontroversial that U2 is false, because there is no single entity which is everyone's self (unless one goes the radical Advaita Vedanta way). So, in that sense, premise AS2 is true. But U1, the more obvious interpretation of U, is *true*, and hence premise AS2, its negation, is false. Everyone does mean the same by the use of the word "I," namely, oneself. The argument is fallacious. It thrives on a deliberately ambiguous way of remarking that our token-reflexive use of the first person pronoun picks out no fixed referent and deducing therefrom that there is no self, ignoring the fixed rule by which it picks out, on each occasion, its flexible reference.

It would be too much to claim that Āryadeva had all these semantic difficulties in mind when he gave this odd argument against the existence of the self. But the argument may be one of the earliest anticipation of the meaning-theoretic difficulties with regard to the pronoun "I." The twentieth-century Indian philosopher K. C. Bhattacharyya has done the subtlest work on our linguistic reference to ourselves and the meaning of "I." The following passage solves the puzzle of the objective yet subjective nature of our use of the first person singular pronoun:

> The word *I* as intending the subject is not definitely either singular or general ... As used, the term has a uniquely singular reference; but as understood, it is general in the sense the term *unique* is general.

The original metaphysical formulation of the Madhyamaka Buddhist argument seems to make the following point. If something is real, it must be the same for all. The so-called self is not the same for all. So it must be unreal. Even after we have exposed the ambiguity and mistake in the semantic version of the argument, we cannot get away from the haunting attraction of this metaphysical insight: *if, objectively, metaphysically, there were a self, would it not be a self for everyone?*

Perhaps there are two distinct insights behind this argument. First, there is a general impersonalist constraint on ontological commitment. Only that entity could be said to exist with that objective nature, which would be recognized to be of that same nature from an impersonal view from nowhere. Second, there is a phenomenological observation about the sense of ego. The self is only a self from a single person's unshareable ego-centric point of view. From every other point of view, it is a non-self.

We could question both these initially appealing claims. It is more usual to challenge the first austere criterion of objective existence. I wish to explore a radical rebuttal of the second, nearly universally accepted, phenomenological claim about the unshareability of the sense of self.

There is some lesson to be learnt from Frege, Wittgenstein, Anscombe, and Madhusūdana and K. C. Bhattacharyya. The self, for sure, is not an ordinary object of reference. The "I" is not an ordinary referring expression. Not a proper name, not a definite description, not an outward demonstrative—"I," after all, is a bit of public language with which we try to include our conversational partners into the most intimate acts of introspection. Even when Hume reported that he entered most intimately into himself and failed to find a substantial ego, his qualification "For my part" was only rhetorically singular.

Of course, everyone is an "I" only to himself, and the same "I" is a "you" or "he" or "she" to others. But since I can think of myself, try to forget about myself, look within myself, and speak of myself to others or even try not to speak or think of myself, I must be able to invoke myself communicatively. Not all invoking as an intentional object is incompatible with subjecthood. Not all agency is incompatible with the role of the accusative. Referring that is vulnerable to error can only happen with respect to the non-self. But there can be kinds of invoking which are non-objectifying. Addressing is one such manner of invoking. When I invoke my friend to greet him or pray to God, I do not need to mean them as objects out there causally extracting this act of reference out of me. I speak to them freely without need for response. I don't speak of them. Similarly when I invoke myself, I am the one who means not the one who is meant, the subject and object of invocation become one, as in noticing my own breathing or feeling my own inner bodily touch during an experienced thrill. This is best realized when in contemplative communication with another I imagine possible role reversals, "I" and "you" converge until I feel your addressing me as my invoking myself. This *aham-tvam* or "you-I" is the "I" which is directly meant by our most authentic use of the first person singular pronoun.

In the spirit of Abhinavagupta we could remark that the first, second, and third persons are all brought together in a communicative union when Krishna addresses Arjuna (=Dhananjaya) in the tenth chapter of the Gītā: "Of all the Pāndavas I am Dhananjaya." In the context of that classic conversation, doesn't this amount to telling his addressee: "I am you"? Incidentally notice how the singling out from a descriptively limited range of alternative objects—the *nirdhāre ṣaṣṭhī* of *pāṇḍavānām*—is done with the third-person proper name, yet the target is the addressee, the you. And the speaker Krishna, who is *aham ātmā sarvabhūtāśayasthitaḥ* (the subject inside every living being), is the first person who is identifying himself with this You-Dhananjaya.

Abhinava insists that even if we try to look upon the other person's body as a mere physical object, the moment "this body" is addressed in communication, it is completely enveloped with the I-feeling of the addressor. The this (*nara, human person*) that is addressed as a you becomes an I-this (*śakti—divine power*). The principle of addressing demands that when I say "Listen You! Standing there," I mean that just as I stand and feel my cognition-will-action manifest itself as standing, you are standing too, thus assimilating your I-ness into my I-ness, and together creating an uninterrupted relishing of subjectivity. This is far from a Being-With or *mitsein* that the existentialist could come up with in overcoming the problem of alterity.

> The sense in which the addressor and the addressee, though different, become one in the addressing is indicative of the *parāparā* Goddess, whose characteristic is identity in difference.[11]

I do not know if Professor Ramchandra Gandhi had been actually influenced by a reading of these passages. The basic insight behind his theory of addressing is present in these and many other passages of Abhinavagupta. Professor Gandhi has characterized addressing the second person as a uniquely non-coercive, non-referential, quintessentially linguistic non-causal invitation of the attention of the other person, while giving notice of his or her freedom not to respond. Abhinavagupta tells us that in addressing the other I address the self in the other, and thereby imagine myself to be addressed. In friendship and love we get an empathic re-discovery of the original unity of all apperception. "The second person which is characteristic of Śakti, shedding its standard divisive use, acquires the aspect of the first person which is characteristic of Śiva, when, for instance, one feels: 'O dear friend! You indeed am I.'"[12]

There are important distinctions between the two theories. But they are both committed to strong non-dualism of consciousness. They both tell us about the convertibility of the I into you and the you into I, through linguistic acts such as addressing and speaking of oneself as another.

Going many steps beyond Ramchandra Gandhi, Abhinavagupta daringly claims that we do not need to speak out loud in order to self the other and other the self. The speech which makes this possible is inner speech, the very nature of self-consciousness which has a questioning and answering, calling and responding, meaning and being meant, at its very heart. To unveil the mystery of this free mutual convertibility of the you, I and the he/she/it, we must turn to the concept of *vimarśa*, as becomes clear from this passage in the IPV:

> The free power of self-consciousness can do everything: it can turn the other into its own self, it can turn the self into an other, it can identify the two, and it can reject even this unification of the self and the other … and this self-synthesis is nothing other than inner speech—a speech that is not ruled by artificial semantic conventions, but is an uninterruptedly self-relishing use of natural signs like head-gestures made inwardly to oneself.[13]

We shall delve into this matter in more depth and detail in the next chapter.

The first person as a Strawsonian person

What, then, is my currently final position regarding the referent of the first person singular pronoun?

In day-to-day use, a particular token utterance of the word "I," I think, refers to the utterer of that very token—a Strawsonian person, a conscious social body and not to a "Smart" brain, nor to a Descartes/Nyāya type soul, nor even to a neurophysiological conglomeration.

So, "I" picks out any one of those self-conscious living beings moving about in space but maintaining a memory-mediated diachronic identity—only one of them at a time—the very one who utters this current token of that term, as long as the token-utterance is not subordinated to and dependent upon another clause

But besides this quotidian self, reference to which often leads to egotism and competitive individualism, and shining through the cracks of our conceptual grasp over the communicative use of this unshareable indexical, there is a deeper self. In personal caring for another, ethical and aesthetic imagination, in seeing I-to-I—as it were—with another person in conversation, this deep I shows signs of breaking the walls between the first, the second, and the third persons. This pure, subjective yet universal unindividuable meaning of "I," when accessed, shatters our egotism and enables us to enjoy a selfless self.

11

The Self at Other Times and in Other Bodies

The case against the existence of the self

There is no self, says the Buddhist. Yet, as far as we know, the Buddha never recommended a radical change in our linguistic habit of using the first person singular pronoun "I" ("*aham*" in Sanskrit). Abolition of the use of the word "I" would make it impossible for a Buddhist to say in all sincerity, "I have no thesis, so I have no fault" (*nāsti me pratijña, tato nāsti me doṣaḥ)* or even, "I take refuge in the Buddha, the Dhamma, and the Sangha." After all, there is a clear use of the first-person singular in the verb-form ("*śaraṇam gacchāmi*").

However, just because the Buddhist keeps using the first-person singular pronoun and believes that she herself—not someone else—is working toward liberation through the therapy of her own desires, the Nyāya champions of an enduring substantial self/soul should not prematurely celebrate a victory. There are many such quick "self"-establishing arguments in the market. One such argument is the following one-liner by P. T. Geach: "If only a self can have illusions, then it cannot be an illusion that a self exists."

But the "self"-repudiator is not so easily silenced. The presupposition that only a self can have illusions is easily rejected by an ancient Buddhist or even a contemporary connectionist fictionalist about the mind. A bundle of *skandhas* can keep making mistakes just as a soul-less computer program can become delusional. And in verbal transactions "I" could be used by and for a community.

The standard Buddhist arguments for proving the non-existence of the self can be classified under the following headings[1]:

1. Arguments from universal momentariness (against an allegedly permanent self, or permanent anything, for that matter).
2. Arguments from mereological reductionism and phenomenalism in general (against external-world realism which is supposed to indirectly require a persistent self irreducible to mental states or sensations).
3. Arguments from the lack of distinction between qualities and quality-possessors (against a substantial substratum of mental qualities).
4. Arguments from non-apprehension (against the perceptibility or direct provability of the self)

The Buddhist critique of recognition or re-identification across times

The major thrust of the standard Buddhist anti-self arguments was not so much against the first person but against the first person's diachronic identity. In response, the ninth-century Nyāya stalwart Jayanta Bhaṭṭa points out that solid evidence for such continuity is right under our noses all the time.

> In sacred rituals, in religious duties, in agriculture and commerce, people successfully make deliberations of the form 'I did this yesterday and the next day I must do this other thing' only because they can re-identify themselves as the same across times. Therefore, surely, each of them is directly aware of one constant person (*dhruvaṃ puruṣam*) in all the states.[2]

Take, for example, the very process of philosophical debate which the Buddhist is so eager to enter into. One has to listen to and understand the opponent's utterances for the sake of responding to them. Let me take a few lines written at least a century later by Abhinavagupta:

> Only if the external and internal objects such as blue and pleasure etc., carried forth by the mouths of the rivers of separate episodes of awareness, all flow and rest in one single great ocean of consciousness which calls itself "I." Can they, then, be mutually synthesized and related to each other? Otherwise how can unconscious material things, or discrete awareness-episodes of them, which remain spatio-temporally limited and insulated inside their own existence, get mutually connected by themselves, because ... if the earlier flash of awareness and the later flash of remembering were simply two events separated from one another then there never would be any recall. Hence through memory one unified Knower-Reality is proved.[3]

Jayanta Bhaṭṭa derives an anti-Buddhist argument for the existence of an enduring self from the very experience of comprehending a long sentence. What follows is a translation of his verse on this process of understanding:

> The phonemes are heard in a sequence. When the traces left behind by the earlier auditory perceptions are all re-awakened at the time of hearing the last phoneme, the partitioning of the total sound-series into words is done along with the activated memory of the learnt conventional meaning of each word. Spontaneously examining the syntactic dove-tailing of the words and the semantic congruence of their meanings, the total sentence meaning is glued together. Now, all of this would be exceedingly hard to explain without postulating a single knower.[4]

Śābara in Mīmāṃsā and Vātsyāyana in Nyāya take this phenomenon of recognition (*pratyabhijñā*) to be the strongest evidence for an identical knower-self continued diachronically. Recognition, by the way, is not to be confused with remembering. It is an *experience* of a present object as identical with something perceived in the past.

But the Buddhist subjects this phenomenon to his usual dilemmatic scrutiny. The following diatribe is my free translation of Jayanta Bhaṭṭa's dramatization of standard Buddhist polemic against the "Nyāya Pro-Soul argument from Recognition."[5]

Is this recognition, allegedly of the form "This (present Object/Self) is (identical with) *that* (the past Object/Self)," one piece of awareness or two? If it is a single awareness, then what is its cause? If it is caused by a sense organ alone, then it could not possibly grasp the past, the *that*-part, for our senses can only grasp the present, and not other times. If it is caused by memory traces alone, then the present part will not be accessible, since memory traces are causally irrelevant to our access to a currently given object. The possibility that the senses and the traces together would produce this single cognition is as absurd as that of unlike causes like a lump of clay and a bunch of threads together producing a hybrid object like a pot-cloth!

So, it must be broken down into two distinct pieces of cognition with two distinct objects, neither of which can anticipate or bring back the object of the other to judge them to be either the same or distinct.

Even if, for argument's sake, we concede that a recognition is a single piece of awareness, what would be the nature of its object? Is the pillar or person that is re-identified a past one, a future one, or a present one? If it is a past one, then the awareness strictly speaking is a memory, which, by the way, even the Naiyāyika does not trust as a proper form of knowledge (*pramā*). If it is about the future persistence of the object, then it is almost like a wish or decision (*saṃkalpaprāyaṃeva tat*). If the recognition is merely of the object as it stands in the present point-instant, so much for your hope that it is going to prove the existence of an enduring object continuing from the past into the future. Thus, recognition seems to behave like a strange ascetic woman who had come with the promise to prove the permanence of things, but goes away proving their momentariness. As for the possibility that the same object could be characterized by both pastness and presentness, the Buddhist (as represented by Jayanta) argues exactly like McTaggart against the A-series: "is past" and "is present" are incompatible predicates, one defined in terms of the negation of the other. How can the same thing satisfy both of them?

Jayanta Bhaṭṭa's metaphysics and epistemology of recognition

Jayanta replies to each of the above objections: is the recognition, that this is the same pillar as the one I had seen yesterday, one cognition or two cognitions? The answer is clear, if we just keep faithful to our introspective report. It is a single identificatory awareness, where sense organs supply one term of the identity and awakened memory trace supplies the other term. As to how these disparate sources could co-operate causally, the fact that they do is experientially undeniable, unlike the implausible analogy of a pot-cloth which no one has ever perceived. If a time-straddling content is presented to all self-conscious knowers, it needs an explanation in terms of different cognitive capacities working together, which is much more intuitive and unsurprising than clay and cotton-threads working together to produce a single effect.

As to the nature of the object of this unitary experience, the accurate description is that it is an object delimited by the present time signaled by *this* and qualified by the past time signaled by *that* (*atitakalaviṣiṣṭavartmanakalavacchinnaḥ ca arthaḥ*). There is no incoherence in its being past and present at once. The same entity *was* present in the past and it *is* past in the present. When the two states of the entity at different times are attributed to it, the difference between the states and the times is very much registered, rather than forgotten. The past figures in this cognition *as past*.

One thing must be noted here. In later Nyāya, a sense organ's direct access to a past (now perished) phase or quality of an object is explained in terms of an extra-ordinary connection between our senses and absent objects where another current or recalled awareness itself works as the connector. It is called "*jñānākṣaṇasannikarṣa.*" Recognition is one of five or six contexts where this kind of extraordinary connection is invoked.[6] But Jayanta does not directly talk about this link through memory here. Instead, he follows the verdict of his intuitive analysis of experience and supplies this rule:

> That a sense organ does not grasp a past object is not its fault just like an ophthalmic disease [would not be]. It is incapable of catching the past time as an independent object, but it does not have any incapacity to grasp the past as a predicate qualifying a current object which is within its range.[7]

Thus, recognition is established to be entirely a variety of sense perception—perhaps with the assistance of the inner sense—where the continuous identity of the object, and the reflexivity of the subject, is evidenced in direct experience.

The Buddhist no-self theorist might still raise a difficulty. The past is, after all, gone and non-existent. How can it figure, even as a qualifier, in the content of a current cognition? Jayanta meets this worry with an intriguing example of counting consciousness. Suppose a glutton has been counting as he is eating some berries. When he experiences the thought, "I have eaten a hundred berries," he *recognizes* the hundredth one as hundredth only in relation—the relation of succession—to his perception of the previous ninety-nine as previous. He need not see and taste all hundred together in order to make that perceptual judgment. Although those ninety-nine fruits are no longer "there," they can "ride on the impression" and thus the bygone past can pervade the present perception of the hundredth fruit. If, at this point, the Buddhist falls back on his general skepticism about all qualificative judgments as mere products of conceptual imagination, and not as knowledge proper (which can be of only pure given particulars), Jayanta would throw up his hands and remark:

> Great Sir, is there anything on earth that you do not denounce as a mere figment of conceptualization? But, long live those (realists) who believe in the knowledgehood of predicative perceptions![8]

Not that a Nyāya realist would consider recognitive perceptual judgment to be infallible. If someone re-identifies one's hair, which has been cut off once and grown back again, to be that very same hair, such re-identification would be mistaken. Seeing a shaven head in the interval between the earlier and later perceptions would dispel this sort of mistaken re-identification. But, in the case of a person's identity across time, there is no counter-evidence of an intervening period when no self was witnessed at all. Intervals of deep sleep and so on are not periods of awareness of absence of self, but period of absence of all awareness.[9]

From non-apprehension to synthesis in recognition

This talk of absence brings me to Utpaladeva's and Abhinavagupta's transcendental argument from the content of perception of absence to the existence of an abiding self.[10] The Kashmir Śaiva epistemologists openly acknowledge their debt to Dharmakīrti and to the Buddhist theory of the reflexive nature of awareness (*svasaṃvedana*). But using the logic of *reductio ad absurdum* proofs, to which the Buddhists appeal so often, Utpaladeva tries to show that if one assumes the theory of momentary self-aware states of consciousness positing their own internal "objects" within themselves, then, eventually, one would have to reject the more fundamental Buddhist assumption that there is no unifying self behind this stream of discreet and object-discriminating cognitive states. One would thus have to commit to a synthesizing enduring self for the purpose of explaining the common practice of communication with other people and remembering other times.

Since the Buddhists, somewhat like Hume, also confess to *not finding* any directly perceptible self or ego besides the passing mental states, the Kashmir Śaiva epistemologists—known as the school of recognition—analyze the phenomenon of *not-finding* or *non-apprehension* (*anupalabdhi*) rather closely.

Before I get into the details of their argumentation, I wish to draw attention to an uncanny occurrence of an argument from non-apprehension given by Frege, where also the immediate context was the proof of a self beyond the mere subjective passing ideas.

Frege's passage starts in a very Nyāya-like vein: "Can there be a pain without someone who has it?" In answer to this insistence on a substantial subject who owns the ideas but is not reducible to them, Frege imagines that the reductionist Humean would say, "Can I be part of the content of my consciousness while another part is, perhaps, an idea of the moon?" This comes very close to Dharmakīrti's account of selfless awareness episodes which, in their reflexivity, create the illusory division within themselves of one part which calls itself the grasper "I" and another part which is felt to be the external object grasped. But Frege quickly rejects this hypothetical error-theory of "ego"-making. He has a series of interesting arguments which I shall not enter into here. But one of his arguments is from non-apprehension. Here is the crucial line:

> I am not my own idea and if I assert something about myself, e.g. that I do not feel any pain at this moment, then my judgment concerns something which is not a content of my consciousness, is not my idea, that is me myself.[11]

Now, back to Utpaladeva's argument against the Buddhist as explicated by Abhinavagupta. Suppose I have an experience that there is no pot here on the floor.

What is the content of my awareness? Ontologically, neither the Buddhist nor the Śaiva admits that there is an additional objective entity characterizing the floor called absence-of-pot. Even if we are talking to a Nyāya-Vaiśesika philosopher who does posit such an additional entity, what would be the phenomenological account of what I am seeing? The empty floor, to be sure. But if the empty floor looks no different from *the floor*, our experience would be the same when we saw *the floor with a pot*, for even there the floor looks the same. Unless we can somehow demarcate the potless floor from the potful floor, we would never have a clear perception that there is no pot on the floor. This demarcation requires comparing and contrasting. Just as in the case of recognition, when one has to bring back the object of past experience and assert its identity with the object of current experience, in non-apprehension too one has to recall what it is to be in the presence of a pot and then find the current experience of the bare floor to be unlike that. Then alone would the floor enter the content of the experience as not just floor-only, but as bare potless floor. How would a mere self-contained unowned un-connected momentary awareness of the floor perform this feat of comparing and contrasting? That, surely, would require connecting back with a previous experience and its different objectual feel.

There is no point in insisting that the non-apprehension of the pot is an indirect inferential outcome from the "prover-sign" (*liṅga*): non-availability of an apprehension of the pot. Abhinavagupta first shows elaborately how this sort of inference would lead to an infinite regress. Second, even inferences require conjunction of a perception of the prover-sign, a recall of the invariable concomitance between the sign and what is to be inferred, and a final unified judgment that such a pervaded sign is present in this case. This gets us back to an abiding self.

Thus, from all possible escape-routes, we are back to the requirement of synthesis and demarcation—comparison and unification—of objects (*viṣayamelanam*), which is impossible without a single thread of a self-aware self running through but not reducible to this passing flow of percepts and ideas. What is true of apprehending absence of a pot is also true of our negative introspective reports of not feeling any pain, or, as K. C. Bhattacharyya calls it, our feeling of a lack of feeling. And I would suggest that we could subject even Hume's negative claim—that when he searched he could not find it within himself—to this phenomenology of non-apprehension. As a result, we could remark that non-apprehension (of a pot, or a feeling, or an impression of a pure ego), which was invoked to prove the non-existence of the self, ends up proving the existence of a transcendental unifier of experiences.[12]

When generalized about all states of object-directed awareness—not just non-apprehension—the full chain of transcendental argument runs roughly as follows:

1. There cannot be a state of consciousness without intentionality, a certain grasping of a definite object, a certain other-directedness.
2. Intentionality cannot be explained without the capacities of demarcation (of one object from others) and remembering or recognizing (as the same object from another experience).
3. Demarcation and re-identification are impossible without mutual comparing, connecting, or synthesis of individual cognitive states. If the states were insulated

within themselves, then they would have no inkling of the contents of one another. Mere causal ordering or impact on one another would not explain how two of them could be about the same object or recognized to be of related or distinct objects.

4. No (more than causal) connecting of momentary cognitive states is possible without a connector which can run through, know all about, distinguish, and hold together all the different cognitive states, and hence is not itself a momentary cognition or their mere collection.
5. Therefore, to close the chain, there would be no states of consciousness unless there were a permanent single knower-self.

What if this sort of idea of the continuous self was a congenital illusion of these cognition episodes? In every case where the Buddhist resists the idea of commonness, either of a continuant across times, or of a property across instances, his last resort is an error-theory, which diagnoses our ineliminable tendency to see sameness in difference as a mistake. Even the transcendental argument, the Buddhist may say, rests on an innate error of positing a synthesizer of the series over and above the series. But Abhinavagupta runs the same transcendental argument from the very possibility of an error. Nothing counts as an error unless it is in principle detected or exposed. The fact that we can even make correction of an error shows that in us there is more than a mere succession of discreet mental states. Suppose we call a particular perceptual experience an illusion. Suppose, for the sake of the argument, that there is simply a causally connected succession of two distinct and unowned representational cognitive states in the form, "That is water over there" (C1), and, "There is just a dry sun-heated surface at a distance" (C2). But how is the second going to cancel the first and prove it to have been an error? If the correction or cancellation happens simply because when C2 arises C1 has perished, then every subsequent awareness will count as a correction of the previous one. Unless there is a single knower who owns them both, refers them both to a single object (*eka-viṣayatayā vinā*), recognizes that something cannot be both a pool of cold water and a dry heated surface at the same time, and also evaluates C2 to be more accurate than C1, detection of error would be impossible.[13] Thus, any perceptual error, or any error, for that matter, presupposes the existence of a non-momentary perduring self.

How much unity can we take? From other times to other subjects

Jayanta was interested only in proving a permanent individual soul, a distinct one in each body. But Abhinavagupta is not content with that alone. Once he has the transcendental argument from synthesis of cognitions to a constant unifier, he uses it to extend that unity beyond a single knower, to include the consciousness of other knowers. A Nyāya metaphysician will find this outrageously over-the-top (*atiprasaṅga*). But Abhinavagupta claims that he is simply generalizing the same argument from synthesis (*pratisaṃdhāna* or *anusaṃdhāna*).

Until now we seem to have proven that all that a single person comes to be conscious of must be somehow interconnected with a self-enjoying creative I-consciousness, which weaves them into some sort of oneness that is tolerant of a projected plurality of objects and places and times. But what about the distinction between one knower and another, between myself and others?

Abhinavagupta gives an argument to overcome even that basic otherness.[14] First, let it be admitted that my own consciousness is known to me directly. I know what it is like to be self-aware and aware of objects. And if, say in the context of an effort at empathy with a friend, I feel acutely that I am *not* quite feeling this friend's own emotions, as a missed feeling, don't I have to subjectively be aware of those emotions, in however inadequate a fashion?

In that sense, could not the unfelt pleasures and pains of another person need to become objects of my direct awareness as what I fail to feel, just as a remembered event is experienced by the same experiencer as what is not now happening? What is it that I ruefully miss when I confess that I cannot feel even my closest friend's own pains as he feels it? *Compare me at other times with the other self now*. Just as in order to remember (and miss) my past as my past I had to connect and re-live the bygone experience with the present one, in order to think of the other person as another subject, I have to connect his subjectivity with mine. Notice that even distinguishing requires connecting.

My self-awareness manifests itself through my bodily activities, and I notice others' bodily activities just as immediately as I notice my own, although there are differences of access set up by our habitual walls of individuality. Now, observable actions of sentient beings are quite distinct from mere physical movements. As Abhinavagupta remarks,[15] "The going of a living being is not like the movement of water, neither is the motionless sitting by a person similar to the motionlessness of a stone." Everywhere it is undeniable that we notice the actions of others as movements or postures enlivened by self-sentient "feels." Just as "He knows" is said as an abbreviation of "He is in a position to say 'I know,'" similarly "He walks" is asserted by me to the extent that I can feel what it is for him to make himself aware that "I am walking." Thus, even others' actions are observed (not inferred) by us to be tingling with the same subjectivity as I feel behind my voluntary actions. We must reject the suggestion that our knowledge of other minds is merely an analogical inference. The word used by Utpaladeva in the context[16] of our awareness of consciousness in other bodies is "*ūhyate*." And Abhinavagupta clarifies: "*ūhyate*" does not mean that others' sensations are merely inferred. To do "*ūha*" is to intuitively extrapolate, directly postulate from "otherwise inexplicability" to make it highly likely. Here, the process is partly a function of our sense organs: we see that the other is in pain, we can feel their pleasure (sometimes more than at other times). Thus, the word "*ūha*" signifies "direct acquaintance."[17]

When we are thus sensuously aware of the power of activity in others' bodies as something cognitive and conscious, this awareness inside others does not appear to us as a "this," that is, as a mere inert material property. To be a "this" is to be not of the nature of light, non-conscious. Whatever the modern brain-mind identity theorist may say, when I say and *see* that my friend is in pain or my daughter is singing happily I don't mean thereby that she is undergoing some physical objective event in her C-fibers or in her amygdala or somewhere else in her body. I mean (even if I don't feel it as mine) exactly the same sort of thing that I mean when I say that I am in pain or I am singing (something as subjectively feelable as that). If a state of consciousness appears as a "this thing out there," then it is not appearing as a state of consciousness at all, hence it is as good as not appearing. But others' states of consciousness are "seen" in their faces and postures and felt through sympathy—to make a Wittgensteinian point, minus Wittgenstein's allergy against the "inner." Therefore, even others' mental states appear to us as subjective, as connected to the "I." The otherness only belongs to the adjuncts and dividers such as these outer bodies, but the consciousness ascribed to them, qua consciousness, rests on the "I"-ness of the knower-in-general, as much as my own consciousness rests on the "I"-ness.

Self-ascription of conscious states may well be dependent upon other-ascription of those states. Unless we are interpreters of others' conscious—linguistic and non-linguistic—purposive behavior, we cannot be self-interpreters. At the very foundation of self-consciousness lie these two kinds of integrative capacities: the capacity to link, compare, and place on a par the subjectivity in others with the subjectivity in myself, and the capacity to integrate the bits of my own states over time into one center of experience. Thus, the argument from the requirement of synthesis, in Abhinavagupta, works for both other times and other people.

Here is his final dramatic clinching of the argument:

> Self-sentience, when it is realized through the medium of another body etc. makes its own awareness-essence known. An awareness never manifests itself as a "this" (mere inert object). Whatever manifests itself has the shape of an "I." Hence, even another person's awareness is one's own self.[18]

Besides our limited—for him, illusory—individual-self, Abhinavagupta "recognizes" a real universal subject, an infinite "I," where all self-regarding and other-regarding concerns rest, the stopping place for all reason-seeking and all conscious craving and relishing and marveling. When the universe is recognized to be contained within this non-individualistic (yet personal) subjectivity of this "all that I-Am," divisive egoistic craving and existential suffering cease and life becomes a perpetual festival. The process of arriving at this boundless unified Self through logical analysis of remembering, re-identifying, distinguishing, non-apprehension, inferring, and error-correction is rather complex. And my hunch is that the argumentation process itself is part of the meditation. After all Abhinavagupta does insist that good reasoning (*sattarka*) is the best of all methods of Yoga!

This brings me back to Āryadeva's ingenious argument examined in the last chapter. Yes, indeed, if what is the "I"=Self for you were an Other=non-self for me, then the category of the "I"=Self would be metaphysically suspect. Let us grant Āryadeva that, although Jayanta or any other Naiyāyika may not admit this. But is it correct that your self is my non-self? Who says that your I is not my I too? When I feel your pain from inside, and even when I register my failure to enter into your experience in that uniquely subjective way, I have to have an identificatory or absence-recognizing grasp of that same subject-hood, the same "I"-ness that you, I, God, or, according to Abhinavagupta, even a worm feels by virtue of simply feeling alive.

To think of consciousness is to think of the "I." This "I" is the same for me and you and others. Its very all-encompassing, relation-making, self-distinguishing, reflexive, phenomenal character resists genuine multiplicity or total otherness. Therefore, it exists, *objectively*, that is, for all of us, but *not as an object*. Indeed, in all its glory and playfulness of projecting numerous others, this consciousness makes an "I" of each one magically-set-up knower and a "You" of all the rest. Pretending that all those others are mere things over there, and then re-identifying them back in oneself—this all-encompassing subjectivity may be all that there really is.

Yet, this identification of the self as both a subject and an object may sound problematic to some. How could it make sense to cling on to the objective reality of the self both as a *subject* and an *object* of awareness? Also, what exactly do we mean by "awareness" in that context? Unless one accounts for such difficulties, any plausible model of the metaphysics of selfhood would remain out of reach. This will be the subject, so to speak, of the next chapter.

12

Does Self-Awareness Turn the Self into an Object?

In both ordinary and academic English, the word "subject" has a wide range of meanings. The edges of some of these meanings seem to be almost at loggerheads with one another. Grammatically, the subject in the sentence is the governor (or ruler) of the verb. It stands typically for (1) the "free agent" of the action that the verb may describe, grammatically the nominative case. But politically, the subject is (2) the governed, the ruled, one of those who are subjected to domination by the powers that be in a monarchy. One may protest that the sense of paradox I am trying to create is phony. Those are distinct words spelt and pronounced the same way, just like "mean" meaning unkind and "mean" meaning middle.

But I am sure the different and even opposite uses of the word "subject" are not quite that unrelated or incompatible. This becomes easier to appreciate if we see how the intermediate meanings shade into one another. Connected to the grammatical sense is the cognitive phenomenological sense of the term, where (3) the first person singular owner of experience is called *the subject*, the "I" of "I think." The self is the subject in this sense. But when a psychologist conducts her research on (4) experimental *subjects*, such subjects are as much treated as objects of observation as they are supposed to feel, behave, and report as subjects of experiences. Then again, the concept of a subject as (5) the topic or subject-matter is closer to the sense of governed or ruled than to the sense of governor or ruler. The topic does not treat or study my thought, talk, or writing. My thought, talk, or writing studies and treats the topic. Yet, it is plausible to take the topic as what determines, limits, and thus rules my thinking or discussion. Thus, the topic is subjected to analysis and scrutiny, although we cannot quite free ourselves from the odd feeling that in a sense its nature dictates our knowledge or thought about it.[1] But the idea of a subject as the principal object of knowledge becomes most prominent when we look at the traditional logical category of (6) a subject as against a predicate of a judgment. If I analyze the content of a normal subject-predicate awareness where some property is ascribed to an object, the object to which the predicate is ascribed, not only can, but must be the subject of the cognitive content. If I come to know that the Pope is Argentinian, the Pope is the subject of my belief and thereby an object of my knowledge, just as the predicated property of being Argentinian is also another object of that piece of knowledge.

When I sit as a subject of analysis in the therapist's couch and try to tell her what I feel and think about myself, I seem to be a subject in at least three of the above senses. I become my own topic. While remaining a subject or owner of my introspection, I make myself at the same time an object of observation, and try to characterize myself as a subject of predication. I subject myself to honest scrutiny, as the agent and patient of the act of looking, at once observer and observed, knower and known. Opposites do not feel incompatible any more. Indeed, once we place ourselves thus in the middle of this range of meanings of the term "subject," it seems quite natural and unremarkable that this should be possible. After all, the ruler and the ruled can sometimes be identical, as in a true democracy where the government is of and by the people. One meaning of "free" is "self-ruled." To be free is to be one's own master, and to be a self is to be free. Analogously, why should there be any incompatibility between being a subject of experience and being an intentional object of experience?

Yet, philosophers of many diverse traditions and times have claimed that there is some sort of a contradiction in making an object out of the subject—that no agent can loop back and act upon itself, and that the knower, literally and directly, cannot be known. Mighty metaphysical structures have been built on the basis of this principle of the putative irreflexivity of the act of awareness, as if the pair "subject" and "object" are like the pair "married" and "bachelor." In this chapter, I want to question this orthodoxy. Although I have claimed that these distinct senses of the term "subject" are not unrelated (in English), I do not for a moment think that they are all the same. I have no non-dualist agenda whatsoever. The subjects of a kingdom are not grammatical subjects of sentences. There is a great difference between being the first person subject of experience and being the topic or subject matter of someone's attention or discourse. But does it follow from these distinctions of sense that nothing can be a subject in both the senses? Take the statement, "This flower is yellow." The flower pointed out is the subject (and object) of attention. It is also the subject of predication. Here the same thing fulfills the role of the subject in two distinct senses. Why then is it said that subject in the sense of the self cannot be the object of perception on pain of a contradiction?

I try to dig for the conceptual roots of the alleged contradiction between these two notions or roles: that of a subject or self of awareness and that of an object or intentional topic to be known. If we cannot find any logical or conceptual incompatibility between the predicate " … is a subject of awareness" and " … is an object of awareness," then we should be friendly toward a realist account of introspection as self-perception. We get such an externalist realist account of introspection in standard Nyāya epistemology, where one treats inner perceptions verbalized as "I am pleased" or "I am aware that it is getting late" as straightforward cases of apperceptions or higher-order perceptions of the self as qualified by the properties of some sensory or propositional awareness. Of course, as long as one has some notion of inner sense, one can adopt this perceptual model of self-awareness without necessarily committing to the Nyāya metaphysics of the self. But contemporary philosophers such as Shoemaker tell us:

> No one thinks that in being aware of a sensation or sensory experience one has yet another sensation that is "of" the first one … And no one thinks that there is such a thing as an introspective sense-experience of oneself.[2]

I want to point out that one of the most sophisticated analytic schools of Indian epistemology thinks precisely that. It would take a very long paper to argue in defense of this much maligned broad perceptual model of self-awareness, especially in the face of Shoemaker's all-out attempt to discredit the idea of an internal sense organ which is so vital for the Nyāya picture of introspection. I want to take out one hurdle for that view, namely that the self cannot be its own object because subject-hood and object-hood with respect to the same awareness are incompatible. Those philosophers who report that they failed to find a self when they entered into themselves, to use an infamous phrase from US politics, must have been looking in the wrong place, at the wrong time, and with the wrong faculties.

Like the word "subject," the word "self-awareness" also has a maddening multiplicity of meanings. Besides its vague non-philosophical uses that may signify a certain heightened or embarrassed sense of individuality, even its technical philosophical use allows for many distinguishable meanings. Let me list four:

A. If used as a synonym for self-knowledge, for which the Upaniṣads and the Delphic Oracle exhort us to strive, self-awareness is a rare achievement of only very few extraordinarily wise people. It consists in knowing all about oneself, and knowing who or what one is, and this perhaps sets one free. I shall not be concerned with this esoteric sense of self-awareness here.

B. The term can mean a strict reflexivity of any state of awareness, whereby an awareness is necessarily self-intimating or self-luminous. This sort of self-awareness does not have any reference to the self or soul as a relatively permanent center of consciousness. It is the awareness, not the owner of it, which is meant by the word "self" in "self-awareness." It is not the agent of the act of cognition but the act itself which is supposed to be self-manifesting in this second sense.

C. Self-awareness could simply mean my direct *de re* perception of myself, or self-acquaintance. Here, the self is the self of the knower. I am self-aware when I know me (not necessarily who I am) to be experiencing or thinking something. She is self-aware when she knows herself to be sad or thrilled, but not in the sense that she has a deep and infallible knowledge of who she is. It is this kind of direct acquaintance with the referent of "I" which Russell had propounded in *The Problems of Philosophy*. There he wrote that the self must be a simple component of the complex "my-acquaintance-with-the-sense-datum," and that every element of a complex that one is acquainted with must be a direct object of acquaintance as well. In his later work[3] Russell rejects this theory because he starts to take Hume's confessed introspective failure seriously, and comes to treat "I" as a description rather than a Russellian proper name like "this."

D. Finally, "self-awareness" could mean simply our awareness of our own mental contents, or *de dicto* awareness that one is perceiving, feeling, wanting, or thinking something. I am inclined to believe that *D requires C, and that C is impossible without D*. I am not going to claim that a bare non-predicative perceptual awareness of the self is possible. I am extremely suspicious of claimed non-conceptual perceptions of anything. The last thing that I think can be perceived barely and pre-predicatively is the self. So, in a sense, C and D are the same for me. But it is important to distinguish them because many philosophers, like Shoemaker and Davidson, who believe that D is routinely possible think that C is impossible.

There are endless debates about the necessary reflexivity of consciousness in the second sense (B) of self-awareness. At least three models of this are available, and each of them triumphantly claims that it does not turn the Self (or the Subject) into an object of perception.

1. The simplest and metaphysically most austere model is that of self-less Yogācāra Buddhist reductionism. A momentary unrepeatable mental state is necessarily self-aware when, in spite of its indivisibility, it imagines itself as having two parts (or aspects): the grasper and the grasped. A sensation of blue comes in the dual-aspect form: the sensation-form, which pretends to be a self-luminous revealer, and the blue-form, which pretends to be some quality outside the sensation and revealed by it. Far from implying the existence of a self, this model of self-awareness is supposed to explain away any substantial or permanent owner of or any external object of ordinary mental states. It serves both the No-Self doctrine and Phenomenalist Internalism. Strictly speaking, there is neither an owner (or subject-center) nor a distinct outer object of this sort of cognition. So the question of turning its subject into an object is doubly beside the point. All that is meant by reflexivity here is, first, that the mental state does not exist unrecognized, and second, that there is no self or higher-order mental state grasping or revealing it. It is manifest but not other-manifested. These causally connected first-order mental states are all that there is. They reveal not only themselves, but nothing besides themselves—no spiritual subjects and no physical objects. It remains a mystery where the psychosis or illusion of bi-polarity comes from, given that we and our environment consist simply of these homogeneous arrays of momentary internal qualia. But intentionality is rooted, upon this account, in this original illusion of the same awareness appearing to itself as both the beam of light and the object manifested by the beam. The diachronically repeated knower-illusion congeals into the permanent error of ascribing more than one mental state to a single knower outside those states and the thing-to-be-known-illusion sets up the error of referring sensations to a single object outside of them.

2. What the first model takes as an error is taken by the Prābhākara Mīmāṃsā model to be the actual state of affairs. There *is* a substantial self in which cognitive states arise and there *are* real external objects of which the cognitive states take notice. But every cognitive state simultaneously illuminates the self, the cognition, and the object, *and* correctly registers these three items to be distinct. Of these three items, only the cognitive state is strictly speaking self-luminous. The self is not self-intimating; it needs the cognition to be manifested. The object too is unable to illuminate itself. It needs the cognition. And at no level does this self-awareness turn either the subject or itself into an object. The anti-reflexivist objection is answered by the following example: if I walk and carry a stone from one place to another, both the stone and I enjoy the fruit of the motion. But I do not make myself an object of my own act of carrying or moving, as I do to the stone. I move as a mover and the stone moves as moved. I lift the stone but I do not lift myself in that sense. The stone has *been* moved. I *have* moved. Thus, when I reveal the object, my self and my act of revealing are also revealed—not *qua* objects, but *qua* agent/knower and *qua* act of consciousness, respectively.

3. The third model is a formulation of the Advaita Vedānta position that consciousness, both in its pure and ordinary object-directed form, is self-luminous.

Colors, sounds, and tastes also appear immediately, but they are presented as objects of sense-perception. Awarenesses are just as directly presented and not inferred or thought out, but instead of admitting positively that they are self-presenting, which may suggest that they make themselves their own objects, they are described as "*not what is known*."[4] So on all these accounts of the second kind of self-awareness, the awareness itself or the self behind it, if any, need not become an object.

But what is this business of being presented immediately but not being perceived? Surely, to be immediately presented is to be perceivable. Jayanta Bhaṭṭa is not convinced by this claim that the self of consciousness is immediately presented (*aparokṣa*), but not perceived (*pratyakṣa*). Whenever I have immediate knowledge of the contents of my mind—for example my awareness that I am hearing the humming of my computer—that awareness involves my direct knowledge of myself. My perception that a hum is coming from the computer is fairly secure, but the inward awareness that I am hearing it to be so is not immune. Both I and the content and quality of my auditory experience are its objects. The sound could exist unrecognized by me if I were deaf. My auditory reception of the sound could exist unheeded if there were too many other sounds. Similarly, I could exist unobserved by myself.

Still, as I stated above, one of the key difficulties raised against self-awareness of type C is that it breaks a logical rule. Making an object out of the subject is considered incoherent. I will now examine whether there is any conceptual impossibility or incoherence in the idea of the self being an object.

Let me call the Śaṅkara-Kant position that there is such incoherence *incompatibilism*. I want to defend a realist *compatibilist* position that there is nothing in the notion of a cognitive accusative to be defined as necessarily other than the cognizer-self, and nothing in the notion of the self to be defined as out of bounds for cognition. The compatibilist can agree that most of our perceptions are directed outward. The sense organs look out, not within. Although I can see parts of my body, vision does not seem to yield any philosophically interesting self-knowledge. But with my inner sense I can sometimes introspect and have direct awareness of my current mental state. The self could be safely claimed to be a possible object of introspective awareness, just like pleasure and pain.[5] I can see the cup as well as its color. I can feel my own pain as well as feel myself feeling it. Wittgenstein wanted to subtract descriptive epistemic content from statements about private mental states, so that he would not have to deal with the "I." The incompatibilists convinced him that the "I" could only exist as an invisible non-object. I can be an object of my own knowledge, my own ignorance, and very often my own error. Again, to know something is not necessarily to know all of it. Most of seeing other bodies or empathically knowing other minds is only catching a glimpse of them. Surely, each of us can always use some more self-knowledge than we have at any given time. The self is not the only object of knowledge but it is an interesting, inexhaustible, albeit elusive, object. The chief gain of my phenomenological and linguistic-conceptual investigation is, I think, that "Subject" and "Object" are not mutually contradictory terms.

From ancient times, the idea of knowing the knower has been compared to a knife slicing its own edge, a finger-tip touching itself, a rider riding on her own shoulder, and other such impossibilities. Nyāya rejects the idea that cognitions are actions. Even so, being an agent of an action does not necessarily preclude being a patient of it.

Take descriptions like the following: "A barber shaves himself." Here one could take recourse to mereological analysis—one part of the barber shaves another. Neither the hand nor the chin can claim to be both shaver and shaved. But what about "The smoker harms himself"? He seems to inhale smoke with the lung he harms. When "The man kills himself," one part does not kill the other. Simple linguistic intuition can go both ways. What about appeal to phenomenological intuitions? When Hume insists that he cannot observe the self and I insist that I can, the debate obviously cannot be settled by checking who is doing the more authentic folk-psychology. What follows is my positive argument for my thesis that self-objectifying self-awareness must be possible, whatever the nature of that self which perceives itself, and whatever the nature of that perception:

Premise (I) If it is impossible to be directly acquainted with *A*, then I cannot perceive that, wonder whether, mistakenly feel that, or come to realize that I did not notice that *A is f*, when "A" is a directly referential singular term.

Premise (II) I can perceive that, wonder whether, mistakenly feel that, or come to realize that I did not notice that I am jealous or I am pleased.

Premise (III) "I" is a directly referential singular term, albeit one which has some unique features and constraints.

Therefore, it must be possible for me to be directly acquainted with the referent of "I."

I have already responded to Anscombe's famous thesis that the pronoun "I" has no reference at all. As such, my premise (III) is justified in assuming that Anscombe is wrong. I argue that identificatory mistakes are impossible to commit with "I." While I could mistakenly think that I am trying to be truthful when I am simply trying to hurt someone, I could not mistakenly think that *I* am trying to be truthful when someone else is. In other words, all mistakes regarding the "I" have to happen in the predicate part—not in the subject-identifying description. It is not easy to see where this criterion of fallible reference comes from. There is an equally strong insight which drives us in the opposite direction. Every judgment or perception or awareness is always infallible with respect to its qualificand or subject-term. It is the predication content which is vulnerable to error and corrigibility. This was the insight behind Russell's insistence that "this" is the only reference-guaranteed proper singular term which picks out exactly what it promises to pick out. Perhaps Wittgenstein would equally disqualify "this."

The point of the exercise is to see whether the self, as an object of introspection, has a status similar to the status objects of other kinds of perception. Surely there are some specialties of self-perception. But if the self is to be a perceptual object in the broad sense, it must be vulnerable to mistakes and to partial occlusion. It must also, in some cases, remain unknown. The self satisfies these conditions. The incompatibilist fears that the privilege of our privileged access proves fatal for the self's claim of object-hood. In what follows I shall address three arguments against the possibility of turning the subject into an object, as proposed by Shoemaker, Śaṅkara, and Armstrong.

Shoemaker argues against the possibility of applying the broad perceptual model to so-called privileged access. One does not talk about perceiving things which are already self-presenting. The chair is said to be seen because, without our noticing, the chair will not intimate its own existence to us.

1. If self-awareness were a form of perception of non-self-intimating cognitive states, then there would have to be some non-self-intimating cognitive states of the self.
2. If cognitive states of the self were non-intimating, then self-blindness must be possible; that is, it must be possible that someone should believe, feel, perceive, and think, but be incapable of being directly aware that they believe, feel, perceive, or think.
3. But self-blindness is in principle impossible, for it would make rational action on the basis of our perceptions impossible and would render Moore's Paradox un-paradoxical.

Therefore, self-awareness is not a form of perception and the self cannot be an object of inner sense.

I will focus on the weakest premise (2), which is based on a modal confusion. Suppose the cognitive states were non-self-intimating, as indeed Nyāya takes most cognitive states to be. Notice that even if a cognition is not-self-aware, it need not remain unknown. Another apperceptive awareness can make it known. If the cognitions are non-self-intimating, and the person is too distracted to look back at what he has just perceived or known, the result may be that he becomes self-oblivious. But self-obliviousness is not self-blindness. A self-blind person is someone who can never directly perceive his own mental states, although he has a clear concept of mental states. Why should the necessary unperceivability of cognitive states follow from their possible non-perception? The Nyāya compatibilist rejects the Prābhākara necessary reflexive self-intimation theory of awareness. But the negation of necessary self-intimation is not necessary non-intimation. It is possible self-ignorance. And Nyāya can live with that, although it cannot live with self-blindness.

Finally, consider now this lethal argument against the compatibilist picture of self as a possible object of direct awareness:

A pot is an object illuminated by a lamp. The lamp is its illuminator. The pot is an object insofar as we notice a difference between the state of the pot when it is not in the vicinity of the illuminator and its state when it is in the vicinity of the illuminator. From darkness it comes to light, from remaining unseen it comes to be seen. Now, although we unthinkingly call the lamp self-luminous because it does not need another lamp to be visible, we cannot call the lamp its own object of illumination. When we try to apply the above criterion of object-hood to it, we fail. X is an object of Y's lighting only if a difference is noticeable between the state of X when it is without Y, and its state when it is in the presence of Y. How can this difference be noticed when X and Y are the same? We cannot even imagine what it would be for X to be without X. We cannot contrast the state of the lamp in proximity of itself with its state away from itself, for its state away from itself is unthinkable. Hence, the lamp can never be an object of its own illumination.[6] This is the closest that Śaṅkara ever comes to giving an independent argument for the conceptual impossibility of self-objectification.

In the above argument, the so-called criterion of object-hood is extracted from an analogy where three rather than two factors and their mutual relations have to be noted: there is the lamp, there is the pot, and there is the viewer. The lamp is not the agent of the illumination but an instrument. And indeed, the role of an instrument, such as a lamp or a pair of eyes, is proved by the difference it makes by being brought to bear on the object or being away from the object. If the appropriate lighting or sense organ is not in contact with the object, then even the present object cannot be noticed. Similarly even if the self is always present to the self, if the inner sense is not in operative attentive connection with the self, the self does not perceive its own qualities or mental states. The main feature of an object as such, namely that it can be wholly or partially occluded from a certain perceiver and that it is not brought about by the activity of the observer, also applies to the self. Of course, the self is not independent of the self. But it is independent of the inner sense or its act of attention. The particular cognitive or emotional state that I know through this inward perception is as independent as any external object in relation to the awareness which registers it, for, upon my account, self-obliviousness is in principle possible. Although many Indian philosophers were suspicious of the claim that the self can be perceived, they did not share Wittgenstein's skepticism about the inner. As for Nyāya, saying that the self can be known only through philosophical inference would not be much of a truce with the incompatibilist: if the subject cannot be the object, it cannot be the object of inference any more than it can be the object of introspection.

Now, I agree with what Armstrong has called the distinct-existence argument against awareness-reflexivism. Even if we admit a sub-personal subjective phenomenal feel about all perceptions, no first-order perception can be said to be its own object. The object of perception is supposed to have a causal role in bringing about the perception. No state can be its own cause. I think the above argument against self-awareness works best against the reflexive self-objectification of a cognitive state. The grasping awareness must be distinct from the grasped object. But the argument is powerless against an awareness of the self by the self. Notice that this "by" is the by of agency and not that of instrumentality. There is an incompatibility between the same thing being an instrument and object of the same act. That is why the sense organs cannot be used to perceive themselves. We must take the concept of an internal sense organ seriously.

We cannot ride on our own shoulders. We cannot even proprioceptively imagine what it would be to do that. Much of our own subjective nature remains hidden, as does much of the nature of material objects near and far away which we nevertheless claim to see, precisely because we do not see all sides of them. But we can most often catch ourselves getting anxious, hungry, or doubtful. These are all glimpses of myself that I can catch. I may make occasional or perpetual mistakes in the predicates I attach to myself. Still, to the extent that these are mistakes about myself, I make myself available as an object to go right or wrong about.[7]

But I have here taken for granted a bit of Indian philosophy of mind that may not be universally acknowledged: the concept of an inner sense, as the mediator between the self as a subject and an object of perception. That organ, known in Sanskrit as *manas*, is the tool by which we achieve self-knowledge.[8] Its existence, however, is not obvious and is in need of defense.

13

In Defense of an Inner Sense

Introduction

Quite a few of us have read as part of our curriculum Plato and the Upaniṣads, Aquinas and Udayana, Kant and Dharmakīrti, Wittgenstein and Nāgārjuna, Quine and Bhartṛhari.[1] But within the insular power-enclaves of philosophy, even a mention of non-Western theories of mind, knowledge, or truth is punished by polite exclusion. Well-preserved ignorance about other cultures and mono-cultural hubris define the mainstream of professional philosophy in Euro-America. In many cases, the discovery of exciting connections, sharp oppositions, or imaginable parallelisms is greeted with condescension or cold neglect.

Although we may lament the misfortune of our purist colleagues who are missing out on this fun, one of the best ways to deepen the collective celebration of culture-straddling contemplation is to reflect, critically and analytically, on the very *sense organ* or cognitive instrument with which we compare, connect, imagine, re-arrange, choose to focus on, desire to ignore or investigate, will to change, like and dislike—or even try to witness without attachment or aversion—disparate traditions of thinking. In this chapter, we shall engage comparatively in such a paradigmatically philosophical reflexive exercise of thinking about the very idea of thinking and cross-sensory comparison.

In Sanskrit, the cognitive and active instrument or faculty is called "*manas*." That word is standardly and not wholly without justification translated as "mind." But for all sorts of well-known reasons having to do with Mind/Self confusion in Western thought, it is safer to translate it as "inner sense." Whatever else it is, the *manas* is never the *ātman* (soul). The *manas* is the organ of attention.

In the earliest Upaniṣads, *manas* is functionally defined in terms of desire, resolution, doubt, memory, and introspection. In Sāṃkhya, Vedānta, and Nyāya, it becomes a distinct sense organ responsible for attention, cross-modal comparison, and reflexive awareness of cognitive and hedonic states. In Aristotle's *De Anima*,[2] such a sixth, inner sense is proposed and rejected, but the idea of a "*sensus communis*" is taken seriously. In Kant, inner sense has a very crucial role to play, but it is distinguished from the common sense which is central to aesthetic reflective judgment. This chapter will go through seven main arguments for the existence of *manas*, show how it does both the jobs of inner and common sense, and suggest a richer theory of a sixth sense organ for imaginatively perceiving possibilities. We shall end with the soteriological role of the inner sense in binding as well as liberating the embodied self.

Philosophy, in both East and West, is uniquely characterized by this inward reflexivity of noticing its own practice and presuppositions, analytically and phenomenologically. So, that is what we shall do: *reflect comparatively on the cognitive and motor organ of comparison.*

The agent-instrument-object model of action

An action performed by an embodied being requires an agent, an instrument, and an object. In case-rich languages such as Sanskrit, the very grammar of our thinking about an action seems to demand an answer to three questions:

- Who does it?
- With what?
- To what?

A tailor could be the agent of a particular act of cutting, in which case the direct object could be a piece of cloth and the tool a pair of scissors. The act of seeing thus requires a visual or auditory organ distinct from both the seer and the seen. This, in brief, may be the conceptual root of the idea of a sense organ (*indriya*), a central idea of Indian philosophies of mind.

Just like touching or trusting, *attending* to the fact that one is touching or trusting something also seems to be a cognitive mental act. It requires an inner instrument or faculty besides the thinker or the agent of volition, desire, attention, or introspection. This job cannot be done by the outer senses. Hence, a sixth sense is postulated.

It is not easy to determine what exactly a sense organ is, especially if we are seeking to map it onto contemporary neuroscience of perception. Even within classical Indian metaphysics of mind, there is considerable disagreement as to what sense organs are made of. While everybody agrees that the retina is not the visual sense organ, but is rather the power to see which is realized by the organ, Nyāya-Vaiśeṣika postulates that the sense organ has to be made of the same material element which it can receive. Thus, the visual organ has to be made of fire or light, the olfactory organ out of smelly earth, and the auditory organ out of ākāśa—the vacuum in which sounds can travel. The Sāṃkhya-Vedānta camp construes sense organs as immaterial, having emerged out of the transparency-dominated aspect of the ego-maker (*sāttvika ahaṃkāra*). But, about the *manas*—the inner sense which receives qualities and acts of consciousness—both camps agree that it has to be immaterial. Surely, even the staunchest materialist will not insist that we can find out with our eyes that we are pleased, or that we can figure out by touching that we are willing or imagining things. We need an internal sense organ. This is what is called *manas*.

Are we conflating the idea of an "organ" (a body part, e.g., a hand) and the idea of an "instrument" (a tool, e.g., a hammer or an axe)?[3] Such an objection helps us penetrate deeper into the general concept of an *instrument* as something in between the agent and the patient of an action. Thus, if we think of the disembodied soul as the agent and the external world as the patient, the body itself is an instrument (like a chariot) which the soul or consciousness (*jña*) wields in order to get things done in the world. If, on the other hand, we think of the embodied organism as the agent and the knife or the brake as the patient, then the hand or the foot is the instrument by means of which the organism moves and uses the tool. If we regard the hand as the agent and the tree as the patient, then that which mediates the former's action on the latter—the axe—itself becomes the instrument. Thus, an instrument literally is the "means"—that which operates in the middle.

On the basis of this concept of the "means," the orthodox (Sāṃkhya) Indian philosophers make deeper use of the agent-instrument-object model of action. It first generates an external organ (e.g., hands) more agentive than the tool (spoon). We use this external organ to wield, catch, cut, move, or grab an object. We then generate an inner sense which is more agentive than the external organ which, in turn, becomes in a way an object manipulable by the inner sense. Thus, the instrument in the middle partakes of both ends. The most abstract notion of an "instrument" (*kāraṇa*) seems to be something which is both an agent and an object used by the agent, functioning as a connector between them. Thus, between the self and the external senses and motor organs, there is the *manas*; between the *manas* and material tools, there are the external senses and motor organs; and between the external senses and motor organs and objects, there are, in some cases, physical tools.

Unlike Vedānta or Vaiśeṣika metaphysics of the mind, early Buddhist meditational psychology has a different conceptual cartography of the sense organs and the *manas*. In the list of twelve *indriya*, the *manas* occurs side by side with separate organs for pleasure, depression (*daurmanasyendriya*), memory, etc.—a list which would look horribly guilty of cross-division from the Nyāya-Vaiśeṣika perspective! The distinctions between the *citta* and *caitasika* dharmas, and the reflective *manovijñāna* are fascinating research topics for any serious engagement with Indian Psychology. Although the Vedic *āstika* schools study the *manas* with a view to liberation, the Abhidharma psychology is closer to an ethically loaded phenomenology of meditational practice.[4]

From the Sanskrit philosophical texts of the orthodox schools, at least seven different arguments can be culled for the existence of an inner sense organ.

Argument from absent-mindedness

It is empirically well-established that sometimes healthy subjects whose eyes and ears are wide open cannot see or hear what is right in front of them. If the well-functioning external sense organs and their proximity or exposure to their appropriate objects were sufficient conditions for sensory perception, then such non-perception would be inexplicable. Hence, there must be an additional faculty or organ, due to the absence or non-operation of which externally stimulated sense organs also fail to register their given objects. This additional sense is the *manas*. If the *manas* is disconnected from the appropriate sense organ where the relevant stimulus strikes, then even stimuli presented to open eyes or healthy ears are not registered.

This argument occurs for the first time clearly in *Bṛhadāraṇyaka Upaniṣad*[5] (ca. 800 BC) where it is immediately followed by a fascinating empirical detail. When someone is touched on the back by another person, the person touched determines, without looking back, whether it is the touch of a hand or a knee. The tactile organ itself does not make those distinctions, since as sheer touch both sensations might feel qualitatively pretty similar. After all, the concept of a knee and the concept of a hand are far richer than merely palpable concepts: they require the articulate recognition of different functionally distinguished body parts conceived in a partly first-person fashion. It is the *manas* which at an imperceptible, but now perhaps measurable, speed reflects upon and discriminates between the tactile sensations in terms of remembered and conceptualized body-schema of other people.[6] Śaṅkara's commentary here is succinct: "If the discriminator inner sense-organ were not there, then how could skin (the tactile sense) alone make such discriminations? That which is the cause of knowledge of distinctions is the inner sense."[7]

Argument from necessary non-simultaneity of all cognitions

Sensory data as well as thoughts and acts of imagination come to us necessarily in a successive manner, one after another. This rule of the successiveness of all mental representations, shared by Nyāya and Kant, has almost the status of an *a priori* principle, for introspection seems to feel, perceive, and think many things simultaneously. But logically, unless two events are perceived at distinct moments in time, how can we tell them apart as two distinct events, especially when spatial locations are not relevant? Thus, perception of succession is impossible without succession of perceptions. Now, let's take our hearing of a sentence uttered, even at a great speed. Unless we hear its constitutive phonemes one after another, with proper pauses, it would become one noise. The same is true, as has been shown by Kant, for our visual perception of an extended object or a long line. Without a sequential perception of different parts of it, we would have no sense of its expanse or length. Now, as far as the visual and tactile sense organs go, both could easily function together. A whole range of objects are simultaneously available to our skin and our visual range. Why is it that we can only go through them one at a time? What breaks up the process to a sequence? The explanation of this is provided by this additional instrument of focusing attention which cannot hook up with more than one sense organ object at a time.

There is a standard counter-example to the "non-simultaneity of awarenesses" rule. When one eats a long twisty fried pastry (*dīrghaśaṣkulī*), he or she may feel the experience of five sensations at once through the five external senses: that it smells good, that it is cold to touch, that it is elongated in shape, that it tastes sharp, and that it even makes a crisp sound as we munch on it! But consider a needle piercing a hundred petals of lotus.[8] It may look as if the needle goes through all the petals at once. But, of course, it goes through them one after another. Thus, quick succession of the attention-function of the *manas* switching on and off from one sensory datum to another creates the illusion of a manifold perceptual data all presented at a single time.

Kant spent a crucial part of his "Transcendental Deduction of Categories" on the three steps of this process of synthesis, including the "synthesis of reproduction in imagination."[9] For experience to be possible, the manifolds of intuition have to be run through and bound together in an ordered sequence. And he postulated the inner sense, parallel to the outer sense, calling Time its "*a priori* given form." But Kant thinks that all synthesizing action must be done by the apperceptive "I think," so inner sense cannot bind and order. Committed to a sacrosanct distinction between thinking and sensing, Kant does not draw the metaphysical conclusions drawn by the Nyāya phenomenologists. It seems undeniable that there is a subjective synthesis of external data that goes on behind the curtain of concept-formation and knowledge of "objects," and that synthesis is rich with qualities accessible to multiple sense organs. What Nyāya philosophers deduce from the same evidence is that there is a fast-moving, constitutionally restless, atomic, unconscious, immaterial substance, other than the external sense organs, but equally able to control the functioning of all of them. It is non-specific to any particular external sense, but unique to each individual conscious body. Not only is the co-operation of that substance needed for the occurrence of any cognition in a body, but the *life* of a conscious animal is nothing but this activated contact between the self and the internal organ. Thanks to the accumulated karmic residues undergoing the process of natural maturation, the sensing, attending, remembering, imagining functions of an individual's life are conducted by the inner sense with the particular mixture of pleasure and pain that they deserve.[10]

The self in Nyāya is regarded as all-pervasive on systemic ontological grounds. Such an all-pervasive self enjoys and suffers experiences only in those regions of space where a particular *manas* keeps contact with it. That *manas* is at the same time in touch with the tactile sense organ spread nearly all over the inside and outside of a specific *karmically-earned* body.

Argument from the perceptual character of our knowledge of hedonic states

Our immediate and unerring awareness of our own pleasure and pain is direct and perceptual. Every perceptual awareness requires an appropriate sense organ as its proximate causal condition. The inner sense is that special organ through which the self perceives its own pleasures, pains, desires, etc. We cannot say that pleasure is nothing but a mode or an intrinsic feature of other external sensations which does not require a special, internal sense organ. Such reasoning can also reduce external qualities into intrinsic forms or modes of cognition. If so, there would be bluish cognition rather than perception of blue color. Objects would become merely adjectival to cognitions.

Since we cannot tolerate such an adverbial reduction of external perception, we cannot also reduce inner perception of pleasure to having some other external perceptions, but in a pleasurable manner. Pleasure must be independently perceivable. The need for sense organs is parallel in inner and outer perceptions. And since we cannot introspect with our eyes or ears, we need the *manas*.[11]

Argument from cross-modal comparison by a "common sense"

External sense organs cannot do the explanatory work done by the inner sense because each of them is limited to a specific kind of quality of physical objects. Eyes cannot smell perfumes; tongues cannot taste sounds. But we make cross-modal comparisons, such as "This sound is more interesting than that sight," "The freezing touch of this ice-cream is not as pleasant as its nice flavor," etc. It is on the basis of these quick comparisons that a subject reflexively makes the decision, as it were, to switch attention.

This involves attaching one's *manas* to a particular sensory stimulus to the neglect of another of a totally different modality.

Obviously, this comparison cannot be done through either one of the mode-specific external senses. So there must be an over-arching non-specific instrument of such sensory comparison.[12]

We can note Karl Potter's description of the function of *manas*:

> It acts as a sort of secretary for the knowing self, passing on one sensation at a time ... the time it takes the self to synthesize its awareness of an object from the data gathered by the senses is due to the time it takes for the internal sense organ to get into and out of contact with each of the several organs.[13]

In his *De Anima*, Aristotle argues against a common sixth sense. He first admits that there seem to be "common sensibles," such as motion, number, and unity which are not specific to any particular mode of external sensation. We can count colors as well as sounds; we can even detect a smell to be moving. But the non-specific recognition of these common qualities can be easily explained by a co-operation of several senses, or by one external sense "incidentally" drawing our attention toward the quality accessible to another external sense.[14] Nyāya too notes incidental non-ordinary contact between the sense of sight and a smell or a taste.

We don't need to postulate a "common over-arching inner sense" for the sake of explaining this. But how can the eyes alone, while making us aware that the wall is white, also make us aware that we are *seeing* that white wall? Surely our cognition of white does not cast an image on the retina as the white wall does! Aristotle anticipates and rejects the hypothesis of an inner sense organ:

> Since it is through sense that we are aware that we are seeing [Notice that he is here talking about *awareness of seeing*, or what in Nyāya is called meta-cognition (*anuvyavasāya)*, and not of seeing as a sensation] ... it must be either by sight that we are aware of seeing or by some sense other than sight. But the sense that gives us this new sensation must perceive both sight and its object, viz. color: so that, either (1) there will be two senses both percipient of the same sensible object or, (2) the sense must be percipient of itself. Further, even if the sense, which perceives sight, were different from sight, we must fall into an infinite regress, or we must somewhere assume a sense, which is aware of itself. If so, we ought to do this in the first case.[15]

Thus, he makes each sense organ self-perceiving, thereby dispensing with the need for a meta-sense organ like the Indian concept of *manas*. The Nyāya-Vaiśeṣika psychologists are aware that if *manas* does the job of a meta-cognition or apperception of the seeing, then it has to grasp both the visual awareness and the color that is the object of visual awareness. But if the inner sense can "see" colors in this incidental fashion (through a *jñānalakṣaṇā* link), why can't we say the reverse, namely that the outer senses also perceive cognitive inner events and that the visual sense organ apperceives itself?[16]

But there is a difficulty present in Aristotle's position, which is not present in the Nyāya position. Once we have given an account of a direct normal perception of a sensible object or quality through its own appropriate sense organ, we can then complicate that story with another sense organ accessing it in an incidental or associative non-ordinary way. Thus, once sandalwood is smelt through olfactory sense, later on one could perceive its smell perhaps even visually. But Aristotle refuses to give us any account of the direct, non-incidental perception of one's own cognitions, and expects the special senses to pick up their own cognitive episodes as they are picking up colors and sounds and smells. He distinguishes two senses of "seeing"—one of which applies even to the perception of darkness.[17]

The reason why Indian psychology can never admit the external senses to be self-revealing or introspective rests on its Vedic roots. The Upaniṣads[18] announce that the Self-born Creator had cut out the sensory holes in such a way that they only open outward. Hence, the doctrine that the sense organs are themselves imperceptible. Only a *manas* can *infer* its own existence, and even the *manas* is not *directly* accessible to itself. The only self-lit (*svayaṃjyotiḥ*) or reflexively self-aware entity is pure consciousness or Ātman. In Nyāya, even the Self is not independently self-luminous—it needs the *manas* to know itself. Aristotle's infinite regress problem does not daunt the Nyāya epistemologist because every act of perception need not be necessarily perceived. But there is a need for an explanation of our direct acquaintance with our own mental states, and Aristotle could not coherently make the tongue inform a wisher that she is wishing. So, Aristotle too ended up admitting a common sense.

Argument from deep sleep

During deep sleep we breathe through our nostrils, keep our ears open, and of course touch multiple things, yet we neither smell, nor hear nor feel anything. What is missing is not the self or its occupation of the body, for we are not dead. So it must be a disconnection between another common cause of all sensation which, during such sleep, leaves all the sense organs and takes rest in a special place. The ancient Indian physiology gave it a name—*purītat nāḍī*. It could be a part of the central nervous system where the *manas* remains in a standby, off-line position.

Argument from memory and imagination

Suppose I am pondering how it would be if we could taste colors, or hear textures. Even if the result is to recognize the impossibility of such a perception, we would need a cross-modal overarching sense organ to feel this impossibility with. Similarly intuitively grasping the metaphorical meaning of a statement, such as "Van Gogh could feel the golden yellow of the Sunflowers on his tongue like a hot sauce!" would require an organ of knowledge that can provide the sensory support for such a cross-modal imagination. This must be a sixth sense!

Not only does the man who has now gone deaf remember sounds, but he is sometimes able to imagine a hitherto unheard combination of tones. We must not forget that Beethoven composed music after going deaf. The hearing organ or faculty, which is absent in those cases, cannot explain such recall and imagination. So we need an inner sense to do the work. Even the somewhat strange list of "nine properties" of the manas found in Mahābhārata mentions imagination.[19]

When we read or listen to poetry, we have to figure out the meaning of such sentences as:

At midnight, butchers convene a conference.
To make sure the proceedings are free from all bias,
They invite a cow to chair it.[20]

In Navya Nyāya semantics, the resulting understanding of meaning is not classified as knowledge by testimony (*śabdabodha*) or information gathered from words, but as make-believe awareness generated by the *manas* (*āhāryamanasa bodha*), which can creatively put together a cow and chairing. Advaita Vedānta classifies memory as a kind of inner perception of the past by the internal sense organ!

Argument from resolution, intention, and desire

Close to imagination is another fundamental function of the *manas*: resolution or intending—"*saṃkalpa*." The verb for imagination "*klṛp*" is present in "*saṃkalpa*" as well, because in order to intend to accomplish a project it must first be imagined.[21] Till today, in the beginning of a Vedic ritual one has to make a resolve—"This is the ritual I am going to perform"—in order to prepare the body-mind of the performer. The following mantra from the *Yajurveda* is called the "*saṃkalpasûkta,*" the hymn of resolution, because it focuses the internal organ of attention to the task at hand:

That which goes up and far ahead for a person who is awake,
That which returns back to him when he is asleep,
That light of all lights, which travels very far,
May that *manas* of mine have this good resolve.[22]

The Upaniṣad mentions the following processes: "A desire, resolution, doubt, trust, distrust, forbearance, lack of forbearance, shame or modesty, wisdom, fear—all of these are nothing but *manas*."[23] The language of the original is worth noticing here: "*etat sarvam mana eva*." This suggests that the functions themselves constitute the *manas*. This functional concept of the inner organ seems more defensible in modern terms than the Nyāya concept of a fast-moving atomic substance wandering around the body hooking up with one sense organ at a time. Actually, the Sāṃkhya-Yoga and Vedānta concepts of *citta* or *antaḥkaraṇa* are concepts of a fluid substance capable of assuming the form of objects and of reversing its flow.[24]

The ancient commentary *Yuktidīpikā* (YD) on *Sāṃkhya Kārīka* develops an argument for the existence of *manas* on the basis of the function of *saṃkalpa* or motivating resolution.[25] In fact YD simply identifies resolve with intention, desire, or thirst, and defines the *manas* as that which does this job.[26] Neither singly nor together can the external senses do the work of wishful resolution, since the outer senses can only grasp what is given to them at the present time. The resolve-making organ accesses the data of all the senses *and* deals with the future and the past. As such, the *manas* is postulated as a special organ of intention.

As life-sustaining functions like breathing are generally attached to all sense organs, one may ask, why can't these functions help the special senses make motivating resolves? YD answers this objection by remarking that breathing, etc., cannot perform the intentional job of resolving because it simply happens in the body but does not take "objects" like a sense organ does. So we need the inner sense organ. Even breathing seems to become intentional when one puts his or her *manas* to it by attending to it as in *prāṇāyāma*. But then it is actually the intention of the *manas* and the breathing is its object.

Since most of our resolutions involve both our inner and outer life, the *manas* stands in between the self and the body, so much that in Sāṃkhya it is categorized as both a *karmendriya* and a *jñānendriya* (a motor and a sensory organ). The *manas* calls into question a rigidly drawn distinction between the sensory and the motor in neuropsychology and between receptivity and spontaneity in Kantian psychology.

Of course, many problems remain unsolved. How can the self know itself, making itself both the subject and object of the act of knowing? How can the agent of introspection get passively and empirically affected by itself? Even if that happens, how can it end up only knowing how it appears to itself and not the real self?

What we can make the manas do and undo

Let me conclude by pointing at an important eighth explanatory function of the concept of an inner sense. There is no doubt that the *manas* is hard to control and perpetually moving. The *manas* is constantly getting attached to and desiring to get attached to this or that external sense organ. But for a Yogin, the *manas* itself is an aid to detachment and control. Kaṇāda, the ancient author of Vaiśeṣika Sūtra, defines liberation in this fashion:

> When the internal organ abides in the self but not in the senses, there results the absence of pleasure and pain which is called Yoga. In the absence of *adṛṣṭa*, which causes transmigration, there is the absence of contact between the internal organ with the self (which results in life), and also non-appearance of another body: this state is liberation.[27]

This brings us to the fundamental spiritual underpinning of Indian psychology. Again, spirituality must not be taken as a denial of the life of the body. Indeed, the *manomayakośa*, the internal organ, along with the cognitive sense organs, is after all an important body that we need to take care of in order to lead a flourishing spiritual life. The spiritual "use" of the theory of inner sense defies the Cartesian division between mind and body, since even the most elementary yogic postures require focusing of the inner sense on parts of the body and on the most spiritually significant bodily function of breathing!

Just as much of Western psychology is proudly applied in nature, much of Indian psychology too is for the sake of application. The goal of that application is a healthy, unsuffering, ecologically, and interpersonally harmonious life, ultimately ending in freedom from frustrating desires. For that purpose, the *manas* is first diagnosed as the cause of distraction, sick desires, doubt, and error and then explored as a possible tool of focused attention which cures those pathological states. There must be such an internal tool of both involvement and withdrawal if the ultimate tranquility and freedom of the self are possible. And the very restlessness and far-imagining nature of the *manas* shows that the religious person seeks such a freedom in the fullness of God or in Omnipresent Self. Since liberation is possible, and concentration is a means to it, the first instrument of concentration, *manas*, must exist.[28]

Unscientific post-script

In his long Middle Commentary on Aristotle's *De Anima,* Ibn Rushd (Averroes) was deeply concerned with the nature and unity of such a *sensus communis* which enables us to distinguish between whiteness and sweetness but which cannot be identified with the eye or the tongue. But in his acute argumentation for the unity of the common sense, he brings in a comparison with inter-personal judgments of comparison:

> If it were possible for that which judges two different things to be itself two, then when I perceived a given object as warm and you perceived something else as white, I could determine that the object which I perceived is different from yours without having your perception, which is absurd … Just as it is necessary that one and the same man be the person who says that "a" is different from "b," so it is necessary that the faculty whereby this individual judges that sweet differs from white be one and the same.[29]

What is most uncanny is how intra-sensory comparison is understood in analogy with inter-personal comparison. For the most controversial original idea that Averroes had about the mind is that there is a single Material Intellect which is the same for every human being, and that individual human intellects and imaginations are fragments of that singularity. Almost no other Hellenistic, Muslim, or Christian commentator supports him in this hypothesis. But the concept comes pretty close to that of a common collective inner sense, or cosmic intellect (*virāt* or *mahān*), found in Vedic, Puranic, and Sāṃkhya-Vedāntic metaphysics of the mind. The following metaphor used by Ibn Rushd resonates deeply with many Sāṃkhya-Vedānta pictures of divine and human intellects:

> Our bodies are like dewdrops, varying in size and shape. The quantitative differences of the glassy surfaces, observable on the dewdrops, may be compared to the passive intellect, that is, to our different individual dispositions. When the Sun, the active intellect, sends out his rays on the dewdrops, the smooth glassiness

> of these drops becomes luminous, capable of mirroring external objects, and this luminosity, a common character in every dewdrop, may be compared to the material intellect. The material intellect, in our comparison the sunny luminosity, is not an emergence from the dewdrops. Water can never turn into sunshine. Rather the material intellect is to be conceived as identical with the sun which radiates actively and is luminous passively, although its luminosity can come into existence only in the presence of the dewdrops.[30]

With the de-individuation of the organ of imagination and emotional cognition, *sensus communis* can re-emerge in the Kantian sense of that common aesthetic sensibility which is the transcendental condition of our claims of taste being compelling across private personal judgments. Such a common inner sense, then, not only tastes the first order pleasures of contact with desired objects, but also feels its own free-play of imagination in re-arranging possible sensory-motor representations. In this, the inner sense becomes an inter-personal creator and spectator of beauty, and indeed of divinity. And the root *div* from which "*deva, devī*, devatā" (deity, divinity) come, Abhinavagupta reminds us, primarily stands for play or sport (*dīvyati=krīḍati*). When freed from its egoistic individual boundaries and interests, our *manas* is not only the instrument with which we worship God by sacrificing our breath in sacred speech or sacrificing our speech in meditative silence, it is also the Divinity whom we worship. Both Śaṅkara and Abhinavagupta tell us, in different contexts, that the deities are just the universalized sense organs in our bodies. The comparing common sense relishes its own playfulness in a divine spilling and crossing over of its own personal and regional limits.

In this sense *manas* is key not only to our cognitive and aesthetic judgments, but also to our spirituality. Yet, there remains the large and difficult problem of the fallibility of the inner sense organ. Could I sometimes be mistaken about what I cognize or are all of my cognitions unerringly self-illuminating? More generally, do I always know that I know? Do I always know when I am mistaken that my cognition is erroneous? The realist's intuition is that we are liable to misapprehend propositions about any domain about which we hold that the laws of classical logic obtain. But how far into our mental life should this intuition extend? For example, must I always know what I feel? To these difficult questions I turn next.

14

Our Knowledge and Error about Our Own Cognitions

One of the jobs of the inner sense is to make us aware of our own cognitions, some of which turn out to be knowledge. According to externalist Nyāya epistemology, for all its "first person authority," our apperceptive cognition of our own cognition runs two kinds of risks. Imagine me smelling and seeing a fragrant flower and thinking "I know that it is champak" when actually the flower I perceive is ylang-ylang (*Cananga Odorata*). This is one kind of error. Another kind of error is when I look within and think I am angry but actually I am afraid. In this chapter, we discuss two issues regarding our knowledge of our own cognitive and affective states. Whenever we actually know something, do we know that we know? Whenever I introspectively ascribe a certain mental state to myself, am I necessarily right about what I am feeling or could I be mistaken even about that?

People often have properties which they do not know that they have. Sometimes those who have a quality may deny or find it hard to believe that they have it. This is not only true of bad things like depression, or conceit. It can be true of talents and virtues as well. Indeed, certain virtues seem to shine better if their possessors are unaware that they possess them. Isn't genius made more marvelous by self-obliviousness?

This may be even easier to appreciate when we remind ourselves that self-ascription of a virtue or excellence is never sufficient for actually having it. And where mistakes are possible, ignorance is possible too. Both are cases of an unsuspected gap between what exists and what is known or believed. When we add to this plausible premise—that possession of a virtue does not entail the possessor's knowledge of that virtue—the premise that knowledge is a virtue, the conclusion that I wish to defend follows irresistibly. Knowledge does not entail knowledge of knowledge.

Knowledge—the crest-jewel of the virtues according to the Gītā (*na hi jñānena sadṛśam pavitram iha vidyate [There is nothing in this world which is purer and holier than knowledge] 4/38*)—like humility or honesty can exist unrecognized by the very person who has it. While others honor him by saying "S really knows that P," S typically may simply *say* that P, *showing* thereby that he knows. Yet, when asked to reflect, S may confess fallibility rather than complete metacognitive self-confidence. Claiming knowledge has never been regarded as a *sufficient* condition of knowing; I want to emphasize that it is not even a *necessary* condition.

What if, instead of the easy-to-refute KK thesis ("S knows that p" entails "S knows that S knows that p"), a more sophisticated view, namely intrinsicism (*svataḥ-prāmāṇyavāda*), is put forward: *the correctness and meta-knowledge of a belief or awareness must be known by the same means which grasps that belief or awareness.* Let us now see how the Mīmāṃsā epistemologists of India argue for three distinct versions of this view.

Intrinsicism about knowledgehood

The veridicality or meta-knowledge of a cognition must be known by the same means which registers the cognition—otherwise there would be no stopping a vicious regress of certifiers of certifiers. Eventually the self-doubter has to stop by trusting her own doxastic resources at some level or another.[1] The apperceptive metacognition which grasps the first knowledge must also verify what the subject and the predicate of that first knowledge are (and their relation).

If I feel happy and my inner perception bears witness that I am experiencing pleasure as pleasure, then that inner perception in effect also certifies that the first cognition was veridical. For veridicality is nothing but a cognition's having a subject which in fact possesses the very predicate that the cognition ascribes to that subject. Therefore, meta-knowledge is recognized intrinsically.[2] If knowing that one believes that *a* is *F* still leaves open the possibility that it may be false that *a* is *F* (which is the fundamental extrinsicist insight), then it should have been possible to think coherently that I know that I am convinced that *a* is *F*, and yet *a* might not be *F*. But it is precisely this kind of thinking that is considered paradoxical and incoherent. Hence, once a piece of knowledge is apperceived, its truth and higher-order knowledge is also known thereby. The metacognition that grasps any cognition which is undefeated by the suspicion of an error also grasps its truth and meta-knowledge. As long as the original cognition happens to be knowledge, there is no way that the witness-awareness can lie about its content, and in reporting indubitably that *a* is believed to be *F*, it also reports that it is true that *a* is *F*, which is indistinguishable from *a*'s being *F*.

The intrinsicist is pointing out that in spite of the appearance of an opaque belief context, the verbalization of apperception actually sets up a transparent context. The statement issued by my witness-metacognition, "I believe that it is raining," does commit me to the truth of that belief. "I believe … " thus seems to be as transparent as the fake opacity-introducer, "It is true that …."

The Dvaita Vedantin Vyāsatīrtha anticipates an objection from the opponent who shows sensitivity to the asymmetry between reporting another person's and reporting one's own cognition:

> Mere after-cognition or apperception cannot prove the meta-knowledge of the cognition that it registers even if it is in fact knowledge. The apperceptive awareness is just like the statement made by someone who has heard the statement of an eyewitness to an event, without himself having witnessed it. Though it reports the same subject and qualifier as the original veridical awareness, and thus

grasps not only the qualificand and qualifier separately but also the fact that they are believed to be cemented together as they really are in the world, it still does not give us a doubt-preventing certainty about the original knowledge. Just as from introspectively registering that I have a desire that that there is a pot of gold in my house, I cannot conclude that there indeed is such a pot. From the mere introspective report that I have a cognition that there is a pot of gold at home, I cannot assure myself that there really is a pot of gold.

I find this objection more convincing than Vyāsatīrtha's reply to it. In reply he repeats the old point that the case of the first-person witness of one's own knowledge is quite unlike the case of the second-hand report which cannot preclude doubt. In responding this way, he fails to notice that the first person is always a biased witness because of our natural fondness for our own convictions and blindness to our own errors. Vyāsatīrtha also shows how he would be ready to trust even a second-hand report when a reliable authority says, "I have knowledge that there is a pot in my house." Then we *are* justified in believing that there is such a pot in his house.

I cannot help thinking that Vyāsatīrtha is fully sensitive to the fallibilism and externalism of the Naiyāyika opponent, but, as a Vedāntin, he has to defend the trustworthiness of the first-person witness because ultimately, even for the Naiyāyika, if we do not want to float away in a skeptical baselessness, we have to stop with self-trust of some sort. Originally designed to protect the intrinsicity of the truth and meta-knowledge of beliefs prompted by Vedic injunctions, and then over-extended to all beliefs, this auto-certification theory of epistemic evaluation does not seem acceptable to me. I think it turns on a deep-seated confusion between a firm believer's inability to question the truth of her current belief, and an objective guarantee of the truth of that belief. We all know how Moore's paradox creates the false impression that it is impossible that P should be true without my believing it to be so—"It's raining, but I don't believe it." The illusion, of course, vanishes as soon as we replace the first person pronoun with a proper name—"It's raining, but Arindam doesn't believe it." Millions of propositions are true while he does not believe in them, let alone know them.

From inside a self-aware believer's point of view, it is impossible to defeat the possibility of objective falsehood; even true beliefs, indeed even reliably obtained justified true beliefs, cannot be known to be knowledge from this internal point of view. Whether one can ever completely step out of this epistemic ego-centric cocoon and assess one's own belief externally as if it were not his own is one of the deepest problems of epistemology. But just as the extreme difficulty of stepping out of psychological egoistic hedonism does not make egoistic hedonism an acceptable ethical doctrine, the pragmatic paradoxicality of my recognizing and embracing a belief while entertaining the possibility that it may not be true does not make *svataḥ-prāmāṇyavāda* (intrinsicism) an acceptable epistemological doctrine.

Against the above doctrine, the most sophisticated refutation offered by a Nyāya extrinsicist comes from Gaṅgeśa:

1. If intrinsicism is correct, then a true cognition is either not grasped at all, or grasped along with a guarantee that it is true.

2. If the cognition is not grasped at all, then no doubt the form, "Is that cognition knowledge or error?" concerning the status of that cognition can arise, for doubt requires that the chief qualificand of the doubted content must be grasped first. If, for example, you do not see any bird at all, you cannot have the doubt "Is that bird a sparrow or a swallow?"
3. If the cognition is grasped with the guarantee that it is true, that too will prevent any subsequent doubt about its truth-value or meta-knowledge.
4. Thus, if intrinsicism is correct, then once a true cognition is registered, it would be impossible to entertain a doubt about whether it is knowledge or error.
5. But in certain circumstances, when for the first time cognition about an unfamiliar object occurs, it is often made the subject of subsequent doubt.

We do not question *that* we see or believe something to be thus and so. We question whether that belief may not be erroneous or unjustified. Therefore, intrinsicism is false, and extrinsicism must be correct. Once the meta-knowledge of a first cognition has been doubted, its truth and meta-knowledge have to be certified by some pragmatic or inferential evidence other than the immediate introspective meta-cognition of the first cognition itself.

Reflexivism versus irreflexivism

Am I necessarily and routinely aware of all my current awarenesses? Are all my cognitive states self-luminous or self-intimating?

This is a live controversy in current Western philosophy and science of cognition.[3] Some answer yes to this question. I shall call them "reflexivists." You are a strong or Cartesian reflexivist if you believe that a state's being a mental state or a state of consciousness consists, at least in part, in its being transparent, that is, in being immediately and incorrigibly known to the subject. A mitigated reflexivist is someone who holds that for rational beings to have a cognitive state is to be introspectively aware of it, although introspection is not another optional higher-order observation of the initial cognitive state. According to this moderately Cartesian reflexivism one may be mistaken or self-deceived about one's own mental states but one cannot be ignorant of them since they are self-intimating. Sydney Shoemaker is a mitigated reflexivist who does not accept the full Cartesian claim that one knows one's cognitive states with unmistakable certainty, but does argue for a certain cautious version of the first person privileged access thesis about knowledge of one's current mental states. Utpaladeva and Abhinavagupta were reflexivists since they argued that all awarenesses are self-aware, and that there is no illumination of an object without self-consciousness (no prakāúa without vimarśa).[4] Even the outward cognition of the form, *that is a pot*, has "*I am aware that …* " entering inside its content.

The Naiyāyika takes a cognitive event to be as external to the subject's mind as any other physical event and therefore capable of happening without the subject's knowledge. When one is aware of one's own perceptual cognition, one must have noticed oneself perceptually but fallibly. I call philosophers who hold such views "irreflexivists." Personally I am inclined to accept irreflexivism just as I am disposed toward extrinisicism about epistemic evaluation. Irreflexivism does not have to say that one's own cognitive states are never accessible to oneself or that knowledge routinely stays unknown to the knower. A totally outwardly-absorbed cognizer who has no clue that cognition has happened cannot possibly even ask herself, "Have I seen or not?" Even irreflexists concede that second-order apperceptive cognition may happen effortlessly on the heels of a first-order perception. They just insist that the existence of the first perception is not dependent on or constituted by any synchronous and necessary self-intimation or meta-cognition by the possessor of the cognitive state.

In classical Indian epistemology, reflexivism famously took the form of the Prābhākara Mīmāṃsā theory of the luminous nature of consciousness. Irreflexivism came in two major teams. The first group insisted that, unlike the brown cat that my eyes could see, my seeing of it is an event or act which even I—the first person—cannot directly perceive. Acts are inferred from their resulting changes, upon this view. The cognitive act, because it is an act, has to be inferred, even by the perceiver herself, from its effect. In this case, the effect is the peculiar feature added to the cat by its being perceived and then noticed in the cat besides its brownness and feline features. It is the occasion-specific feature: presentedness or cognizedness, *prākatya or jñātatā*.

The other irreflexivist group rejected both the self-illumination theory and the opposite view that cognitions are imperceptible even by the subject herself. They held that with a distinct but equally perceptual awareness-episode operating through the inner sense, my own perception of the cat can be known and ascribed to myself by myself. The first cognition is verbalized as "That is a brown cat," and the second apperceptive cognition is verbalized as "I see a brown cat." Thus, perceptions are neither self-intimating nor only inferable. They are accessible by a second "look within"—a kind of metacognitive glance.

Defending different kinds of self-luminosity

It is true that a knife does not cut itself and that the eyes don't see themselves. But, unlike material or sensory tools, awareness is conscious and self-luminous. Its job is to reveal. How can an awareness reveal and present its external intentional object to the subject if it itself remains unrevealed and unpresented to him? Generally it is only self-lit lights which can illuminate other things. If I don't know *that* I have known how would I know *what* I have known? All awarenesses arise in the form "I am aware of this" and not "some awareness of this object has occurred" or "this is presented." In the context of this primary immediate awareness, I, this, and the cognition itself are all at once illuminated. The only difference is that the self and the object are other than the grasping awareness, whereas the awareness is identical in the roles of both the illuminating and the illuminated. Having said this, the reflexivist hastens to add that the awareness does not actually become an accusative object. The anti-reflexivist objection that self-illumination theory claims to "enable a finger-tip to bend back and touch itself" is wide off the mark because the cognition is not illuminated as its accusative (*karma*) but only as an immediate enjoyer of the fruit of the cognitive act.

This point is made with the example of carrying a stone, which I presented in the chapter "Does Self-Awareness Turn the Self into an Object?"

Similarly, when I disclose an object with the light of my awareness, both the object and the awareness get disclosed together (therefore not as identical). They are bathed by the same light but their distinction shines loud and clear: the object is an accusative of the verb "to cognize," while the cognition is the very constitutive meaning of that verb. The object is opaque with a shape and could exist uncognized. Even when cognized it is not self-intimating. The cognition is transparent, without any shape of its own and self-intimating. It cannot exist uncognized. So the reflexivist is rejecting the externalist observational model for our knowledge of our own cognitions.

Kaṭha Upaniṣad tells us that our senses have been hewn in such a way that they only grasp their objects outside but cannot perceive the self inside. Extrapolating from this, one can arrive at the doctrine that at least perceptual awareness is not self-aware in either sense: when we see a green leaf we neither see ourselves nor see the awareness-episode, since we are totally focused on the leaf. The colorless, shapeless self is not the right sort of object for visual perception. Yet both the Yogācāra sect of Buddhists and the Prābhākara Mīmāṃsākas hold the view that awarenesses are self-aware. "A cognition that is itself unperceived cannot be proved to perceive an object"[5] is an oft-quoted Yogācāra Buddhist principle. The two most crucial differences between the Yogācāra Buddhist and the Prābhākara Mīmāṃsā version of self-illumination theory relate to the ontology of the perceived object and the perceiver subject:

1. The Yogācāra Buddhist (a subjective idealist) thinks that an awareness has no object other than itself. What appears to be an object is nothing but the received part or object-end of a two-part structured self-sensing awareness. The Prābhākara Mīmāṃsā (a staunch realist) believes that the external object is revealed by the cognition along with the cognition itself.

2. Having no self in his ontology, the Buddhist cannot mean by self-perception perception of the self. But the triple object theory of awareness that the Prābhākara upholds precisely requires that my perception of a cup illuminates at once the cup, my awareness of the cup, and the self that perceives the cup.

Without entering into the intricate debate between the Prābhākara view of the relfexivity of all awareness and the rival Bhaṭṭa Mīmāṃsā and Nyāya views of strict non-reflexivity, let me simply record their differences. Just as the tip of the finger cannot touch itself, said Kumārila, no awareness can reflexively be its own object. We already saw above how Bhaṭṭa Mīmāṃsā sticks to the inferential view of cognition via the acquired property of cognizedness noticed in the object. A perception cannot notice itself because it is a cognitive act, and acts, themselves impercetible, can only be inferred from their results. That is the Bhaṭṭa view.

Nyāya does admit the possibility of internal perception of mental events or qualities. This introspective apperception of an awareness (or pleasure or wish) is called a higher-order awareness or metacognition (*anuvyavasāya*). Although it routinely follows a perception, it is not constitutive of the first cognition of an object, and is not phenomenologically necessary or mandatory. If someone falls asleep immediately after having heard a sound, one may never apperceive that one had heard anything. Like any other real event, a mental event can go unperceived. It is this non-necessary character of the distinct apperceptive awareness that saves the doctrine from an infinite regress. The verbalization of my first (determinate) sensory awareness of a cup, according to Nyāya, is not "I see a cup" but "This or here is a cup." It is the meta-awareness that takes the form "I see a cup" or "A cup has been seen by me." In this second perception, the operative organ is not the visual sense but the inner sense (*manas*) which is in touch with the soul where the cognition has arisen and is waiting for an extra moment as an inherent occurrent quality to be perceived.

There is one wrinkle here. Just as the eyes cannot see the inner cognitive state, the *manas* is not supposed to introspect the cup. Yet the introspective meta-awareness includes within its full content-complex the cup too! This problem is solved by an ingenious appeal to the special non-normal connecting link called *jñānalakṣaṇasannikarṣa*. The previous moment's awareness itself works as the link between the *manas* and the cup which is after all an object hooked by that first awareness. A reflective awareness of an awareness is partly normal and partly non-normal perception by the inner sense.

This complication does not affect the doctrine of apperception of hedonic qualities such as pleasure and pain which do not themselves include any "objects." The pleasure of good food is due to the food but is not "about" the food in the same way that my cognition of a wall is about the wall. One consequence of this distinction between a non-intentional state of pleasure and an intentional apperceptive awareness of pleasure is a sharp disagreement with Yogācāra Buddhists who equate pleasure and pain with our cognition of them. For them the idea of an uncognized pleasure is unintelligible. Not so for the Nyāya-Vaiseṣika philosophers of mind.

The idea of self-illumination assumes a different phenomenological dimension with the Advaita Vedānta characterization of witness-consciousness as self-aware.[6] Witness-consciousness is self-aware not in the sense of being its own object, but in the sense of being "shown" in immediate linguistic behavior while remaining purely subjective.[7]

An argument against reflexivism

There are many standard arguments in the anti-Prābhākara traditions which refute reflexivism. Here I have tried to formulate my own argument against it:

1. Assume Reflexivism: A cognition of O is constituted by the same cognizer's cognition of the cognition of O. Thus, cognition of O = cognition of cognition of O.

2. Cognition of a blue pot (Cbp) = cognition of cognition of a blue pot (Ccbp) or cognition that one is aware of a blue pot.

3. The cognition that one is aware of a blue pot is not the same as the cognition that one is aware of just a pot. With the introduction of each additional qualifier to the content, the cognitions themselves change (even if the external object of the cognitions remains the same).[8]

4. Thus, cognition of a blue pot (Cbp) is not identical with cognition of a pot. Otherwise, the former (being identical with CCbp) would be identical with the cognition of the cognition of a pot (CCp)—which it is not (by [3] above). So Cbp is not identical with Cp.

5. But we know that a blue pot is also a pot. Outside of our awareness, the multiply qualified object is not distinct from the same object poorly described.

6. There is a pot, such that whoever is cognizing it as a sheer pot is cognizing the blue pot, and whoever is cognizing the blue pot is also cognizing a pot. This obtains regardless of whether the cognizer recognizes this identity. So at least in this one case, cognition of bp is identical with cognition of p. Thus, Cbp = Cp. Between 4 and 6, we have a contradiction. Therefore, our assumption, namely reflexivism, must be false.

If the reflexivist is simply claiming that there is a certain subjective feel to being in a mental and hence in a perceptual state, I have no objection. But the subjectively experienced phenomenal quale is far from self-intimation. Apperceptive metacognition is representational. It represents a piece of cognition as thus and so. Just as cognition of a pot is distinct from the pot, metacognition of cognition must be recognized as distinct from its object.

The above argument against reflexivism construes it as a HOT (Higher Order Thought) theory of consciousness where to have a cognitive state is to be aware *de dicto* that one is in that cognitive state. This may be an unfair characterization of the more plausible versions of reflexivism. The Advaita picture of self-intimation, for example, is neither a HOT theory nor a luminosity claim. It is simply the negative claim that a certain immediate phenomenal awareness is never an object of any awareness, not even of itself, and that it does not depend on any other awareness. Perhaps some part of the dispute between the reflexivist and the irreflexivist may therefore be talking at cross-purposes.

In the next section, we shift our attention to a related but distinct question: can I be mistaken about my own current mental or cognitive state?

Can I detect my own mistake while making it?

Room for mistakes is what sets the normative apart from the descriptive. Only where there is a standard to reach is there a risk of failure. Counting, for example, is a normative activity with a positively valued goal to reach exactness and a negatively valued risk to avoid miscounting. Headaches, on the contrary, cannot be accurate or inaccurate. Is my judgment that I feel angry more like a headache or more like counting objects? Is first person awareness of current mental states normative or descriptive? This is the question I would like to start with.

At first, it may seem quite easy to answer. Even if mental events themselves are not normative, *my judgment* about my mental events must be. If I can misperceive, misremember, and mispredict other things, people, and times, why can I not make mistakes now about myself and my own current perceptions, feelings, and findings?

But matters are not that simple. Even before we come to the slippery topic of "my mistake about my current feelings," the very idea of "my mistake" has a *ring* of paradox, somewhat like the idea of "my death." It can happen, but can I witness and detect it happening? What would it be for me to commit an error while knowing it is an error? Would it not amount to making and detecting the mistake at the same time? Is that possible, without dividing myself into two? As long as a certain awareness or judgment is mine, it is not possible for me to treat it as erroneous. For to treat an awareness as erroneous is to reject it, disown it, and make it cease to be one's own. Thus, if it is (taken by me as) mistaken, it is not mine. When it is mine, I could not find it mistaken.

We regularly encounter perceptual illusions and make mistakes with respect to the external world. But how is it possible for us to make mistakes about our own current mental states? And even if it is possible that we make such mistakes, is it even conceivable that we could detect such mistakes from a first-person present-tense point of view? *Can I assert coherently that right now I mistakenly think that I am feeling calm?* We seem to be on the verge of unintelligibility! Traditionally, whatever way one has of immediately being aware of one's own current mental states is called "introspection." So, the harder question boils down to: *How can introspection be self-detectably erroneous?*

Normally the question of a correct *take* or *mistake* arises only if there is some object, property, or state of affairs out there for us to have a (sensory or doxastic) take on. Since the takes themselves are detected by introspection, it is assumed that the taker at least cannot mistake the take itself.

A complicated version of this theory of infallibility of apperception is found in the Dvaita Vedānta (Madhva) doctrine of *sākṣin* (witness). One can make a mistake in seeing silver where there is only mother-of-pearl, but one cannot be mistaken in the self-awareness that one is excited to see silver because the "inner witness" is immune to error. Why? Because the inner witness is the same as the Self. It is a kind of consciousness which functions like an additional apperceptive sense organ, but it is actually none other than the eventual mistake-detector. Once you allow this witness-self itself, on some occasions, to bear false witness as to even what (erroneous) content it is experiencing, you lose the possibility of firm exposure of error, let alone confirmation of knowledge. To distrust this ultimate court of appeal is to open oneself to unstoppable doubt not only about whether it is so when it seems to be so, but even about whether it even seems to be so.

But the alleged infallibility of first-person authority is not the only ground for claiming freedom from the risk of error. There is another easy argument to prove that awareness of our mental states could not be erroneous. If my anger is itself more like a headache, and my awareness of anger is indistinguishable from it (in other words, if there is nothing "higher order" about the introspective awareness), then the non-normativity of my first-order mental states would render my self-cognitions non-normative and thus incapable of being assessed for truth or error. Headaches could not be non-veridical. Awareness of a headache would be indistinguishable from that headache. Hence, awareness of headache could not be non-veridical. It is hard to deny the first premise, according to which occurrent mental states themselves are natural events.[9] So the counter to this argument has to attack the second premise: the collapsing of awareness of a pleasure to the pleasure itself. Unless one insists that awareness and undergoing of the pleasure are distinct, one cannot make sense of mistaken awareness of current pleasures.

Yet we do, undeniably, make mistakes of different sorts in assessing our co-occurrent mental, hedonic, somatic, and proprioceptive states. We may think—and tell ourselves—that we are not annoyed when we are. Many different kinds of mistakes fall under the general category of "errors about one's current mental state." Some inward or higher-order self-ascriptions of cognitive states "inherit" the error of the outward judgment that they reflectively register. While having the rope-snake illusion, as yet undetected, one could introspect, "I am seeing a snake now." The error of the outward judgment, "That is a snake over there," contaminates the introspective awareness, "I am seeing a snake now," rendering it erroneous insofar as the claim is taken as existentially quantified: "There is a snake which I am now seeing."

Once we have some systematic account of the different sorts of mistakes, we can commit even about current first-person perceptual hedonic or cognitive states, it should be quite interesting to see in what sense we can have states or contents about which we also could be in error!

Self-presenting states such as *it is seeming to me now that I am being appeared to orangely* were deemed immune to error because it was thought that there is not enough "give" between it seeming so and being so. The only room for correction was supposed to be linguistic, for example, using the wrong word for a feeling while putting the introspection into words.

However, introspection of alleged immediate self-awareness makes much wider claims than these "seeming to seem" pronouncements, and therefore makes more than verbal mistakes. As Jay F. Rosenberg has noted,[10] with these "It seems to me … " types of statements we don't express any beliefs at all—we express *retreats* from belief. And a retreat from belief cannot be incorrect because it cannot be correct like a failure to believe could not be true or false. So it is misleading to describe these "It seems to me … " utterances as expressions of infallible first-person reports.

If we do treat them as positive reports rather than mere "showing that one is withholding full objective commitment," then their content is much wider than the internal appearance of appearance. A report of my introspective belief involves committing to the existence of the intentional object(s) of my belief. As we shall see, with wider content, the error-accommodating "give" between our take on our mental states and the mental states themselves also expands. This inner leeway for mistakes then becomes part of the "space of reasons"—even if not all regions of it are equally public. Between this larger "give" and our epistemically riskier "take," there is room for ignorance, deception, exaggeration, underplaying, and other kinds of misconstruals, even after a certain kind of first-person privilege is conceded.

How can self-awareness be erroneous?

Let us remind ourselves of the point we started with. A storm cannot commit an error. A person's judgment can. Hence, the latter admits of emendation and improvement.[11] It makes sense to try to get better at it. The mind-training traditions which propose to improve our ability to know ourselves must admit the possibility of substantial—not merely verbal—mistakes in our effortful or automatic introspective cognitions.

If the real existence of its intended object makes a cognition veridical, how can non-veridical cognition have any object at all, and without an object what would it err about? How can one resist the threat of "all is error" pan-illusionism without falling into "if it is genuine perception then it is immune to error" infallibilism? These questions are thought through in Indian epistemologies, but the problem-terrain is not so well-charted even in sophisticated contemporary Western philosophy of perception.

One could put the "privileged access thesis" this way: I am not only the sole authority on my soul. I am the only unchallengeably reliable authority. If it appears to me that I am feeling happy now, I must be feeling happy.

I would like to argue against the claim of infallibility of first-person present-tense ascriptions of mental states. My bottom line is this: if introspection has to count as a cognition of anything at all, and as a cognition which sometimes qualifies as *knowledge* (*or perceptual knowledge* of one's own mind), then it must take the risk of error just like any other knowledge of objective facts. If I have to claim credit of being mostly right about myself, I must be ready to take the blame of being wrong sometimes. I could be wrong about what exactly I am feeling or what exactly caused what I am feeling.

By errors of introspection I don't mean false beliefs about oneself which span over longer-term dispositional claims about what sort of a person one is. It is well-known that people can be deluded about their own temperaments or characters. An irritable man may believe that he is a very calm and patient fellow. This kind of mistake is interesting but is not our concern here.

As with any error, error about one's own current inner state cannot be concurrently detected. The correction has to be retrospective. Of course, the detection—and hence elimination—of the introspective mistake has to be done by the mistake-maker herself. But in some cases, one can get help from others. Suppose I ask myself at t_1 whether I am jealous of X, and find that I am not. Later on at t_2, I might think back of the time t_1, and realize that while I convinced myself that I was not jealous of X, I was, even then, annoyed at the news that X got an award that I never got, but explained away the annoyance as simply being disturbed by the injustice of an undeserving person getting an award. I may then, at t_3, weigh and balance my conflicting self-assessments at t_1 and t_2, and come to the true conclusion that I had made a mistake in thinking at t_1 that I was not feeling jealous of X. I was.

Self-knowledge is thus a rare commodity, the path to which is paved with many mistakes masquerading as incorrigible privileged access. Sometimes, we must be capable of knowing our own minds, for otherwise it would make no sense to detect the occasional mistakes we make about our own minds.

When foundationalists like Roderick Chisholm tried to give our knowledge claims about the external world a non-defeasible justification, they depended heavily on "self-presenting states" which could not occur without the person to whom they occur being aware of them. According to one strong version of the self-luminosity thesis, these states and our awareness of them are the same. And thus our beliefs about them would count as basic beliefs which could never go wrong. The infallibility of these beliefs was thought to follow directly from the special privilege that the first person has about her own inner states.

The debate between fallibilists and infallibilists about introspective self-ascriptions of mental states has now boiled down to the deeper debate between internalism and externalism in epistemology and philosophy of mind about mental content. There are different shades of internalism and externalism, and there are different levels of controversies involved in the debate. All we need to remember here is the simplest common internalist claim: the content of a mental state is entirely determined by the inner life of the subject whose mental state it is. Naturally, if cognitive content referring to external objects were wholly determined by internal conditions of the cognizer, content about one's own inner states would be wholly within the self-conscious access of the subject whose inner states they are.

What makes our introspection falter?

In more recent times Paul Churchland has rejected the infallibility thesis about introspective reports by pointing out at least three kinds of influences which mislead us when we look within. First, we can make mistakes based on our expectations. Second, even sensed distinctions may be unnoticed when each difference in sensory stimulus falls below the threshold of what Titchener called "just noticeable difference." Over a certain duration, we tend to think that our experience has remained the same. Third, if some long-standing neural damage suddenly gets cured, even though new sensations start happening, habit-memory can inhibit second-order acknowledgment of newly acquired sensory abilities.

Of course, the infallibilists could analyze these alleged errors in such a way that the mistake would be accommodated in the objective reference aspect of the inner experience. In this way, they would keep the core of self-consciousness in the inward look free from the possibility of error.[12] But if the nature of the seeing itself becomes the object of the seeming, then seeming need not be any safer from possible error. If I can ask what it is that I am seeing or hearing, I should be able to ask what it is that I seem to be seeing and hearing. And the correct answers could be different.

Take for example the famous Müller-Lyer Illusion (see Figure 2):
Presenting someone with the below figures, we could ask two distinct questions:

Q_1. Is the top line shorter than the bottom line?
Q_2. Does the top line look shorter than the bottom line?

If someone measures and already knows the correct negative answer to Q_1, she could become biased by that and answer "No" to Q_2 as well. But, then, we tell her to look again, and this time judge not the lines but how they look or appear. Strangely enough,

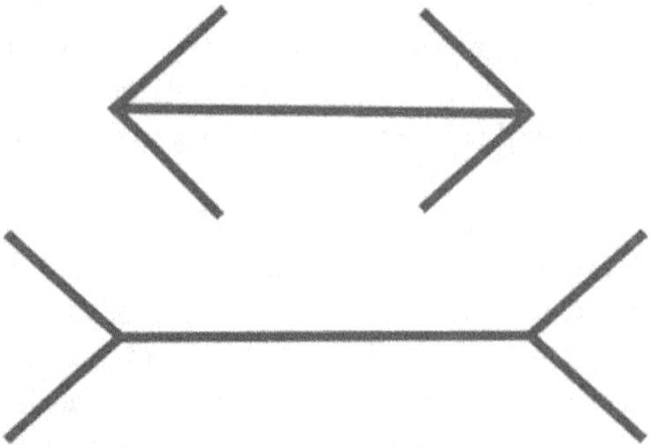

Figure 2 The Müller-Lyer illusion

we often need to unlearn how our mind or eyes or their habits add, distort, or touch up external stimuli in order to properly introspect the mind's verdict. Such mind-ignoring self-perception is sometimes called "open-eyed introspection," whereby simply taking a fresh look at the object we learn about how we are perceiving it. When one notices with a second look that one visually finds the bottom line longer than the top line, then one can go back and detect that the first, intellectually compensated, judgment that they look equal was a mistake about one's perceptual content even though it was correct about the lines themselves.

The very possibility of perceptual doubt points at the possibility of perceptual error: is the top line shorter or not? I could vacillate about this and therefore I may erroneously think it is shorter when it is actually not. Analogously, when there is doubt about whether the top line is *appearing shorter to me*, there must be the possibility that when it is actually appearing shorter, I may think that it is not appearing shorter. This is to say that when I think I am seeing it to be shorter I may not be actually seeing it to be shorter. Thus, I could be mistaken about my current visual experience itself! As A. J. Ayer comments, "But in allowing that he may be uncertain how a thing looks to him, we have already … drawn a line between the facts. And his assessment, or description, of them."[13]

Two things must be noted with care. Ayer is talking about mental, sense-experiential facts. Normally we call such facts "subjective." But once we draw the distinction between those experiential facts and the subject's assessment of them, the experiential facts claim a certain objectivity: anything the subject could be wrong about must be objective. So, then, is the fact that I am feeling impatient now a subjective fact or an objective fact? My feeling impatient is directly self-intimating to me, it seems. But I could misdescribe (silently, even to myself) this feeling as a feeling of fear (e.g., the fear that I shall be late). I could be wrong about it and no one may ever know whether I was impatient or afraid. In that case, this is an objective fact, which can go completely unrecognized. So it is both subjective and objective.

This discomfort seems to stay with Ayer till the end. Is a misdescription a verbal error, a misuse of words, or a substantial assessment error? In the latter case, my use of words is accurate: I am genuinely misjudging my objective (real)—subjective states!

A certain stripe of internalism and foundationalism insists that such first-person errors about current mental states could not be more serious than mere linguistic slips. Our experience of our own experience, unclothed in social language, must be intrinsically immune to error. Unless a minimal infallibility of the first person's clear and distinct judgment about her own current inner states were granted, there would be no difference between our knowledge of our own minds and our knowledge of others. Yet, the very "mineness" of my own states seems to consist in my word being final about their nature.

Externalism and our more-than-verbal errors about ourselves

In the face of obstinate internalist refusal to admit clear cases of illusions of introspection, I will propose my own externalist arguments. They aim to prove first, that the very distinction between factual error and verbal error is questionable, and second, that I am not the sole authority on the content of my own thoughts and feelings.

Let us remind ourselves of W. V. Quine's life long insistence that the line between claims about sense-experience (synthetic claims) and claims about meaning of words (analytic claims) is not hard-and-fast. Semantic decisions are not entirely free from the impact of our experience of the world, and observational decisions are not entirely free of semantic conventions.

If this is correct, then even verbal mistakes could be factual mistakes. If I misname my current feeling of anxiety as exhaustion, I cannot whitewash my introspective error as simply my misusing the word "exhaustion." If my use of the word does not match the social norm which governs the use of that word, then just because no one else can confidently tell whether the mistake happens at the name-giving level or at the experience-recognizing level, I cannot insist on drawing such a clear distinction between verbal and recognitional error. The incorrect application of a linguistic category amounts to incorrect classification, hence incorrect cognition, of my own mood. To call anxiety "exhaustion" is a mistake, and in many cases it is pointless to ask whether it is a verbal or a factual mistake. The only reason to insist on such a distinction would be to beg the question on the issue of the infallibility of introspective reports.

Here is my final externalist argument to prove that even when I am introspectively certain that I am thinking about gold, I could be mistaken because I may be thinking of something else. It's true that my thoughts may be generally and specially accessible to me. Nevertheless, I may make and correct mistakes about what I think I am currently experiencing because the identity of the thought depends often upon its external object and my mistake about it would infect the veracity of my self-ascription.

Suppose John has grown up most of his life on planet Earth where gold is the shiny yellow metal named by the chemical abbreviation Au. Now he is transported unbeknownst to him to Twin-Earth where there is an identical looking yellow metal whose chemical constitution is quite distinct—XYZ—but it is called "gold" there. A Twin-Earth dweller shows him a piece of XYZ, and tells him, "Now close your eyes and think about this piece of gold." When John now thinks of this piece of gold, he is thinking of XYZ and not of Au, since his first-order thought is constituted through the memory-demonstrative "that bit of metal" by the actual sample outside, which is of XYZ. But if he now introspects about what it is that he is thinking of, he would come out with the verdict, "I am thinking of a piece of gold," and since in his vocabulary "gold" means Au and not XYZ, he would be mistaken in identifying his own thought. We cannot rescue this introspective self-ascription from substantial error by calling it a mere verbal mistake.

Of course, there is one kind of mistake from which, most probably, introspective self-reports are immune. While I may be mistaken whether I am having a pain or an itch, whether I am hungry or greedy, or whether I am experiencing love or lust, I could not be mistaken about who it is that is undergoing these introspected mental states. If I am introspecting that I am in state F, then I must be right about the fact that it is I myself and not someone else mistaken to be me. It is not just bizarre, but scarcely intelligible to suggest that I could be introspecting into someone else's mental state and mistakenly ascribing it to myself.

But counter-examples to the infallibility claim have been proposed even on this topic of the alleged immunity to error due to misidentification of first-person self-ascription. Let me mention one such funny counter-example (which I have already used once in chapter 10 above) and leave it to the reader to decide whether even the bearer of an inwardly recognized mental state could be mistakenly taken to be oneself. This was suggested in a fascinating paper by Hogan and Martin:

> Paul is a super-macho male. He has never acknowledged to himself that he ever felt fear. His father must have brought him up as a fearless hero. He undergoes psychotherapy and learns to recognize that when he is angry in a certain way, either or both of two things may be happening: he may be actually afraid and he may be totally identifying with his daughter. Once, after he learns this, he finds himself feeling that kind of befuddling anger. As a result of his inductively acute self-assessment he naturally has a clear feeling that either he or his daughter is now afraid. Over-correcting himself, he introspects that it is he himself who is afraid. But he gets it wrong. This time it is his daughter who is afraid. His self-ascription of fear is not immune to error due to misidentification of the subject. He got the fear (predicate) right, but he made a mistake about whose fear it was (subject).[14]

As we saw in "On Referring to the First Person," even if there is something counter-intuitive about Hogan and Martin's example, the Wittgenstein-Anscombe thesis that when we make judgments of the form "I am feeling M," we are not making any singular reference to anything by the use of "I," is even more counter-intuitive. The price we pay if we accept Wittgenstein's conclusion that self-ascriptions of inner states are like mere groans and grimaces is the concession that "I am sad," "You are sad," and "She is sad" are *not* substitution-instances of the same sentence-frame "X is sad." Even when people tell me what they are feeling, upon this view, they are not saying anything *about* themselves, so I cannot claim to understand what they are saying about themselves. When I tell my daughter, "You must be disappointed!" and she agrees, "Yes, I am disappointed," under this non-referential account of first-person self-ascriptions, she is not agreeing with me. First, she is not making or endorsing any assertion, but is simply expressing disappointment as she would have done by drooping her lower lip. Second, she is not predicating anything about the same self about whom I had predicated disappointment. First- and third-person reports of mental states then would never express the same propositions, for the first would not express any proposition at all!

Now, one kind of self-awareness may be universally automatic, and another kind may be proverbially hard to get, but to buy Wittgenstein's argument is to concede that the very idea of knowing or being aware of oneself is nonsensical. That is not a price but a penalty. I am not ready to pay it. I would like to keep the ideas of self-knowledge and self-reference intelligible, even if difficult.

One can run a Parfit-type thought-experiment with teletransportation in order to generate a misidentification of the subject, rather than the object or property. Suppose John is teletransported to Mars (in the branch-line manner, without destroying the original Earth John) at the age of fifty. Shortly thereafter Earth John thinks, "I currently feel that I shall not like to be on Mars for more than a year," and thinks that he is referring to the Martian Replica with his use of the first-person singular pronoun. But, he is mistaken. He is still habitually tied to thinking about and through the persona of his Earth Original and is reporting the discomfort of that earthling, accidentally correctly, because the earthling may be "simultaneously"(!) having such a future-directed feeling. The predicated discomfort is veridically ascribed, but to the wrong self—to the wrong John-replica. Of course, to Parfit the distinction would not matter; hence, it will be a negligible mistake. But for a strict, Thomas Reid sort of personal identity realist, it is a big mistake due to misidentification of the bearer of the mental state. Precisely from this mistake introspection is thus proved to be not immune.

There could be all sorts of controversies about the value of such thought-experiments. But no one could call the error of thinking that I, the replica, am feeling like F, when actually I, the original, am feeling like F, a merely linguistic mistake. If they do, then linguistic mistakes are substantial mistakes. (I owe the insight behind this example to Mark Siderits.)

Our inadequately clear perception of our own affects

Our mental states, especially affects or emotional states—which might permeate all of our cognitive states if Sāṃkhya psychology is to be trusted—are too complex for us to figure out in detail simply by a reflexive look within. A peremptory introspection runs all the risks of carelessness. Even a painstakingly deliberate look tends to let in all sorts of biases and distortions. Just as the largely ignored field-part of external perception renders possible the attention-illuminated focus-part to have the borders that it does, a currently neglected background cluster of feelings may make it possible for us to focus sharply on one salient feeling. Someone may be unnoticeably feeling deep love and an occasional sulk toward a friend, along with boredom. The unnoticed field of feelings is making it possible that she is finding a friend boring on a particular summer afternoon. But she may actually have to deny, consciously, the love and the sulk so that one could emphatically feel that one is *simply* bored by this friend. That one is bored is not inaccurate. But the error of omission pollutes the truth claim: one tells oneself erroneously, and somewhat perversely, "No, I am just bored, I am not sulking at all and I don't love him anymore. I feel nothing but boredom." The introspective focusing or highlighting blocks out the introspective peripheral vision.

Feelings—even our own feelings—are like coffee-mugs and buildings. They have a front which we see because they have a back which we don't. The occlusion of the back by the front makes them objective well-rounded complex feelings, not just façades of feelings. But to that extent, it is best not to claim that what we apperceive of them is all that is there to them. What we see is *not* all of what we might have seen. Emotional self-knowledge is rare because the combination of partial ignorance and epistemic conceit sometimes yields the error of denying the hidden back-sides of our own feelings.

I would rather preserve the value and rarity of self-knowledge by keeping open the possibility of all kinds of substantial errors that we, subjects, are subject to about our current mental states. Our mental states, whether they are identical with, supervenient on, or functionally thrown up by our brain-states, with all their subjective qualia, are things we can remain routinely partly or occasionally wholly ignorant about. Hence they are possible objects of ignorance and error. Perhaps nothing that is not an object of ignorance could be an object of knowledge. It should not be just a joke about a behaviorist but common practice of epistemic humility, during times of great emotional confusion, to go up to a friend or a mentor and ask, "Tell me, how am I feeling today?"

My goal here was to show why we shouldn't be so haughty about the content of our introspections. But this thesis is open to an unhappy misunderstanding: I am not claiming that *all* of our mental lives are so fundamentally different from what they seem to be that no statement about them could be true. Such error theory about introspection may nonetheless insist that our linguistic practice be preserved for practical purposes, or, as Buddhists would say, as a piece of useful fiction. I now turn to a discussion of such a thesis, hoping to show why I find it untenable.[15]

15

Fictionalism about the Mental

Introduction: What exactly is fictionalism about the mind?

Physicalists who believe that our talk of persons, sensations, emotions, beliefs, desires, consciousness, etc., is convenient fiction sometimes appear to tolerate folk psychological claims. While neuro-physiological discourse states hard facts, their argument goes, ordinary first- or second-person consciousness attributions deserve "soft" or "as if" truth-status. In Mādhyamika Buddhism and Advaita Vedānta, there is a long tradition of metaphysical double talk, which serves to distinguish between levels. The Mādhyamika Buddhist asserts the existence of permanent selves carrying the imprints of past actions and desires from one life to the next life as an empirical, ethically important, transactional truth, but admits no such self at the level of ultimate truth. Candrakīrti, the Prāsaṅgika Mādhyamika commentator on Nāgārjuna, similarly asserts the ontological status of physical objects, albeit only at the transactional empirical level.[1] Yet, this assertion of direct realism about physical objects is, in the ultimate analysis, a kind of fiction.

My aim is to show how fictionalism about the mental (FM) is imperiled by insincerity and self-refutation. If appearance-talk is mind-talk, then the fictionalist cannot deny the existence of mental states, attitudes, dispositions, and events by diagnosing all thinking as merely appearing to think. His denial would then be also inside the folk-psychological fiction, since neurons cannot deny or accept, or appear to deny or accept, anything. His denial would be merely a set of occurrences and dispositions of his brain. If a realist (anti-fictionalist) about mental events tries to point out the contradiction in maintaining

1. that thinking is nothing but neural activity,
2. thinking is fiction, but
3. neural activity is not fiction,

then the fictionalist could respond as follows: the inconsistency disappears if we rephrase (2) as "thinking, as anything distinct from neural activity, is fiction."

---

[1] "I deplore the philosophical double talk, which would repudiate an ontology while simultaneously enjoying its benefits." W.V.O. Quine, *Word and Object* (Cambridge, MA: MIT Press, 1960), 242.

A nominalist tolerates our discourse about common properties, but only as a conventional "manner of speaking." The innocuous reference to time in the oft-uttered sentence "My time is valuable" does not commit the busy man to the existence of Time as a separate metaphysical category. Those who do not believe that abstract numbers exist over and above concrete collections of as many objects might still speak of numbers. Another common type of utterance could be perfectly literal but not used for stating facts. When we "speak of" Sherlock Holmes as an addict, we need not believe in his existence. There is yet a third way, besides metaphor and fiction, in which we can speak of things we do not believe exist: reporting of other beliefs. A modern social scientist who has no belief in souls could state that the Christian soul is not reborn like the Hindu soul.

With respect to philosophy of mind, the fictionalist either descriptively diagnoses our first-person introspective reports or qualia-ascriptions to others as "really" figurative, ontologically non-committal utterances, or prescriptively recommends the revision of our ontological commitments such that we treat all mind-talk with meta-metaphysical levity.

FM faces a destructive dilemma. It either fails as a translation of folk-psychological sentences about first- or second-person mental events, or gets trapped in the incoherence of saying that between a statement and its correct translation one is true, and the other is false. Fictionalists, it seems, deny that there are any irreducibly mental facts. But then they hasten to add that we best keep talking as if there are. Irreducibly psychological events cannot be mere make-believe, because *application of the concept of make-believe presupposes the real happening of mental events.* A mental eliminativist asserts that mental events really do not exist. Amicably, neuro-materialists call their own natural mind-talk "folk psychology." Contrary to folk psychology, they tell us that upon thinking nothing really occurs except frontal lobe events and synaptic connections. They sincerely claim to *think* so, and expect us to understand the *meaning* of their claims. Some of them, inspired by the example of how we can do mathematics and science without the slightest ontological commitment to numbers or functions, adopt a sophisticated position called "Fictionalism about the Mental" (FM).

What is fictionalism about the mental (FM)?

In classical Indian philosophy, Yogācāra metaphysicians were anti-realists about mereological wholes, substantial diachronically identical selves, universals, and external physical objects of perception. These philosophers developed varieties of fictionalism with great sophistication against formidable Buddhist and anti-Buddhist realist objectors. However, one big distinction between Buddhist anti-realisms, reductionist or otherwise, and contemporary fictionalism is that Buddhist anti-realisms do not privilege empirical or theoretical sciences over common sense. Except for the extreme "Emptiness School," no Buddhist questions the reality of phenomenal qualia or the existence of momentary mental episodes. Buddhist subjective idealists were not fictionalists about the mental; they inevitably render any sort of adopted fictionalism in terms of the thorny "doctrine of two truths."[2]

In recent Western philosophy, the version of fictionalism that has been most rigorously developed is a form of anti-realism about numbers.[3] Hans Vaihinger earlier interpreted Kant's "Ideas of Reason" as indispensable fictions that human understanding needs to keep positing, while disciplining itself never to treat them as knowable facts.[4] Indeed, we might read into Kant's "Paralogisms of Rational Psychology" the idea that taking oneself as an enduring experiencer and one's mental states as objects of inner sense betrays an incorrigible error. Such a strongly anti-realist interpretation of Kant's "Empirical Psychology" might read as an early anticipation of FM. Perhaps the slogan "empirically real but transcendentally ideal" points to a fledgling "two truths" doctrine in Kant.[5]

The word "fictionalism" occurs, perhaps for the first time, in Vaihinger's *The Philosophy of As If* in a footnote to the following quotation from Schiller: "In error only there is life, and knowledge must be death."[6] Since then, connection between fictionalism and error-theory has been close. In mathematics, physics, political economy, and morality, Vaihinger claimed that the imaginary (the absolute, the perfect, the ideal) is indispensable and justifiable, in spite of its unreality.[7]

Some define fictionalism as eliminativism combined with a motivated and pragmatically useful protection of our ordinary "folkways." Others take as fictionalist the Daniel Dennett-like stance that while neuroscience gives us the real picture of human consciousness, incompatible with folk psychology, we can continue to be "realists" about beliefs, desires, and other intentional states, although no place remains for them in strict scientific ontology.[8]

The most rigorous characterizations of fictionalism tend to show internal incoherence or double-think.[9] Gideon Rosen writes:

Fictionalism about a region of discourse is defined by three basic contrasts:

1. As against the instrumentalist or the non-cognitivist, the fictionalist maintains that claims made within the discourse are genuine representations of how things stand, and that they are therefore normally capable of truth and falsity.
2. As against one sort of reductionist, the fictionalist maintains that the language of the discourse is to be interpreted "at face value." Claims made within the discourse genuinely imply what they are most naturally taken to imply.
3. As against one sort of realist, the fictionalist maintains that the ultimate aim of discourse in the area is not (or need not be) to produce a true account of the domain, but rather to produce theories with certain "virtues"—virtues a theory may possess without being true.[10]

Now, there is a tension between (1) and (3). If statements such as "I had a rush of rage which I am now regretting" are genuine representations of how things stand, it seems perverse to insist that existential generalizations that follow from reality-representing assertions such as "There exist such mental events as surges of anger and bouts of repentance" are not aimed at truth but are instead designed to produce "virtuous" theories. The tone of (3) sounds clearly instrumentalist whereas (1) builds in a contrast with (one sort of) instrumentalism. The three criteria together are not strictly inconsistent, because of these cautious "one kind of's" added in each clause.

But a non-instrumentalist view taking certain discourse as representations of how things really are seems to gravitate toward realism of some sort or another. And the third contrast makes it clear that a fictionalist about sentences putatively referring to X-type entities is not a realist about X-type entities, and does not take assertions in that domain to state plain truths or falsehoods.

Let me try to give a simpler sketch of what FM may amount to. Let us suppose that an ontological debate ensues concerning the existence of a class of entities X. The fictionalist about X recommends, either descriptively or prescriptively, that all sentences S which seem to ontologically commit one to X should be reinterpreted as sentences that are *not* ontologically committing and not fact-stating. In addition, the fictionalist explains why these sentences prove useful, and therefore employable. Such a proposal of reinterpretation of statements about Xs with the recommendation that we should take them metaphysically lightly—as useful fictions—is called "Fictionalism about Xs."[11] Sentences like "Necessity is the mother of invention" (N) are not to be taken as of the same form as the sentence "Hillary is the mother of Chelsea." We do not speak of Ms. Necessity who gave birth to Mr. Invention. According to the fictionalist about the mental, much of philosophy of mind sets out on a similarly misguided search for the exact ontological location of subjective states spoken of in sentences like "My desire is stronger than my belief."

Another kind of talking that philosophers often engage in makes it impossible to assume the existence of the apparent topic of conversation. This happens when the existence of the topic itself is in question. One speaker denies, another affirms, and yet another remains doubtful of the existence of the subject under discussion. Not just the fictionalist, but also any brand of eliminativist or strong anti-realist about entities faces one tough question: *what* exactly do they deny the existence of? What semantic value should we attribute to terms such as "physical objects of perception" or "numbers" or "inner mental states" when used to designate contentious entities? When some believe that the terms stand for real entities and others believe they do not stand for anything, what would their common agreed-upon use of those terms stand for? Michael Dummett had suggested that we speak of disputed classes of statements rather than disputed entities as forming the common topic of realism/anti-realism debates. Even terms cannot be fixed as the pivot of a metaphysical dispute. If we disagree about the very existence of mental states, what single set of things can we point to about which we disagree?

FM's special awkwardness and disingenuousness

Even if we provide a clear account of fictionalism, FM remains a particularly precarious position to formulate. The central problem is that the two parts of FM, the eliminativist and the instrumentalist, assume an appearance-reality distinction. But this distinction presupposes the concepts of error, pretense, or make-believe, which remain incompatible with the purely physicalist ontology. And the diagnosis of why we cannot live without this pervasive folk psychological story does not make the case for its being a universally shared error any stronger. Neurons do not make mistakes because they cannot be held to any normative standard of truth. Synapses do not mean anything and need not entertain false beliefs to function efficiently. *We do*. If we cannot describe, say, at the electrochemical level, the error without presupposing real mental events, then mental events cannot be less real than electrochemical impulses. Calling the appearance mere fiction only works by straddling levels of discourse, which the fictionalist's mutually insulated "scientific" and "folk" levels cannot permit.

Statements such as "I missed you" or "Brenda hates Aaron" are made and understood without spelling out "missed" and "hated" in terms of neurophysiological states. Common sense takes them to be statements about mental episodes or dispositions. One can at best draw a distinction between *de dicto* or statement-realism and *de re* or term-realism about "missings" and "hatreds." But as users of common psychological vocabulary, we take dejections to be as factual as digestions. Introspective reports are not meant as elliptical or fictional statements about the speaker's behavior or brain-states. Some verbs seem to stand for non-physical relational properties or mental acts, just as an existentially quantified statement such as "Some happy memories cause more pain than any unhappy memory" seems to range over the nonphysical entities we call memories and pains. But if one insists that only spatially locatable physical entities exist (in the ontologically committed sense of existence), then one cannot be a realist about mental events, acts, properties, relations, or things.

Michael Dummett has taught us that realism about mental entities, such as pains and memories, takes statements referring to these entities as lending themselves to a truth-condition theory of meaning, rather than a justification-condition theory. Determinate recognition-transcendent facts or truth-makers, by virtue of which such statements prove true or false, exist even if we lack decisive evidence justifying the assertion or rejection of such statements. Thus, a realist about the proposition "Brenda hates Aaron" must insist that even if no neuroscientific test and no observable behavior can justify or confute the proposition, it's true if and only if there exists a tendency toward or a mental state of disdain for Aaron "inside" Brenda. A realist should also be ready to call that statement false, if and only if no such negative emotion exists "in" Brenda, however perfectly she may sham and consistently behave in a disdainful manner. Thus, the realist remains committed to the existence or absence of interpersonal amorous or affective facts as truth-makers of our first-second-or third-person avowals and assertions of love or hate, and of our ascription of psychological attitudes toward one another.

But what if one is not a realist about mental states or events? One could then take up the extreme position that the meaning of "Brenda hates Aaron" has to be understood quite independently of its truth conditions because it has none. An eliminativist about mental properties or actions would say that statements such as "Some happy memories cause a lot of pain" is as false or truth-valueless as "Some tame unicorns cause phlogiston to attain an astral aura."

To call some controversial things "fiction" and to call our talk about such things plainly false sound deceptively similar. The former, while more polite, proves metaphysically more damaging. "A creator God is just an ancient piece of fiction" could be stated as a rhetorical variant of "The ancient belief that God created the world is false." Yet fictionalism, as a technical term in metaphysics, wants to say something very different from "eliminativism" or "error-theory." So what dissimilarities can we find between these two kinds of dismissal? First, we must reject a plain falsehood the moment it gets exposed. But we can tolerate and retain fictions in an ersatz way as long as we do not claim truth for them. Let us call this the *bearability* of fiction. Second, even though fiction has no truth-value, it may have some other kind of value, for example, charm and heuristic usefulness, which a plain falsehood does not have. Let us call this the *seductive usefulness* of fiction.

Now, one cautionary remark is in place here. At first blush, fictionalism may sound a bit like pragmatism because both appeal to useful discourse and both seem to share a certain ontological light-footedness. But actually they maintain dissimilar if not mutually incompatible stances. Fictionalism about a certain class of sentences regards them as *useful but false*. Pragmatism insists that such sentences are *true because useful*. Appealing to Horwich, John Daly claims that fictionalists distinguish between: (1) Theory T is true, and (2) T is useful.[12] So according to the fictionalist one can believe (2) without holding (1). The garden variety pragmatist would see (2) as equivalent to (1).

Another key feature of fictionalism is what I will call its *ontological innocence*. This refers to the fictionalist's point that pretending as if a fictional entity such as that the Tooth Fairy exists does not carry the same kind of ontological commitments as believing in a falsehood such as that Osama Bin Laden was the Anti-Christ. Remembering these distinctions, we could one more time try to define FM as accepting the bearability and seductive usefulness of our ordinary auto-phenomenological and hetero-phenomenological assertions about mental events, while remembering their ontological innocence or referential toothlessness.

We accomplish in the epithet "folk" what we used to accomplish by calling something "naïve" or "common sense." A folk-theory is thus one that science revises while letting it rule ordinary language and day-to-day communication. FM responds to the problem of *how best to save folk psychology and our ordinary belief-desire talk in light of the overwhelming success of neuroscience*. The more we know about the brain, the less we need the mind!

After Kant, metaphysics has had to curb its enthusiasm into a sort of fictionalism in most sectors. We metaphysicians must talk about ordinary middle-sized dry goods "as if" they exist mind-independently. Both Kant and modern physics seem to take mountains and mangos as mere appearances put together by human understanding—as inter-subjectively agreed-upon fiction. Thus, common-sense talk of cardinal numbers, minds, and mental events has been tolerated as various folk-ontologies.

Yet what Strawson calls descriptive metaphysics could not be underwritten by transcendental idealism, because transcendental idealism is an error-theory and is therefore revisionary metaphysics. Such fictionalism, if it is one, can be likened to a certain kind of ontologically bashful anti-realism about the external world. A mental fictionalist may claim seriously that each of us is a conscious self with some measure of freedom to choose and with a stream of intentional cognitive and affective states. But then, in the face of the mighty materialism of physics and neuroscience, she back-peddles and says, "I am just *saying* these things, because that is how we communicate and act as if." But when she takes one step forward toward direct realism about consciousness, selfhood, and freedom, and then two steps backward into anti-realism, she seems to get caught in self-refutation. If one "freely accepts" the revisionary fictionalist's recommendation, then one *really chooses* to act. Since appearances are all we have to live with, if this appears to be a self-refutation, then it is one. Or at least we are compelled to act as if it is one. If, as I believe, compatibilist freedom of the will is central to the mental, fictionalism about the mental, thus, turns out to be an operationally inconsistent position.

Can phenomenality be a mere appearance or a cultural construct? Here too one needs to draw a robust distinction. How exactly one feels in the presence of a bright orange sunset may depend upon cultural and individual contextual conditions, but *that one would be feeling some way or another* is a brute reality and not a matter of convention. I am not appealing to infallibility of first-person reports of experience. One can be mistaken even about *how* one is currently feeling, but not *that* one is feeling a certain way, unless one is in deep sleep.

Refutations of FM

Argument from presupposition

Fictionalism of any sort presupposes usefulness, bearability, and ontological innocence. Hence, it presupposes *finding* one set of beliefs indispensable or more useful than others, and *thinking* to oneself that, and *talking* to others as if, one is having conscious experiences and making conscious decisions. But FM entails that events such as finding and thinking and freely communicating do not happen. The fictionalist turns out to be a subtle eliminativist. If there are no meaning-bearers in axons, dendrites, nuclei, or synapses, and there is no other reality except the neurophysiological one, then nothing really means anything. When the mental fictionalist goes on to propitiate the feeler in scientists and nonscientists alike, by telling us what we *really mean* when we say, "I am sad," or "You love me," he contradicts himself.

Argument from appearance

FM amounts to denying the possibility of anything appearing any way to any consciousness. But as fictionalism about X, it also implies the usefulness of believing X, and therefore it ineluctably seems as if there are Xs. Thus, FM either involves a contradictory pair of claims about appearances, or commits appearances themselves to appearances, which is absurd. That things appear a certain way (while they are not) cannot itself be an appearance.

Eliminativism contradicts pretense argument

If we take FM as the conjunction of eliminativism and pretend truth claims about mental states, then it incurs several counts of self-refutation.[13] As suggested above, pretense or make-believe remains central to the concept of fictional truth.[14] But pretense and make-believe are folk psychological notions. The first conjunct sweeps out folk psychological entities from our ontology, while the second conjunct invites them back via the notions of pretending or simulated belief.[15]

Argument from failure of translation

If the two descriptions "I feel like scratching my back" and "The prefrontal cortex over here is sending motor signals which, unless inhibited, will result in this hand landing up on that expanse of flat skin behind it and the contraction of its finger muscles" are logically equivalent, then how is it possible that one of them is false and the other true? Buddhists would reduce the apparent referential character of the "I" to a usefully erroneous reification of a series of psychophysical strands and cluster-streams. No Buddhist who recommends painstaking mind-watching meditation would be ready to eliminate episodic inner—not neural—mental events as a mere manner of speaking.

"No fakery without real mentality" argument

If there were no real conscious states, there would not be any state—material, functional, computational, or neurophysiological—that would masquerade as a conscious state. When coupled with argument B above, the underlying principle "No fake f without a genuine f" has especially persuasive force.

A philosophical revision of our folk beliefs always presumes the possibility of someone reasonably changing her views. The above exposure of the incoherence of FM is, in a similar way, meant to appeal to the reason of the interlocutor. Just as you could not ban banning, on pain of operational self-refutation, you cannot be a fictionalist about the mental, because fiction-making or pretending or *making believe as if* cannot happen in a world where there are no irreducibly mental facts. The distinction between "behaving in one way while thinking in another" can happen only in a world where thinking non-fictionally goes on. Fictions do not happen at the level of neurons. Fictions, make-believe, and imaginings happen and are shared in real consciousness.[16]

Conclusion: a diagnosis is not a proof of fictionality

It is true that certain fictions have such hold on our imagination that even after recognizing they are not factual we are compelled to go on talking as if they are. But a very credible "diagnosis" as to why we need to speak as if, say, the Sun really rises (P), or as if the Earth is larger than the Moon (Q), can never prove that P or Q is false. One of them is indeed false, the other true, and the diagnosis of why both are entrenched in language does not tell us which is which. When the mental fictionalist gives a convincing diagnosis of why "the error" of thinking that we have consciousness and phenomenal qualia is so widespread and indispensable given the presence of such a vast and nuanced psychological vocabulary in all human languages, she provides no argument to prove that it is an error in the first place (unless one presumes that all widespread beliefs are false, a presumption which one should be embarrassed to own up to).

Take the very special and difficult issue of the ontological status of a mental image. When I call up an image of a golden palace on a hill, I can drop my entity-multiplying search for a pretend-object of inner perception by simply rephrasing the act of imagining as pretending to perceive a golden palace rather than perceiving a pretend-golden palace. But how does one go about simulating or acting as if one perceives a golden palace? Presumably, one does something a whole lot similar to seeing a golden palace, except that no palace stands nearby. But how does the fact that my conduct remarkably resembles someone who genuinely experienced something show that I am not experiencing something? Saying to someone who believes that p, "We know why you cannot help believing that p" may betray a snide way of telling her that p is false, like saying "You wish!" in response to someone's assertion. But this does not serve as substitute for a good argument proving that p is an excusable piece of falsehood.

Both positive arguments *for* a Dualist or a Parallelist or a Neutral Monist or an Anomalous Monist position, as well as negative arguments *against* folk psychology befit serious metaphysicians. But anticipating the metaphysical light-footedness of the fictionalist, certain Buddhist philosophers spurned all metaphysics, encouraging a tradition that engages in relentless negative dialectics against all possible philosophical positions. The resulting position has been sometimes described as pan-fictionalism or absolute skepticism, but it sounds dangerously close to what the Buddha described as the philosophy of the eel-wrigglers. The pan-fictionalists end up finding their own claim of the emptiness of the common sense world empty. They do not pound the table with assertions about ultimate reality. But neither can they make too big a deal of their own non-table pounding and yet sacrosanct distinction between two levels of truth. Instead of examining the folk-metaphysics of common sense realism and finding it good, they end up, albeit self-dismissively, recommending an unexamined life as the only relief from that suffering we lovingly call philosophical analysis.

Perhaps this view amounts to a form of metaphysical humility, as it commits itself to a limited range of real items, if any. Its epistemology, however, is not humble—unlike that of the realist who celebrates the fact that there is so much outside of our knowledge. The anti-realist's metaphysical austerity naturally embraces FM and FM naturally extends to fictionalism about the self, seeking to remove it from our final ontology. It seems as if much of this second part of the book would be pointless without the real existence of a self. What is the self anyway, and how could we defend it? As long as we do not dismiss all a priori philosophical reasoning as otiose unless contemporary physicalist neuroscience endorses its results, Nyāya has much to say about that most important piece of the puzzle of subjectivity.

16

Nyāya Proofs for the Existence of the Self

Introduction

It was clear to a Naiyāyika as ancient as Uddyotakara (*c.* sixth century CE) that negative existential statements cannot be truly made by the use of genuinely referential simple subject-terms. It is by presupposing the existence of tigers[1] that we can assert, "Tigers growl," whereas we cannot so presuppose the existence of unicorns when we say, "Unicorns are fictional." This old philosophical problem about subject-terms of existence-denying statements recurs in many contexts, especially between the Nyāya and the Buddhists in their debates concerning the existence of God,[2] the reality of the external world, the possibility of a supporting example for the contra-positive of the Buddhist definition of existence,[3] and the need for a proof of the existence of the self. The basic semantic principle with which the Naiyāyika operates is stated rather plainly by Uddyotakara as follows: "*Na hi ekam padam nirarthakam paśyāmaḥ.*"[4]

Since *artha* (as against *pravṛtti-nimitta*, etc.) is usually the term for denotation or reference, here he is actually expressing the Russellian assumption of the Nyāya semantics, namely, that every genuine single (i.e., simple) expression must denote an object. Accordingly Uddyotakara cuts what Quine has called "Plato's Beard" by analyzing "The rabbit-horn does not exist" into "The rabbit bears no causal relation with horns" or simply "No rabbit has horns." This resembles Russell's policy of breaking up all apparently empty subject-terms into non-empty predicates like " … is a rabbit" and " … has a horn," except that the technique used is not a formalized language of quantifiers of a predicate-logic. Later on, the development of the regimented language devised by the Navya-Naiyāyikas made perspicuous techniques available for expressing such a denial.

But the expression would always be—however technically circumspect—in what Carnap would call "the material mode," namely, in the idiom of an absence and its counter-entity. Another vital difference between Uddyotakara and Russell would be this: while Russell's criteria for being a reference-guaranteed singular expression were too stringent to allow any ordinary noun to qualify as genuinely singular, Uddyotakara does hold "the self" (or at any rate "I") as a genuinely singular term which *cannot* be coherently used as the subject-term of an (absolutely) negative existential. That is why he diagnoses "The self exists" as tautologically true, "The self does not exist" as self-contradictorily false, and "Does the self exist?" to be as pointless as "Is that tree a tree?" Obviously, he does not think that it is the full-fledged notion of a Nyāya-Cartesian pure-ego, which is in this sense uncontroversial. What one cannot significantly deny is the existence of the referent of the term "I." Even if one is a physicalist and refers to the body whenever one uses "I," one is not a doubter of the *existence* of the self but is simply a disputant of the spiritual-substance theory of self. Gautama seems to avoid even this trouble of taking "the self" as genuinely singular. His proposed proof of the self does not take the form of an inference which establishes that there is existence in the locus of the Self because of the presence of some other existence-pervaded factor in it—i.e., it is not *a sattā-sādhyaka, ātma-pakṣaka,* something-hetuka inference. Such an inference even if construed might be at once rejected by the opponent as *āśrayāsiddha* since the opponent challenges the very existence of the *pakṣa*—viz., *ātman.*

When we come to this controversial use of the term "the self" (the uncontroversial use made "Self (= I) exist(s)" trivially true) Gautama would analyze it in a Russellian fashion into: "The X such that is a substance other than the five elemental substances, the *manas*, space and time." By proving that such a substance is the referent of the "I"-usage in all our self-ascriptions of consciousness-predicates (e.g., in "I wish," "I know," etc.), Gautama would claim to have proved that the *self* of the typical Nyāya (Vaiśeṣika) kind exists. In his ontology *ātman* is just a surrogate for "the non-corporeal substance other than *manas* and the sense-faculties to which emotions, cognitions and volitions belong."

The topic of controversy: the nature, not the existence, of the self

The Cartesian line of argument was not at all foreign to the Naiyāyika. That the Indian philosophers were aware of the absurdity of denying the existence of the subject who does the denial is *amply* attested to by later discussions.[5] As in contemporary Western philosophy, the exact nature of the self-refutation incurred by such a statement as, "I do not exist," was subjected to careful analysis. Udayana made distinctions between *self-contradiction,*[6] *self-act-nullification,*[7] and *self-refutation.* That is why Uddyotakara does not prove that what is referred to by the pronoun "I" exists—on that score there cannot be any significant disagreement. *Na kaścidātma sadbhāve vipratipadyate.*

It is only the specific metaphysical nature of the self that is the subject of controversy. Thus, one can maintain that the same-seeming subject (which Kant called *the synthetic unity of apperception*) *relying* on which we recognize objective continuity (in the form "*the person I* who experienced an object visually am now experiencing *the same* object tactually") is really

1 Nothing over and above the distinct (and momentary) bits of experiences—each distinct from another.
2. A bundle of such experiences (or perhaps a series).
3. Some substantive entity other than the experiences.[8]

Or

4. Is identical with the body of an individual to which these experiences are ascribed.

A decision between these alternatives must be made, if at all, by means of arguments or inferences, for as Hume's "intimate entrance" into himself showed, one cannot directly perceive (as least in normal introspection) anything more than these inner states themselves.[9]

In the main argument, therefore, the only empirical premise is the intuitively self-evident proposition that there *are* states of consciousness, for example, wish, aversion, effort, pleasure, and pain.

In the Cartesian dictum we cannot straightforwardly take the *ergo* as a sign of inferential passage, because Descartes considered *sum* to be a primitive certainty and leaned heavily on its self-evident character. It would be a gross mistake to think that Descartes was deducing "I exist" from a general major premise such as "Whatever thinks exists."[10] Even for the Naiyāyika, there is no property F such that whatever has or lacks F has or lacks existence. They were constantly criticizing the Buddhist attempt to *define* existence in terms of causal productivity, *because* there is no way of *proving* any such generalization as "Whatever Fs exists." But one seems to find evidence that Descartes too sometimes formulated the *cogito-sum* in the form of an *inference*. If I am to stop with what is immediately and incorrigibly given to me, I cannot assert anything more than Lichtenberg's tag, "There is a thought."[11] From this, if we are to pass to a thinker, which Descartes explicitly says is *not* identical with his or her thinking,[12] we must take recourse to an inference. This is precisely the inference Descartes divulges in the face of Hobbes' third objection, which constitutes at least part of Gautama's intended proof. "It is certain," says Descartes, "that thinking cannot exist without a thing which thinks, or generally, that any accident or activity cannot be without a substance of which it is an activity."[13] This sounds like an echo of Vātsyāyana's argument,[14] except that what Descartes loosely calls "accident or activity" is classified by Vātsyāyana as *quality*, and that Descartes cannot, without inconsistency, show up the "derived" inferential nature of the conclusion that the self exists.[15]

Symbolizing Gautama's argument

Gautama's own argument, as spelled out by Vātsyāyana, is most naturally taken by Uddyotakara and Vācaspati as a couple of arguments riveted together. But it is mentioned in the *Bhāṣya* as *one* complete argument exemplifying the *sāmānyatodṛṣṭa* type of inference. A formal proof of the validity of the argument may be given as follows:

Sx: x is a substance
Qx: x is a quality
Ixy: x inheres in y
Cx: x is a conscious state (e.g., desire)
Bx: x is a body (or *manas* or *dik or indriya*)

Adopting the above symbolism, the premises can be written as:

1. $(\exists x)Cx$ [There are states of consciousness or mental events]
2. $(\forall x)(Cx \supset Qx)$ [States of consciousness are qualities]

3. $(\forall x)[Qx \supset (\exists y)(Sy \,\&\, Ixy)]$	[All qualities inhere in some substance or other]
4. $(\forall x)[Cx \supset (\forall y)(By \supset {\sim}Ixy)]$	[Conscious states do not inhere in any corporeal substance, e.g. body]

Hence the inference:

5. Ca	1 EI
6. $Ca \supset Qa$	2 UI
7. $Qa \supset (\exists y)(Sy \,\&\, Iay)$	3 UI
8. Qa	5, 6 MP
9. $(\exists y)(Sy \,\&\, Iay)$	7, 8 MP
10. $Sb \,\&\, Iab$	9 EI
11. $Ca \supset (\forall y)(By \supset {\sim}Iay)$	4 UI
12. $(\forall y)(By \supset {\sim}Iay)$	5, 11 MP
13. $Bb \supset {\sim}Iab$	12 UI
14. $Iab \supset {\sim}Bb$	13 Trans, DN
15. Iab	10 Simp
16. ${\sim}Bb$	14, 15 MP
17. Sb	10 Simp
18. $Sb \,\&\, {\sim}Bb$	16, 17 Conj
19. $(\exists x)(Sx \,\&\, {\sim}Bx)$	18 EG, Q.E.D.

Notice that the conclusion only proves that there is some substance other than the body, etc., which amounts to "there is a self." This representation of the argument as a *single* one proving the contention that qualities like desire inhere in a substance other than body, etc., also accords with Jayanta's formulation.

A two-part argument?

If, on the other hand, we follow the suggestions of Uddyotakara and Vācaspati, we interpret the argument as two-tier. The first step is a clear BARBARA of the Aristotelian syllogistic mood:

1. All qualities call for a substance to which they belong.
2. Desire, aversion, cognition, pleasure, pain, volition are qualities.
3. Desire, etc., call for a substance to which they belong.

Both the *Vartika* and the *Tātparyaṭīkā say* that *this* is the genuine *sāmānyatodṛsṭa* inference. Since this proves only the dependence of the consciousness-qualities upon some other substance—*icchādī guṇānām pārātantryaṃ*, says Vācaspati—it must be supplemented by a further *s' eṣavat* argument to the effect that this *other* substance is no other than the spiritual substance or soul. This suggested complementary second step is a disjunctive syllogism:

4. The substance to which desire, etc., belong is either earth or water or air or fire or *ākāúa* (or a conglomeration of these), or space or time or *manas* or it is some *ninth* substance different from all these.

5. Neither earth nor water … nor *manas* is the substance to which desire, etc., belong.
6. Some ninth substance different from all these is that to which desire, etc., belong.

To complete the argument we have only to add the verbal decision of calling that non-physical non-psychological substance, to which all of our conscious experiences are ascribed, the Self or *ātman*.

The major premise of the first step in the above argument, namely that every quality is predicated on a substance, has been often challenged by phenomenalists and by those whom Strawson calls no-ownership theorists. Such philosophers say the so-called inner-states as well as the posited objects of those states need not necessarily be *owned* by or *belong* to something beyond themselves. In the external world, such a supportless show of (naturally unsharable, hence private) sense-objects leads to a sort of solipsistic flux-doctrine. But, in the inner world, non-ascription of experiences might give rise to bizarre interjections such as: "Here is a nice piece of jubilation! There, a bit of jealousy, and lo! What a clear act of belief!" The explanation of experiences having the logically unwashable stamp of being *someone's* in terms of their happening around a body does not always work: certain unlocated conceptual thoughts are simply not ascribable to the body. Still, the general premise that qualities have to be ascribed to something stands unchallenged. A Naiyāyika argues elaborately against the objection: *na guṇa vyatiriktaś ca guṇī nāmāsti kincana*—"This is no quality-possessor over and above the qualities."[16] Premise [B] has also been challenged: qualityhood does not belong to desire, etc., so the conjecture of a substratum is superfluous: *guṇatvamapi nāstyasya yato 'dhisṭhāna kalpanā.*[17]

Uddyotakara supports their categorization as qualities by an eliminative argument. Since mental states are usually short-lived (none of them are eternal), they cannot be either universals, ultimate particularities (residing in atoms), or the relation of inherence. There are other technical reasons for not classing them as either actions or substances. They can only be qualities. Once we admit [A] and [B], [C] follows logically. Now, to be a substance in the Vaiśeṣika and Nyāya framework, something must be either any of the eight already admitted types or a new, ninth one. So [D] is analytically derived from [C] in the Nyāya ontology. The most interesting and controversial move is [E] which cancels the candidature of body, *manas*, and other sense faculties as the owner-substance of desire, etc. This is the Naiyāyika's battle against physicalists of different shades.

Why anything material cannot be this self

Since nobody ever takes earth, water, fire, or air to be individually the support of states of consciousness or to be possessors of P-predicates, the Naiyāyika also does not consider them separately. Fire cannot feel pain, entertain beliefs, plan actions, or have thoughts. Both Praśastapāda, the Vaiśeṣika commentator, and Kaṇāda show how such a thesis would lead to the absurd position that the referent of the terms "I" and "earth" (etc.) are the same.

It is only through the human body, their joint product, that corporeal substances have maintained their age-old rivalry with the spiritual substance. Materialistic theories of self-body identity have sprung in all ages from common speech-forms like, "I am overweight," from the logical necessity of giving ground to our ascription of mental predicates to *other* persons of whom only the body is surely cognizable to any of us, and from other reductive behavioristic considerations. The Nyāya rejects the thesis that consciousness is a property of the physical body on the following grounds.[18]

a. If a quality (like color) belongs to a body, it inheres in it as long as the body lasts, unless some new antagonistic quality (falling under the same *determinable)* comes to replace it. But consciousness is not found in the body at death, when often the body stays intact and no other opposite *(pratidvandvī)* quality of the same category supplants consciousness, which is just found missing.

We cannot explain this fact by an analogy with speed (*vega*), which is a quality of some bodies *at some times*, but may not continue to be in them as long as the bodies exist. Speed is *caused* by some other factor, *namely motion*—a sort of activity (of going, *gamanam) of* the same body with whose ceasing speed ceases. We cannot find any corresponding cause either in or outside the body to be held responsible for the occasional emergence and disappearance of consciousness. It is tempting to argue against this since for the Nyāya theorist even the soul does not contain consciousness-attributes during its career as a substance. In liberation, the soul is said to shake them off. The same *ayāvaddravyabhāvitva* will then disqualify consciousness for being a special attribute even of the soul. But it is only about the special qualities of *the body* (not *all* qualities of *all* substances) that the Naiyāyika forms the *vyāpti* that they are *unlosable* by the physical substance. This weakens the objection.

From the general point, later summed up by Viśvanātha as *mṛteṣu vyabhicārataḥ*, one can develop a more neutral argument to the effect that if Mr. X's body is the same as *the same* Mr. X who felt the wish, *knew* the propositions, planned the action, etc., why can't we point at the body and say, "That is Mr. X over there!" after Mr. X's death, when for all practical purposes Mr. X's body is still there?

A similar argument has been hinted at by Kripke in the following footnote:

The simplest Cartesian argument can perhaps be restated as follows:

Let A be a name (rigid designator) *of* Descartes' body. Then Descartes argues that since he could exist even if A did not, $\Diamond$(Descartes≠A), hence Descartes≠A.

> Those who have accused him of a modal fallacy have forgotten that 'A' is rigid … On the other hand, provided that Descartes is regarded as having ceased to exist after his death, "Descartes≠A" can be established without the use of a modal argument; for, if so, no doubt *A survived Descartes* when A was a corpse. Thus A had a property (existing at a certain time) which Descartes did not.[19]

Obviously this last formulation goes against the immortality of the self, but we state it as "*A survived a vanishing of the mental states*."

b. Since consciousness is present *all over* the body, any part of it (because parts of a substance are also substances) must be called "a conscious substance" or a "feeler" or "a wisher," if we are to attribute consciousness to the body at all. But this leads to the absurd position that one body contains multiple conscious subjects, which participate in each other's private experience.
c. The final and weightiest argument is from the observation that consciousness cannot be an attribute of the body because it is basically *dissimilar* to bodily qualities. Color, sound, weight, etc., however dissimilar to each other, are either available to external perception or are totally imperceptible, because they are *dispositional* and are to be inferred. *Occurrent* conscious states are neither publicly observable by external sense organs nor completely imperceptible, but are *internally perceptible* only through the "*privileged access*" of the subject of those experiences.

Besides privacy, there are other respects in which a mental state is generically different from a physical state, for example, intentionality *(saviṣayakatva)* and unlocatability (but for somatic sensation). We cannot sensibly ask, "Does your knowledge measure four square feet?" or "Is your remorse to the west of your sulk?" By this very argument, we may hope to explore the most plausible behaviorist or central-state materialist theory. However close correlation and unfailing agreement in presence and absence one may show between a reported mental event and a recorded physiological event, one cannot identify the two or say that the pang itself is that particular event in the autonomic nervous system. The strongest evidence of positive and negative concomitance between two phenomena does not establish that the one is *due* to the other, or is an inherent quality of the other. While the pang is felt or perceived internally, the physiological event is either inferred or externally observed in the laboratory (most normally *by others,* not by the subject himself).[20]

If the central-state identity theory were correct, I could never know, except by subsequently inferring from X-ray plates or by trusting the authority of physiologists, that I am having a painful experience or even that I am angry because what happens inside my central nervous system is simply not perceptible by me. All of Ryle's rhetorical tricks fail to account for the patently occurrent and directly perceptible feeling we have of, for example, a flashing solution to a mathematical problem. To account for these kinds of phenomena, we must bring in a "*private stage*," for we do not observe them by seeing ourselves or infer them from physiological reports. Not *all* mental states are explicable as *dispositions* to behave in a certain fashion. Later the Naiyāyikas also stressed the point that only states like knowledge or wish can be *directed toward* or *about* an object, whereas no bodily qualities are such.

Can the inner sense do the job?

To establish the status of the self as a ninth independent substance, one must show that its job cannot be done by the *manas*. The *manas* most naturally demands "mind" as its English equivalent, because that word *does* carry that sense in most non-philosophical contexts.[21] But to the Western philosopher in general, no distinction between mind and self, or *soul*, is intelligible. There is no talk of a mind or an internal sense organ over and above the self. The necessity of admitting both entities (*ātman* and *manas*) emerges in the course of Vātsyāyana's arguments against the thesis that the *manas* itself can be the *substance* which we are looking for as the owner of conscious states.

If we simply *call* the possessor of desire, etc., *manas* or "mind," that would be an uncontroversial nomenclatural decision. Thus, it is of no importance to observe that in Western philosophy, "The self comes in contact with the mind" makes for an idiomatic howler, whereas in Indian philosophy of mind, the *ātma-manaḥ-saṃyoga* is a necessary condition of all kinds of cognition. If, of course, we go further to identify the *knower* of the inner states with the *instrument* of our introspective cognition, we shall be making an unwarranted exception to the general rule (which we *have* to admit in the case of external sensation): there is a substantival knower besides the instrumental organ (= faculty) in every case of perception.

If we do not require a *mantā* (minder) over and above a *mananakriyākaraṇa* (the instrumental cause of the act of minding), why should we require a *draṣṭā* (seer) over and above the *darśana krīyākaraṇa* (the instrumental cause of the act of seeing, i.e., the visual sense)? Yet we are compelled to posit some "seer" over and above the eyes. As Socrates cautions Theaetetus, it is not the eyes that see but we (or our souls) that see through the windows of the eyes. It is this soul which survives the loss or damage of the sense-faculties and remembers its once-collected *data*. It survives and remembers because it is *not* identical with the sense organ itself, hence the general rule of distinguishing the instrument from the subject of a sensation or experience.

When showing the need to posit a substantial perceiver distinct from the perceptual organs, Vātsyāyana makes a Ryle-esque distinction. The common speech-forms "A is X-ing with B" implies a distinction between A and B. Sometimes, this implication is just a false linguistic illusion. Vātsyāyana's example for this could have fitted snugly in the last few pages of the *Concept of Mind*: "The building stands by its pillars." From this sentence, we cannot correctly infer that the building is some separate substance *quite* other than the pillars which are just *instruments* for its action of standing. It is, in Vātsyāyana's words, "A statement regarding the whole and its parts, and not regarding one and another thing."[22] But sometimes the suggestion of duality is based on a real distinction. In the sentence, "The cutter is lopping the tree with his axe," the cutter and the axe are surely two different things. With this preface, Vātsyāyana proceeds to inquire whether when we use sentence like "I am seeing with my eyes" or "He is introspecting with his inner sense," the "I," and the "eyes" and the "He" and the "inner sense" are to be interpreted after the 'building-pillar' model or after the 'cutter-axe' model.

How he rejects the former model and finds only the latter suitable for our reports of mental acts is partly indicated above. A further argument for the object-neutral (*avyavasthita*) common subject distinct from the object-specific (*vyavasthita*) sense-faculties is derived from the important intuitive evidence of feeling by touch and seeing by eyesight the *same* object.

In a significant sutra, Gautama proves the self non-identical with any specific sensibility or any aggregate of sensibilities: *darśana sparśanābhyāmekārtha grahaṇāt*.[23] Both the *unity* of the *object* and the *unity of* the *subject* are proved by a transcendental argument which strongly resembles Kant's argument in his first version of the Transcendental Deduction. There must be an object which supports both the visual and the tactual qualities and is continuant enough to be reidentified by different sense-reports (hence the objection to the momentariness or nonexistence *of* the external object of perception). Similarly, I cannot account for such introspective data as belonging to the same myself who had touched the object and is now seeing it, unless there were some *subject,* some *unity* of apperception behind all these sense experiences. This explains why, when Nyāya combats the Buddhist theory of the non-existence of external objects, it also attacks no-soulism. *kṣaṇabhaṅgavāda* and *nairātmyavāda* are taken care of by the same sort of arguments.

One subject cannot conceivably remember the experience *of* another, but the fact of *synaesthesia* shows that a sense-datum appropriate to one sense often arouses reaction in another—e.g., the very *look* of once-tasted food may stimulate some sensation in our palate. Furthermore, if the sense of sight in one were a distinct *perceiver* itself other than the sense of touch or the inner sense, the following introspection would be impossible: "I am touching this coldish paper, perceiving its white color, and also thinking these thoughts." This happens because, as Praśatapāda says, "There is one on-looker who can look at different things at the same time through its different windows."[24]

Putting the two parts of the argument together again

The question of the supporting substance of consciousness being *dik* (space), *kāla* (time) or *ākāśa* (aether) does not arise. They are introduced into the ontology to serve specific purposes, namely, of accounting for our valid cognition of spatial determinations, our sense of duration and change, and our auditory sensation.

Thus, we have equipped ourselves with the negative premise for the residual (*parīúeṣa*) argument:

> Body, *manas*, sense-faculties *dik, kāla*, or ākāśa are not eligible to be the holder *of desire*, etc., which, being *bhāvas* (cognitive states or at *any* rate mental qualities) cannot be unreceptacled, hence the soul has to be admitted as the ninth substance which supports these qualities.[25]

But to honor Vātsyāyana's original intention, we may also represent the whole argument as *one sāmānyatodṛṣṭa* inference and typically so, since the relation between the *liṅga* (mark/reason/*hetu*) and the *liṅgi* (to-be-inferred *object; anumeya*) is not accessible to perception (*apratyakṣe liṅga-liṅginoḥ sambandhe*) and since the *anumeya* gets established through its community with some other *feature*, namely the substance-demanding parasitical nature of all qualities. Note that Vātsyāyana was operating with a notion of *anumeya* which is not quite the later concept of *sādhya*. In his inference, the *Self* itself is the thing to be inferred and the logical structure of the inference is *less* articulate. The qualities like desire are the *liṅga* or *marks* from which the *marked* or *liṅgi,* that is, the self, is inferred—although it is by itself absolutely intrinsically imperceptible[26]—hence the classification of the whole unbroken inference *sāmānyato dṛṣṭa*.

Jayanta, who shows how we *can* reformulate any inference to make it look like *pûrvavat, seṣavat*, or *sāmānyatodṛṣṭa*, gives us a rigorous *unitary* picture of the inference with the Nyāya-scholastic device of sandwiching more than one *hetu* to prove a compound *sādhya*:

> Qualities like desire, etc. [= *pakṣa*] inhere in some substance other than the body, etc. [= *sādhya*] because, they are qualities of such a type that there are logical obstacles in taking the body or any other substance as their substratum.[27]

Other supporting proofs of the self

Although Gautama explicitly mentions only cognition, conation, aversion, desire, pleasure, and pain as marks from which we can infer the self's nature and existence, we can prove it also from many other *hetus*. The *Nyāyamañjarī*, for example, suggests a handful of alternative reasons why it is incumbent upon us to admit a non-corporeal self. The self can be inferred from the instrumental nature of the sense faculties which need an agent to wield them, from the goal-seeking behavior of the human body, from the self-heating, self-developing, unique nature of a living organism which points to an interested *person* inhabiting it who, as it were, "looks after his own house," or from the analysis of any *of* the processes of valid cognition—which consist in bringing together successive mental acts. Jayanta explains how even the undeniable fact that any of us can understand the meaning of words used by another points to the existence of one cognizer who takes heed of all the sounds, builds up the meaning systematically, and yields a complete cognition of sentence-meaning.[28]

The latest theories of understanding a language as a kind of implicit *knowledge* which, however *inchoate,* is an *inner* disposition of the listener are strikingly similar to Jayanta's account of our grasp of meaning. Both point to *a knower* who abides. These last seven chapters attempted to elucidate what the existence of that knower—the self—entails. We are brought back to the simple question about intersubjective perception that drives this book. That question has been partially analyzed: we discussed the object of your and my perception and the nature of subjectivity. We now must address the problems of the second person—the other I—for our project to be complete. How do *I* know how *you* feel since I am not you? The second-person singular pronoun demands the kinds of selfhood and uniqueness which I recognize in myself, but places them outside of me. And yet, you, as a second subject, are not merely a part of nature. This trouble—the trouble with you—is what I turn to in the first chapter of the last part of the book.

Part Three

Other Subjects

17

Knowing You from the Bridge

Introduction

By "you"- I mean any second person whom I can address. The main trouble with *you* is that you are a *self*, but not *myself*. This may be the root of the better-known "existential trouble" of human relations: I want You, but I cannot stand You. In this chapter, I would like to address a different yet equally troubled relation between the first and the second person: our epistemic access to the second person's inner, especially emotional, states.

The trouble with You can be traced back to a more basic trouble with I: its demand for uniqueness that it cannot rationally refuse to share with other similar uniqueness-demanding subjects. Yet, what could it mean to *share uniqueness*? If both you and I must be unique with respect to the single property of being "the self," there seem to be only two alternatives: either (1) to strictly, numerically equate you with I because such identity follows from both being equated to a single Self, or (2) to take turns and sometimes recognize the Ego alone and sometimes the Other alone to be the only self. But neither option constitutes genuine "sharing," let alone "facing each other," whatever that seductive phrase means.

The I is in "trouble" insofar as it desires a You. Both the ancient Upaniṣads and the modern Immanuel Kant give voice to this logico-emotional dilemma of *needing* and *fearing* a second.[1] Kant calls this "the unsocial sociability" of human nature.[2] The Upaniṣads call this the self-imposed veil of ignorance of the self.

In certain kinds of suffering, I feel so alone in the world that I have to let others know about my loneliness. The basic trouble is that I understand you best when I stand next to you in your troubled times and confess to you that I fail to understand you fully. I somehow open myself to your wound just when I feel most acutely that it does not hurt me quite the way it hurts you. To feel your separateness from me, I need to imaginatively fill up the hollow of your foreignness with the kernel of my subjectivity and face you as if I am facing myself. I must empty myself of my first-person-ness and give all my I-ness to you.

It is well-known that solipsism cannot expect endorsement or acknowledge disagreement. Despite this logical awkwardness, doesn't each of us, independently of the use of the first person singular pronoun, feel imprisoned in a solitary bubble?

I am not myself unless I recognize my qualitative identity with and numerical distinction from you. I need you to speak to me, listen to me, or ignore me. I learned calling myself "I" from your calling me "you." When my teacher says to me, "You are confused," I correctly interpret him as saying that I am confused. There must be some translation rules from the word "you" to the word "I." Yet I am not one with you (in the singular), and I am not one-of-you (in the plural).

We are distinct as ego and non-ego, but we are the same as self or subject, and that is why when I refer jointly to you and I, I don't say "you" in the plural, or "the two of you." I say "we" or "the two of us." Together we are two or more *first persons*. When a second or a third person joins the first person in a group, they become members of a first person plural group; but apart, I alone am I and you are another. Much of this may well be a linguistic muddle—but not all of it.

The other connected epistemological trouble with you is that when you are angry sometimes (but not always) I *know* that you are angry but I still don't quite feel your anger. If I did feel, your anger would be *my* anger, and therefore not your anger. Sometimes I can see that you are feeling an emotion when you really are, without myself having those emotions. But, in a puzzling way, your annoyance, when immediately felt by me, becomes my (having your) annoyance. Yet, the only emotions I seem to directly experience are emotions I have. It seems perfectly possible for me to see your nose without having your nose, but somehow not so easy for me to experientially and immediately feel your rage without having that rage too.

Dharmakīrti's argument from analogy with the first person

How can I know that you are listening? I know that you are distracted. How do I know that? The classical answer given by Dharmakīrti is an argument from analogy.[3] His account is slightly different from John Stuart Mill's formulation, which simply says that since some of my bodily changes and actions are correlated with introspected inner feelings, at least some of another's observed bodily changes must also be preceded by inner stirrings.[4] When I run toward an object, I first feel a desire for that object. Therefore, the other must feel a similar desire when running. Dharmakīrti puts it more cautiously and negatively:

> Since the movements and actions experienced in another body are not caused by any will or cognition within my/this stream of consciousness, they would either be uncaused, or caused by a will or cognition which is outside this stream of consciousness, belonging to another stream. Since we cannot coherently call such observed actions uncaused, there must exist other streams of awareness.[5]

Four hundred years after Dharmakīrti, another Yogācāra logician named Ratnakīrti wrote "Refutation of the Other Stream-of-consciousness" (*Santānāntaradūṣaṇa*), which exposed fatal fallacies in justifications of inferential claims about other minds. I will run just a simplified version his complex refutation here.

In Indian logic, all inferences from sign F to unobserved property G must be based on prior knowledge of a universal concomitance of the form: *wherever there is an F, there is a G, such that G cannot be absent where F is present*. Now, what is the prover-sign (*hetu*) for my inference that there is another stream of beliefs and desires in you? It has to be your talk, your tone of voice, your facial expressions, your movements. What is the basis for the supporting universal concomitance? Well, it must be the agreement in presence and absence I observe in my own case. When I do not introspect any believing and desiring states in myself, I do not see any corresponding conversation or conduct either. Now, failure to perceive something is not proof of its absence. Only non-perception of that which is perceptible is taken as proof of absence.

Ratnakīrti challenges the I-to-You generalizer: is this desiring mind which I wish to prove inside Your body visible or invisible? If Your desire is visible but never seen or felt by me, it must be non-existent. If, on the other hand, it is in principle invisible (like an electron), then the mere fact that I do not see it will never prove that it is not there. But if we cannot be sure of its absence, we cannot establish *agreement* in absence. So how could we be certain that wherever there is absence of desire and cognition, there is absence of movement and talk? The only way I could confirm the universal concomitance between the external signs and the internal states to be inferred would be to observe the presence and absence of internal states (even outside myself) in many cases in the presence and absence of the external signs. But that would involve direct perception of the inner states of others. Clairvoyant ability would render the analogical inference process redundant!

Ratnakīrti then proceeds to show the intrinsic incoherence of the very idea of a phenomenal subjective state outside of the first person. If other streams of mind-states were possible, I would always observe myself as either (1) distinct, (2) non-distinct, or (3) neither distinct nor non-distinct from these other streams. But surely the last two options are unacceptable. I do not perceive myself to be non-distinct from You—my very being myself consists in not being You or He—and to be neither distinct nor non-distinct is a logical contradiction which I cannot ascribe to Your mind-stream. So the first option is the only plausible one: I perceive the series of my own mental states as distinct from your series. But a distinction between one thing and another cannot appear unless both appear distinctly. Yet, by our own admission, I can only see or feel my own stream of perceptions, emotions, desires, pleasures, and pains. I can never see yours. Thus, the distinction between my stream or its waves and your stream or its waves cannot clearly appear to me. Since none of the three possible consequences of its assumption can be accepted, the other stream of mental states is not even a coherent possibility. Not only you do not exist as a conscious being other than me, you are also not even consistently conceivable!

But the point of this exercise was not to prove solipsism. The point was to show that inferring the existence of other feeling and desiring minds is useless.

Strawson's devastating critique of the argument from analogy

Peter Strawson raised objections against the analogical argument for other minds.[6] It is too mild a complaint to say that the analogical inference is a bad inductive argument given that it is from a *single case*. Strawson insisted that even in the single case of myself the mental predicate cannot be coherently applied, unless I already know how to apply it to others. If a P-predicate (psychological predicate) is ego-centric, it is not a general predicate at all. The skeptical question that Dharmakīrti answers with the analogical argument cannot be coherently *posed* because the concept of a person—a "*santāna*," or "stream," in the Yogācāra Buddhist case—would not be a concept unless there was more than one instance of it. The consciousness predicates, in order to be self-ascribed, have to be other-ascribable because of the generality constraint on any intelligible predicate.

Strawson shows how we do not need to reduce your inner state of depression to your depressed behavior. Neither should we be skeptical like the typical dualist or obsessed with first person privileged access. Although I know that I am depressed by direct first person introspection, whereas I know that you are depressed by using your depressed behavior as a "criterion" for my ascription of that predicate to you, the predicate retains its sameness of meaning across these two sorts of application-rules. If it did not, it would not be a P-predicate. According to Strawson, if psychological predicates were only mine, then they would not even be mine.

I could not tell others that I am depressed in my private language and expect to be understood. "x is depressed" is a predicate which I feel from inside when I attach it to myself, but observe from outside in you.

Two competing contemporary theories of second person mind-reading

The contemporary Western scene in cognitive science and philosophy of mind is roughly an ongoing tussle between two competing theories of our apprehension of the second person's mind.

Theory-Theory

Mental states are *theoretical posits* like electrons or magnetic fields, and are equally unobservable. Around the age of four, a child starts manifesting his or her tacit knowledge of a set of causal-explanatory conditionals by connecting current behavior with future or past or current behavior or mental states. For example:

If she is so red in the face, she is going to cry.
If he came back from the door, he must have forgotten to take his keys.

Hundreds of such conditional interpretation-rules constitute the child's rough-and-ready theory of mind, which is also known as "folk psychology." One major rift within the Theory-Theory camp is between empiricists such as Paul Churchland[7] who claim that a folk psychology is entirely learned by the child from its human environment, and innatists such as Peter Carruthers[8] who argue that the child is born with a core theory of mind, whose law-like connections it could not pick up by merely observing and interacting with others.

Simulation theory

Šimulation theory is in competition with Theory-Theory. The core idea is enshrined in the popular idiom of oneself getting into someone else's shoes in order to figure out how he or she feels. If A notices B in a certain condition and "understands" that B is nervous, anxious, or embarrassed, the steps of simulation are supposed to be the following:

- A observes B in an uncomfortable position with certain bodily changes.
- A imagines himself in B's (bodily contextual) position and imagines having such overt changes.
- A simulates, impersonates, pretends that he or she is B.
- A (in the role of B) undergoes some feelings, experiences, beliefs, desires, etc., as if they are A's own.
- A de-links these mental states from his or her own ego-involvement.
- The outputs of this simulation process are taken and tagged on to B.
- A knows or has some justification to believe that B feels afraid, anxious, embarrassed, etc.

What is the most vital distinction between these two accounts of mind-reading? It seems that they have split between themselves the two insights that originally prompted the analogical inference view. Theory-Theorists seem to adopt the inferential figuring out part but ignore the analogical "what if I were you" part. The mind-reader need not introspect or play at introspecting on this account. In the simulation-theory, my similarity to you is crucial. To the extent that I can make you myself, in this make-believe re-enactment, the rest of the inner story is supposed to automatically unroll—following no set of theoretically articulable connections—as detachable narrative of my own pretend-branching-out life.

Theory-Theorists treat others as living objects of explanation, study them in interaction with each other, and ascribe them mental states in the functionalist sense of the term. Simulationists, on the other hand, remain under the common Cartesian spell that subjective mental states are best apprehended in oneself, and then grafted on to others.

Abhinavagupta on other minds

Abhinavagupta first reconstructs Dharmakīrti's version of the analogical inference for the existence of other minds:

> It could be said that in myself I observe voluntary actions such as utterance of words, invariably pervaded by a wish of the form "let me speak" assuming the causal role. Now, such actions as speaking must therefore be preceded by such inner wish even in the body of Caitra—the body which is not mine. By self-awareness I have established the connection between my will and my action. From another's action I can infer back a will outside the stream of my consciousness, therefore the existence of another stream of consciousness is easily established. Couldn't we say that?[9]

Then subsequently exposes a fatal logical error:

> Here, one who infers has two types of experience of utterance of words. At the time of establishing the rule of universal concomitance (*vypti*) the drawer of the inference correlates the experience or phenomenon describable as "I am uttering words" with the subjective experience "I have a desire to communicate."[10]

But in applying the rule of *vyāpti* to the case of the other body, he at best has the experience or the sense-datum "That other body is emitting words." Now, this new phenomenon, "that body utters," unconnected with the subjectivity of the one who draws the inference, is quite distinct from the sign which has been established as concomitant with an inner desire, since that sign was "I am uttering." The first person cause (*my inner desire*) may explain the occurrence of the first person effect (*my utterance*). How can it explain the distinct type of third person effect: *his utterance*? And if I know that what I have to infer from your utterance is not my inner desire but your desire to speak, then I must have already formed the concept of you as another person capable of having desires. In that case, the whole inference to the existence of the other stream of consciousness is rendered redundant.

Abhinavagupta thus threatens the classical analogical inference with a dangerous dilemma: either (1) the inferential sign "uttering of words by the other body" is inconclusive, or (2) the argument begs the question. In (1) the sign is inconclusive because it has no pre-established general connection with the inner states of wishing, etc. The inductively generalizable sign is based in one's own case and would thus be "uttering of words by me" connected to "my meaning something." The alleged inferential sign "emission of word-sounds from that other body" is entirely unlike the felt first person phenomenon of my uttering words, which means that the inference fails. In the alternative case (2), one has already learned to treat "he utters words" as a special case of "I utter words" ("I" here is a mere place-marker for general subjectivity). Thus, the existence of a first person—a self-in-the-other body—is already established. As such, the analogical inference is not required. It follows that the so-called proof of other minds is either inconclusive or circular.[11]

Post-Cartesian Western thought finds the problem of the Other Mind challenging and the very presence of the Other existentially constraining and self-annihilating. Abhinavagupta, on the other hand, finds the You to be a foundational middle-reality between the pure Self and the apparent non-Self, in contrast and community with which the Self discovers its own playful knower-hood.

Perhaps this proves that what a single person comes to apprehend and imagine is woven into a single self-enjoying creative I-consciousness that is tolerant of a projected plurality of times—my past, my present, and my future. But, as we asked in Chapter 11, what can we make of the distinction between one cognitive-emotive agent and another?

We saw that Abhinavagupta argues against such otherness.[12] Distinguishing itself presupposes knowledge of the distinguished, and is thereby brought within the light of I-ness even when the distinguished is another self. Thus, even the awareness in/of the other is indeed one's own Self![13]

Did Abhinavagupta anticipate the recently discovered developmental link between mirror-neurons responsible for gestural mimicry and language ability in a child;

between the sense of self and empathy; or between action, interpersonal affect, and conscious cognition? He surely embraced a Max Scheler type "direct perception" view of our knowledge of other people's feelings. But more speculatively he gestured toward a transcendental argument from the very possibility of genuine empathy and interpersonal communication to the underlying unity of all sentience.

It turns out that our isolation may not be so deep and existential if it is bridgeable through conversation and empathy. Conversation and empathy are made possible by language, which has a function beyond referring to and stating truths about the world or expressing thoughts. Many languages have a vocative case: a distinct grammatical form of addressing other subjects and drawing them into relationship with the speaker. For this reason, neither the vocative case nor complex epithets deserve to be ignored in translation. This power of addressing as a subjectifying move will be the topic of the following chapter.

18

The Grammar of Calling the Other

Calling

We do not only speak *of* other people, we also speak *to* them. Often instead of starting with a "You," which still awaits disambiguation between two or more addressees, we start with a vocative use of a personal proper name. "Roger, will you be free for lunch tomorrow?" we may say. In this chapter, I shall try to tackle some of the philosophical issues, not regarding the referring use, but regarding this vocative use of personal proper names.

In the first round of the game of philosophy of meaning, proper names appear to be meaningless tags or identifiers. If someone calls their car "Cleopatra," they can call their friend "BMW." In a particular context of use, "Whitehead," "Baghdad," "Mahatma," or "Jack-the-Ripper" picks out a particular historic or fictional place or person, but connotes nothing. That, at least, was the influential view upheld by John Stuart Mill and later revived with some frills from modal logic by Saul Kripke.

But what happens to proper names when they are used not to *refer* to the topic of conversation but to *address* or call someone? Consider the use of names in the following:

(a) "John, I am leaving"—or, more fatefully, "I am leaving you, John."
(b) "Kṛṣṇa! Keśava! Save me."

I am not referring to John or Kṛṣṇa here because, as Ramchandra Gandhi[1] has argued, the speech-act of addressing someone—in conversation or prayer—cannot be reduced to speaking of or about him or her.[2] If referring is an objectifying move, addressing is a subjectifying one. Even "you"-ing is subjectifying. Abhinavagupta suggests that in saying, "Listen, stones!" ("*śṛṇuta grāvāṇaḥ!*") one discovers one's own consciousness in the inert (i.e., outer) other, by giving that other some of one's own subjectivity. So, in addressing Kālī, I am not referring to Kālī. Neither am I *asserting*, nor am I *presupposing* her existence outside my speech-act. This, incidentally, is why non-believers can pray, and can pray for faith. Invocation can precede belief.

If the only meaning of the non-connotative proper name were its referential function of picking out the individual and if that function is lost in the vocative use, then "John" in (a) would have mere pragmatic use, but no semantic content at all—like hitting a wineglass with a fork to draw attention. But whose attention? And is calling "Kṛṣṇa, killer of Kaṃsa" semantically equivalent to calling out "Kṛṣṇa, Kṛṣṇa"? What about allusive or jocular occurrences:

(c) "John, I hope you are not a Baptist!"
(d) "John, can I use the John?"

In responsible translation how does one preserve the meaning of the vocatively performed proper name, if it is supposedly so entirely bereft of meaning? For a translator, there is of course a simple default strategy: transliterate! That at best makes the common *sound* hop into the space between languages, and the sound is important. But there is much more to calling your interlocutor by her name than just the mouthing of the sound of the name. In Sanskrit, the name is inflected in the vocative use: "*Durgā*" becomes "*Durge*," "*Hari*" becomes "*Hare*." How should we transliterate? Should we restore the name in its uninflected form?

The sense of the name seems, after all, all important. One is supposed to get the humor in:

(e) "Gayatri! Please protect us with your singing."[3]

As Tagore says, the infant who calls the mother just out of addiction to the name ("*shishu jemon māke, nāmer neshāy dāke*") does manage to call *her* by using and not merely mentioning or quoting the word "*mā*." Unlike in the grammatical aphorism "*agner ḍhak*," the vocatively inflected word "*agne*" in "*agna āyāhi vītaye*" does not refer to the word "*agne*." It refers to nothing, but *means* (helps us address) fire. There must be something fishy about Mill's merely denotative theory of singular names. It crashes completely in front of the addressing use of proper names.

Translating exclamatory address in the Gītā

This philosophical issue becomes a practical problem in the context of translating the Gītā. The following verse contains two vocatives:

Klaivyam māsma gamaḥ pārtha, naitat tvayy upapadyate,
kṣudram hṛdayadaurvalyam tyaktvottiṣṭha paramtapa!

One vocative is clearly a proper name (*pārtha*). The other has descriptive content (*paraṃtapa*). Usually the former is left untranslated, while the latter is translated with "O! Scorcher of Enemies" (One who makes the other [*param*] suffer [*tapa*])." But why not translate Pārtha as "Son of Pṛthā"?

In her introduction to a recent translation of the Gīta, Laurie Patton explains that she chose to translate the epithets Arjuna and Krishna use for each other because those epithets "function like nicknames in the *Gita*, where Kṛṣṇa and Arjuna engage in a kind of ironic banter on the subject at hand."[4] Indeed, I would go further. *The play of vocatives breaks down the distinction sacrosanct to post-Millian analytic philosophy between names and descriptions*. Take Arjuna's impassioned response to Kṛṣṇa:

> *Killer of Madhu*, how will I fight back Droṇa and Bhīṣma with arrows in battle?
> How will I fight these worship-worthy men, *Killer of the Enemy*?[5]

Let us see how two standard English translations deal with the almost identical vocatives "*madhusūdana*" and "*arisūdana*." Sargeant uses the ubiquitous "O" which is supposed to do the work of the vocative (zero-) suffix:

> How can I kill in battle Bhīṣma and Droṇa, O Slayer of Madhu?
> How can I fight with arrows against these two venerable men,
> O Slayer of The Foe?[6]

Barbara Stoler Miller simply ignores the sense (*Sinn*) of the vocative and replaces it with reference (*Bedeutung*) preserving "Kṛṣṇa" and clipping off the second vocative: Kṛṣṇa, how can I fight against Bhīṣma and Droṇa with arrows when they deserve my worship?[7]

What none of the English translators notice is that traditional Sanskrit commentators pay much more attention to the specificities of the vocative epithet/names. One of them famously comments under this verse: "the two vocatives '*Madhusūdana*' and '*Arisūdana*' should not be taken as the defect of repetition because they show how emotionally unstable Arjuna is by the fact that by the end of the sentence he has forgotten how he had addressed Kṛṣṇa at the start of it."[8] And of course, harping on Kṛṣṇa as being a killer of his enemies has the implicature, "of course YOU will want me to kill even these venerable folks."

It is well-known, thanks to Frege and Quine, that in an intensional or opaque context co-referential expressions are not truth-preservingly interchangeable. We cannot rewrite "Oedipus desired that Jocasta should sleep with him" as "Oedipus desired that his mother should sleep with him." Of course, the question of truth-preservation cannot be raised because, as we shall see later, vocative addressing use of names and definite description does not enter into the asserted content of the sentences. But the question still remains whether co-referential vocatives are interchangeable in the addressing context. Can we translate "Pārtha! Give up this small-hearted weakness" as "Arjuna! Give up this small-hearted weakness"?

Bhartṛhari on the semantics of the vocative

From Bhartṛhari onward, Indian philosophical grammarians considered two major philosophical issues regarding the vocative.

- Is it a "*kāraka*," a proper *case*—role directly semantically related to the verb as the nominative, accusative, instrumental, dative, ablative, and locative cases are?
- If it is not, is the meaning of the vocative at all part of the sentence-meaning?

In Vākyapadīya, part III, on the kārakas, Bhartṛhari remarks:

> *Sambodhana* is known as nothing but the function of making that which is already accomplished (the commandee or addressee) turn toward oneself (the speaker). Once the self meant by the noun-phrase is made to face the speaker, it is then employed to the action meant by a verb in the imperative mood, etc. Thus, what is meant by the vocative is not (part of) sentence-meaning. That is the tradition coming from the ancients.[9]

Bhartṛhari then argues that the assertion that Arjuna actually scorches his enemy is no part of the imperative sentence-meaning of "Give up this small weakness of the heart, and rise, Scorcher of Enemy!" In "John, please shut the door" the vocative "John" also stands outside the sentence meaning. Exegesis is not mere exposition. Helārāja argues against Bhartṛhari:

> Since the addressee is known independently of syntactic awaiting of other sentence-forming words, the vocatively meant is said to be no part of the sentence-meaning. But, just as with an implied but unspoken verb when even a single word such as "tree" could become a sentence, even a vocative must become [part of] the sentence-meaning.[10]

Clearly Helārāja has in mind cases in which the vocative "John!" means a warning or a plea: "John, beware" or "John, please don't!"

The "O! Krishna" predicament of the Bhagavadgītā translator

In one passage of the Gītā, Arjuna himself apologizes for his rash *vocative* use of epithets for Kṛṣṇa. In *A Critique of Post Colonial Reason*, Spivak focuses on these verses with great sensitivity. After being awestruck by the sublime vision of his friend Kṛṣṇa in the cosmic all-devouring form of Time chewing off all past, present and future kings and warriors, Arjuna shivers with joy and fear, and says:

> Taking you for a friend, whatever rash words I have spoken, calling you
> "Hey Kṛṣṇa," "Hey Yâdava," "Hey pal," clueless about your greatness, out of affection or error, please forgive those.[11]

This shows that the Sanskrit "*He Kṛṣṇa*" cannot be mechanically translated as "O! Kṛṣṇa," for the former sounds reverential and misses the past intimate frivolity. It would be ridiculous for Arjuna to apologize for his reverence. Mere "Kṛṣṇa" may be mistaken as a meaningless proper name standing outside the sentence meaning. So perhaps something like "You, of the Yadu clan" better communicates Arjuna's teasing informality. The exercise of translating the Gītā from Sanskrit reveals the spuriousness of the distinction between connotative epithets and non-connotative names and between performing the act of addressing and qualifying the action meant by the verb with the speaker's intended manner of drawing the hearer's attention.

After a certain point, the translator's obligation to deliver readability in the target language must bow out to her obligation to preserve the richness of the original. English should happily change in order to receive those qualifiers and epithets which make Sanskrit so rich, ironic, and allusive. Without slipping into archaisms, English can and sometimes does sacrifice its cool neglect of the performative content of vocative uses of descriptive and suggestive names in order to accommodate Sanskrit poetic content. When translating technical logico-philosophical Sanskrit, one is always frustrated by the no-win choice between inelegance and inaccuracy. When I translate technical Anglo-American philosophy into Sanskrit, I do not expect to write charming Sanskrit prose like Patañjali the grammarian or Śaṅkarācārya the nondualist. The whole point is to break down distinctions of the target language by unidiomatic uses from the base language.

Bengali, Hindi, or Sanskrit devotional or mystical poetry often involves addressing one's own mind. One scolds oneself, one draws attention of oneself, one faces oneself to praise or shame oneself. There are phrases often found which are best translated as "O, my mind!" Should we care if it sounds weird in English? That is a different self-Othering "can of worms" which—if self-addressing is permitted, I should say—"Listen, my loquacious mind!—you better not open now."

One grammatical point that remains supremely important from the theological point of view is that the vocative is not a case; it is not a "*kriyānvayi kārakam*." Even if I invoke Kṛṣṇa or Durgā by saying "Save me" or "Give me peace," the vocative "Hey Kṛṣṇa." does not stand for the nominative of the verb "save" or "give." As Kṛṣṇa says in the Gītā, God's doings do not make Him a doer. By keeping the vocative outside the case-structure of the sentence, Sanskrit grammar not only honors divine "*akartṛtva*" (non-agency), but also keeps the addressee outside the world while inaugurating a prayerful conversation with the Divine. Standing apart from all referring-describing speech-acts, the act of addressing (*sambodhana*) makes intimacy with the transcendent possible. By revoking our referential ambitions to talk *about* God, we can start invoking God to talk *to* Him.

I have attempted to show the irreducibility of the vocative as the grammatical tool of addressing another subject. Acknowledging the subjecthood of another also involves acknowledging that he or she is an agent not only in the metaphysical or ethical sense but also in the epistemic sense: other subjects know propositions. They often know more than we do. We can learn from them. The next two chapters discuss some issues raised by the roles that other teller-subjects play in our individual private knowledge.

19

Knowing from the Words of Others

From understanding others' words to learning from them

Words are sometimes said to clothe our thoughts and beliefs. But like clothes, they sometimes reveal more than they conceal and impose shapes, which our ideas might have lacked in their naked state. Beliefs put on the dress of language not only when they are exhibited but also when they travel from one person to another.

Perhaps, this sartorial imagery is wrongheaded. The very notion of a belief in its prelinguistic nudity may be a myth. Still, the phenomenon of expressing our thoughts and beliefs through our utterances has been given ample attention whereas the major role of language in instilling information and generating knowledge has remained relatively neglected, at least in twentieth-century Western epistemology. Too busy with explaining exhibition, we had forgotten about the *transmission* of knowledge through the medium of speech. True utterances in a certain language are not only caused by pieces of knowledge acquired by the sincere and competent speaker, but also can in turn *cause* genuine knowledge in an audience trained in that language. That the fire in Yellowstone National Park is spreading is information obtainable perceptually or via verbal testimony. As H. H. Price pointed out, not only do we trust such facts as how old each of us is, but even our knowledge of what day of the week or date or year it is today is based on the evidence of testimony.[1] Because of the increasing sophistication of the specialized branches of science and technology, we have to swallow more and more information from reliable say-so rather than from firsthand inferential or directly perceptual knowledge.

Yet, even now the proposal to count testimony as an independent avenue of knowledge on a par with but not reducible to perception, inference, or memory seems to smack of dogmatism or gullibility. Until recently, it was counted as a standard complaint against some classical Indian theories of knowledge that they recognize "report of the reliable" as an accredited source of or evidence for knowledge. After the "linguistic turn" in the West, comparative philosophers, many of whom used to feel apologetic about the hardheaded Nyāya's concern with word-generated knowledge, defensively started to discover echoes and anticipations of contemporary issues in the ancient and medieval discussions of Indian philosophers. There is a wealth of dialectical materials on issues like the meanings of empty subject-terms and existence denials, sentence-holism versus word-atomism, secondary (metaphorical) versus literal (first) meaning, the role of the speaker's intention in meaning-determination, the meanings of words, sentences, quantifiers, pronouns, proper names, imperatives, and so on. Among the many confusions that have arisen out of these reinterpretations of classical Indian epistemology and philosophy of language, lack of clarity about the concept of word-generated awareness (*śābdabodha*) is an important one.

The Sanskrit word "*bodha*" is derived from the same root as "*buddhi*", which is announced to be synonymous, at least in the relevant philosophical tradition, with words like "*jñāna*" or "*upalabdhi*." The latter mean (usually episodic) awareness, cognition, or apprehension.[2] But as we look carefully in the literature, we find that what in Western philosophy (and common English) is meant by "understanding of a sentence" is quite different from what in Nyāya philosophy goes by the name of "the awareness generated by the sentence" (alternatively called "awareness of the relatedness of the meanings of the individual words in the speaker-intended order"). My point may sound merely terminological. Upon hearing you say that p, I come to know that it is the case that p. I am thus having word-generated knowledge that p. But this knowledge is by no means reducible to my understanding of your utterance "p." My understanding of your utterance consists of my knowledge of what you mean to say, whereas my word-generated knowledge consists of my knowledge that what you say is in fact the case. However, the phrase "knowledge of what you mean to say" can be misleading. That is why once this terminological confusion is clarified, the issue goes deeper. The more or less received wisdom of contemporary Western theory of language is that when a hearer listens to the utterance of a sentence by a competent speaker, she first comes to recognize the force and content of the utterance and then goes on to either accept or reject the content. Let us roughly call this picture "understanding followed by trust."

About both kinds of putatively speech-generated awareness—namely, understanding and trust—we could ask the following two questions: (1) Does it deserve the title of "knowledge"? and (2) Is it reducible to sense perception, inference, or memory, or is it a unique kind of knowledge?

But the most momentous contrast between the classical Western view above and the classical Indian view of the matter lies in the latter's tendency to reject the "understanding followed by trust" picture. The Nyāya—like many contemporary philosophers—does not admit intentional entities like meanings, propositions, or Fregean senses. Unless we admit a beliefless noncommittal state of apprehension (which we might call "mere comprehension"), it becomes difficult to answer this question (1) without losing sight of the distinction between word-generated awareness (roughly, trust) and the so-called understanding. So, Nyāya regards the trusting reception of information as the primary cognitive attitude to meaningful, nonfictional, nonfigurative speech.

I shall address the following three issues:

1. Is word-generated awareness (in the sense sketched above) classifiable as perception, memory, or inference?
2. Does the Nyāya account of the content of word-generated awareness in the general terms of qualificand (subject) and qualifier (predicated property) fail to work in the case of sentences in non-indicative—especially imperative or optative—moods?

3. Is the Nyāya's refusal to accept the "understanding followed by trust" picture based on a mistaken defense of gullibility?

On being told

One significant definition of the verb "to tell" is "to make known." Under normal circumstances S can make p known to H only if S herself knows that p—hence the idiom "transmission of knowledge." Through the words of a language, a piece of information travels from the true-believing speaker to the inquisitive hearer who has mastery over that language. This was once described by John McDowell as the phenomenon of contagion of knowledge: "If someone knows that p and says that p, then typically someone who hears and understands him is in a position to know that p."[3]

Of course, not all telling is knowledge-generating. The speaker herself could lie, joke, or make a mistake. When explaining the concept of *āpta* (reliable authority) Vātsyāyana reveals two important things[4]: First, it is not enough to know the truth. Someone may know the truth, but lack the motivation or skill to communicate. But as long as there is no reason to suspect mistake, delusion, or deception, the speaker can be taken to express purport and communicate facts. Second, the admission of words as a source of knowledge is no defense of credulousness or gullibility. It is the recognition that religion, common morality, historiography, and even science would be impossible without this straightforward method of handing down knowledge through language. It is not in spite of, but rather *because* of the progress of science that more and more premises, theories, and results of experiments must be taken on authority or learned from (uttered or printed) words. If each individual or generation had to directly perceive, inductively verify, or deductively arrive at every piece of knowledge from scratch, then, as a famous Sanskrit couplet goes, "This world would be immersed in total darkness of ignorance, deprived of the light which we call 'speech."

Unfortunately, the so-called communication-intention theorists, in their enthusiasm to explain the sophisticated manipulative use of speech, have tended to ignore this basic knowledge-yielding employment of our linguistic repertoire. McDowell reminds us of the evolutionary survival value of the capacity of sentient creatures to spread important news by making significant noises. The alarm cries of some birds at the sight of a predator are surely not used just for the purpose of inducing in the hearer a recognition of the squawker's intention to alarm. Such cries are meant to pass on the beneficial results of one individual's perceptual data to other individuals.

Of course, we cannot forget the characteristically human exploitative tendency to cry "wolf" when there is none! Michael Dummett remarks somewhere that we fully master the practice of speech only when we can tell or suspect lies. Yet we must not lose our grip over the basic insight that, after all, words stand for objects, assertions are primarily used to record facts, statements get their meanings from the standard practice of intending and taking them to be true, commands are intended to be obeyed, questions to be answered, and so on. We cannot but take the truth-telling, knowledge-transmitting, information-instilling use as the standard use of language. When the real wolf comes, we have no other choice but to cry "wolf" again!

From utterance to uptake

Let's consider Mathurānātha's story of the genesis of a standard utterance[5]: (1) At first, speaker S comes to apprehend a certain state of affairs (which will eventually be the complex meant by the sentence). (2) S becomes aware of his or her own awareness. (3) S desires that another person (hearer H) should also acquire that piece of awareness. As S recognizes that the utterance of a certain sentence would produce this desired belief in H, (4) S wishes to utter such a sentence. Realizing that the exercise of the appropriate vocal and other anatomic apparatus is both within his or her powers and conducive to the fulfillment of this desire, (5) S tries to perform those phonetic acts. (6) From the latter emerges that string of articulate sounds, which we call the utterance of a sentence.[6]

The story on the receiving end runs somewhat as follows: Sometime earlier, hearer H had come to learn (either spontaneously or by training) a series of meaning-rules of the form, "From this word that thing is to be understood." In the preceding formula, "word" includes parts of speech (nouns, verbs, etc.), their inflected forms and particles, and even other kinds of morphemes (prefixes, suffixes, etc.). "Thing" includes particular substances, qualities, relational properties, universals, actions and events, numbers, and so on. Hearer H has learned such meaning-rules about all individual words in the sentence uttered by speaker S. H must have learned how to decode semantic features of the sentence, identify implicit contextual factors, disambiguate equivocal expressions, and determine the speaker's intention. In addition, H must have cultivated a general sense of what sorts of objective combinations of things, properties, and relations meant by the words are (or are not) fit to be entertained as actually obtaining. Now, as H hears these words, his or her episodic or dispositional memory of their individual meanings presents the meant items, first individually and then as held together. After H comes to hear the last phoneme, he or she apprehends the contiguity of the mutually relevant words, perceives their mutual syntactic, grammatical, and semantic dovetailing, believes or at least suspects the meant complex to be fit to be actual, and then firmly believes that those meant entities are in fact related to one another in the alleged order by the intended relation. If the entities are actually related in the way described by S, then the resulting belief in H amounts to knowledge; if not, it is an error.[7] In either case it is a special sort of belief or awareness obtained through listening (with comprehension) to the well-formed utterance of a communicative speaker.

In answer to a self-enquiry (How did I/you know this?) or to an epistemic challenge ("Why do you believe this?") one must reflectively offer an honest introspective report. The standard form that report takes is, "I heard it" or "I was told." Appeal to the reliability of the speaker or to any coherence criteria comes at a subsequent stage. According to Nyāya, then one is justifying not what one knows, but instead the claim that one knows it.

What is it that we know when we understand the meaning of a command?

There is one problem likely to loom large in any project of interpreting traditional Indian materials in the idiom of contemporary Western epistemology: the problem of the cognitive content of non-indicative utterances. Imperative or optative sentences like "Bring the cow" are given in Indian epistemology as illustrations of knowledge-generating utterances quite indiscriminately, along with straightforwardly indicative utterances like "Buffaloes are grazing by the side of the river," or mixed statements like "Here comes the son of the king; let the man be driven out of the way!"

This juxtaposition of commands and assertions is by no means careless or accidental. There were schools rival to Nyāya (upon which we are basing our account here), which regarded only religious and moral injunctions—hence utterances in the imperative mood—to be knowledge-generating. Without going into intricate detail concerning their views about scriptural (Vedic) sentences, we can just note here that such imperatives were taken, on the one hand, to be uncaused (or unuttered) by any human or divine author and, on the other hand, to be conveying the absolute obligation of certain ritual-performances or the prohibition of certain actions. As such, these commands could not possibly be true or false, nor could their content be known by any other direct means. Perception or generalization therefrom could hardly tell us what ought to be done in a deontological sense. Some modern interpreters of such classical Indian views think that the replaceability of its evidence makes testimony unworthy of epistemic prestige when it comes to statements of fact but that the irreplaceability of its (scriptural) evidence in the case of categorical imperatives makes it respectable as a source of duty. It was novel of Nyāya to extend the domain of *śabda* (word) as a source of knowledge to ordinary matters of fact. Nyāya deliberately flouts the stricture imposed by other schools of thought as to the assignment of specific sorts of knowables to specific ways of acquiring knowledge. One can come to know that there is fire on the hill by walking up the hill to observe the fire for oneself, by inferring it from a distance by seeing an invariable mark of fire (smoke), or by trustfully understanding an eyewitness's utterances to that effect.

Let us come back to our original uneasiness about the informational content of commands or requests or moral injunctions. For one thing, we must notice that the verb "to tell" is used most naturally in the context of an imperative utterance. Just as someone tells me what happened, someone tells me what to do, where to go, what to bring, and so on. So the notion of "what is told" must somehow include both states of affairs, which can or cannot be the case, and actions which should or should not be done. The Nyāya theory of action has a general rule: from cognition flows desire, from desire volition, from volition effort, and from effort the actual performance of the action.

The standard case of action-motivating desire comes from a triple awareness: (a) that performance of the action will produce desirable results, (b) that it will not produce undesirable results strong enough to counterbalance the former, and (c) that such an act is within the power of the actor. Now, when S tells H to "bring the cow," H learns immediately that the addressee has to be an agent of the act of bringing the cow. Since information or messages received from utterances must be capable of turning into knowledge—and knowledge is essentially linked up with the truth of the content—the informational content must be such that it can be true (or false) on standard appropriate occasions. As we know from the now-notorious problems of the separation and marriage of assertoric force and neutral content in the Western analytic tradition, the only form suitable to bear truth seems to be the indicative. Thus the embedded content even of imperatives has to be construed in the qualificand-qualifier form, which is the Nyāya substitute for the Western subject-predicate form of "basic combination."

Orders are not as such capable of being true or false; hence Dummett suggests that we modify their correctness condition as obedience conditions. So the troublesome bit—namely, "a has to be F," or "make a become F"—in our initial construal of the content of an imperative utterance is reparsed as a kind of predication. Then the predicated property is not apprehended as already actually residing in the qualificand (or subject), but as "intendedly" or "commandedly residing" therein. We must realize, of course, that for F to commandedly reside in a, it need not actually reside in a; all we mean is that a is asked or desired to have F. Hence the truth-biased reconstrual of the message passed on through "bring the cow" runs as follows: the addressee is the seat of the commanded/desired agency, which is conducive to the action of bringing, which has the cow as an accusative. To use Matilal's notation here, the content will look like this:

Q (you, Q (agency, Q (bringing, Q (accusativeness, the cow))))

However, we must be cautious to interpret the second "Q" as standing for a special intentional qualification. It remains difficult to imagine how the conditions of knowledgehood of a belief resulting from an imperative sentence will be enunciated upon this allegedly uniform account of meaning. Obviously, it would be quite ludicrous to insist that for the command to be "correct" (that is, for it to be knowledge-generating) the addressee should already have the agency toward the action he is asked to do. It is the *absence* of agency, which normally qualifies the addressee to be asked to do something. You can be asked to run only if you are not already running.

But here again we seem to have missed the mark. We were not looking for the conditions under which there exists a point to issuing the command. The point of the utterance has to be distinguished from the message encoded in it. In this case, the message seems essentially to involve the idea of the addressee's being desired to perform an action. Hence the command is rightly understood if and only if one knows what action the addressee is desired to perform. Translated into the technical language, the action denoted by the verb must be understood to be "injunctively" qualified by the particular result the addressee is expected to bring about, just as, in case of an assertoric sentence, correct understanding requires that the subject term is understood as being qualified, in fact, by the predicated property. This is, roughly, how uniformity of interpretation is achieved across indicative and imperative utterances. When I read the command "Press start" on the computer screen, I know that I am supposed to press the "start" key. Quite straightforwardly I (the addressee) am the subject (or qualificand) and "being supposed to press the start key" is the predicate or qualifier. Thus the awareness generated by the imperatives doesn't necessarily bring the speaker into the content.

Is testimony an irreducible knowledge-source?

We can now approach our central question: is verbal testimony an independent way of acquiring beliefs (and, derivatively, knowledge)? Gaṅgeśa rejects the suggestion that testimony is not a source of knowledge rather summarily with a quick pointer to a self-refutation. The hypothetical discreditor of testimony tells us that "words can never give us knowledge." But how are we to take *that* statement? Do words uttered by an antagonist of word-generated knowledge give us any knowledge? If they themselves do not convey any knowledge, then the statement is simply not true. If that statement is true, that is, if those words themselves convey knowledge, then words do, on this occasion at least, generate knowledge in us. From this follows the falsity of the contention. There is a patent performative contradiction in stating in words that words can never arouse true beliefs.

But easy victory was not to Gaṅgeśa's taste. He considers the possibility that those words of the skeptic or heretic arouse in us as a sort of awareness, which is itself not a directly word-generated belief but is still capable of revealing the unreliability of directly word-generated beliefs. All we have to prove in order to evade self-refutation is that such an awareness is a kind of perception or inference rather than a piece of special testimonial knowledge. Thus the question of whether testimony is at all an admissible avenue of knowledge eventually reduces to the question of whether all alleged cases of knowledge by testimony are reducible to cases of memory, perception, introspection, or inference. Before we take up this issue as it was discussed in late medieval Indian epistemology, let us look once more at the corresponding Western scene.

Hume attempted a sustained account of knowledge from testimony. His discussion in the section on "Miracles" in the *Enquiry* is regarded as the standard take-off point. He does not dispute the point made, later, by J. L. Austin that a statement made by someone in a position to know (an authority) is a source of knowledge.[8] All Hume insists is that our reliance on witnesses, historians, reporters, and experts is derivative of our reliance on inferences based on inductive generalizations from observations of constant co-occurrence. Thus the threat to testimony, even here, is that of reduction to inference or to customary observation or experience.

But as Coady has argued,[9] Hume's program of reduction can be damaged by a destructive dilemma. When Hume argues that we trust others' words because we have in the past experienced them to be true, what does he mean by "our experience"? If he means the experience of a single person, then the diagnosis is simply false. The range of observation of a single person hardly justifies any such claim to know a general connection between assertions and facts. Simple reports like the content of a letter mailed by a friend could not be trusted with any degree of certainty if one had first to ascertain by individual observation all relevant types of facts involved in the postal path of the letter. As we pass on to more specialized scientific information, the observational responsibilities implied become too absurdly enormous to be discharged by a single individual with limited time, expertise, and cognitive equipment. The only other alternative is to include others' experience. But then we beg the question about our trust in testimony because the only standard way we come to know of others' experiences at such a sophisticated level of confirmation requirement is to hear and trust their avowal or verbal reports. So the Humean attempt to reduce testimony to empirical reasoning is either completely unrealistic or circular.

Another sphere in which testimony is almost irreplaceable is our knowledge of the meanings of words. At the superficial level, we have no conceivable way of challenging the authority of dictionaries and language teachers. To insist that one can "look up" the vocabulary on one's own, or "observe" usage instead of relying on the instructor's words, would once again be circular. Here the role of perception in "looking up" or "seeing" is deceptive. When we figure out "what means what," we trust the expert's explicit or implicit, formulated or contextual, definitions of word meanings. At a deeper level, Putnam's notion of division of linguistic labor clarifies the role of testimony in language acquisition. When the chemist tells me "This is sodium sulfate," pointing at a substance, I immediately come to know what that term means. How? By testimonial evidence, to be sure! Such facts about meaning actually determine our knowledge of facts about the world in ways much discussed by Quine, Davidson, and Putnam. Both sorts of facts are thus known through distrustless comprehension of the utterances of competent speakers. We need not establish the separate trustworthiness of the source; it is enough if no evidence to the contrary is already available. So the question is not at all whether testimony is a source of knowledge. It is simply dishonest to doubt that. We cling to perception despite the fallibility of our sensory equipment and meet skepticism about the validity of inductive inference with naturalistic or pragmatic responses. It would be sheer prejudice to refuse testimonially acquired beliefs the title of knowledge on the ground that all understandable utterances could be generally false. Indeed, as I shall argue later on, understandable utterances could *not* be mostly or generally incorrect. We must therefore suppose that testimonially acquired beliefs do merit as much general presumption of truth as do our direct reports of perception. But the question at hand is whether they constitute an independent source of knowledge.

Why knowledge by testimony is not a form of perception

The Cārvāka school of classical Indian thought did not recognize means of knowledge except sense perception. Naturally, its followers either had to reject most of our nonperceptual knowledge claims or reduce them to perception. Now, the best way to classify knowledge obtained from hearing and comprehending as perception is surely not to insist that through the words we actually see, touch, taste, smell, or hear of the objects talked about. No ordinary contact between the sense organs and the objects about which information is verbally received could be postulated. Hence perceptualist reductionists resort to extraordinary contact called contact-through-memory-awareness (*jñāna-lakṣaṇa-saṃnikarṣa*). Perhaps on some previous occasion the hearer perceived individually the items or kinds of items talked about by the speaker—his memory of those objects (including substances, qualities, relations, etc.) aroused by the use of the relevant words establishes an extraordinary contact between his senses and those items themselves. Thus, the communicative intent becomes perceptually presented by his listening to the utterance, given that he is semantically trained.

Against this suggestion, at least three strong arguments have been given. First, there is phenomenological, introspective evidence that what we learn from a sentence is not immediately afterward felt as something we have seen, or otherwise directly perceived, but as something we have "heard" in that nonsensuous sense of hearing in which we hear messages rather than noises. Although after some vivid verbal explanations we make the remark "I see" or "I can almost feel it," our reception of verbally communicated information is not intuitively felt to be direct or presentative in nature.[10]

Second, the order or direction of qualification involved in the complex content of the qualificative awareness resulting from hearing a sentence is irreversibly determined by word order, nominal case endings, and other inflective marks. Thus, from an utterance of the sentence, "The table is brown," we shall never have an awareness where the color brown figures as subject and inhering in the table figures as qualifier. It must be an awareness of the table qualified by the brown color. But had the experience been perceptual, the qualification structure would have been reversible as long as the captured fact remained the same. When I see that the cat is on the mat I can be correctly described to have seen that the mat is under the cat. Direct access enables us to rearrange empirical content while testimonial knowledge remains bound to the order dictated by the words.

Third, once we rely on memory-assisted perception, we have to include in the content of our alleged testimonial knowledge all that one is reminded of at the time of listening to the utterance. In perceptual experience, the subject is well known to be helplessly at the mercy of the senses. When the links of stored past experience are added, the chances of being perceptually presented with data for exceeding the bare meaning of the utterance are high. We might be reminded of some accidental feature of the speaker (that he is a Californian, for instance) by the special accent or tone, which we cannot help hearing along with the utterance. If the utterance were, "Oxford is a boring city," the resulting perceptual content would be something like the proposition that a Californian believes that Oxford is a boring city. But that is not the word-generated belief that we wished to capture by the perceptual reduction.

Actually, perceiving the mere words never gives us the putatively perceptual knowledge of the reported fact. We have to be aware of the contiguity of the words uttered, of their syntactical "expecting" of each other, and of their fitness to represent a situation, which is not known to be nonactual, and so on. If all these conditions are fulfilled, we need not construe the resulting knowledge as a memory-linked, extraordinary perception artificially confined only to the properly word-recalled objects. We can more parsimoniously admit that this was a noninferential, nonperceptual, word-generated awareness of the meant relation between just the meant entities—no more, no less.

Knowing from words is not simply remembering

If it is not reducible to perception, then our putative knowledge from another speech should not be regarded as a straightforward case of remembering. We can come to understand and have true beliefs about situations, which we never witnessed perceptually before we heard the sentence which describes the situation. If testimonial knowledge were to be a subclass of memory cognition, then we could claim to be informed only by sentences which describe a state of affairs which we have ourselves directly experienced before. The whole point of telling others about places, subjects, events, etc., of which the listeners have no direct experience would be foiled.

Why reduction to inference fails

We can now consider a few of the attempts to reduce word-generated awareness to inference. Two types of inferences have been proposed by Indian philosophers who subsume testimony under inference: (1) those which revolve around the words or the utterance itself and (2) those which revolve around one or more of the objects whose mutual relatedness is asserted by the utterance and grasped by the audience.

To consider the first type, let's suppose that the sentence uttered is, "That cow is white." The inferential reformulation of the knowledge generated by this cluster of words will run somewhat as follows.[11] The words "that," "cow," "is," and "white" (i.e., the place) are uttered due to an awareness (in the speaker) of the purported relation between the purported qualificand and the purported qualifier (i.e., the inferable), because they constitute a string of words connected to each other by syntactic and semantic expectancy, compatibility of meanings, and so on (i.e., the mark).

But even if the inference goes through, it only makes us know that the speaker himself, before uttering the sentence, must have believed that the cow is white. How does that generate in the hearer the same belief?

The features of a sentence which serve as the "mark" of an inference must be known and firmly believed for the inference to be epistemically effective. We never arrive at the conclusion of an inference from a shaky awareness of the reason, ground, or mark. Yet it is well-established that we need not be certain about the mutual expectancy of the words; it is enough if they, in fact, have that feature. We definitely need no prior firm belief in the factual fitness of the meant content in order to acquire knowledge from the utterance of the words. It is enough to entertain the possibility of the individual meanings of the constituent words to be factually combined. We do not receive any information from a sentence like, "Mrs. Clinton had three wives," because we have a firm belief in the unfitness of the content.

The preceding inferential reconstrual therefore yields a belief with more *and* less content than the belief which it was expected to account for. It is richer in content than the alleged testimonial knowledge (about a cow) because it is a belief about the speaker's belief and not about a cow. Each time S utters the sentence, "a is F," S does not manage to or want to say that S believes that a is F. The latter involves references to S and S's mental states (his belief) besides a and F. Here Gaṅgeśa anticipates the problem of the referential opacity of intentional contexts. He thinks we cannot argue that in knowing S's belief about a's being F, we also come to know that a is F. This seems to be required if one follows the Nyāya account of the causal mechanism of all multiply qualificative cognition. We could not be aware of a multiply complex qualificative content unless we were first aware of each embedded qualified qualificand and qualifier. Unless you believe that the stick is red you cannot come to believe that the man is carrying a red stick. Similarly, if you read all awareness in a *de re* manner, then to be aware of S's awareness of a's being F, you have to know first that a is F, because the content of the belief about S's awareness will be: Q (S, Q (awareness, Q (a, F))).[12] In order to arrive at the whole content you must causally and epistemologically work your way back from the innermost qualified content.

But to this Gaṅgeśa objects that if this were always required, then whenever we ascribed a mistaken belief to another person we would ourselves be mistaken. Thus, God, who is aware of all our errors, will be in error Himself. This demonstrates why the conclusion of the inference gives us less information than what the sentence conveys. Hence, our inference about the utterance U being generated by the speaker's belief that p would not take care of our word-generated awareness that p is directly generated by our listening appropriately to the utterance U.

Let us look now at the other type of inference. Here the meant entities themselves figure as subjects or places where some relevant properties are inferred. Take the sentence "John is ill." This generates in anyone who has mastery of English, who knows who this John is, and who does not question the credibility of the speaker, the belief that John is ill. Is this belief inferentially obtained? Could it be an inference about John, whom the hearer has seen before and now is reminded of by the utterance of his name? Could it be an inference to the effect that he has the property of illness such that the predicated property is the inferable and John is the place (or subject) of inference?

What would serve as the mark for such an inference? The features of words like contiguity, expectancy, and so on could not be marks, because the marks and the inferable must be capable of residing in the same locus; at least the mark should reside in the subject of inference. But features like contiguity and expectancy are syntactic and semantic features of the utterances, which cannot be looked for in John or in any of the meant entities. So the mark will be essentially faulty.

In response to this difficulty, we could manipulate the mark so that this defect of unavailability does not vitiate it. We could dress up the inference as follows: John (= the place) has the property of illness (= the inferable), because he is recalled by the word "John" in a sequence of words where the other words "is ill," meaning what they do, have the property of "expecting" the word "John." But to tighten up this inference into a valid form, we must add the semantic feature of "fitness" of the meant entities—once again, because we can never validly infer the actual obtaining of the state of affairs reported by an utterance by merely arguing on the basis of syntactic or grammatical features. Once we presuppose knowledge of such a semantically strengthened mark, we shall actually assume, within the premises of the inference, a prior knowledge of the truth of the information, thus rendering all knowledge from testimony into a reknowing of the already known. The inferences become epistemically circular. The essential freshness of testimonial knowledge is lost.

What do we know when we understand what others say but do not trust it

I began by distinguishing between understanding and word-generated knowledge. The distinction is not drawn in terms of truth or falsity or correctness or incorrectness. There is no tendency in Nyāya to hold that word-generated awareness is always knowledge. We can have false belief generated by believingly comprehended false sentences. The contents of such false beliefs are explained by the general Nyāya technique of assigning misallocated intentional roles to bits of the real world. Even such false beliefs are word-generated beliefs. So the problem is not with false awareness of contents but with unbelieving awareness of contents. Nyāya also has an account for a sort of unbelieving awareness of contents which may result from a sentence known by the hearer to be semantically unfit or patently false. This is the notion of a conniving or mock awareness. Take, for example, one's attitude toward a contention which one intends to refute. Fitness is no longer a condition; it is rather a firm awareness of unfitness that causes such fictional apprehension of unfit contents. But it seems like a lacuna in Nyāya philosophy of language that nothing like a propositional content is ever admitted to serve as the object of a belief-free grasp of the meaning of a sentence.

It has been established almost without controversy in Western epistemology and philosophy of language that we must grasp the content before judging the content to be true. Although Frege himself drew our attention repeatedly to the informational vacuity of the adjective "true" so that knowing that p, and knowing that p is true, could always collapse to the same thing, it was he who insisted upon a distinction between the three acts of (1) apprehending thought content, (2) judging it to be true, and (3) asserting it to be true. More recently, Gareth Evans has explicitly formulated the principle of belief-independence of informational states.[13]

But the examples he gives are of illusions and false impressions, which persist even after clear recognition of or firm belief in the non-veridicality of the experience. It is unclear, however, how without positing ontological entities like Fregean thoughts or propositions (subsisting but not existing) one can call such states "states of knowledge." If such beliefless understanding is called knowledge, then what is it knowledge of? To answer that it is the knowledge of meaning gets us nowhere. If we want to retain our robust sense of reality, then we cannot claim to have knowledge of some entities called "meanings" without believing that such meanings are there in the world for us to know them. If we continue to insist that the being-there of the meant content does not constitute the existence of the fact, which the sentence would have pictured if it were true, we are left with only one alternative apart from the unpalatable Fregean third realm of the senses: Wittgenstein's Tractarian notion of states of affairs which might or might not exist.

I am inclined to do justice to the phenomenon of the ontologically noncommittal language games of giving and receiving information without the full load of belief in their reality. Yet it seems unavoidable to have the believing awareness of content as the standard case, and to build our theories of unbelieving understanding derivatively upon them. This murky state of belief-free presentation of contents seems to be inviting obfuscation! I am sure that we do unbelievingly understand a lot of utterances, but it is too much to argue that all knowledge of facts through testimony has to go through this noncommittal state of belief-free information intake.

It is only when we have a two-step theory like the one I have been arguing against that we tend to treat the end belief of the credulous audience as inferential and often inadequately warranted. Interestingly enough, Fricker calls the so-called second step (coming to believe that the grasped content is actually the case) first-level hearer's belief. Her notion of second-level belief is, of course, different from that of understanding; it is not belief-free. It is a belief not about the world, but about the speech act performed by the speaker. Nyāya will have no trouble with that. Surely when I hear you utter a sentence, I perceptually recognize that you have made an assertion with a certain content. This could be perception. I can also make an inference from this to the effect that you meant to tell me something by the use of that sentence. But this is not what Nyāya would mean by "word-generated knowledge" because your words did not say, "I am making an assertion that ... " To be informed by your assertion is to believe that what you assert is the case. And this belief turns out to be knowledge when the assertion is true and when my apprehension of it follows the intention of the speaker and the grammatical and lexical rules of that language.

The skeptical pressure to think that all intelligible speech could be consistently and systematically taken as false may induce attachment to the view that my knowledge that an assertion has been made is securer than my knowledge that what has been asserted is the case. Fricker draws the corollary from her inferential account of first-level hearers' beliefs (the Nyāya *śābdabodha*): "That it is perfectly coherent to suppose an individual who understands others' utterances perfectly, and yet never believes what they say."[14] She says that such an individual would indeed be "odd." This word of disapproval is misleadingly mild. I think it could be shown that entertaining such uniform unbelief would deprive the distrustful interpreter of his capacity to interpret correctly.[15]

Of course, knowledge is not easy to come by. But the skeptical possibility of the entire web of our beliefs about the world being massively mistaken is no more genuinely threatening to testimony-transmitted beliefs than to our perceptual resources or our non-deductive inferences. If this sounds like a defense of gullibility then gullibility needs some defense.

Having discussed the nature of testimony, we now face another set of problems. Even if we admit that we can learn propositional content from others, can they teach us understanding? A negative answer implies that understanding is a solitary affair. In the following chapter I shall argue that we are not warranted to accept this 'solipsistic' view so quickly. Knowing from the words of others may naturally lead to real understanding which teachers and friends may initiate as well as deepen.

20

Can Another Person Teach Me What It Means?

Introduction

Whether she learns from reason, from experience, or from inspiration—the ideal learner in the West gathers knowledge all by herself. Plato says in the *Theaetetus* that there may be teachers who can persuade someone else to accept a truth but no one can plant knowledge in the head of someone else. Why? Because to cause me to believe (even truly) is not to bring me to understand, and without understanding there is no real knowledge. There is only one person who can bring me to understand something, viz. myself. Centuries later, John Locke likens received learning to borrowed wealth, admonishes that the floating of other men's opinions in our brains makes us not one jot the more knowing, and concludes that men must think and know for themselves. Thus, both rationalists and empiricists deny the phenomenon of transmission of understanding or knowledge through teaching. In contrast, the classical Indian knowledge-seeker invariably turns to a epistemic lineage of masters-and-disciples. Whether it is for something as trivial as learning the meaning of a word or for something as momentous as knowing how to live wisely, one is required to submit to a teacher. "The learning of those who have not sat at the feet of earlier scholars ... does not attain complete definiteness," says Bhartṛhari in his seminal work *Of Sentences and Words*. Torn between such opposite paradigms of knowledge gathering, we start to see the point of our initial question: Is there any education in understanding except self-education?

What is it to understand?

What is this supposedly unteachable understanding? One obvious answer is this: *understanding is knowledge of meaning*. Standing somewhere between the grandeur of wisdom and the triviality of informational knowledge, understanding could be characterized as a deep, connected, and re-applicable knowledge of the reason, cause, principle, or mode of functioning of something. We can be said to understand a remark, a joke, a mathematical proof, a theory, a person, a society, a work of art, a kind of music, and a whole lot of other things. Anything which fits into a structure or admits of explanation or interpretation can be said to be understood.

I will concentrate on linguistic understanding primarily because the truism "to understand S is to know what S means" suggests to me that if one could determine the exact variety of knowing that involves knowing the meaning of a bit of speech one would also get a clue about the nature of other sorts of understanding. Second, grasp of a concept which seems to be crucial for any kind of justified belief or structured thought can best be handled theoretically in terms of our understanding of a word, especially a predicate. Third, one of the classical forms of philosophical enquiry has been to ask for the exact meaning of a word like "real," "true," "good," "know," or even the word "meaning" itself. It seems that understanding of such key words constitutes the core of philosophical knowledge if there is such a thing as philosophical knowledge.

Fourth, if we trust Bhartṛhari or Quine, we acknowledge that all knowledge is in a deep sense linguistic. Since linguistic communication opens up other people's minds for us and since the very concept of an objective world which gives content to the notion of belief, truth, and justification is the concept of a public world equally available to all as a target of reference and description, cracking the mystery of understanding speech would indirectly amount to cracking the mystery of all knowledge claiming objectivity. So the narrowed down question is this: "Can one person teach another person what a certain expression means?" Once again the question sounds trivial. The answer, it seems, should be an obvious "yes!" Strangely enough, St. Augustine answers the question with a clear "no" in his early dialogue *De Magistro*. He argues that no teacher ever teaches us anything. He takes knowledge of the meanings of the words as his chief example and tries to prove in the first part of his dialogue that nothing can be taught without signs. In the second part, he argues that nothing can be taught with signs. So nothing can be taught. If "learning" means picking up genuine knowledge from the instruction offered by other people, then none of us ever learn anything from others.

An obvious difficulty is this: don't we learn something, at least that teachers teach us nothing, from Augustine's own writings? Is not his dialogue operationally self-defeating? Augustine anticipates this objection and responds: if at the end of reading the dialogue, the reader's understanding comes to agree with Augustine's, that is because the inner light within the heart of the reader has seen the point of each step of the argument on its own.

The logical structure of the *De Magistro* argument

The structure of the argument in *De Magistro* is as follows:

DM1.If the meaning of a word could be taught at all, it could be taught either by ostension/exhibition or by words.

DM2.Through ostension/exhibition meaning cannot be taught because ostensive definitions could always be misinterpreted. Besides, many important words have meanings which cannot be exhibited or pointed at.

DM3.By words we cannot be made to know anything that we do not already know by firsthand experience.

DM4. Therefore, the meaning of a word cannot be taught at all.

The second premise of this argument anticipates a crucial point about the inadequacy of ostensive definitions, which we find in Wittgenstein's *Philosophical Investigations*.[1] Although we do try to convey what is meant by a proper name like "Jesus" or a color adjective like "red" or a common word like "rabbit" or a mental-state-word like "pain"—all by pointing at things like a picture of Jesus, an arbitrary sample of a red surface, an instance of the rabbit-kind, or a physical manifestation of the state of pain—such gestures run the risk of misfire, ambiguity, indeterminacy, and misinterpretation.

The most contentious premise, however, is the third. It denies the possibility of conveying any knowledge through words, and especially denies that the meaning of a word could be explained and thereby imparted to another person verbally.

A sub-argument for this premise could be reconstructed from Augustine's text as follows:

A. When words are uttered, either the hearer knows their meaning already or he does not.
B. If he already knows their meaning, then the words do not give him any (new) knowledge.
C. If he does not know the meaning (of all or some) of the words, then the words only generate a sensation of noise—which is not even knowledge of words as words of a language.
D. Therefore, in either case, when words are uttered nothing new is known by the hearer.

Thus, the understanding of a word remains un-teachable, period.

Now, it is one thing for us teachers to feel utterly baffled from time to time by the difficulties of explaining concepts to students and quite another thing to concede the nihilistic conclusion that no linguistic understanding is conveyable through instruction. The conclusion of the Augustinian argument must be false. Yet the argument and the sub-argument look formally valid. Therefore, something must have gone wrong in the premises.

I propose to question the very first premise (DM1) which claims that there could only be two ways of teaching meanings—by verbal explanation or by ostension/exhibition.

There is a way of teaching by exemplifying the use of an expression which is neither of these two ways. This is how most of us learn our first language. Parents do not try to point at or exhibit or enact the meaning of a verb like "walk" or "sit," neither do they start explaining in other words what walking or sitting mean. Instead, they use the word in the right context and let us watch them use it. Augustine anticipates this way of resisting his first premise with his example of the bird-catcher who teaches by simply using his bird-catching equipment in the presence of an onlooker.[2] Apart from the weak protest that even this way of teaching is open to the same incompleteness and indeterminacy as teaching by ostension/exhibition, Augustine more or less agrees that knowledge of language can be imparted through this method of demonstrating the use of words rather than demonstrating what is meant by them. But perhaps that would not count as teaching in the strict sense. After all, the teacher is totally passive and the learner is left to figure it out on his own.

A lot of weight is attached to this notion of passive teaching in classical Indian theories of learning. Taken to an extreme, it leads to such metaphorical expressions as: "The tree has taught me tolerance." An eager Ekalavya learned archery just by watching Droṇa train the princes and later on just by imagining that the statue of Droṇa was teaching him. The problem with this third way of teaching is this: from the fact that A learnt from B it does not follow that B *taught* A. The converse failure of entailment is witnessed by all of us teachers quite often: from the fact that B taught A, it does not follow that A learnt from B.

I shall, therefore, assume that the first premise is correct—that there is no third way of explicit teaching of meaning—and try to attack the anti-teaching argument more directly at a different step.

The real sophistry of Augustine's argument lies in the third premise, which tries to prove that with words no new understanding can be effected. This is proved on the basis of a simple trick with the plural "words" which could mean single words taken distributively or a sentence as a string of words.

Suppose I tell my daughter: "Cats eat rats." She knows what each of those words means, so by uttering those words I have not given her any new lexical knowledge. But she does not know that cats eat rats, which is the fact meant by the entire sentence and hence by those words. Thus, her knowledge of a new fact about feline diet is something for which I as a teacher can claim credit. We can see how a new knowledge of meaning can be transmitted through old words already understood by the learner.

But Augustine's complaint against teaching by words goes deeper. It springs from the Platonic distrust of testimony as a source of knowledge. Augustine claims that even sentences of the Bible give us useful true belief rather than knowledge. Until my daughter sees a cat eating a rat, her belief in the content of my words is not knowledge. By the same logic, testimony to the effect that the word W has the same meaning as M can at best give the learner of a language a true belief that W means M, but in order to understand W the learner has to see what W means in actual use by her own light and work it out from there.

As a general epistemological thesis, this distrust of testimony is, I think, quite wrong-headed. I have argued for the irreducible respectability of knowledge from words in the last chapter. Without engaging in the debate here, let me say just this: if the autonomous knower sticks rigidly to her principle "know it yourself," then she cannot make use of any public language even to preserve or classify information for her own future use, let alone for posterity. One can consolidate and deepen one's knowledge of semantic value by noticing further connections in usage, but for the primitive connections between noises and what they stand for in a certain language it is foolish to ask for any more justification than that the speakers of that language tell us that those noises stand for those sorts of things. Since the only possible languages are public languages, the person distrustful of other's teachings about meaning is left with no language whatsoever. It is impossible to participate in any human social transaction without implicitly accepting native speakers of a language as habitual true-believers and truth-tellers. Our experience of the world will be severely impoverished if we cannot claim that a certain flower is a rhododendron because that is what we were told it is called.

The basic fallacy in the Augustinian argument may stem from an equivocation on "teaching." Notice the following two uses of the verb "to teach": "The Gītā teaches us that the soul does not die" and "P. K. Sen taught me logic." It is clear that we can substitute the former use of the verb "teaching" with the verb "telling." "The Gītā tells us that the soul does not die" is perfectly fine. But we cannot do that for the second use: "P. K. Sen told me logic" does not make sense. Conversely, we can rewrite the second sentence as "P. K. Sen taught me how to solve logical problems" but there can be no "teaches-how-to" equivalent of the first statement. When somebody tells me that something is the case, he does not usually give me any recipe for future creative use. Teaching logic is thus not just teaching-that or telling, it is teaching-how or training. Now we can safely formulate the following principle about rules in general and meaning-rules in particular:

i. A has successfully taught B a rule only if, after being taught, B can figure out the results of a particular application of it in a fresh case on his own.

Now,

ii. if B has figured out something on his own then no one, not even A, has taught him that.

From these two premises, it seems to follow that

iii. If A has taught B how to apply a rule, then A has not taught B that in a particular untaught case the rule yields such and such specific results.

If we ignore the distinctions between teaching-how and teaching-that, we could state this conclusion with misleading brevity as: "If A has taught B then A has not taught B." This may appear to prove that for all A and all B, A never teaches B, as long as A and B are distinct persons.

Is understanding knowing-how or knowing-that?

Of course, my rebuttal of one particular argument against the possibility of teaching does not conclusively establish that understanding can be taught. But positive possibility-proofs are as hard to come by as positive existence-proofs. All I can do to make my positive case stronger is to spend more time on the exact nature of understanding or knowing what a word or sentence means so as to clarify what is done when such knowledge is imparted. I have implied just now that understanding may be conveyable by teaching-how rather than teaching-that. A tourist guide can teach an American tourist that in Hindi "*Main videshi hun*" means that I am a foreigner. But just gathering that information will not give the tourist *understanding* of even that sentence, let alone the language.

Now teaching-how presumably imparts knowing-how. But is the understanding that I pick up from linguistic training just skill or mastery of a practice? Of the two classical modes of knowledge—practical skill and propositional awareness—which one fits the nature of understanding better?

Michael Dummett has argued that the practical-versus-theoretical dichotomy is spurious when applied to a speaker's knowledge of a language.[3] I shall rehearse in my own way some of his arguments to prove that grasp of meaning is neither exclusively theoretical nor exclusively practical knowledge.

We could claim that to understand the Sanskrit sentence "*Gaṅgā nīlā*" is to know that the sentence "*Gaṅgā nīlā*" in Sanskrit means that the Ganges is blue, which is not to know that the Ganges is blue but is still to know a proposition. But this claim fails to preserve the important identity between what the sentence means and what is known when a sentence is understood. For, that "*Gaṅgā nīlā*" means that the Ganges is blue is not the meaning of that Sanskrit sentence. The meaning of a sentence does not include the sentence once again. The threat of a vicious regress lurks here.

Shall we therefore drop the idea of knowledge of what a word or sentence means in the sense of awareness altogether and reduce the speaker's or competent hearer's understanding of a sentence-meaning to a mere ability or competence? Our understanding of an individual sentence as a consequence of our mastery over the language to which it belongs is often episodic. This is not possible with mere knowing-how. Beyond this, our mastery of basic vocabulary has a deeper inner side than externally detectable skills. Of course, we no longer believe in a psychologistic Lockean code-conception of meaning where to understand a word is to call up an idea associated with it and to speak is to translate one's private mentalese into English, Hindi, or Japanese. Our mastery over concepts must be manifestable in overt linguistic or non-linguistic practice. But to be manifestable in practice is not to be reducible to practice. A perfect parroting of cooking would be cooking, but a perfect parroting of speaking French will not be speaking French. Understanding Sanskrit is not merely the ability to utter some sounds and react appropriately to the utterance of some sounds. If it were, then one could know what it is to speak Sanskrit without knowing Sanskrit. But it takes nothing short of knowledge of Sanskrit to enable someone to know what it is to speak Sanskrit. Therefore, understanding is not just knowing-how.

Dummett's own suggestion is that it is a unique third kind of knowledge, namely *knowing-what*. On his account, it would be a mistake to treat "what the sentence means" in the case of "The speaker knows what the sentence 'Clinton is bald' means" as a noun-phrase standing for the object of understanding-knowledge. Dummett thinks that knowing what the sentence means cannot be broken up like that: it is not knowledge of what-the-sentence-means but knowing-what-the-sentence-means.

The nature of this peculiar knowing-what is still unclear, but it seems highly plausible that this is the sort of knowledge—neither *techne* nor *episteme* but a bit of both—that *we* try to generate in our students when in a philosophy class we try to teach them, say, the meaning of Hume's sentence "Whatever is, may not be" without necessarily agreeing with it. If a student memorizes all that I have told her but cannot tell, on her own, how the fallacy of *svarūpāsiddhi* (or "the mark's absence in the subject of proof") happens in cases other than the hill, smoke, and fire—then my teaching of Indian logic of Inference has failed. Now, there is a part of this teaching which remains unsaid, just as there is a part of conveying the sense of a word which remains unspoken. The teacher of philosophy can teach best by actually doing philosophical thinking aloud in class and letting the students watch her do so. This need not be passive teaching insofar as the teacher's choice of the style, topic, etc., would be actively geared to the pupil's specific needs. But this teaching-how to handle proofs, concepts, and distinctions would at best give the student something like a knowledge of rules. One cannot and should not supply further instructions as to how in each case to apply these rules. This should be left to the judgment of the student. Kant calls this judgment the faculty of application of rules or "the specific quality of so-called mother-wit" and remarks that it is a "peculiar talent which can be practiced only cannot be taught."[4] This mother-wit, I claim, is what Bhartṛhari called "*pratibhā*." It comes in the form of a generative transformative capacity for rule-following as well as in the form of the flash of synoptic understanding. It is partly innate, and partly emergent out of proper training. I like to call it knowledge by contagion. Even the mother-wit needs a nudge now and then—a skillful teacher follows no particular set of rules in deciding how best to give these nudges. Philosophical understanding is an emergent symbiotic effect of my teaching-how, the pupil's mother-wit, our joint belonging to a self-changing continuous tradition of thought, and the student's submissive-subversive immersion in that tradition.

This way of teaching is often compared to shining a light. In darkness we cannot see what is really there. A teacher is eulogized in Sanskrit as one who removes the blinding darkness of ignorance. This invokes the intuitive association of darkness and ignorance. But are shadows and darkness absences just like lacks of knowledge or are they visible physical entities of a sort? Also, is there an ontological difference between shadows and darkness? These are questions to which the following chapter turns.

21

Shadows of Ignorance

The puzzle of shadows

Shadows do not only scare children at night, they also threaten philosophers and their smugly drawn distinctions between substance and quality, presence and absence, real and illusory, objective and subjective. In what follows, I shall outline a few different positions regarding the ontological status of shadows. Those of my readers who cannot wait to ask "Why bother about shadows?" will have to be patient. At the end of the chapter, I shall discuss the *importance* of shadows in Plato as well as in Advaita Vedānta.

Our intuitive assumptions about shadows lead us into some paradoxes which are not easy to resolve. It is this puzzling indeterminable nature (*anirvacanīyatā*) which makes a shadow such an excellent analogue of *avidyā*—that primordial gloom of ignorance, which, according to the non-dualist school of Vedānta, explains the superimposition of illusory multiplicity of objects over the undifferentiated unity of all subjective consciousness. One Ṛigvedic hymn considers the universe to have emerged by way of uncovering the veil of ignorance (*avidyā*). This ignorance also allegedly has the power to project our plural world on the screen of non-dual pure consciousness.[1]

Let us call one of the puzzles, "The Paradox of Cast Shadows."[2] The paradox starts with some initially plausible assumptions:

1. An ownerless shadow cannot exist, i.e., a shadow must be cast by something.
2. An object upon which no light falls cannot cast a shadow.
3. A shadow cannot pass through an opaque object and be cast on a surface behind it.
4. If a shadow is cast by two physical objects A and B, e.g., when my fingers plus the pencil I am holding cast a continuous shadow, A casts part of it and B casts another part.

Given these uncontroversial-looking assumptions, we seem to be trapped in the following paradox (referring to Figure 3).

1. Physical objects A and B are arranged in such a way in relation to a source of light that they seem to throw a single shadow S, which would be identical to the shadow cast individually by each of the objects A and B.

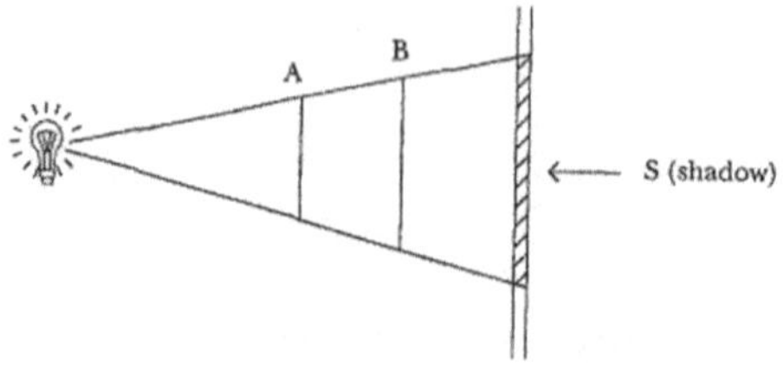

Figure 3 Shadow of What?

2. Shadow S is not owned by B because no light falls on B.
3. Shadow S is not owned by A because through the opaque surface of B, A cannot cast its shadow.
4. Since neither A nor B casts any part of S, S cannot be cast jointly by them.
5. Since S is not cast by anything, it is ownerless.
6. But being ownerless, according to assumption 1, S cannot exist even though it is seen. Seeing something nonexistent should count as hallucination, but as a normal seeing of a shadow it is most definitely not such a case.

Several "obvious" solutions suggest themselves. We may be tempted to drop assumption 3 because it is based upon the confused notion of the casting of a shadow through another opaque object. But there are independent reasons for not letting A pass as *the* owner of S, since S *would have been there* even if A were not present, as long as B were there. Unfortunately the same sort of consideration disqualifies B as well. Perhaps the very idea of "the owner of a shadow" has to be given up. I shall return to this puzzle at the end of my ontological excursion.

Some distinctions

The word "shadow" has two easily distinguishable uses: to mean *reflections* and to mean what I call *contoured relative darkness.* When Wordsworth says, "The swan in St. Mary's lake floats double swan and shadow," he is talking about a well-lit, richly detailed mirror image of the swan on the clear placid water of Yarrow's lake. This is not the sense I am concerned with now. My investigation is of the exact category into which we can fit dark silhouetted murky images cast by opaque objects on unmirrorlike surfaces due to obstruction of light. This is the sense in which "The zebra's shadow has no stripes."

There are two other words which are akin to "shadow" in this sense: "darkness" and "shade." I don't usually call the interesting shadow cast by my moving fingers on the wall "shade." The shadow cast on the ground by a big tree is properly called "shade." But actually, shades are typically borderless—notice the metaphorical idiom "shades off"—whereas shadows have more or less well-defined boundaries. When painters talk about light and shade as visual cues for convexities and concavities of surfaces, they do not mean by the term "shade" what we call a "cast shadow." I shall also leave aside the further ambiguity of the word "shade" due to its use signifying distinguishable hues of the same color.

There are two straightforward ways of establishing the distinction between the darkness-related notions, *shade* and *shadow*. First, if I bring my hand to a source of light, one of its surfaces will be in light and the other in shade. The darker side is shaded (or in shade), but it cannot be said to have a shadow on it. Whose shadow would it be anyway? A surface cannot cast its own shadow onto itself. The shadow-casting surface has to be lit by that very light the lack of which is suffered by the shadow-hosting surface, and no surface can both have and not have the same light shining on it at the same time. Michael Baxandall calls shades "self-shadows," apparently defying my rule above that nothing can cast its shadow onto itself and blurring the distinction I am so eager to draw.[3] But actually there is only a terminological difference between his usage and mine insofar as he too attaches importance to the separation between self-shadow (i.e., shade) and projected shadow (shadow).

Second, a realistic painting of a well-lit spherical surface would demonstrate that the distinction between light and shade is relative and without a cut-off point. It is difficult to count shades, whereas one is generally able to enumerate shadows. Shade is standardly a visual cue for depth and dent, but shadows by themselves are usually not so. Shades used in the depiction of undulations on drapery could be so sharply set off against highlights as to be strictly *visually* indistinguishable in color from cast shadows; yet *conceptually* shadows are purely visual objects caused by or causing no tangible difference in the texture or shape of the surface where they fall.

Is "shade" then just another name of darkness? Of course, the word "darkness" is itself ambiguous. The term "dark" is used most often as an adjective of a *place* or area with respect to its condition of illumination. Sometimes, it is also used as a qualifier of a color, as in "dark blue" when it seems almost interchangeable with "deep." Now *this* latter sense of darkness has little to do with lack of illumination. A light blue when seen in gloom does not *look* deep blue, and surely a rich dark green is not just a less well-lit pale green.

Wittgenstein, I suspect, gets himself trapped in this ambiguity. After treating *darkness* in the second color-qualifying sense by noting that a ruby can get darker red without ever becoming cloudy, he remarks, "In paintings darkness *can* also be depicted as black." Taken by itself the remark is trivially true. But taken as a remark about saturation of a hue, it goes flatly against the point about darkness as color depth.

If we confine ourselves to the notion of darkness which deals with lack of light rather than with saturation of hue, we might be tempted to identify it with shade. But even here Turner draws a useful distinction. "Light," he writes, "is a body in painting of the first magnitude and reflection—the half light; while shade is the deprivation of light only, in the deprivation of reflection likewise it becomes darkness."[4] Turner illustrates this point with Titian's bunch of grapes. Except for the central focus of a highlight every other part of each grape is depicted as in shade—in relative deprivation of reflection—yet the visible front of each grape is in full light. There is no *darkness* on them.

Perhaps Turner's distinction is drawn more rigidly than the way common users of English would draw it. But the concept of sheer darkness, carefully considered, I think, turns out to be distinct from both that of shadow and shade. Leonardo da Vinci makes this point with two definitions: "Darkness is the absence of light. Shadow is the diminution of light."[5] What descends on a natural forest after sundown (especially if the night is moonless) can be called "darkness." Complete absence of light (the phenomenon of dark-adaptation aside) makes us feel as we might imagine a blind person always feels. Hence, the Sanskrit word for darkness: *andhakāra*, literally meaning *blind-maker*.

However, like complete vacuum, complete darkness must be hard to achieve. But if it were achieved, it would not be discernible as shade or shadow, for both shade and shadow require light. No shadows can exist under the condition of zero illumination. To see the difference between shade and darkness, imagine carrying an umbrella inside a pitch-dark tunnel. Darkness seems to make shade impossible. Switch off the light and all the shadows in a room (after dusk) are gone. The property of being visible without the aid of light figures crucially in (classical Indian) metaphysical argumentation about darkness and surely does *not* belong to shadows.

Seeing darkness or not seeing light?

Of course, these are just *prima facie* distinctions. No one can deny that the three notions of darkness, shade, and shadow are closely interlinked. Having made these distinctions, I shall often in what follows speak interchangeably of shadows or darkness or shade, all of which can be perceived to be "out there."

I just said that darkness could be perceived. Some philosophers would stop me right there. If darkness is just lack of light and a lack is a negative thing—a gap in reality rather than a bit of reality—how could it have the causal power or the appropriate effective relationship with a sense organ to generate genuine perceptual experience? The absence of a beloved person can figuratively weigh you down, but literally, absences cannot act on you or, for that matter, on your retina. When we seem to be perceiving darkness, these reductionist enemies of absence would insist, we are just *not* perceiving light. It is not that we see lack of light but that we fail to see light.

However plausible this may sound, the suggestion has the following awkward consequences. First, when we close our eyes or sleep without a dream, we are not seeing anything; hence, we are not seeing any light either. When with our eyes wide open we are seeing darkness, even then, according to these philosophers, we are merely not seeing light. The experiential content of these two states ought to have been identical. But they are in fact significantly different, if, that is, the not-seeing counts as having any experiential content at all.

Second, there is a rule of thumb that if a certain object is perceived by a certain sensory faculty, then its absence should also be recognized by the same sense. When a singer misses a note, we have to *hear* the omission; when a soup lacks a flavor or taste, we cannot *visually* experience such a lack. Now perceptions themselves are mental or inner states, unlike colors or sounds. Perceptions are perceived by the inner sense. If we have to register lack of a perception, we have to do that as well by introspection through the inner-sense—the same faculty that would have noticed a perception had it been there. But we cannot sincerely confess to noticing shadows or darkness through introspection. Hence, seeing shadows cannot be identified with not seeing light. Shadows must be visible things and not mere lacks of vision.

Third, when from inside a dark room I look outside and *simultaneously* notice the gloom in the room and the sunny outdoors, I would have to be described as not seeing and seeing at the same time. A more coherent description of my experience would be seeing light in one place and privation of light in another.

However, to echo Russell,[6] there lurks in the deepest core of our robust sense of reality a tendency to resist the admission of such negative entities as lacks, absences, cessations, etc. Russell had to struggle against it when in his lectures on logical atomism he took a strong stand in favor of the objectivity of negative facts. But even Russell, I'm sure, would have felt squeamish about the claim that we are as directly and perceptually acquainted with the absence of an object as we are with the presence of an object. Yet our acquaintance with shadows or darkness seems to be *visual* and *direct.* If shadows and darkness are mere lacks of light, then must we not admit the actuality of sensory acquaintance with absences?

Perception of an absence has to be distinguished from a mere non-perception of the absentee. Whenever I do not see an elephant (for instance right now), in the ordinary case I am not seeing the absence of an elephant either. In order to see the absence I have to somehow think of and miss the absentee, *qua* an elephant. A born-blind man does not see darkness because he does not have any idea of what it is a lack of, and also because he simply does not see. Seeing a hole in the wall is not to be equated with not seeing the wall at a certain point. It is more than that. It is a distinct positive act of perceiving the fact that a bit of the wall-substance which should or could be there is missing. An eighteenth-century scientist called shadows "holes in the light."[7] If holes are seen, shadows are seen too.

Before I return to darkness and shadows, let me add two important cautionary remarks about absences in general. First, the most common mistake is to conflate the absence (*abhāva*) *with* the absentee (*pratiyogin*), the negative fact with a non-existent state of affairs, the not being there of a thing with the thing which is not there. Absences are not Meinongian non-existent (but subsisting) objects. That the Eiffel Tower is not in Seattle is *a fact.* It is not a piece of fiction like *The Eiffel-Tower-of-Seattle.* The absence of light which we wish to call darkness is never to be confused with the missing light. One may have independent reasons to balk at the absence theory of darkness, but fearing that thereby we flout the Parmenidean warning against thinking of non-beings would be foolish.

Second, from the fact that we do not *perceive* absences unless we somehow remember or think of the absentee, we may be tempted to conclude that absences are cooked-up by our expectations. But we must resist that temptation. Thought of the absentee is a prior condition for someone's *recognition of* an absence, but it is not a condition for the existence of the absence. The negative fact is discovered by thwarted expectation or denial of an entertained false proposition, but it is not invented by those cognitive acts. The absence-theorist of darkness, therefore, is *not* committing shadows to the subjective realm.

The absence-theory of darkness and its difficulties

Like holes, then, are shadows distinctly perceived absences? Are they simply lacks of light? That, at any rate, is the usual view about both contoured and uncontoured darkness. Notice the peripatetic work *De Coloribus:*

> There are many arguments to prove that darkness is not a color but merely privation of light, the best being that darkness, unlike all other objects of vision, is never perceived as having any definite magnitude or any definite shape.[8]

Of course, the argument fails completely in the case of shadows with well-defined shapes and measurable magnitudes. If shadows did not have definite location, shape, and size, sundials would be quite useless. But then how can absences have sizes and shapes? Apart from general ontological worries about the identity criteria of absences, there are serious hurdles to the view that shadows are mere absences of light.

Shadows can overlap or occupy the same area of space, but still be easily enumerated according to the number of obstructing bodies and/or the number of sources of discriminable illumination. Absences, on the other hand, are much harder to count. A vacant chair seems to house countless absences corresponding to all the likely and unlikely persons, animals, and objects which might have occupied it. Usually absences are individuated in terms of distinct absentees or counter-positives and not in terms of their locus. One single absence has numerous locations. But there are cases where this principle of identity of absence on the basis of identity of absentees becomes less obvious and we have to count absences on the basis of the number of locations. Thus, the identity criteria of absences seem foggier than those of shadows.

Second, absences, such as the absence of color in air, are incompatible with their own absentees. David Keyt and David Keyt's absence cannot coexist on a chair. But shadows can coexist peacefully with *some* light. Even deep darkness can easily tolerate the flickering light of fireflies. Strictly speaking therefore, a shadow or darkness cannot be the total absence of light.

Third, absences do not bear properties like color, shape, and movement. Shadows, on the other hand, have all kinds of properties. On white surfaces, shadows of physical objects against the sun usually look blackish or bluish grey in color. But actually the color of shadows varies enormously from surface to surface, depending upon the color of the light and condition of the weather and atmosphere.

Leonardo's notebooks abound with instructions to the painter as to how best to depict colored shadows. Among the French impressionists, Seurat made the most strenuous effort to articulate the colorfulness of shadows even on sunny afternoons. As a pointillist, Seurat would most probably draw a distinction between the apparent color and the real color of the (parts of the) shadow. But it would still be odd to think of an absence of light as having a real color!

About creating colored shadows with artificial illumination, Goethe in his *Theory of Colors* suggests the following:

> Two conditions are necessary for the existence of colored shadows: first that the principal light tinge the white surface with some hue; secondly, that a contrary light illumine to a certain extent the cast shadow. Let a short lighted candle be placed at twilight on a sheet of white paper. Between it and the declining daylight let a pencil be placed upright so that its shadow thrown by the candle may be lighted, but not overcome, by the weak daylight: the shadow will *appear of* the most beautiful blue. That this shadow *is blue is* immediately evident; but we can

> only persuade ourselves by some attentions that the white paper acts as a reddish yellow, by means of which the complemental blue is excited in the eye.[9]

Notice that Goethe does not commit himself to the view that under those conditions the shadow really "*is blue*," although he uses those words once. He explains how it can be made to *appear* blue with the surrounding white paper appearing reddish yellow and a complementary blue *being suggested* to the eye. One could definitely argue that the blueness of the shadow is doubly illusory. First, the real color of the surface which is covered by the shadow is white. Just as the yellowness is superimposed on the rest of the white paper by the candlelight, its whiteness is concealed by the shadow cast by the pencil. Upon this already falsified color of the paper apparent blueness is superimposed, existing because of the contrast effect upon the cones in the retina. So the shadow is not *really* colored. But is anything really colored?

Of course, all colors are strictly speaking subjective. Colin McGinn ascribes even to current common sense the view that color-predicates are dispositionally understood in terms of our reactions as against shape-predicates, which common sense takes to have direct objective content. I cannot agree with that. I think, in spite of the normal dose of physics and physiology, that all of us take "red" to be more like "square" than like "scary." So when I ask, "Do shadows have colors?" I don't want to get entangled with the larger issue of the objectivity of colors.

A second kind of temptation to paraphrase has to be resisted as well. When a shadow looks bluish, we should not report that the part of the surface on which the shadow is cast looks bluish. Even the most unreflective viewer does not think that the lawn looks partly green and partly bluish grey when it is sun-dappled. The *shadow* looks bluish grey.

But the absence-theorist cannot even concede that shadows have secondary qualities because absences cannot have insensible parts by the frame, figure, texture, and motion of which they have the power to produce in us visual sensations of colors. Only substances can have primary or secondary qualities. But we cannot *presume* that darkness is a new sort of substance in order to defend that it has or appears to have color especially because, as we shall see later, possession of color itself has been used as the main premise for the conclusion that darkness is a substance.

Finally, the absence-theorist of shadows faces fresh troubles from the phenomenologically undeniable evidence that shadows *move.* Can absences move? If motion is defined as successive production and perishing of *contact* with different regions of space, absences—which are never in the relation of contact with anything even according to metaphysicians who take absences with utmost seriousness—should be logically incapable of motion.

Once again, this ploy for treating shadows as positive entities may turn out to be rather weak. One could argue that it is the contour of the patch of light which changes and it is the motion of the light which is falsely superimposed upon the area where there is relative absence of light.

Of course, the motion of the light is not the only cause of the illusory motion of the shadow. In his notebooks Leonardo observes *five* kinds of motions of shadows. The first is that in which the derivative shadow moves together with its opaque body and the light causing this shadow remains immobile. The second is that in which the shadow and the light are moved, but the opaque body is immobile. The third is that in which the opaque body and the luminous source are moved but the luminous source with greater slowness than the opaque body. In the fourth the opaque body is moved less swiftly than the luminous source. And in the fifth, the motion of the opaque body and the luminous source are equal to each other.[10]

It remains a deeper philosophical question how to take these causal explanations of the movement *of* shadows: do they explain away the apparent motion *of* shadows *as* visual illusions like the motion of trees or the river-bank seen from a speeding boat? Or do they give the causes of what we really and veridically see as *out* there?

One could appeal to the shaky generalization that whatever can be the substratum of an erroneous superimposition must be positive in nature. However, the mainstream philosophical attitude is to take linguistic usages such as "shadow grows longer" and "shadow moves" as unnoticeably metaphorical just like the phrase "the sharp rise in death-rates."[11]

If he does not take seriously the color and motion arguments against the negative nature of darkness, the absence-theorist has a tough time articulating what sort of *not-being of light* darkness is. Not-beings are divided into two major kinds: not-being-the same-as (or *otherness*) and not-being-there (or *lack*). There is no question of identifying darkness with *otherness* from light. We perceive all sorts of bright objects like tigers and teapots as distinct from light. We do not thereby see them as displaying darkness or shadow. Lacks, on the other hand, are either atemporal or temporal. Atemporal lacks are usually absolute. The lack of fire in ice is *complete*. Shadows are never such absences of light. Even what is known as a pitch-dark night generally has some light particles or waves which start affecting the retina once the latter gets used to the darkness. Temporal absence is either prior or posterior. It seems arbitrary to label the darkness at nightfall as the prior absence of the future morning light, rather than as the posterior absence of the past daylight, or the converse. Prior absences are beginningless and posterior absences are endless. Since a shadow or a patch of darkness has both a beginning and a terminal point, neither can be either of those absences.

If we define shadow or darkness as relative deprivation of strong perceptible light, rather than as absolute or temporal lack of any light whatsoever, then we can even explain the following observation made by Goethe in describing some landscapes of the Venetian School:

> The sunlight brought out the local colors dazzlingly, and the shadows were themselves so light that they could have served as lights in another context.[12]

The part of a body which is in shade or darkness can easily be at the same time illuminated by visible light. Even when we adopt a sophisticated version, the absence theory of darkness faces grave epistemological objections. Perception of an absence, we have already noted, necessarily presuppose awareness of the absentee. It also presupposes awareness of the locus. The fully fledged form of the alleged absence-perception would be: "The *a* which is F is not there in 1"—where *a* is the absentee, F can be technically called "the property limiting the absenteehood" and 1 is the locus.

Now, sometimes we do perceive darkness in this way. When lights go off suddenly at night we perceive the posterior absence of those very lights in the room. But one can imagine a person who has always lived in a dark chamber who nevertheless has full eyesight. He would see darkness without having an idea of the lack of light he is witnessing. When enveloped in gloom, one sees darkness without identification of the place where it is seen. Thus, even the requirement that the locus of absence be identified is not satisfied by the perception of darkness.

Finally, there are philosophers who stubbornly question the division of entities into presences and absences. If light and darkness are opposites, why not think of light as absence of darkness? Leonardo observes:

> Shadow is of greater power than light, because it banishes and completely deprives bodies of light and light can never wholly chase away the shadows of bodies, that is to say of dense bodies.[13]

If Leonardo is correct (I suspect he is not), then it would be implausible that darkness is privative or that light is more ineliminable from the manifest image of the visually available world than shade.

We have discussed the absence-theory and objections to it at some length. I shall now flesh out some of the alternative *positive* account of darkness as an entity.

Positive theories

The English word "darkness" with its ness-y ending suggests that it is a positive *quality*. One account holds that like blueness, darkness itself is a color. Shadows are just patches of such a color which can appear to be a different color because of the color of the surface and light condition of the surroundings, etc. Now, all of us who have struggled with sense-data theories of various kinds know that the word "patch" in "a patch of color" hides quite a lot of confusions.

In his *Commonplace Book,* G. E. Moore wonders why you can have blue and yellow patches of light but not a black patch of light.[14] Yet black surely can be the color of something that appears on a movie screen. Moore asks: "What name is there for the '?' thrown on the screen in a cinema?" At the end of the entry, he decides to call the "?" "images." But is "images" any clearer than "patches"? Moore rules out the possibility that what we see on the screen when a color film is shown are *shadows* of translucent surfaces.

One can try to prove that shadows are colors from the other side of the equation. Goethe quotes Athanasius Kircher, who held the view that "Color itself is a degree of darkness."[15] We can understand the appeal of this view in the following manner. In order to create dark*ness* or to cast a shadow, we usually need to obstruct the light with an opaque body. But if we start making the obstructor less and less opaque, it would still prevent some light. The *shadow* of a panel of stained glass will be a collage of patches of color. This helps make sense of calling color itself a degree of darkness. The baby physics behind the theory could be this: colors are results of the selective absorption of parts of the spectrum by different surfaces. Any color other than white must therefore be a result of some sort of obstruction eating up parts of the light falling on the surface. Thus, our experience in watching a color film can be just an enriched version of the experience of shadow-play. If colors are bits of darkness, then it may *seem* easier to agree with the view that darkness is color, although I suspect that the identity here is not symmetric.

But this view is not at all popular among phenomenologists of shadow. First, there is an unclarity in the very notion of colors. Are they universals or particulars? Modern Western philosophy has tended to treat colors along with all qualities as universals. I myself prefer the view that colors are objective particular qualities or tropes specific to the surface where they belong.

Now, if colors are universals, then shadows cannot be colors. The visual perception of shadows clearly points to particular two-dimensional unrepeatable entities. I am not assuming that universals are imperceptible—perhaps all shadows share the universal of *shadowiness*. But I find it counter-intuitive to think of shadows themselves as abstract entities.

What if colors are particular qualities? Even then, there would be *two* strong arguments against treating shadows as colors. First, the same single shadow can consist of different discriminable patches of color, when it spans across different surfaces. Take the shadow of the lance on the admiral's dress in Rembrandt's *The Night Watch*. We see different colors within the same continuous shadow, and those particular colors are individuated according to the distinct dress-materials in which they inhere. But the shadow is individuated by the light source and the shadow-casting object. We *see* one shadow, but many colors.

Second, take this neat and naive little argument: colors do not have colors, shadows have colors, hence shadows are not colors. That shadows *have* colors—however questionable it may be—has been also used as a perceptually well-grounded premise for the somewhat strange view that shadows are *substances* rather than qualities.

Entire schools of philosophy—Vedānta, Mīmāṃsā, and Jaina—in ancient and medieval India upheld the view that darkness is an independent substance on the basis of arguments such as the following. Whatever has the capacity to cover another substance is itself a substance, for example, a curtain, a lid. Darkness can cover any substance on which it is cast. Hence, it is itself a substance. Only substances can have qualities like color and shape. Darkness has color and shape. Hence, darkness is a substance.

The objections that (1) it does not physically clash with other substances, or (2) that it cannot be *really* colored or contoured because all really colored or contoured objects are touchable, have not dissuaded these substance-theorists. A beam of light can also be passed through without any clash, and a shadow, after all, does get distorted if a hand or stick goes through it. In scorching summer days, shadows feel cool to the *touch*—so it is not obvious that they are only accessible to *one* sensory faculty. And in any case, the converse generalization that whatever has touch has color fails in the case of air. The rule that all colored substances are tangible may also admit an exception, viz. darkness.

The strongest argument against shadows being colored substances has been the following:

A. All substances which are genuinely colored need the help of light to be seen, e.g., a cherry.
B. Darkness can be seen without the help of light. Hence, darkness is not a genuinely colored substance.

We find premise A clearly formulated in early and late Vaiśeṣika texts on metaphysics and in *De Anima*. Aristotle observes:

> Not everything that is visible depends upon light for its visibility. This is only true of the 'proper' color of things ... That is why without the help of light color remains invisible.[16]

After Aristotle, both Leonardo Da Vinci and Goethe talk about colored shadows and make the presence of light of a specific kind a necessary condition for the visual perception of colored shadows. In the Indian context, A has been challenged by the counter-example of light itself which does not need the help of light to be visible. Also premise B does not hold true at all about colored shadows.

The robust point behind this standard argument, however, remains true. A colored substance, even a black surface, can be better observed in brighter light, although perhaps one can never see its *real* color under any condition of illumination—maybe it has none. But it is foolish to try to observe the real color of a shadow by illuminating it with a beam of light. Of course, we can illuminate the *painting* of a twilight scene, but that does not entail that darkness itself can be seen better with the aid of light.

Finally, material substances which are accessible to external perception are supposed to be divisible into particles. But talk about particles of shadow seems out of place outside of a Seurat canvas. Yet Jaina ontologists talk fearlessly about darkness atoms clustering together to form visible darkness.

Contemporary astrophysicists are talking seriously about dark matter. The most famous physicist of our times, Stephen Hawking, wrote in 1990:

> We can measure the rate at which objects are moving apart, but the amount of matter we can see in the universe is not enough to slow down this rate of expansion significantly. So there are two possibilities; either our understanding of the very early universe is completely wrong, or there is some other form of matter in the universe that we have failed to detect. The second possibility seems more likely, but the required amount of missing 'dark' matter is enormous; it is about a hundred times the matter we can directly observe.[17]

He also speaks of black holes and dark baryonic matter and states unambiguously: "We can imagine that the particles of shadow matter might form shadow atoms and molecules."[18]

I have always been suspicious of current scientific parallels of ancient metaphysical speculations. The dark matter of current physics of course has nothing to do with ordinarily perceived shadows—which most probably are a form of absence of light.

Are shadows illusions?

All these quarrels about the ontological status of shadows might finally lead us to believe that they are, after all, public optical illusions like the "rising" sun, or the "broken" stick immersed in water. Against the view that shadows themselves are illusory appearances, one could argue that sometimes we hallucinate shadows rather than really see them. Consider the optical illusions where in the white gaps between a series of separated blocks of black squares we regularly hallucinate patches of darkness. The converse illusion can also happen. A shadow on a white shirt could be mistaken for a piece of dirt. We might try knocking it away, only to realize that it really was a shadow. Could shadows be mistaken for something else and falsely perceived to be there unless they were sometimes veridically perceived? In the absence of some perceiving entity, wouldn't an erect stone still cast its shadow on the ground on a sunny afternoon?[19]

Shadows cannot be so easily wished away as illusory or as any more observer-dependent than other visible objects. If we regard them as objective perceptible absences of light, then we must provide an account of perception of absences as separate countable entities, because we have seen that seeing a shadow cannot be reduced to failing to see light. A correct definition of "seeing" is immensely difficult to come up with. But if shadows are lacks of light and are *seen* and if seeing essentially involves a causal relation between the object and the sense organ, then we have to start thinking about the causal efficacy of lacks. Negative things like lacks or absences have not been much favored by ontologists in the recent Western mainstream. Given that Nyāya-Vaiśeṣika metaphysicians and contemporary thinkers alike conclude that a shadow is a "local relative deficiency in the quantity of light meeting a surface, and is objective,"[20] a reconsideration of this bias in favor of the positive seems warranted. negative things like shadows, shades, and darknesses most definitely exist mind-independently and can cause us to see them directly. Indeed, without seeing *them*, we would not see undulations and grainy textures, cracks and holes, spheres and edges, dawns and dusks.

I promised to say something about the importance of shadows and darkness in the history of philosophy. Let me mention two glaring examples: shadows in Plato's cave and darkness as Śaṅkara's analogue for ignorance—a positive *presented falsehood*.

In Plato's cave

In Plato's *Republic*[21] shadows seen by the prisoners in the cave serve as analogues for illusory objects or mere appearances. Once outside the cave, the liberated lucky realize "that what they had formerly seen was meaningless foolery." The Greek original here uses the word "*phluarios*" which has been translated by Julia Annas as "illusion."

Now, it is one thing to call shadows insubstantial but quite another to call them illusory. The popular Greek idiom "wrangling over the ass's shadow," which is alluded to in Plato's *Phaedrus* and in Aristophanes's comedy *The Wasps*, understandably takes shadows as less *important* than their originals but not as less real. Even Plato calls them "silly trifles" in the context of the cave—though perhaps for Plato to be real is to be valuable and hence unimportance may not be that far from unreality! But let us see how appropriate it would be to call what the prisoners saw mere appearances or silly trifles. Of course, if a prisoner saw a silhouette of a man blowing a bugle and judged, "That is a man blowing a bugle on that wall," that *would* be a pretty silly error. But for that error to be possible, doesn't he need to have seen correctly a man and a bugle sometime before? The elements of the content of a misperception have to be severally available to him through some veridical experiences of the past. Given that unlike a mirror reflection a shadow would not look like the prisoners themselves (supposing that they could barely see themselves), it is hard to imagine how such an error could actually be made. It is understandable, however, that since the light source or the effigies in wood or stone were not seen or suspected by the prisoners, they could not see the shadows *as shadows*. So they could be making some misjudgment. But what they saw on the surface of the wall were objective entities, even if they were a bunch of absences or superficialities like holes and cracks. Even in the sunny world outside the liberated should meet with real shadows cast by real people and real trees! What then could be the rationale for using shadows as illustrations of mere appearances?

One answer can perhaps be found in Thomas Aquinas's commentary on Aristotle's discussion on the different meanings of "falsity." Shadows are called "false" insofar as they are "fitted by nature to appear to be other than (what) they are."[22] Here also Aristotle's example of a "shadowgraph" reminds us of Plato's parable. Dreams, on the other hand, are false because they "appear as things which do not exist." It stands to reason therefore that those "other things" (whose shadows might mislead us into thinking that we see when we only see their shadows) *do exist*. Real shadows can only be cast by real owners of shadows.

Let me at this point return to the initial puzzle of cast shadows. A shadow is a relative privation of light. Now, a certain located absence of light (the end-shadow) due to an intervening opaque object is such that within the conical range marked by the apex which is the source of light and the base which is the surface hosting the end-shadow, any arbitrarily placed obstruction of the appropriate size and shape would have caused the *same* end-shadow. Thus, a single shadow could "belong to" a number of distinct obstructing objects—if more than one of them are actually present within the shaded volume of space then no one of them has any special claim. Yet a shadow always raises the question, "Whose shadow?" because *it is a parasitic entity*. It needs an owner but in this case it cannot legitimately be assigned one. As an ontological orphan, in spite of its objectivity as a visible absence, it gravitates toward a misleading appearance. One of our assumptions creating the puzzle was that an ownerless shadow cannot exist. The solution of the puzzle lies in simply giving up this assumption. As mere absences which require an absentee (the light from the source) and a locus (the host surface) but no determinate blocking entity *(vāraka dravya)*, shadows with no (specifiable) owners do exist.

The analogue of positive ignorance

A famous passage of the post-Śaṅkara Advaita work *Vivaraṇaprameyasaṃgraha* tries to establish the "existence" of a positive veil of ignorance on the basis of the following inference. A freshly obtained veridical awareness must have been preceded by an ignorance, just like the illumination of a first-lit lamp in darkness is preceded by a positive, concealing darkness substance distinct from mere prior absence of the light. Both the light and the knowledge manifest that which was hitherto unmanifested. Although this inference heavily depends upon the positive substance theory of darkness, which Advaita Vedānta borrows from Mīmāṃsā and which thereby lacks strength insofar as that theory of darkness fails to hold water, we can appreciate the analogy between darkness and ignorance (shadow and doubt) that underlies this inference. The phenomenological significance of the introspective state expressed as, "I do not know (see, understand, remember or feel) anything that I seem to suffer (or even enjoy!)" is sometimes as immensely valuable as the darkness in a Rembrandt painting. Without this surrounding "field" of nescience, the revealing "focus" of knowledge would not have been discernible. The just-woken person's retrospective report seems to point toward the existence of such a felt antecedent darkness during deep sleep. Advaita metaphysics compares darkness and ignorance, and suggests this ignorance (like the play of shadows in a three-dimensional field of vision) gives delineation and body to the empirically known objects. Every object is known by being fished out of an ocean of beginningless unknowing. But the exact nature of this concealing ignorance is indeterminable. It is neither ultimately real nor totally unreal. The contradictory pulls of intuition felt about the cast shadows inside Plato's Cave, when explored, lead us equally well to this ontological twilight of indeterminacy. Advaita Vedānta captures this indeterminacy through the concept of *māyā*.

If darkness is comparable to ignorance, then what is the light of knowledge? "To know x" may mean at least three things: to have a direct perception of x, to possess the concept of x, and to have a word for x. The relationship between these three levels of knowledge: experience, thought, and linguistic understanding, is a separate and difficult problem; For example, can perception be pre-conceptual or can concepts be pre-linguistic? What is the extent of overlap between sense-perception, thought, and language? This important question at the confluence of epistemology and philosophy of mind motivates the next chapter.

22

Concept Possession, Sense Experience, and Knowledge of a Language

Two connected questions

Can someone possess the concept of a flower without knowing the word "flower" or any word for flower in any language? Can someone see or notice a flower without having or applying any concept whatsoever?

I shall try to defend an affirmative answer to the first question and a negative answer to the second. I shall also try to excavate a link between these two answers. Most of our garden-variety perceptions are loaded with concepts picked up at the time of language learning. But once we recognize that prelinguistic possession of concepts must be possible, it becomes easier to admit that preconceptual perception is a mere myth.

Between two suspect notions, viz. nonlinguistic grasp of a concept and nonconceptual experience of particular objects, the latter—the source of the Myth of the Given—surely deserves a decent burial and for the sake of that the former merits a cautious resurrection. Knowledge of the sense of a word requires knowledge of that word and knowledge of at least that fragment of the particular language which determines its use. An unverbalized (but verbalizable) predicative perception of *a* as F does not seem to require perceiving *a* as falling under the extension of a kind-word of any particular language. It is the fear of meeting such a steep requirement which has often made philosophers expel concepts from the contents of nonverbal perceptions, and suspect even simple predicative perceptions as experience adulterated with verbal and hence nonnatural thought. Once we make room for possession and application of concepts which need not be grasped *merely* as senses of words, we can frankly admit the role of such concepts even in our most primitive noticings of our surroundings. Mythologizing about inexpressible pre-predicative immaculate perception of pure particulars can then be clearly recognized to be otiose. Recognition of the purely perceptual character of concept-enriched experience, thus, makes us ready to embrace the sort of direct realism about ordinary propertied particulars defended by Peter Strawson.

Wordless experiential concepts?

In the age-old epistemological schism between passive perceptual cognition through the senses and spontaneous rumination, belief formation, and communication through language, *concepts* were always thought to belong to the language-faction. It is more realistic, in both the technical and colloquial senses of "realistic," I suggest, to affiliate concepts—at least some basic concepts—with the perception-faction. The indescribable aroma of a new blend of coffee which we smell quite obviously as of a definite *recognizable* kind and intensity is not perceived as a bare particular stripped of all general features. The aroma may be nameless but it is not therefore featureless. We could not be groping for a word for that *sort* of smell unless we already fitted that particular whiff to an olfactory sort or concept. The smelling goes wordless not because it is concept-free but because no word has yet been found to match the *concept* with which the smell was smelled.

John McDowell writes, "In experience one finds oneself saddled with content. One's conceptual capacities have already been brought into play, in the content's being available to one, before one has any choice in the matter."[1] Years before, Strawson wrote, "The ordinary human commitment to a conceptual scheme of a realist character is … something given with the given."[2] Strawson also gave a Kantian-style explanation why this is so. In order that fleeting and subjective events like our sensations could be taken as caused by and pointing toward objective and enduring bodies, we need to possess and apply *concepts* of distinguishable and reidentifiable objects. Thus, our actual intake of perceptual experience is said to be "soaked with or animated by, or infused with … the thought of other past or possible perceptions of the same object."[3] But this concept-saturated character of all experience is often taken as evidence for the fact that our language permeates our perceptions—that our experience is as much caused by convention-guided speech as it is by the world knocking at the door of our senses. To take Strawson's convincing example, "I hear the clock strike twelve. Could I hear *this* without grasp of the concept of a clock and of the number-system? And whence does this grasp derive? … Perception, *our* perception, is *powered and driven by the word*."[4] Now, this may be true of the rather sophisticated "hearing" which is involved in the above example, but to insist that any *seeing* (or hearing or touching or tasting or smelling) is seeing plus implicit employment of speech is but one step away from the idealistic thesis that the world opened up by predicative perception is constructed by us through some kind of linguistic social contract.

Sensing things without making sense?

Let us look at the matter in the form of a typical philosophical puzzle: each of the following three propositions seems to be initially plausible.

1. No adult perception is imagination-free or nonconceptual.
2. Concepts (roughly equated with Fregean senses) are nothing but ways or rules of using words.
3. Some adult perceptions (e.g., of an unfamiliar smell) are causally and contextually nonlinguistic.

Yet, it looks as if these three could not be true together. If no perception is possible without concepts and no concepts are possible without some actual or implicit use of language, then no perception should be free from linguistic loading; that is, proposition 3 must be false. Making a distinction between belief-independent perception and judgment based on perception, Gareth Evans[5] would perhaps drop the first claim. He openly pleads for nonconceptual content of perceptions. In ancient and medieval Indian Philosophy, standard Nyāya would also reject (1) by putting forward the distinction between prejudgmental indeterminate perception and determinate predicative perception. We should not forget that even indeterminate perception was postulated as the prior acquaintance with a property like Fness which would take up the role of the qualifier in the determinate cognition "*a* is F." But Naiyāyika-s would emphasize that even the content of determinate perception, including the particular to be characterized, the qualifying property, and their characterizing tie, is wholly perceptual. Determinate perception is not perception partly generated by words. Bhartṛhari solves the puzzle by rejecting (3): nothing counts as a cognition of an object, according to him, unless it is a distinguishing illumination of it, and nothing but a linguistic grid can enable us to illuminate and distinguish. Matilal, while discussing Bhartṛhari's view, quotes Sellars in rather vehement support: "all awareness of sort, resemblance, facts etc.—in short, all awareness of abstract entities—indeed all awareness even of particulars—is a linguistic affair."[6]

I suggest that we solve the puzzle by rejecting (2). My suggestion involves amending the traditional Nyāya position in lines suggested (but not fully developed) by Matilal, and developing Strawson's picture of perceiving itself as involving demarcating, classifying, recognizing, and identifying. Let us stop regarding some basic empirical concepts as mere meanings of bits of speech and acknowledge their anchorage in direct sense-experience. All animals, says Aristotle, "have an innate discriminative capacity called perception." And when a lion has many memories of individual oxen, it has a concept of an ox, although it has no ability to give reasons for calling something an ox or to ascribe possession of this concept to itself. But as Sorabji has wondered, even we humans do not give further reasons for all our concept-applications.[7] Our command over the concept of *pain,* for instance, must be as independent of language use and as experiential as a beast's multiple-memory command over the concept of pain. With due respect to Wittgenstein's "public language argument," the ability to use the word "pain" in the right circumstances is no essential ingredient or manifestation of that command.

The path to such a language-independent account of concept possession is rather thorny. It bristles with powerful objections and often falls into thickets of confusion. I shall have space to consider only one powerful objection. But before that, let me clear up some of the confusions.

Learning to perceive by mastery of language?

Suppose in early childhood my father pointed to a cow and told me, "That is called a cow." At that learning moment I did have to see the cow and also understand what he said in an accepting manner. It was a case of knowledge from testimony assisted by perception. Does that mean that now in my mature experience of the world when I see and claim to see an animal as a cow I am only telling an ungrateful half-truth if I say that I know it is cow because I simply perceive with my eyes that it is a cow? Should I rather say, each time, that I knew it was a cow on the basis of what I saw and what my father told me? If the latter answer were more accurate, then all predicative perception which could be reported by using words (common nouns, proper names, or verbs) that one originally needed to learn would indeed be awarenesses jointly produced by words and the senses. And insofar as arbitrary human semantic conventions would substantially contribute to their content, no predicative perception would ever reveal the world as it really is. It was to reject this covertly antirealistic construal of all judgmental perception that the adjective "nonlinguistic" *(avyapadeśyam)* was added to the general definition of perception in the *Nyāyasūtra*.[8] Vātsyāyana's commentary on this tricky word unambiguously shows that he was not regarding it as applicable only to the allegedly preconceptual indeterminate variety of perception, but was taking it to cover fully predicative perceptions as well. Of course one could not *say* what one saw or heard before learning some language or other. But the content of what one sees or hears after learning the word does not necessarily differ from that of the time when one had not learnt the word (*tadarthavijñānam tādṛgeva bhavati*). Jayanta goes further. Even if training in a language does enable us to see differences and similarities which go unnoticed by speechless brutes or babies, the resulting concept-applicative perception is not knowledge of the word any more than the seeing of a book lit up by a candle is seeing of the candle. Like the candle, the word or its memory is at best an aid to the senses. We see with help of rods and cones in the retina—do we therefore see rods and cones? Even Vācaspati, who restricts the application of the epithet "nonlinguistic" only to the so-called unverbalizable pre-predicative perceptions, clearly recognizes that the feature that is meant by the remembered generic word is also first independently perceived by the senses. The word remains neutral and uninterfering as far as the content of the experience goes.

Jayanta argues for the thesis that mastery over the use of the word "cow" cannot be presupposed by our perceptual ascription of cowness to a particular object. The argument runs as follows: such a mastery itself presupposes a prior grasp of the concept of a cow or a capacity to recognize cowness when faced by it. Even when the first instructor tells the novice "Such animals are called cows," she must be assuming that the novice has already seen the ostensively identified body as a sample of the bovine ilk but has no knowledge of the name of the ilk. If the learner has not done so and asks "Which animals?" it would be a joke empty of all information for the teacher to answer back "Just the ones which are called cows." To give a primarily linguistic account of universals is to commit two fallacies. First, there would be reciprocal dependence which is one form of circularity: the limiter of qualificandness and the predicated property being identical, the language learner's newly acquired information will take the form: *"red" stands for whatever it is that "red" stands for,* which is no information at all. Second, if, on subsequent occasions, to see a surface as red were to actively invoke one's knowledge of the meaning of the word "red," then every word would in effect mean itself because the complex object of the dispositional understanding or occurrent recall of the meaning of the word would include the word itself as the chief qualifier of the complex. This would make every word self-allusive, which is intolerable.

Both of these fears, of course, could be considered baseless. The guidance given to the first learner can remain linguistic without going round in a circle repeating the word to be taught. The instructor can just use synonyms or explanatory phrases to teach the use and hence the meaning of the word. But this rejoinder does not satisfy the realist who has independent reasons to find an extralinguistic home for at least some basic universals. To use McDowell's phrasing, we don't want to reduce our conceptually enriched picture of the world to a "frictionless spinning in the void" of a large circle of intertranslatable words none of which make any direct contact with the world we speechlessly encounter. Of course, Bhartṛhari or Quine would say that to be speechless is to be worldless; accordingly, Bhartṛhari would make a virtue out of the second fallacy. He welcomes the consequence that every word would stand for itself because on his theory the form or "own universal" of the word itself is its primary meaning. Couple this with his doctrine that the real word is the word-type or some internalized version of it, and you get the result that a word primarily means itself. Since neither his view of reality as evolving out of some eternal Speech-essence nor his view of language as an indivisible inner and innate endowment common to all sentient beings is recognizable as common sense, we have excellent Strawsonian reasons to set aside such rejoinders to Jayanta's arguments as revisionary and esoteric.

Why all concept-possession cannot be based on word-mastery

Jayanta's circularity objection against a uniformly linguistic account of concept-possession strikes me as uncannily similar to Dummett's complaint against modest theories of meaning:

> We are being told that an understanding of the word "sheep" consists in a knowledge of the proposition expressed by a certain sentence, that a knowledge of this proposition requires grasp of the concept of a sheep, and that a grasp of that concept by a speaker of the language in question will consist in his understanding of the word "sheep." Since (this is patently circular), we may conclude that the conception of a modest theory of meaning is a phantasm.[9]

Unfortunately, in spite of his insistence on the full-bloodedness of our account of knowledge of a language, Dummett would suspect any language-independent theory of concepts of the mistake which he calls the code conception of meaning and which he has attacked *ad nauseam*. So the first powerful charge against my suggestion that some concepts must be at our disposal before we can begin to learn any language would be this: once we make it possible to grasp a bit of sense or think a bit of thought antecedently to our command over the bit of speech-pattern which would eventually capture or express that sense, there is no escape from the psychologistic associationist picture of concepts as coming before our consciousness and before the dispensable clothing of words. It is well-known how Dummett finds this popular mentalist picture guilty of a category mistake, a vicious regress, and a skeptical invitation to the damaging idea of a private asocial mastery of a language. But as recent development in pure theories of thought has demonstrated, to make room for a basic prelinguistic ability to see actual shared and distinguishing features of objects and therefore to credit humans along with some other retentive action-planning animals with the power to have world-directed thoughts prior to and independently of language is not necessarily to embrace a code conception of language.

Which comes first: language or thought?

Apart from Dummett's own nagging doubts about what he labels the cardinal tenet of analytic philosophy, viz. the explanatory priority of language over thought, I can hint at a new way of cashing out the opposite priority. Why don't we forget this confusing equation of concepts as possessable by individual thinkers with Fregean senses which are not possessed but apprehended anyway![10] Instead, let us take the more daring step of going back to Frege's own use of the word "concept" and start talking about properties without considering it impossible to recognize a property perceptually. What I am proposing is a Fregean realism about properties without Frege's Platonist baggage that properties could only be thought but never perceived. Strawson, who recognizes that it is more natural to report that one saw a gait or heard a tune than to claim to have perceived particular instances of these universals, still has a hard time believing that we could literally see universals.[11] If we can give a sophisticated account of sensing universals as inhering in spatio-temporal particular exemplifiers—such an account already exists in Nyāya—then we need not be afraid of slipping into any mentalism about concepts.

If we underplay his earlier animus against the demand of full-bloodedness, then John McDowell's defense of the idea of concepts perceptually thrust upon us by the external world can help us strengthen this claim that we do not need to invent or impose universals as mere meanings of words. In order to fit words, concepts need not have a wordy origin. A common external world can be the mother of both perceived properties and meanings of common nouns and adjectives. There could be a deep connection between *senses* as the avenues through which the world impinges on our consciousness and *sense* as that which is grasped when a word is understood.[12] Surely we need a trained mind to be receptive to such sighted rather than blind intuitions. But there is no reason to think that what is received by such a "second nature" is tampered-with data. Concepts do open up the possibility of *error*; for they make *truth* possible. The mythical blind or raw intuitions which were supposed to be preconceptually received *would not have given us any truer picture* of reality. They would have given us no picture at all. The concept exists before the word, but there is nothing before the concept because the latter has a truth-value.

I take this restoration of the full prestige of genuine perception to verbalizable but not word-generated experience saddled with concepts to be welcome fall-out from Strawson's open rejection of the two-step theory of perception.[13] After this it is easier to offer a right-minded affirmative reply to the question "Would we have experienced the world as containing white snow and green grass, mothers sitting and dogs running fast if we did not have words like 'snow,' 'grass,' 'mothers,' and 'running'?" In order to say a long-overdue "yes" to this, I'm afraid we have to make room for concepts which are not due to words but nevertheless lie ready to be put into words.

Our use of publicly understandable words, whether made correctly or not, seems to depend on our prior familiarity with concepts. The relationship is not just one of causal dependence. There is a certain purposiveness to acquisition of new recognitional capacities, and to tethering those capacities to convention-sanctioned patterns of using words. Learning words—or concepts, for that matter—seems to have a clear future-oriented teleology. What would be the point of learning any skill unless one can look forward to its future practical use? The common sense belief that we learn for the sake of our preparedness for a different time from now must be basically correct, even though it opens another can of worms in metaphysics: "What are other times for us now?" or more specifically, "How real is the future?"

23

On What There Will Be

Introduction

Quine answered the central ontological question "What is there?" in one word: "Everything." This answer is closely linked to his slogan, "To be is to be the value of a variable." The question I want to answer in this chapter is straightforward: Do wholly future entities have a place inside Quine's nonhierarchical unrestricted world of everything? Is the future part of that "objective nature" over which our existential quantifiers range?

Given his lifelong crusade against propositions, mere possibilities, abstract entities such as kinds of all kinds, and all properties except those that could be reduced to classes of classes, one feels fairly certain that none of those possible gunmen that can turn up in the next fifty years at the doorway of the Taj Mahal will count as entities that his variables will ever take as values. But what about the actual ones who will? When we try to find the causes of our future sufferings, we look at sufferings that will actually occur. Right? Yet, surely the endeavor to prevent future suffering assumes that there is a chance that those sufferings will not be actualized! What are we then trying to prevent? Are objects of successful prevention parts of everything in nature?

A large part of our mental and linguistic lives consists of hoping, fearing, guessing, forecasting, warning, promising, planning, preparing, worrying, waiting—all of these refer to the future. Indeed planning ahead is supposed to be more rational than lamenting the bygone; getting ready for tomorrow makes more business sense than nostalgia about yesterday. Yet, to refer to *x* according to Quine's logic is to presuppose, if not actually claim, that there is an *x* to be referred to or definitely described. But the future is not there yet! Does that mean that a large part of our mental life—indeed the more rational part of it—is spent in *doing what cannot really be done*?

There have been at least four kinds of views among philosophers about this. First, there is *eternalism* (or spatialization of time): the view that past, present, and future are all equally real, tense is just a grammatical prejudice, and the "there is" of existential quantification means there was, is, or will be. Other times are just like other places. The dead and the unborn are elsewhen instead of elsewhere. Quine calls this the four-dimensional view and endorses it in the entry on "Future" in his *Quiddities*. J. J. C. Smart and, I am told, Einstein also believed in this view. Neither the uncertainties of quantum mechanics nor the Christian fuss about the evil-explaining freedom of the human will could shake Quine from this four-dimensionalism.

Second, there is *neutralism*: the view that the past and the present are real and that the future simply does not exist. This was the view of the Cambridge philosopher C. D. Broad. A milder form of neutralism does not commit the future to the realm of fiction. It takes the form of an asymmetry thesis: the past cannot be promoted or prevented but can be known or singularly and securely referred to. The future can be promoted and to some extent prevented but cannot be known or genuinely referred to or named.

Third, there is *presentism*: the past and the future are equally unreal; only the present truths are truths; present existents truly exist. To be is to be current. This view is unabashed in its Heraclitian indexicality.

Fourth, there is what could be called *non-presentism*: only the past and the future are real. This view is reported and refuted in the first century AD in Gautama's *Nyāyasūtra*. The present does not exist because it is a vanishing interval between the gone and the path to be traversed. I shall, for the most part, examine neutralism and eternalism.

The metaphysical question

"Is time real?"[1] has been a perfectly respectable metaphysical question discussed (and answered either way) by philosophers of all times and climates. Since the future is taken as one segment of time, "Is the future real?" should have at least an equal claim to being a substantial metaphysical question. Our question can thus be introduced as the inquiry: whether the yet-unelapsed stretch of time itself from now to ever after is real or not. For example, as specific instances under that general question we can ask, "Does the day 15th of October 6090 A.D. have any reality?" Due to the level of philosophical generality at which we ask our question here, all such questions should be answered the same way, affirmatively or negatively, as long as we choose to answer "yes" or "no" to the big question about the reality of the future as such. In this sense of the question, we cannot say that *tomorrow* is real but 4000 years after today is not real, because then our answer does not depend upon treating a future bit of time *just* with respect to its absolute futurity and nothing else. That is the first meaning that I can give to our question. But I must quickly confess that in this sense the question remains embarrassingly unclear. Of course, in daily discourse we give names (e.g., dates) to times as distinguished from events happening in those times. And I don't think that asking about a certain particular year or day whether it is real or not is completely unintelligible as a speech-act. One common use of the word "real," for instance, is to contrast something with imaginary items. We do talk about imagining a day or imagining a certain period of time both in the past and in the future—although it is hard to tell how we can *distinguish* in imagination between a day 2000 years *ago* and a day 2000 years *afterwards* without filling in the idea of the first day with the thought of some known event of history of the world around that time or some connection therewith! Works of fiction often place their plot in what can be safely called imaginary stretches of time. Perhaps we have to take all such talk about real slices of time as against imaginary ones—*reductively* in terms of real *events* and imaginary *events*.

Now consider the statement: the future set of events is not real. This could mean that the events, which will happen after now, have not yet happened and therefore that they are not real *now*. Or it could mean that no events will happen after now—we are just living in the terminal moment of the history of the universe. The first interpretation makes it an exceedingly uninteresting trivial statement, viz. that the future is neither the present nor the past. That just tells us what we mean by calling an event a future one. It does not tell us whether such an event exists or not. The second sense makes the negative view empirically so implausible that it is seen to be false almost while it is being stated: a negative future tense sentence mentioning a particular event (e.g., "A building will *never* be built on this site") may be hard to verify, but the statement "No event will ever happen after now" will refute itself by the very assumption of being understood or assented to by the hearer after it has been put forward. When reacting to a paper by J. J. C. Smart on the subject, Strawson remarked:

> So we offer the theorist of the unreal of the future a choice between a thesis ("Its all over") which he will certainly repudiate as false and a thesis ("What is yet to be is not yet and had not yet been") which he would certainly regard as too trivial to be worth embracing. When he rejects both, we invite him to be more careful, *in future*, expressing his sense of how it is with things.[2]

Nevertheless, I do suspect that there is something more than trivial in the non-apocalyptic version of this negative view. For one thing, although it may turn out to be a mistake, it is not an unpardonable logical howler to take the "is" in "The future is real" in the temporal sense. And this is what C. D. Broad does in *Scientific Thought* with his view that only the past and the present are real and that the future is *nothing* at all. He even suggests, by comparing speaking about *Puck* or any fictional item and about a future event or object, that the future has the same status as fiction (or maybe worse!—viz. because the fictional object in one sense bears its unreality on its face).

Before I rehearse and reject one of his own arguments for the view, let me conjecture how a Fregean can be misled to *agree* with such a view. In Frege's ontology tables, football matches, apples, and live people have *actuality* because they can act upon things in the spatio-temporal world, whereas numbers, senses of words, thoughts expressed by true or false sentences, value ranges, and classes are all objective entities but do not have any actuality—i.e., any role in the world of causes and effects. Nevertheless, these non-actual entities *are* there: they can be values of variables which are bound by the "there is" quantifier "(Ex)."

Now, Geach has always insisted that it is this *actuality* which is *lost* when something goes out of existence; for example, when a person dies or when an entire island is wiped off the face of the earth. By parity of reasoning, he should also say that it is this Fregean actuality which is *earned* by a baby when it is born or by a bridge when the last rivet is knocked in. Will he then not also say that unlike past events and present events which have either had their effects upon the world or are now changing the world somehow, the future is still causally barren and hence non-actual? Indeed, the Buddhist doctrine of momentariness is based upon a definition of existence or reality which exactly echoes the Fregean definition of actuality. To exist is to be *able* to produce effects. The Buddhist logicians rejected the modal notion of "potential capacity," so "ability to act" translates for them as "actually acting." Thus, one could hold that since no future event or item has *actually* acted upon us because of the impossibility of backward causation, the future is non-actual or unreal. I am not saying that all the Buddhists have actually said this. One famous commentator on Nāgārjuna remarks, "The future is that which has not yet attained its own nature." This suggests committing the future to nonexistence; but we have to remember the wider context of the remark which is a defense of universal emptiness and lack of own nature of everything. However, not all Buddhists adhered to the Emptiness school. The more realistic schools have much reflected on the metaphysical status of succession as such and the nature of the absolute past, present, future distinction (i.e., roughly, McTaggart's "A series" and "B series"). Their views have varied from a kind of empirical realism about all the three segments of time through a kind of *presentism* to absolute anti-realism about all times and temporal properties.

Now back to Geach. Frege looked upon actuality as a *losable* and *earnable* property just because he took actuality as a first-level property of *objects* (unlike tenseless-being which is supposed to be a property of concepts). We cannot argue that Geach must be wrong. Frege seems to divide his ontology roughly into the following three realms:

a. The realm of *actual objective* things (e.g., trees, people, physical events)
b. The realm of *actual subjective* things (e.g., ideas, mental images, pains)
c. The realm of *non-actual objective* things (e.g., numbers, classes, thoughts.)

If Geach were right, then we would have to take death reports or other reports of the cessation of material objects as describing the journey of an item from the first to the third realm. But that is patently implausible. By dying, I shall cease to be alive but shall not cease to belong to the category of living beings. By ceasing to exist, an actual object does not become an *abstract* object. Indeed, nothing but an actual and animate object can be (now) dead. A consumed cake does not now inhabit the realm of Fregean senses! Actuality, though a first-level property of only *some* objects, is an unearnable and unlosable atemporal property of them like any other categorical property—e.g., being a physical object. Thus, by a future event we don't mean an event which now lacks actuality; we mean a timelessly *actual* event whose effect on the spatio-temporal world will exist at a time relatively future to itself. Even the Buddhist-sounding criterion of causal efficacy need not be applied in the question-begging manner to mean "only that is real which has already mothered a change." Future things will exert their causal impact on more future things and can therefore be timelessly called *actual* and real.

Let us now examine one quick argument given by Broad. Since the present is by definition most recent, Broad argues:

a. The present event does not have a successor.
b. A future event is by definition a successor of the present.
c. Therefore, a future event is the successor of an event which is without a successor.

This is meant to reveal an incoherence in the very notion of a future event and is reminiscent of the classic example of an empty term in Indian logic: "the child of a childless woman."

Now, this is obviously mere sophistry. It is easy to see how the "does not" in premise "a" is used tensefully to mean "does not as yet," whereas the "is" in premise "b" is used tenselessly. The moment we rewrite the second definitional truth in a tenseful language ("The future event *will be* the successor of the present event") and add a little "now" to the first premise, the alleged incoherence vanishes. Every woman is at some point childless. Does that make all of us children of childless mothers?

But behind this apparent sophism lies a deeper worry or, rather, assurance. We can never *contemporaneously* identify an event as a future event. Maybe we can make or try to make demonstrative reference to the immediately adjacent future moment or event. But I suspect that even that reference cannot afford to be genuinely singular. The negative answer to our original question is a metaphysical expression of the semantic doctrine that we cannot demonstrate, pick out, name, or otherwise singularly refer to an item or event which lies wholly in the future in order to state about it truly that *here* is a future event. So we cannot point to a future event now.

The reference-theoretic sense

This yields the second reference-theoretic sense of the question "Is the future real?" which is: Can we make genuine singular reference to an item lying wholly in the future? I hold that we cannot. Before I defend this view, let me neutralize a possible source of an unqualified affirmative answer, which challengingly asks "Why not?" In the crucial sections 40–43 of *Philosophical Investigations*, there is a semblance of an argument to the effect that the name for a tool can continue to be used with the same reference even after the tool (the referent) has gone out of existence. We can also imagine using the name of a nonexistent object meaningfully. Take the following passage:

> But has for instance a name which has never been used for a tool also got a meaning in that game? Let us assume that 'X' is such a sign and that A gives this sign to B—well, even such signs could be given a place in the language-game and B might have, say, to answer them too with a shake of the head (One could, imagine this as a sort of joke between them).[3]

Now, commentators like Baker and Hacker have conjectured that in this passage Wittgenstein might have been arguing in the following fashion:

1. If we can name past items, then we can name future items.
2. If we can name future items, then we can name fictional items.
3. We can name past items.
4. Therefore, we can name fictional items.

I shall try to show that the first premise of this argument is not compelling. Although antenatal nonexistence and postmortem nonexistence are equally varieties of temporal nonexistence, our singular reference to the deceased seems to go rough such that our references to forthcoming items remain at best attempts awaiting ensured success. The use theory of meaning of proper names *might* be extended to cover fictional proper names on independent grounds. But the argument for that extension cannot be based on our use of names of things which have not yet come to exist.

We must remember that we are still arguing about what we can or cannot name or talk singularly about in plain world-talk. This game does not allow us to make a committed reference to the Tooth Fairy because there is no such person. Yet, even in this game, it seems, we have to admit that we can and do refer to Socrates when he is dead and not there at all. Do we *understand* his name completely if we just know how to use it and how to respond behaviorally to someone else's use of it in a sentence? Don't we have to know someone who in particular is being talked about? And how do we who live thousands of years after his death manage to do that? Since we cannot avoid singular reference to the dead, we must, it seems, give up the rule that existence at time n of an object is essential for our reference made at time n for it to be successful. But once we lift that restriction we immediately face the question whether our attempted reference to future items—equally lacking existence—can be consummated in advance of their actual emergence. Of course, we try and pretend to use ordinary names and definite descriptions purportedly referring to not-yet-existent items: the typical medieval example was the name "Anti-Christ." Hindus believe that "Kalki" is a name which now picks out the tenth reincarnation of Lord Vishnu who is going to be born a few thousands of years from now. Such names *claim* to be more than just surrogates for definite descriptions. The sentence "Kalki will ride a horse" is not meant to be about any old bearer of that name who happens to be the unique satisfier of all the specifications mentioned in the holy books of prophecy. Unlike Kalki, whichever child is first to be born in the twenty-third century may be the reference of the artificial designator "Newperson I." But Kalki is supposed to be *one precise* individual rather than just *precisely one* individual whoever it may be. One way of looking upon our use of such names could be to *pretend* that we are already in the designated future time where Kalki has been christened and that we have been handed down his name from a relatively past usage. But that would be to talk *fictionally* about Kalki. In actual religious usage, there is no such pretense involved in a believer's utterance of the singular sentence "Kalki will ride a white horse." While sincerely talking about the actual world, believers *wish* to be able to express singular thoughts about Kalki before his advent. But it seems that logic would not grant this wish. We could not apply a causal theory of reference to such names without implying that a future occasion of ostensive dubbing of the object determines the name's present employment by backward causal links. However epistemologically undecidable, unavailable, or irretrievably lost the past may be, we can always coherently assume that the present use of Socrates' name goes back to or is causally determined by the original use made by the presence of its bearer. The future, on the contrary, is not only unknown but is metaphysically open. Even the determinist cannot insist that an actual item of our fixed future enters the genetic history of our *present* use of its name. That is why even if some of our predictions involving definite descriptions fitting future items come true, we cannot argue that those predictions were about those items. We cannot have names *of* future items. We can only have names kept ready *for* them.

This view has been reenforced by the distinction between names and rigid designators. All names are rigid designators, but all rigid designators are not names.

My name picks me out at every possible world, even at worlds where my parents have not met and I do not exist. Once it *has been* used as a name of an object in the actual world, we are able to say from the perspective of the actual world that it is true at such I-less possible worlds that Arindam Chakrabarti does not exist in them. In order for this proposition to hold true at that possible world that name must designate me *at* it, though it cannot designate me *in it*, because I am not in it. But such strict namehood pertains only to names which have been actually used for actualized individuals. "Newperson I" has not been so used. Even if we keep that rigid designator ready for the firstborn of the twenty-third century and claim foreknowledge of the trivial truth that "Newperson I" will be the first to be born in twenty-third century, we cannot claim to have known a truth *de re* about "Newperson I."

Commentators of Wittgenstein should be warned that alleged names of future individuals not only lack a referent but even lack a use (as a name) now. Baker and Hacker asked: "Why is it not possible to name a future individual? Does logic prevent it?"[4]

If we accept Bob Adams' account, then the answer should be "yes." Singular posthumous reference is possible because the dead leave their thisness (haecceities) behind. But antenatal reference can never manage to be singular, for the thisness of an individual cannot precede the existence of that individual. It would be overhasty to generalize from the case of naming the broken tool that an author's chosen name for an unwritten work has as much *use* in the language-game of serious world-talk *qua a name* as the names of expired entities.

There are two reasons why a future item cannot be genuinely named. First, the openness of the future makes it as much vulnerable to failure of uniqueness as in the context of possible worlds. Prophecies about already existent items can come true singularly about them but prophesies apparently about precisely named not-yet existent individuals could equally well be fulfilled by a plurality of exact satisfiers of descriptions. Since no *one* of them has a better claim than *another*, the definite description backing up the name fails due to the failure of the "at most one" condition. The force of this argument can be best brought out by the following example of Prior's:

> Suppose some gifted gipsy goes into a trance in 1850 and says "Next century there will be a person called A.B. with such and such a character and history and a person called M.N. with such and such different character and history" and then suppose the man gets worried and says "No perhaps it is the second man I meant who is going to be called A.B. and have the first character and history and the first will be called M.N." and then gets still more worried and says "Perhaps I am even more wrong than that; it is neither of the persons I meant who will do and suffer these things, but two quite different individuals altogether." These worries are surely senseless.[5]

If you reject the descriptivist theory of proper names, then the alternative is to embrace some sort of a causal theory. Under a causal theory future objects have even less of a chance of being named. Let us use the example of the complete unassembled lectern-kit from which, following fully specific instructions for assembly, only one particular lectern can come into existence. Can't we dub that lectern now, before it has been put together, at least for the purposes of asserting its pre-originatory absence? Suppose we call that would-be lectern "Tubee." Will "Tubee does not yet exist" count as a genuine singular statement? Now, there can be two sorts of reasons for refusing to assign the status of a genuine name to a name-like expression. The first involves the lack of specificity of the intended *name*. Such was the trouble with the possible satisfiers of the fictional descriptions of a certain character. Since too many objects turn up with equal claim to fit the associated descriptions, the uniqueness-demanding proper name refuses all of them. But in the case of some future objects' lack of specificity, this can hardly be a problem. Only one unique lectern can come out of the members if the instructions of assembly are accurately followed and if they do not leave any alternatives for the assembler at any step.

The second reason for rejecting the claim of namehood is causal. According to the causal theory of singular reference, the name, or at least the particular use of the name, has to be an *effect* of its referent. Now, however specific the future lectern might be, it cannot cause a past use of the name "Tubee." If the actual history of that particular use of the name "Tubee" does not involve the lectern itself, then just by uniquely fitting the description, the future lectern does not become a genuine dubee. Incidentally, this explanation also covers our failure to be able to use names for merely possible entities which will in fact never come into existence. Suppose the lectern-kit that we talked about earlier is never assembled and is burnt off. As a set of past objects, we can still refer to those once-existent parts and specify the only possible table that would have come out of it. We can try once again to name it "Tubee." Tubee, in this case, will be a merely possible nonexistent. But, according to Kripke and other causal theorists, "Tubee" will not count as a genuine proper name.

Still we cannot quite consign the future or the merely possible lectern to the realm of fiction. "Tubee" may not be a name, but Tubee is not *unreal* like Sherlock Holmes' pipe. That is because no one shoots a fantasy-film about Tubee the lectern. Kaplan asks: Even if we do not allow singular reference to future objects, shall we permit quantification to range over them? Quantizing over future or merely possible entities surely will not be as revolting as quantizing over fictional or impossible objects! But the consequence here will be that within ordinary world-talk "it would then be natural to add a *narrow existence predicate*"—a predicate which will be true of past and present particulars but false of wholly future or merely possible values of variables.

We can playfully call this narrow existence predicate the "Broad existence predicate" after C. D. Broad, whose ontological whittling down of the future can now be reinterpreted in terms of the narrow existence predicate being true of only past and present referents of genuine names.

So it seems that we are left with a choice. We might reserve full-blooded reality only for items which can be publicly named and referred to singularly. In that case, we will hold with Prior, Ryle, and Geach that future items do not have this kind of reality, whereas past and present items do because:

a. We cannot genuinely *name* a forthcoming item (a forthcoming work mentioned in a Curriculum Vitae surely carries less cash value than work cited as already out).

b. Our knowledge of the future can never be definite *de re* knowledge strictly *about* the items that it pretends to be about.

Alternatively, we might argue in the following fashion: Why must reality require strict nameability and richly textured definite knowledge about it through singular propositions? After all, where in ordinary parlance do we have bare reference or properly proper names? Shouldn't we Quine away singular terms and be content with definite descriptions so that as long as something is a value of a variable it (tenselessly) is there? Thus "with objectual quantification we can have reference without naming." After all, how richly textured or fine grained is our knowledge of the past or even of the perceptually inaccessible bits of the present about which we are so eager to affirm some sort of concrete reality? It was this sort of appeal to the Minkowski interpretation of special relativity, which roughly treats time as another dimension of space, that made J. J. C. Smart maintain that "to be real is to be part of the universe, and if the universe in the twenty first century contains a certain thing or event then that thing or event is surely real."[6] And of course, to be part of the universe is to be an F such that (Ex)(Fx) with a tenseless quantifier and a tenseless manner of being F.

I have already revealed my sympathy with the former view. The spatializing of time upon which the latter view depends seems counterintuitive. Events situated in other times (in the same place) are not like events happening in other places at the same time. It is not a mere medical impossibility that we are incapable of travelling to the future and coming back to the present or of talking *de re* about events which are going to happen. Dummett has in one place compared parts of times with *roads*. I consider the analogy misleading. A road exists at a distance before it has begun and after it has come to an end, whereas walking along the direction of an increasing numerical order of streets, I can stand on the junction of 7th and remark strictly *about* the 22nd street that it lies ahead of me. But before a human being is born or a statue is made, I can at most record the generic absence of *a* human or any statue. Imagine Lorenzo de Medici looking at an uncut chunk of marble and telling Michelangelo "Ah! I see your David is still unmade." If he was referring to the very same David which we now see in the Academi in Florence with the full weight of the existence-assumption, then which existence was he coherently denying by calling it "*unmade*"? There is a sense in which when a road finishes, it does not perish—but at death a human being does. Before an entity comes into being it seems just poetry to think that it *lurks* somewhere out there in darkness. I must however emphasize that calling the future nonexistent (using the *narrow existence* predicate) in the second sense has *nothing to do* with the apocalyptic metaphysical view we rejected. Of course, there are, albeit will be, infinitely many chapters of real history to be unfolded after now, but when we say that it is still up in the air, we do not mean that these chapters are all written up in detail somewhere up there. Maybe the very general features of that yet to be unrolled scroll of time are determined by logical and natural laws. But conscious agents along with unconscious but freakish forces of nature can significantly affect the specific features of the future in a way that they cannot do to the past. Of course I can introduce some Cambridge changes in the past now: a twentieth-century American philosopher can bestow on an obscure fifth-century Indian logician the property of anticipating an insight which became famous after 1500 years by unknowingly rediscovering the same philosophical point. In *Quiddities* Quine has given a moral argument in support of his spatialized view of time which entails that future entities which will actually exist are real as actualized past and present entities.

He first poses a dilemma: environmental ethics demands that we should conserve energy, vegetation, and atmospheric balance in the interest of future generations. Now, surely we cannot work for the interest of nonentities. So future humans *do exist*. On the other hand, birth control, which is necessary to stop overpopulation, would involve denial of the right to life if a potential human exists as a future entity. But we know that birth control does not involve deprivation of life for anyone, hence *future humans do not exist*. His solution is based on his well-advertised hostility toward the merely possible. The fetus which is not allowed to come into existence would never have developed into a human, so such a human individual does not exist even in the future. Hence it is not a member of the existent future generation for whom conservation remains our duty. Future-born humans are as real as past and present ones, while unborn ones are figments of modal logic.

Apart from a gut-reaction against drawing metaphysical conclusions from fixed moral decisions, I find this dilemma suspect. Both its horns are weak. True, we cannot be asked to work for the benefit of fictional entities or nonentities. Members of future generations—actual *and possible*—must be entities. But in order to be an entity, something need not *exist*. Abraham Lincoln and the Holy Roman Empire are entities. They are not figments of fancy. Yet they no longer exist. Secondly, the second horn of the dilemma seems to concede a big point to the pro-life protesters against birth control. A rationally taken decision not to have a baby or to engage in nonreproductive sex might be justified on independent grounds which have little to do with non-killing or fear of overpopulation. A fetus can be conceived of as identical with a possible human, whereas right to life could be restricted to only the actual ones.

In any case, that strikes me as a rather flippant defense of a panrealist view of time or an omnitemporal view of existence. Upon my view, future babies, whether actual or merely possible, are not real now. Whether a currently actual fetus should be destroyed or not, or whether other measures of birth control should be taken is a distinct issue. Future humans—babies or adults—cannot be disallowed to be born, harmed, or killed *now* because they are not real enough to be dealt with roughly or tenderly.

Generally speaking, there *are* some future humans (most probably) but none of them *exist* specifically enough to be named or singled out individually.

The meaning-theoretic sense

Till now I have examined two senses in which the thesis of unreality of the future could be put forward. I rejected the thesis in its first, straight metaphysical sense but accepted it in its second, reference-theoretic sense. So the future is real, but one cannot name anything in it because it is not identifiable. Something or other will keep happening after now. If actuality or realness is defined as an ability to bring about effects, then to insist on the unreality of the future is to render the last moment of the present causally impotent and thus to take away actuality. So, *metaphysically* future things in general should be quite as actual as their present and past ancestors. Having concluded this, can I consistently go on to deny the future—the "narrow" existence predicate which is applicable to an item only if it can be successfully picked out by a genuine singular term? This second sense of reality, I explicitly acknowledge, is intimately connected with language use, especially with the epistemic backdrop of singularness of reference. The richly textured knowledge of a particular referent which we can possibly claim in support of a name of an already actualized (past or present) bearer of a proper name is *in principle* unavailable for a name kept ready for a forthcoming referent. Why, one could ask, should that make the actual future any less real? What does singular reference have to do with reality? Whether someone recognizes use of referring expressions as genuinely picking out determinate individuals of a certain class has often been relied on as a mark of whether that person is a *realist* about items of that class. By making the distinction between the metaphysical and the reference-theoretic senses of the question of reality, I wanted to make it consistent to hold that some future item or other exists but that no particular items do and we could never single out which ones will.

I shall now discuss a third and meaning-theoretic sense in which reality of the future could be questioned or defended on the basis of considerations regarding what it is for us to *understand* a future tense sentence.

To hold that a certain type of thing is not real is to refuse to be a *realist* about that type of thing. A realist about the future, in this technical sense, is one who believes that contingent sentences about future events or times are either determinately true or determinately false independently of our capacity to establish or recognize their truth-value. An anti-realist about the future, in this sense, is one who believes that the sentence "There will be a sea-battle in the Persian Gulf in 2050" is neither determinately true nor determinately false at this moment insofar as we have no way of ascertaining the occurrence or nonoccurrence of the event in virtue of which it is supposed to be true.

There is just not a state of affairs which renders that such statements are either determinately true or determinately false. When a human agent talks about a future performance of a voluntary action in the first person (e.g., "I shall meet you tomorrow at noon"), the anti-realist would typically interpret her as expressing a current resolution or intention rather than describing an objective future. In either case a statement about the future does not *have* a verification-transcendent truth-condition. The prediction of the naval battle would be true, false, or neither only insofar as present checkable propensities make it so. The personal promise or resolve would have sincerity conditions to be given in terms of the agent's present genuine intention. Adopting this last view could constitute calling the future unreal in our third meaning-theoretic sense.

But we have to be cautious in setting out our philosophical options here. Let us proceed by listing the alternative views which could be coherently adopted. Doing so will show that at least some of the usual assumptions made about the logical connections between determinism and realism about the future and reductionism and rejection of bivalence about future contingents are quite incorrect.

Here is a list of the *usual assumptions:*

1. It is often taken for granted that to believe in ontically free will (i.e., not only freedom based on ignorance or knowledge of necessity) is to be an anti-realist about the future, and, consequently, that the one way to be a realist about the future is to be a determinist. I shall show that this is false.
2. It is also generally believed that to give up the law of bivalence about future tense statements is to be an anti-realist about the future. This is false too.
3. I have suggested above, with my characterization of a meaning-theoretic anti-realist about the future, that such a view always takes the form of a reductive thesis. This might typically be the case. But taken quite generally here as elsewhere, anti-realism need not necessarily come with a program of translation or reduction.
4. It is also quite common to suppose that anyone who understands predictions, warnings, promises, and forecasts in terms of present tendencies and present intentions must be an anti-realist about the future. I suspect that even this assumption is questionable. Unless many of these four sorts of assumptions were false, the following four views *could* not even be consistently proposed. Without arguing for any of them I shall set them out as initially *consistent* semantic views.

We may have to question one or more of these common assumptions when we try to sort out clearly the available alternative positions we can take with respect to the question: Is the future real?

Non-reductive realism with and without bivalence

I can believe that future tense sentences like "The United States will start World War III in 2027" are just like past tense sentences, either timelessly true or timelessly false. They are made true or false—independently of our ability to determine their truth-value—by those very future circumstances to which such sentences explicitly allude. Now, does this necessarily mean that one is a determinist? Of course, a determinist will say the same thing. And the fatalist will somewhat inconsistently add the frill that it *was* always fixed which truth-value that sentence will have. If disjunctive statements about a certain topic can be taken as being *about* that topic at all, then it is easy to construct compound sentences about the future which *now* looks quite definitely true. Here we are well advised to take the adverb "determinately" seriously. It is possible to regard the future as metaphysically *real, yet open*. In this case, one can disjunctively assert jointly exhaustive and mutually exclusive alternatives about the future in the form "*a* will be either F or G or H, etc." without committing to *the* deterministic claim "*a* will *determinately* be either F or G or H, etc." Some philosophers have then distinguished between the analytic law of excluded middle and the synthetic law of excluded middle. The former is compatible with freedom, while the latter is not.

At this point I want to consider the possibility of another sort of realism about the future. This realism rejects the thesis of bivalence and yet does not reduce claims about the future to claims about present tendencies, expectations, or intentions. This will be the position of someone who believes in an objective *third* value such as "indeterminate" which could be assigned to any statement just as "truth" and "falsity" are assigned to it. If a statement's possession of any one of these three truth-values is conceived of as quite independent of our ability to ascertain which truth-value it actually has, then there could easily be *a realist-indeterminist* about the future. Such a position is clearly suggested by Boethius in his second commentary on Aristotle's *De Interpretatione.* It is not because of our shortsightedness, such a believer in objective chance might hold, that the actual truth-value of a future contingent is undetermined. Rather, there is no determinate truth or determinate falsity that *actually* attaches to the proposition now. As Boethius puts it, it is essentially *unknown not only to us but to nature.*

Accordingly, for such a realist-indeterminist, God's knowledge of everything is quite compatible with God's not knowing that the future sentence is either determinately true or determinately false. Indeed, God would be *mistaken* if he projected back the actual future situation which will obtain X-branded future tense propositions either true or false. The metaphysical nature of "everything" includes the indeterminate truth status of the contents of our singularly expressed hopes, fears, resolutions, and warnings about the future. As such, knowing everything entails knowing such future-involving propositions to be indeterminate. The coherence of this position shows that the first two of the above-mentioned assumptions are false.

Reductive realism

One could also hold that future tense sentences should be understood as emphatic and picturesque ways of talking about present propensities, decisions, preparations, trends, etc., and that like our statements explicitly about present or past facts, they are either determinately true or determinately false. A realist about *trends* can hold that a trend either exists or does not exist—independently of our recognitional capabilities. An actual defense of such a thesis is rare in the philosophical literature, perhaps because few philosophers have looked upon tendency statements as *barely* true. If someone were to be a realist about Lockean secondary qualities, while regarding them as powers, one would have to give a similar defense. Nevertheless, it seems perfectly consistent, on the face of it, to reduce all talk about what is going to happen into talk about present potentialities and to retain mind-independence and bivalence about statements about potentialities. Doesn't this show the fourth assumption to be questionable?

Non-reductive anti-realism

One could quite consistently believe that the future is metaphysically *unreal* and that *that* is why our talk about it cannot be reduced to any other statements definitely about objective reality. Anti-realism in this strong sense need not and perhaps could not take a reductive form, as long as one remains a realist about the reductive class of statements. Someone who refuses to admit that fictional utterances express genuine thoughts need not take them as oblique ways of talking about the real world, e.g., about what the author of the fiction wrote or imagined. Analogously, we need not understand future tense statements as first translatable into statements about present propensities and resolutions and then regard them as either true or false. Such radical anti-realism about future tense sentences would still require an account of what we grasp when we understand forecasts and promises. But that account will eschew any reference to truth or even to assertability conditions: the speech-acts of predicting and pledging would have to be understood in terms of how sincerely one is taking the risk of being proved wrong or insincere, etc. In any case, anti-realism about the future need not be reductionistic. This proves the third assumption to be incorrect.

Reductive anti-realism

Finally, there is neutralism, which takes a reductive form. A neutralist thinks that future tense sentences should not be understood as made true or made false by what is *in* fact going to take place. There just is not any definite future which renders every such statement determinately either true or false. Notice that the neutralist does not slip into the absurdity of maintaining that the future does not exist in the sense that the present moment is the terminal point in the history of the universe. Nor does he merely underline the triviality that what will happen has not yet taken place. Future reality is still in the making. Our statements about it, says the reductive anti-realist, can be intelligible only if taken as statements about present tendencies, hopes, fears, promises, and resolutions. Such a view would be the future-related counterpart of the phenomenalist view about the past once held by Russell and Ayer: our statements about the past are to be understood as made true or false (or left undecided?) by present memories and observable traces of other sorts. Notice that the mere adoption of a reductive view does not make the neutralist an anti-realist unless she also takes the further step, on the strength of this reduction program, of rejecting the principle of bivalence for statements about the future. There may not exist either a present tendency confirming or a present tendency against a given prediction, in which case the prediction can be taken as neither true nor false.

K. C. Bhattacharya's metaphysic of the future

We find a form of neutralism in the work of K. C. Bhattacharya. He starts his searching paper (titled "Reality of the Future") with the provocative remark:

> The future, if expected without a ground, cannot be said to be known as real. If expected on a known ground, it is believed to be real. Really, however, we infer at least that B *can* be and only expect non-cognitively that B *will be* … What we may claim to know or infer is that B can be, that there is a tendency for B to be.[7]

From this he eventually concludes that the future is real only to our active will or to our irrational faith. Any statement about what will be is understood as a statement about what is currently being looked for or being brought about as an intended object of expectation and effort. In holding this view, K. C. Bhattacharya was going against the mainstream Indian view of the time, which was unmistakably deterministic and externalistic. Another contemporary traditionalist Indian philosopher has given a rather original exposition of the ancient Sāṃkhya view of causation. The argument runs as follows: the future jug which will come out of a lump of clay must be real (even before it has emerged in the form of a jug). Why? If the future jug were not real, futurity, which is a genuine temporal property of the jug, would have no bearer. With this and other standard arguments, the Sāṃkhya Vedānta camp has tried to establish that the yet-to-exist must be as real as its material cause which precedes it in time. Otherwise the two could not be so intimately related.

K. C. Bhattacharya, on the other hand, recognizes that the relation expressed by "comes out of" is as intentional as the relation expressed by "is expected by" or "is desired by." He therefore maintains that we cannot argue from the determinate reality of the second term in relation to that of the first. However complete our causal preparation for a certain expected outcome might be, what K. C. Bhattacharya calls the "principle of objective indetermination" tells us that we can never be certain that there is nothing to counteract the actualization of the *specific* outcome which was visualized. That is why we can never *know*—in the richly detailed way in which we can claim to know the present or the past—the *exact* absentee to what Indian metaphysicians have called a prior-absence. After the thing has come into existence we can retrospectively identify its prior-absence *as* the absence of this thing. But as long as *the* absence prevails we can only speak of the absentee in general terms.

It is this essential resistibility of contingent future events which explains why singular reference to the future cannot be allowed. Suppose that we are planning a party next week which we call "FUN 92." If "FUN 92" is a genuine referring expression, then the party next week cannot *not happen*. Now, since every party in the future, however well planned and securely guaranteed can eventually not happen, "FUN 92" is not a genuine referring expression.

After noticing that future tense sentences are to be taken as expressing belief about present tendency or as expressing the will to bring about something, K. C. Bhattacharya notes that these two uses of "will" often clash. Someone may sincerely wish to do something while firmly and with good reason believing that she will not be able to accomplish the task. Thus it might be odd but consistent to say "I am going to finish my book this month but I am not going to finish it this month." The first conjunct talks about the willed future and the second about the believed future.[8]

However plausible the above neutralist view might sound, it leads to several grave difficulties:

First, at least in its straightforward reductive form, it leads to inconsistency of the truth-value of the same statement. Take the statement "A football match will be played on the 20th of April." Since this does not involve any individual indexical expression, what proposition it expresses or what statement is made by it should not be determined by who utters it and when—as long as it is uttered before the 20th of April. Now perhaps on the 15th this is true because the relevant tendency and resolution exist most definitely on that date. On the 18th the game is called off (due to sudden illnesses), but the tendency and resolution may yet be reversed. On the 19th no definite trend either way exists, for the decision makers are in a tie. The chances of the match being played are fifty-fifty. In this case, the disputed proposition "There will be a football match on 20th of April" would be true on the 15th, false on the 18th, and without any truth-value on the 19th.

This will hardly daunt the anti-realist about the future. It is only the realist who wishes to retain bivalence and the properties of being *simply* true or *simply* false for the relevant class of statements. Yet a nagging doubt remains. It is one thing to be ready to admit that a certain statement is neither true nor false because it is undecidable, but it is quite another thing to hold that the same statement is true at one time, false at another, and truth-valueless at yet another time. Perhaps we should conclude with Dummett:

> [J]ust because, on his (the neutralist's) view there is no constraint on the different truth-values the sentence may have at different times, there is no serious sense in which he is taking it to make the same statement on the different occasions of utterance.[9]

This looks like an unpalatable consequence to me. It seems counterintuitive that at various times of utterance an unambiguous future tense sentence without any token-reflexive word should serve to make different statements.

Secondly, Dummett points out that if we take this reductive view of future tense statements, then our existing practice about how to settle a wager will call for drastic revision. As we commonly understand a bet, like "Oxford will win the boat-race in 2027," it is lost when 2027 comes and Oxford does not win. But if all I mean by that statement is that what renders the statement correct (if it is correct) is that there is a definite tendency in principle ascertainable for Oxford to win the 2027 race now, then the bet should be settled immediately by calculating the odds right away. To this, the neutralist may answer back in the following fashion. Since present tendencies might exist unperceived, a reduction to talk about present tendencies need *not* make bets about the future either immediately settleable or any easier to win. But this reply is not actually available to the neutralist. If the neutralist regards facts about present tendencies verification-transcendent, his position boils down to what I have called reductive realism.

Finally, there is a shadow of circularity in the neutralist's reductive program. Insofar as the reductive clan of present tense sentences will include statements about *intentions* and insofar as such intentions are unintelligible except as intentions directed toward the actual future, the present tense translations would involve ineliminable reference to future events. Even if this reference were nonsingular, the neutralist reduction can never expunge talk about present tendencies or resolve talk about the future. If, as Dummett originally insisted, we demand of the reductive anti-realist that statements belonging to the reductive clan be intelligible independently of any statement of the disputed claim, then no satisfactory translation or reduction could be given of future tense statements in terms of present tense statements regarding intentions. There can be no intelligible characteristic of intentions without ineliminable allusion to the future objects to which they are directed.

Even if neutralism can be salvaged from these difficulties, I have very general qualms about the standard Dummettian[10] way in which the case for anti-realism regarding such undecidable sentences as "There will be a sea battle in the Persian Gulf in 2027" is made. Since I cannot make up my mind between these four alternative meaning-theoretic views about the future, let me end by recording some of these qualms.

In my view, if we fully understand a sentence and yet do not know how to prove or disprove it, that shows that our understanding of such a sentence does not consist in knowledge of verification conditions. The meaning of the sentence "There will be a World War in 2027" is perfectly clear to me. Yet I have no clue as to how to go about establishing or confirming it. Doesn't that seal the fate of the thesis that grasp of meaning is knowledge of verification conditions? Of course, the knowledge of truth-conditions that a realist thinks we do possess with regard to unambiguous non-vague future contingents might be impossible to *manifest* or *display* in a manner which will satisfy Dummett. But such unmanifestability will be a problem even for our knowledge of verification-conditions in case of most undecidable sentences without some phony allusion to hypothetical powers of proof. Shall we then say that we just do not know the meaning of future tense contingent sentences? But, surely, we do! A verificationist might respond that we could evince our knowledge of the meaning of a future tense sentence by the practice of *rejecting* bad proofs, thereby showing that we know what does *not* establish the sentence as true. But when faced with two equally undecidable sentences with completely distinct understandable contents, the mere practice of rejecting certain verification-procedures as inconclusive would never constitute adequately scrutable evidence that a certain language user understands the two sentences as having distinct meanings. In any case, the verificationist seems to be in no better position to give an account of what it is that mastery over the meaning of an unverifiable future tense sentence enables us to do. Although we are at a loss to offer behavioral criteria for distinguishing between someone who does understand an undecidable future contingent and someone who does not, we cannot deny that we do understand them. This combined fact seems to be a reductio of the view that full manifestability of knowledge of meaning is a constraint on any adequate account of meaning. Dummett fears that one bad consequence of accepting a realistic truth-conditional account of the meaning of such problematic sentences would be that even someone who does not really understand the sentence "World War III will happen in 2027" could pass himself off as grasping its meaning by producing its so-called homophonic truth-conditions or by producing a translation of it which he equally fails to understand. Thus understanding will become fakeable. Whether one knows the meaning of a sentence or not will remain a matter of private first-person introspective authority. Now, that is a consequence which is better avoided. But a *realist* about the future could easily be a realist across the board and insist that, like the truth-condition of the above sentence, the truth conditions of the sentence "S knows the *meaning* of the sentence 'World War III will happen in 2027'" are also recognition-transcendent. In other words, S could actually understand it without anybody else ever being able to decisively make out whether he does or does not.

A global realist will not be threatened by Dummett's manifestation argument because it's very first premise (that knowledge of meaning must lie open to public view) assumes anti-realism about understanding-ascribing sentences. Whether one agrees with Dummett's manifestability argument or not, it must be acknowledged that it offers a fertile ground for a discussion of the realism links that have been the subject of this book.

In what follows I will try to show how God's omniscience could be the key to realism about the external world, that is, how a belief in external objects seems to entail theism and vice versa.

24

Is There a World Out There? God Knows

On the very idea of an external world

"Out there" is an unanalyzable adverbial idiom of English. Its meaning is best given by its use, and not by a lexical breakup, as in the case of an idiomatic adjective like "out to lunch." But philosophers addicted to analysis could find a lot of juice by chewing on "out" and "there." The word "out" points at externality and mind-independence, especially if you take it as an ellipsis for "without." "There" or "being there" signals bare existence. To be there is to be real *simpliciter*, with a tilt toward being located in space. To be there is to *be* and to *be somewhere*. Insofar as an ordinary opaque object of perception has a back side which the front side occludes, the unseen side poses a mereological threat to the naïve realist who insists that the whole object is directly seen. Since the back of the object exists unperceived, the word "back" potently captures the realist spirit. Berkeleyans are lampooned about risking the perishing of valuable items or people they have left "back home" unless God keeps an eye on them. Realists about the past have to find an ontological asylum for traceless events that took place "back then." So, the richest characterization of a realists' world (inclusive of realism about the past) would have been "the world out back there." Unfortunately, that is not a permissible English idiom even in the outback.

By excavating common sense and ordinary usage, we can detect at least eight different elements in our concept of a "world out there" or what is in effect the same concept, the concept of *the way things are in themselves*.

a. Collection of all real objects of perception or of other possible varieties of knowledge (objects which are accusatives of those very cognitions that they cause)
b. The totality or unity of all facts, when by "facts" we mean true propositions
c. The infinite sum of all events/processes past, present, and future
d. Set of all such facts which would be the case even if any particular individual did not think of them or did not know them (mind-independence, cashed out as ignorance-tolerance)
e. A physical cosmos made up of space-occupying particulars and their properties and relations
f. Totality of all objects which cause or can cause our perceptions of them and can exercise causal power on each other

g. The common focus or shared objects of the perception of different human individuals who may not know each other's minds
h. The common place inhabited by and actively and adaptively negotiated by conscious living beings of different species, human and nonhuman, the place where they perceptually locate objects and each other's bodies.

An anti-realist about the external world repudiates one or more of the above concepts as incoherent, redundant, or confused.

Five ways of being an anti-realist

There are at least five distinct ways an anti-realist about the external world could repudiate the many-faced notion of a world out there. Some of those ways are called "idealism"—a term notorious for its many and sometimes incompatible meanings.[1] Anti-realism is a safer term, which may be stipulatively used for any of the following five views:

A1. The existence of mind-independent objects in space is doubtful or unprovable because from within perceptual experience there is no way of telling if one is dreaming or awake, and dream-perceptions do not require the support of any external objects (Kant calls this "problematic idealism").

A2. The idea of an object existing without being registered in any consciousness is incoherent.

A3. An object of awareness and the awareness of the object are identical, because the one is never found in isolation from the other.

A4. Since we can explain every feature of our language and experience without assuming an external world, it is parsimonious to hold that there actually *is no* such external world.

A5. Since to understand a material object-statement is to come to know the conditions under which we can prove, verify, or justify it to be true or false, rather than to know its recognition-transcendent truth-conditions, we must be ready to recognize such a statement as neither determinately true nor determinately false, in case it cannot be proven, verified, or justified to be either.

Realists in early modern or twentieth-century Western philosophy and in classical and medieval Indian philosophies have refuted at least the first four versions of anti-realism. Before exploring the connection of these realism-debates with the debates about the possibility or existence of an omniscient entity, let me rehearse two lesser known refutations of A3, the idealistic thesis that a heavy shell is identical with someone's awareness or idea of a heavy shell because the two are necessarily and inseparably co-cognized.

Before discussing the first millennium CE Indian realist rejoinders, let me summarize Frege's 1918 refutation of idealism:

(i) The heavy shell is indistinguishable from the idea or perception or awareness of the heavy shell (assume anti-realism).
(ii) Weight (heaviness) is a property of the shell.

(iii) Weight is a property of the idea or perception or awareness of the shell. (If $X=Y$, then for all F, if F is a property of X, F must be a property of Y.)
(iv) Weight cannot be a property of any idea or sensation, since ideas or sensations could not be heavy or light.
(v) Weight *is and is not* a property of the idea of heavy shell (iii and iv, Conj).

Since (i)—assumption of "idealism"—leads to a contradiction, it must be false. Therefore, everything that exists is not a subjective idea, the heavy shell is not identical with the idea/perception/awareness of the heavy shell.

Suppose, here, the Idealist questions premise (ii) and says: "It is not the weight which is a property of the idea of the shell, but the idea of weight, since everything is an idea. When you substitute "the shell" with "the idea of the shell," you must also substitute, uniformly, "weight" with "the idea of weight." What is the problem in taking the idea of the weight to be a property of the idea of the shell?" Frege's answer captures the basic flaw of any anti-realist reduction of external object to subjective experiences or ideas or possibilities of perception: a conflation between parts and properties.

The relation between these two mental entities is this: idea of weight and idea of a weighty shell would at best be the relation of part and whole. The more complex idea includes the simple idea as a part. But a part is not a property. In the entirely subjective realm, only part–whole relationships hold, if any relations hold at all (Udayana shows that if we take the full consequences of Buddhist pan-mentalistic reductionism, no relations survive). There would be no room for genuine exemplification and substance-property relationship in a world of mere ideas. Externality of objects of cognition, thus, is closely connected to the *generality* (and instantiability) of properties and the mind-independence of exemplification (or inherence) as a relation. You cannot be a realist about particular objects without being a realist about properties and exemplification-relation.

Among many anti-realist arguments put forward by Yogācāra Buddhists, the most interesting one is a version of A3: *an awareness of a patch of blue and the patch of blue itself must be identical because they are inseparably apprehended together*. If two things are constantly co-cognized such that one of them cannot be apprehended without the apprehension of the other, the two must be one and the same thing, such as the two moons in case of the double moon optical illusion. The point is the same as Berkeley's Master Argument: the impossibility of proving the existence of an unapprehended object. Dharmakīrti, who proposes this argument in both *Pramana Varttika* and *Pramana Viniscaya*, has an error-theoretic explanation of why the object is projected as outside of the mental apprehension. Our consciousnesses, which are streams of momentary self-aware mental quanta, have an erroneous tendency to divide the grasping part and the grasper part of themselves as distinct. The grasper parts are lined up inside as permanent egos, while the grasped bits are lined up outside as external objects. Hence the aptness of the optical illusion analogy: one moon of reflexive self-sensation misperceived as two moons, the subject and the object.

If one feels uneasy with the "positive instance" of the double moon because one is not sure whether both of these moons are to be judged illusory or only one of them, then the Buddhist logician would welcome the unease. For, it is this very duality of the grasper and the grasped which is illusory. In their example, the moon itself is perfectly real; it is the misperceived twoness of the moon which is a result of a diseased double vision.

The Indian realists have simply riddled the anti-realist's "Master Argument" from invariable co-cognition of object and awareness with holes of fallacies. For example, they point out that the Yogācāra Buddhist has used a hostile *hetu* (*inferential sign*), a counter-probative reason property which proves the opposite of the target property, identity.

Yet we have to live with the predicament that we cannot put our finger on a barely real event or object without somehow touching it with our language and thought. We cannot imagine an unimagined world without us. Some famous refuters of idealism have themselves ended up with a profounder entanglement with idealism. Kant and Śaṅkara's refutations of subjective idealism have been underwritten by a metaphysics which relegates both the mental and the material world into merely empirically real appearance. Some sort of direct access to the external world has been ensured at the cost of reducing outer space to a subjective form of sense perception.

What does God have to do with it? Does liberation bring omniscience?

The realism debate, we saw, is about the bare existence of unknown objects, of objects tolerating our ignorance of them, or as J. N. Mohanty (developing the Advaita Vedanta concept of positive ignorance) and James Frederick Ferrier[2] would put it, about real *objects of ignorance*. The more we know, the smaller becomes the shadow of our ignorance but sharper are the contours of that shadow. Any comparison between less and more knowledge logically entails an unsurpassably maximal degree of knowledge. What no one—which means no one like us—knows would be knowable to that paradigm of epistemic perfection. God is no one and to be someone is to focus on certain things to the neglect of other things. To be real is to be accessible to an ideal unsurpassable epistemic excellence. This is how the realist Yoga philosophy of Patañjali arrives at the idea of God: "*There, the seed of (possible) omniscience becomes unexceedable.*" In another part of the Yogasūtra IV.14–17, Buddhist anti-realism is explicitly refuted and a real object (vastu) is described as "known-unknown" or "known as partly unknown" to individual minds with object-directed intentionality.

Davidson's use of the possibility of an omniscient interpreter

A simple-minded realist thinks that idealism is sheer arrogance. In saying that all of reality is within consciousness isn't the idealist claiming that he knows everything? Not only does the naïve idealist say "What I don't know is not knowledge," he further says that if he is not aware of something, then it does not exist. Compared to such epistemic megalomania, which claims to have made the emerald green by the color of one's consciousness, the realist's stand seems cognitively humble: things can and do exist totally uncognized by me or by any center of consciousness. To be a realist is to *defer*[3] to the existence of unknown realities. But the simple-minded idealist points out a contradiction in the realist position. When the realist says: there exist lots of things which I don't know and which perhaps no one knows—all those blossoms born to blush unseen, she could not be asserting such objective existence unless she implied that *she knows* that there exists such unknown things. So, in effect, the realist claims that lots of things exist which neither I nor anybody else knows but I know that they are there. Kant tried to remedy this contradiction by making it explicit that the existence of unknowable things in themselves is not a matter of *knowledge* but was only a matter of *thinking* and taken on trust.

Russell tried a better solution by clarifying that *knowledge that something exists* is one kind of knowledge and *knowledge of that thing* is another kind of knowledge. The latter can be absent, while the former is present. I don't know my great great-grandfather but I know that he existed. This seems to save the realist from the peril of self-refutation. Yet, this question of facing our own ignorance, which is at the heart of the debate between realism and idealism, remains an open question. Even if we claim indirect knowledge by description of all that exists, if all real things are essentially knowable, are we not denying the possibility of existence beyond the limits of human knowledge? When I know that I do not know something, what exactly is the object of my knowledge?

It is here that the concept of omniscience becomes directly relevant to the realism versus anti-realism debate, albeit in a maddeningly hairy way. The concept of omniscience is not merely of theological interest. Naïve idealism is the claim that what we do not know does not exist. A realist, on the other hand, claims that even what we are contingently or necessarily ignorant about may and does exist objectively. Since omniscience is the logical negation of partial ignorance—to say "S knows all things" is to deny that there are some things that "S does not know"—the very idea of knowing everything is crucially and contentiously connected to the perennial philosophical dispute between idealism and realism.

After gathering dust in the infrequently used section of philosophical theology for almost a century, the concept of omniscience came back to the fashionable mainstream of Western analytic philosophy in the late 1970s. Donald Davidson helps himself to the concept of an omniscient interpreter who knows everything about the world and about what causes us fallible users of language to assent to any sentence. He does not assume that there actually is one such all-knowing individual but claims "there is nothing absurd in the idea of an omniscient interpreter." Davidson has a two-step proof against the skeptic who tells us that all or most of our beliefs about the world could be false. The first step shows how I cannot identify your beliefs and therefore single out some of them as your false beliefs unless I share most of your other beliefs. Thus interpretation breeds concurrence. But why would it not be possible that this shared coherent network of our beliefs is massively mistaken? It is here, at the second step of the proof, that Davidson needs the consistent possibility of an omniscient interpreter. If such an interpreter can understand us by maximizing shared beliefs, then, given the first step, we must be capable of sharing most of our beliefs about the world with a being who has all and only true beliefs. Thus most of our beliefs must be true. In this way, the possibility that we are in massive error is ruled out.

There have been at least three kinds of critical response to this unexpected use of possible omniscience to bridge the gap between being interpretable and being largely true. The first line of criticism is that Davidson needs not an omniscient but an infallible interpreter. The second objection identifies a modal fallacy in the argument. If it is merely possible that there is an omniscient interpreter, then it is merely possible that we have a largely true network of belief—a conclusion that the skeptic can easily agree with. But Davidson claims to have proved that our network of beliefs is largely true. The third line of criticism accuses Davidson of begging the question. Since interpreting requires maximized sharing of beliefs, and fallible people cannot share most of their beliefs with infallible people, it is the very omniscience or infallibility of that fictional individual which will disqualify her as an interpreter of error-prone earthlings. Thus, a skeptic will balk at the apparently innocent idea of an omniscient interpreter. To assume that these two descriptions are compatible is already to assume that our beliefs about the world are truth-prone rather than error-prone.

Although I am just as intolerant of global skepticism as Davidson is, and I think Davidson answers the first two objections, this last criticism may be lethal. I am not so worried about begging the question: metaphysical ascetics lives on question-begging! But there is deep trouble *within* the notion of omniscience toward which this last objection against Davidson draws our attention. Mere infallibility would not serve Davidson's purpose because it is perfectly consistent for an infallible being to confess that she cannot make sense of us at all. All that she believes is true, but all that is true she need not believe. If Davidson's objector is right that an infallible person would not understand us, then an omniscient person would both know and not know what we mean. He would know because he is omniscient and not know because he cannot interpret massively mistaken people.

Davidson may find a way out of this impasse. But the larger questions remain: Can an all-knowing unerring person know what we fallible folk groping in the semidarkness of some flicker of knowledge in the midst of a general cloud of unknowing mean, feel, or believe? If such an omniscient Buddha or God spoke to us, like Wittgenstein's lion, could we understand him? Would it be appropriate to ascribe any beliefs to him, let alone beliefs shared by us? We shall see in the next section how both heterodox Buddhists and Orthodox Mīmāṃsāka-s rejected the idea of "eternal knowledge." One who does not *come to know* from once not having known, they would say, simply does not know. Could we recognize omniscience given that we lack it? And, if we could not understand or speak to him, how could he be our interpreter? Yet the very notion of omniscience demands that, among other things, he also knows English—if he knows all, then he has to know all languages—and knows that we mean that snow is white when we utter the sounds "Snow is white."

Davidson never calls the omniscient interpreter "God." But as even a cursory excursion into Buddhist and Jaina concepts of omniscience should show, one does not have to believe in a world-maker God in order to believe in an all-knowing World-Teacher. Jaina and Buddhist defenders of the possibility of effortful attainment of omniscience provide us with the richest arsenal of anti-theistic arguments. A theistic school like Nyāya or Yoga attributes omniscience to the primal teacher and legislator of semantic rules or the teacher of all teachers of Yoga but also recognizes the possibility that by disciplined practice of yoga a human being can attain detailed simultaneous knowledge of all things in all their possible aspects.

There is a trivial sense in which every time we make or assent to a universally quantified claim, each of us knows something about everything. Even without going into the quaint Nyāya epistemology of aspectual acquaintance with all members of a class through perceptual contact with their shared universal in an exemplary member, we can read knowledge that for all x, Fx implies Gx as knowledge that everything is such that if it is F then it is G. One such knowledge of unrestricted generality which all of us, except Meinongian "Priests" of Free Logic, can claim to have is that everything exists or everything is self-identical.

Furthermore, under one interpretation of Tarski, whenever we know that a certain sentence is true, we know that it is satisfied by the universal set of all infinite sequences, which is to know something about all things. Such knowledge about the universe, luckily, does not require us to be divine or Buddha-like. As Tarski and Davidson never tire of reminding us, in order to know that the sentential function (with zero free variables), "Arindam is garrulous" is satisfied by all infinite sequences, all we have to know is Arindam and his inability to keep quiet. Philosophers like F. H. Bradley once held that every true judgment has the whole of reality as its subject and the entire judge-able content was predicated of it.

While developing a nuanced notion of Buddha's omniscience, the anti-realist Buddhist philosopher Śāntarakṣita alerts us to an ancient objection to the very idea of unrestricted universality. Whenever one says "all," the question arises: "all what?" Universal quantification must be restricted to a domain, such as "all human beings," "all natural numbers," or "all edible stuff." Thus, an *omni*vorous person need not eat Higgs' bosons or the binomial theorem. The Buddha, Dharmakīrti says, is called omniscient because he knows all that is important for eliminating suffering, not because he knows the exact number of microbes floating in air. Knowledge is not knowledge unless it is usable in relieving pain—an old theme of what can be called the Buddhist "pragmatism-of-compassion."

Different concepts of omniscience in Indian philosophy

At least ten different concepts of omniscience are available in the arena of classical Indian epistemology and philosophical theology. The first two concepts are both attributed exclusively to God, who need not be a creator ex nihilo of the world.

O1. As we have mentioned above, anticipating Aquinas' Fourth Way of proving the existence of a perfect being, Patañjali in Yogasūtra 1.25 argues:

> Any quality which admits of variation in degrees must attain a maximum (*kāṣṭhā*). Among human beings we see more and less degrees of knowledge. From that we must infer the existence of an epistemically unsurpassable being[4] who has direct non-sensory perception of even (humanly) imperceptible past, present and future things and events.

It is this omniscience that qualifies and urges such an all-knower to be the first teacher of all earlier teachers of spiritual sciences.

O2: Once the existence of a God who makes the material world out of preexistent atoms is established, by a causal argument in Nyāya metaphysics, such a God has to have detailed knowledge of each atom out which, step by step, according to the merit and demerit earned by the beginningless karma of living beings, God builds the material world, because a master-builder must have knowledge of his own raw materials, especially since the first motion in atoms is caused by the bodiless will of this world-maker. This omniscience, for systemic reasons, has to consist in one single direct timeless *de re* knowledge of all things. (Notice that neither of these concepts of omniscience involves knowledge of *true propositions*.) If the first is a teacher's omniscience, the second is the maker's omniscience of God.

O3: For every human being, there is, according to Jaina ontology of souls, an innate natural potentiality for knowing everything if all the dirt of ignorance, attachment, desire, and aversion is fully cleaned up. For a transparent soul, complete relational knowledge of one single thing in the universe should yield knowledge of all things in the universe because they are all interconnected.

O4: In the context of solving the "problem of induction," Nyāya theorists of knowledge postulate a kind of un-ordinary but direct perception, where the sense-organ can use the connecting link of the universal reproductive property shared by all X just while observing a few X and thereby *perceive* all of them with respect to that general property. Now, one universal, the property of "realness" (*sattā jāti*), is shared by all real entities. If one sees that universal in a few instances, then Nyāya seems to have no trouble admitting that very generic perception (*sāmānya-lakṣaṇa pratyakṣa*) of all realities, as real, is possible.

O5. With a special spiritual-analytic exercise of distilling the meaning of the Vedic "awakening text" "I am Brahman, or all that exists," in Advaita Vedanta, one can know the universe by knowing the Self when the self's false limitations melt away. This is a non-dualistic omniscience where to know oneself is to know all.

O6. For a Mahāyāna Buddhist of a kind, a mirror-like consciousness, by concentrating on the truths of universal suffering, universal impermanence, universal essencelessness, can attain to a generic knowledge of everything through contemplative perfection.

O7: Dharmakīrti, the world-teacher Buddha, did not necessarily have detailed identificatory knowledge of the life-experiences of each living being, but he knew "all" in the sense of "all that is needed to be known: what is to be eliminated (dukhka or misery), what is to be striven for (nirvāṇa, extinguishing of the ego), and what is the means of attaining that freedom from misery. This is practical or ethical omniscience.

O8: In order to emphasize the humanity of the Buddha, early Mahāyāna Buddhism described his omniscience as a sequential effortful knowledge of all the practical, theoretical, and spiritual sciences to distinguish it from an intuitive flash of omniscience and from an innate divine gift of vast knowledge.[5]

O9: There is another notion of detailed and simultaneous intuitive knowledge of all "feels" and "flavors" of all objects of knowledge that is attributed to the Buddha at the consummation of his spiritual pursuit (*sarvākāra-jňāna*).

O10: In the Yoga-sutras of Patañjali, there are many descriptions of a special Yogic attainment, a "*vibhūti*," a dawning of direct awareness of the past, present, and future of the universe which is called *"prātibha" or "prasamkhyāna."* Liberation comes not from that special omniscience but from a lack of interest in it, from looking at all of *prakrti, natura naturata,* and setting it aside with disinterest as "that is what pure consciousness is not" to achieve perfect aloneness or *kaivalya.*

Questioning the very idea of omniscience and a new eighth-century paradox of omniscience

Kumārila gives many powerful arguments against the very idea of omniscience, human or divine. Let me go through them very briefly:

I. The Inductive Argument: The natural laws regarding what means of knowledge can access what sorts of objects remain more or less unchanging through time. For example, however much you may increase the power of the eyes they never could or will grasp sounds. In our own times (even in 700 CE in India) we do not see supra-sensuous perceptual knowledge, e.g., of other people's past and future ethical record. Therefore, there never was any such clairvoyant all-seeing person.

II. The Ascription-Impossibility Argument: The only possible evidence that someone is omniscient could be either his or her own claim to that effect or a non-omniscient person's claim. Self-ascription of omniscience is hopelessly circular, to put it mildly. Non-omniscients cannot ascertain another person as omniscient. Mutual endorsement is also questionable. Kumārila shook the very foundations of Indian thinking about religious or scientific authority with this question: "If the Buddha is all-knowing, where is the proof that Kapila (the teacher of Sāṃkhya) is not so. If both of them are all-knowing, how come they disagree on fundamental matters?"

III. Limits of Range-Extension Argument: Intense practice can perfect and enhance a certain epistemic virtue or faculty or skill, but it cannot go beyond certain limits. But eyes, even if they become very far-seeing, cannot see tastes or events happening in the future. Therefore, no amount of intense practice can make a person omniscient.

IV. Argument from Definition of Perception: Perception can only grasp what is presented to the senses. The past and the future are, by definition, not present, hence never presented to the senses. No perceptual knowledge of the past and present is possible by a human (or a divine) eye. If direct vivid awareness of past, present, and future objects is meant by "omniscience," then omniscience is impossible.

A junior contemporary of Kumārila, Maṇḍana Miśra, gives an ingenious argument against the very concept of omniscience. What is this "all," asks Maṇḍana, by knowing which God or the Buddha is said to be omniscient? This "all" cannot be each isolated object unrelated to another, to be known one at a time, nor could it be a whole bunch of things tamed by a universal (*sāmānya-vaśīkṛtah*). What if "infinite" in its primary sense is meant by "all"? If the time of knowing is a present moment in between neither going back infinitely into the past nor going forward infinitely into the future, can you encompass "all" because these two infinities would exclude each other. After exploring many different kinds of infinitude, finally Maṇḍana asks again: What is this infinitude? Let's say it is unlimitedness, being devoid of any delimitor. But if you say: "This infinite magnitude, this much is the extent of God's knowledge which is limitless like the sky or space itself," then there is danger.[6] Claiming that, one raises the unwanted ghost of God's ignorance by the very pacifying ritual of establishing God's omniscience. To make this paradox clearer, let us ask the question: Does God know the entire extent of all his own knowledge? If he does not know, then he is ignorant of something. If he does know, then his knowledge is not infinite because he knows the limits of his own knowledge. He knows this much and no more.

This is not a paradox of omniscience in the weaker sense that God's omniscience would be incompatible with human freedom or with openness of the future sea-battle's option of happening or not happening. It is a paradox *within the very notion of knowing all*. It should give us a pause whenever we use the notion of "all knowledge" or "knowledge of all." This complicates further the relationship between realism about all that is the case and the postulation of a possible or actual all-knowing someone or no one.

Another very plausible-sounding objection against God's omniscience is raised and answered by Udayana. God's alleged omniscience is self-defeating. Insofar as God must be aware of all the errors we humans commit, he has to share our false beliefs and therefore cannot be infallibly knowledgeable. The reply is straightforward. In order to understand others' mistakes, even know what it is like to be mistaken, one does not himself have to be mistaken.

The last realism link?

But what about God's token-reflexively rich knowledge of past, present, and future as past, present, and future? If his omniscience is a view from nowhere, from outside or above Time and Tense, doesn't that deprive God of the view from here and now?

Michael Dummett, the notoriously hard-to-follow anti-realist who battled against Davidson's realism, came up with a peculiar argument for the existence of God. In his earlier writings on McTaggart's proof of unreality of time, as well as in the very last section of his *Logical Basis of Metaphysics*, Dummett held on to offering a choice between only two alternative approaches. Either we retain Einsteinian realism and the absolute conception of reality and a possibility of perspectiveless omniscience, but give up reality of time; or we keep the A-series of now, before, and after and the reality of time as we experience it, but reject omniscience as an incoherent notion. Kumārila and the Mīmāṃsākas seem to have elected the second option, insofar as they define "real existence" as "being related to an A-series time" (*astitvam kāla-sambadhitvam*), and consistently with that, find the concept of omniscience incoherent.

In the last stage of his metaphysical reflections, Dummett comes to a third compromise position, preserving both anti-realist and realist insights. The only way to preserve the (realist) idea of *things as they really are in themselves* while remaining faithful to a justificationist (anti-realist) theory of meaning, Dummett submits, is to postulate the existence of an omniscient God such that a proposition's being true independently of any ordinary mortal's being able to justify or verify it consists in God's thinking (knowledge?) of it. Dummett's reasoning starts from his commitment to three of his best-known insights:

1. A realism–anti-realism battle must be fought in the field of theories of meaning and not by airing ontological convictions baldly and question-beggingly.
2. To be a realist about the past, about numbers, about the external physical world, etc., is to insist that our understanding of statements about the past, numbers, or external objects of perception consist in knowledge of truth-conditions rather than our knowledge of justification conditions or proof-procedures, *even if we have no way of knowing whether those truth-conditions obtain or not.*
3. Since understanding must be manifestable in public linguistic conduct, and we cannot manifest a knowledge we do not have, it cannot consist in knowledge of recognition-transcendent or ignorance-tolerant truth-conditions. Therefore, our theory of meaning/understanding must be justificationist, hence anti-realist.

When he adds to this the idea of one common world, a world that it makes no sense to think of as utterly knowledge-independent, his reasoning reaches the following semantico-metaphysical crescendo:

> This one world must be the world as it is apprehended by some mind, yet not in any particular way, or from any one perspective rather than any other. How God apprehends things as being must be how they are in themselves. *But now we must say the converse: how things are in themselves consists in the way that God apprehends them.* [7]

The argument crucially depends upon the Fregean equation of facts with true propositions, but incorporates an un-Fregean notion of propositions as made of mental/cognitive concepts which have nothing to do with Frege's *Begriff*. The full-fledged argument can be broken down into the following steps:

1. The world, as it really is, is a totality of structured facts, not a bunch of unconnected things or events.
2. A fact is a true proposition (an actualized state of affairs).
3. So the world is a totality of true propositions.
4. Propositions are made of concepts.
5. So, facts—and hence the world—are made of concepts.
6. There cannot be concepts without some sentient thinking being that understands and employs them.
7. Therefore, there cannot be a world without some conscious mind that understands and uses the concepts which constitute the world (by constituting the facts).
8. The concept-constituted world of humans and that of nonhuman sentient beings (such as owls, bats, meerkats, or centipedes) are more or less drastically different, according as the sensory/cognitive mechanisms of these creatures and concepts/recognitional capacities available to each are more or less different.
9. Hence, we cannot equate the world as it really is in itself with only the human world (the world as constituted solely by human concepts).
10. Therefore, the world as it is in itself is independent of and outside our human thought and knowledge. That is, the existence of the world (and its parts)

tolerates our ignorance thereof. This is the sense in which the world-as-it-really-is must be independent of human and nonhuman finite minds and conceptual schemes.

11. Therefore, the world as it is independently of human thought must be made up of true propositions made of concepts in the mind of some being other than any being inside the world; that is, the (concept-constituted) world has to be in some mind outside the world.
12. An all-encompassing overarching mind (which has no bias toward any human or creaturely conceptual system) must exist, which cannot be a human or nonhuman individual personal mind.
13. That impersonal mind, unconstrained by any particular bodily or sensory structure, is called God.
14. So God exists.

Conclusion: Is there a real world out there?

For the last couple of decades, I have been pursuing a research program which I called "Realism-Links." I argued that realisms about the external world, about a self as distinguished from passing mental states, about universals as distinguished from particular instances of them, entail each other. My hunch is that commitment to the existence of an omniscient God, who is not one individual subject inside the world but is "higher" in the sense of Tractatus 6.432 (God does not reveal himself in the world), is somehow linked to at least one kind of realism concerning the external world. Since God, if any, would not be one of us, not a being limited by a body, he could be described as "No*body,*" or to emphasize his unknowability, God could be and has been called "Who." That could be taken semi-seriously as an explanation of why common parlance sanctions the substitutability of *"Who knows!" "God knows," and "Nobody knows."* To be a realist about the world out there is to insist on such a world being knowledge-independent in the sense that it is the object of such a no one's knowledge. A new question now begins to raise its scary head. What if there simply is no world at all for any omniscient God or Buddha to know? Is the possibility that reality is one big hollow—an infinite void—even intelligible? Before concluding the book, let us peep into this metaphysical hole of absence and nothingness.

25

Absence, Non-Existence, and Other Negative Things

What is nothing?

The Nāsadīya Hymn of Beginning opens with these three words: "Not nothing was." It appears that the last two words propose a prima facie theory of the origin of everything, which the first word negates. Where did this universe come from? Before this universe (anything) existed, what was there? If "the universe" means all that exists, the logical answer should be, "Nothing." But it cannot be true that nothing was there before anything was there, for in sheer nothing no world can originate. Yet, the deepest philosophical question "Why is there something rather than nothing at all?" inexorably pushes us to the notion of "nought," as if all positive entities push out the ontologically prior nothing. But what is this nothing?

The possibility that the universe might not have existed has appealed to some philosophers in recent times.[1] In ontology and semantics, questions about the existence of negative facts and the meaning and truth conditions of expressions about "nothing" remain relevant. All of this, of course, sprouts from the presence of negation (or at least of correction, which amounts to negation) in all languages. Neither the negation nor the negated is touched by unreality or fictionality. There are no snakes in Hawaii, and there is no nitrogen in pure water. These lacks are absences. Neither the snakes nor nitrogen must be non-existent in order to be absent in a place. In Sanskrit, absences are called "*abhāva*" (literally: not-being). They are real, unlike non-existent entities which are termed "*asat*" or "*alīka*." Turtle-hair is a typical *asat*. But the real *abhāva* of real hair on a real turtle-shell is *sat* (real).

What if one takes this notion of absence and applies it to the universal set of things? Could we make sense of "nothing" as the absence of all things? We shall see in what follows that every absence requires both an absentee and a locus or site. One problem about the absence of everything would be that it could not be hosted by any site, since all things are its absentees. The other problem is that we cannot imagine the absence of everything. If we commit some item to unimaginability, don't we first need at least a concept of that thing in order to know that *that* thing is unimaginable? In that case, the absence of all things seems to have some kind of conceivability. Nothing may be unimaginable but it surely has to be conceivable insofar as we know what it is we are supposed to try and fail to imagine.

Utterly different from both total non-existent(s) and absences are the Buddhist *śūnya* and its abstract cousin *śūnyatā* (emptiness). Emptiness can be achieved through rejection of all positions and disputations in philosophy or through contemplative non-conceptual ineffable experience of "being no one" beyond the four logical options of real, unreal, real-and-unreal, and neither. We need, therefore, to distinguish very clearly between absences, nonentities, and emptiness.

Besides all this, there remains the simple phenomenon of a felt lack of feeling. Expressed in negative introspective reports, for example, "I am not in pain" or "the excitement is gone," a happy relief or a lamentable lack is often felt. I will discuss the positive claim of this sort at the end of this chapter. It seems apt to *end* the book that began with an analysis of the notion of a 'thing' with an analysis of the notion of 'nothing'. Endings, too, are absences of a sort.

Real not-beings: the logic of lacks

Let me begin by drawing some distinctions. Distinctions, by the way, are themselves negative things. An ant is distinct from an antelope and this consists in the ant *not being* an antelope. This is true of both type-distinctions, where otherness is delimited generically, and token-distinctions, which turn on haecceity. But otherness is not the only form of absence—the primary form of absence is the lack of something *in* some place or something else.

Lacks are not-beings, rather than non-beings, because lacks are there whereas non-beings are simply not there. If there is no object in a room, the object not-being in the room is real and the object in the room is a non-being. Non-beings are "manufactured" in language and in imagination. The combination of two concepts can generate an intersection set that is a null set. The intentional objects of our unfulfilled, sometimes unfulfillable, desires are often constructed in this way. For example, the desire for a dog combined with the desire for a pet with wings generates an intersection set (winged dog) that is also a null set (a fictional non-being). Whereas a not-being is either not-being-there, such as the actual absence of the Statue of Liberty in Pakistan or not-being-the-same, such as Obama's not being Bush. The absence of color in air is not an imaginary fictional non-entity. The only "reason" why someone may think that such an absence is imaginary is confusion between the absence and the absentee. Air's color is imaginary, not the fact that air is colorless.

Gappy entities seem to be unavoidable in an ontology that stays faithful to commonsense and ordinary language. Even in the metaphysics of actions, which would be deeply connected to our sense of responsibility-attribution and agency-ascription for reprehensible or laudable acts, omissions or non-doings seem to claim equal status as doings. Indeed avoidance itself is a negative act. The act of desisting is a practical void.

In the face of objections from Buddhist and Prābhākara Mīmāṃsāka foes of negative facts, some Nyāya and Bhāṭṭa Mīmāṃsā thinkers consider lacks real.

Lacks are not-beings. Not-beings come, mainly, in two forms: x's *not being in* y and x's *not being* y. The former, lack of residence, is called absence (*samsargābhāva*) and the latter, lack of identity, is called mutual absence or mutual negation. The latter is simply *otherness*. That John Searle is not in the Sahara desert is a kind of not-being-in (*atyanātbhāva*); that he is not Jacques Derrida is a kind of not-being-the-same-as (*anyonyābhāva*). For perspicuity, let us call lack of residence *absence* and lack of identity *otherness*. From now on, I shall only speak of absences as lacks and forbear mentioning otherness.

Absences everywhere

Holes, silences, intermissions, omissions, gaps, recesses, waits, blanks, voids, bald patches, clearings, slits, gaping apertures, the eye of the needle—the observable world around us is replete with real *lacks*. Why do metaphysicians hesitate to list lacks in a catalogue of real things? One alleged and errant reason is an elementary confusion between not-being and non-being. "Non-being"—against which Parmenides warned philosophers—can itself be used in two different senses. First as a count-noun: Pegasus is *one* non-being, Sherlock Holmes is *another*. Since neither exists, they can be, in a second sense, said to enjoy the same phony property, namely non-being or unreality, shared as it were by all non-beings in the world. But Quine has cautioned us that there can never be any legitimate individuation criterion for such fictional entities. There remains, of course, the worry that the various origins of fictional entities preclude us from considering two or more the same null entity. But non-beings are, undoubtedly, metaphysically messy. Existence can be permitted universal status, but nothingness cannot be taken seriously as an ontologically permissible universal.

Now, what I call "a lack" has nothing to do with these non-beings, unreal entities, or their shared nullity. In a manner of speaking, such things as color of air—a non-existent—can be said to be absent from the face of the world. But this, to say the least, is a very misleading manner of speaking. A much saner description would be "the absence of color in air." Lacks are plainly such things as I discover when I look into the fridge and see that there is no milk in it.

We have already introduced locus, absentee, and absence. Suppose the cap of my ballpoint pen is missing. Three things must be distinguished: the pen—the *locus* of absence, the cap—the *absentee*, and the pen's lack of a cap—the *absence*. All three are real. Even if the missing cap is now destroyed, it has not been reduced to a figment of imagination. It is absent, not non-existent.

Pieces of veridical awareness which come in the form "x is not in y" or "x does not bear the relation R to y" (or "x is no longer in y" or "x will be in y" or "x is not yet in y") do not represent presences, but nor do they fail to represent. They represent absences. Aside from idiomatic usages, a *presence* can be identified with *what is present*. But an absence cannot be identified with *what is absent*. That is why it is a mistake to identify a negative fact with *what is not the case*.

What is not the case is a nonexistent state of affairs—and I believe that there *are none* in the world. That there is no elephant in this room, on the other hand, *is the case*. Its absence in this room is not a basic particular; that is, it is not a substance, event, or unrepeatable quality. Absences are not universals either. As their representations in language and awareness reveal, they are complex entities individuated by what they are absences of-absentees-, locations, relations, and properties which delimit the relevant absenteehood. The limitor of the absenteehood of a given absentee is the relation between that absentee and the absence in question.

Although it makes sense to call absences negative facts, if only the *presence* of a relation between objects and properties counts as a fact, absences should not count as facts. Even Russell, while giving the strongest defense of negative facts, warns us, "It must not be supposed that the negative fact contains a constituent corresponding to the word 'not'."[2] The negative fact that makes the sentence "The Taj Mahal is not in London" true has only the *Taj Mahal*, the city of London and the *relation of being located in* as its constituent items. Negation, we must insist, is not another object or item participating in it; it is just the way these three are placed with respect to each other that establishes the negative fact..

Analytic philosophers in the twentieth century and Indian philosophers in the eighth to thirteenth centuries have come up with four powerful arguments against the admission of negative facts into ontology. The four arguments are (A) absence as a category is ontologically redundant because it can always be reduced to the bare locus, (B) an absence is imperceptible hence it is only a creature of conceptual construction, (C) the absence of any *x* can always be reduced to the presence of some *y* which repels *x*, and (D) absences subjectively appear due to thwarted expectations of the mind.

First, let me say a few words on the bare locus theory. Anticipating David Lewis's move of reducing the holes in cheese to the cheese itself, Prābhākara proposed that the lack of a pot on the floor is nothing but the bare floor. This, naturally, provoked a quick rejoinder from pro-absence realists: if the floor by itself constitutes the absence, then even when the floor has a pot on it, we should still perceive the absence because it is the same floor or chair. To block this absurd consequence, the reductionist has to articulate what it means by the "*bare* locus." It is not the floor as such but "*only*" the floor without the pot on it which constitutes the absence. But isn't it obvious that "only" and "without" are negative words reintroducing the abstract element of lack? So we have to perceive the floor plus its potlessness to perceive the absence. Thus, the bare locus theory fails to avoid the positing of real lacks.

Let us consider Demos's repulsion theory of absence: The lack of the color purple in a buttercup is reducible to the presence of yellow which repels purple. To take Dharmakīrti's example,[3] we feel lack of warmth because we feel coldness, which is incompatible with warmth in the same locus.

The repulsion theory of lacks has the following two profound weaknesses. First, I can know that X's being yellow entails X's not being purple only if I know the fact that it cannot be both—which is a negative fact. Second, we often have no idea about the so-called "positive and repellent" quality of an object and yet we can know for sure some negative property fit. In other words, we can know a negative fact in advance and without reference to some repellant force.

Fourth, there is Bradley's view that *negation is subjective.* Lacks cannot be objective, the argument goes, because they are posited by human imagination and language only to express a thwarted expectation which would not be there if human thought did not try to represent the world. Negative facts earn psychological and conversational significance by virtue of reference to possible error. Hence, negative facts are looked upon as second-order comments on the truth-value of an affirmative one, and hence never on a par with the latter. As far as the psychological/conversational contrast is concerned, the occasion for a negative assertion can be simply a question to be answered, rather than an error to be exposed. And a subjective failure to get the facts straight in any case does not amount to a subjective negative judgment. If I judge that X is not in Y but I fail to remember where X is, that failure is subjective but X's failure to be in Y is not.

In one strict Kantian sense, wherever there are prediction and judgment, there is some combination of thought and theory. Ascription of a predicate to an object is one sort of conceptual processing of the data of experience, and rejection of a predicate with respect to an object is another. If we regard the lacks as man-made holes in a nonporous reality because negative awareness is qualificative rather than non-conceptual, then we have to dismiss most of our positive pictures of objective reality as subjective. But facts should not be confused with finding of facts. In facts, objects fit into each other precisely because the possibilities of such combinations are their formal properties. Facts are not man-made constructions. They are the stuff that the world is made of. If the world were not *in itself* the totality of positive and negative facts, then it would not be a totality of facts at all.

Heterologous absences: constraints on real and spurious absences

Indian Logic is a logic of things and their properties. One infers from the reason-property H (*probans*) to the presence of the target-property (*probandum*) S, in the site P, on the basis of the invariable concomitance or universal co-location informally formulated as "Wherever there is H, there is S, as in the corroborating instance U." The problem in logic then is to define this rule of invariable concomitance—a required feature of a good reason (*saddhetu*).

If invariable concomitance (*vyāpti*) is defined as "*not* occurring in places where the target-property is *absent*," we run into a difficulty in counting as valid those inferences which involve universally present target-properties, because a universally present property is nowhere absent. According to Nyāya, "This must be nameable because it is knowable" is such an inference. The inference relies on the invariable concomitance between knowability and nameability, both omnipresent properties with null exclusion range. If something like this cat is knowable, it must be nameable as well. Provisionally, to solve such problems, it has been proposed that we construct absences even of omnipresent properties like existence and knowability. But how can we find the absence of even an omnipresent property? We can talk even about a present (never-absent) thing as absent if we delimit the absenteehood of the absentee by a property which does not belong to the absentee. Existence which is found in everything that exists is still not a color. Existence could be missing from any particular existent thing, if we search for it under the wrong sortal, say, for example, as a shade-of-grey![4] Nothing—not even existent grey things—possesses existence-as-a-hue just as hours cannot be four meters long. Analogously, since knowability does not technically *inhere* in what is knowable, even in things which possess knowability, we can miss that feature and find it absent as an inherent property. Such an absence of something whose absenteehood is delimited by a demarcator property non-co-located with the absenteehood is called "heterologous absence."[5]

Gaṅgeśa rejects such heterologous absences as artificial and redundant. Our cognition of absence, according to him, always has a doubly qualified content. If a copper pot is missing from the cupboard, then the cupboard has (is characterized by) an absence. The absence in turn is qualified by the pot's absenteehood, which is again delimited by the property of being made of copper. If the qualification of the pot with the property of being made of copper is an error or make-believe, then our awareness of such an absence is also an error or make-believe, corresponding to which no real absence can exist. Heterologous absences do not exist because their absentees are necessary non-entities. This shows how absences have to be absences of real things and properties.

Raghunātha[6] distills Gaṅgeśa's reason for throwing out such absences. Our statement or judgment of an absence does not have three independent constituents: the absence, the absentee and the (de)limitor of absenteehood. It is only as a qualifier of the absentee that we recognize the limitor of absenteehood.

This investigation should have shown us one suggested but unpopular non-Meinongian way in which Navya-Nyāya could handle our *talk* about the non-existence of fictional entities without getting committed to their shadowy existence in some fictional realm. The underlying connection between logical insight, phenomenological evidence, and ontological decision-making is clarified by this debate.[7]

Ancient nihilism: from exclusion to universal unreality

In *Nyāya Sūtra* 4.1.37, Gautama poses, as the opponent's view, a nihilist position similar to the extreme skepticism Sextus Empiricus distances himself from, namely, that nothing exists. "All is non-being," the nihilist contends, "because in every being one can find (establish) the non-being of another." Determinations are negations. Insofar as things are differentiated and excluded from one another, all entities are negations of one another. What is interesting is that in this nihilistic position we hear a vague anticipation of a powerful exclusion (*apoha*)-theory of meaning that later on would become the foundation of Buddhist nominalism and negative semantics.

Gautama rejects it with the following argumentation. First, the proposition to be proved is patently self-refuting. There is something positive called "Everything." And here is a two thousand-year-old definition of universal quantification: "For all x" means "for a plurality of x.s without any remainder." So the nihilist extremist's own word "all" means many real entities. How then could the presence of these many reals, exhaustively enumerated, be equated with absolute absence of everything? Surely there is no plurality, let alone remainderless plurality, in zero. Second, even if we somehow make sense of the conclusion to be proved, the reason proffered is incompatible with the thesis. If all *bhāva*s have mutual otherness or exclusion among themselves, then they are *bhāva*s—positive entities.

Gautama proceeds in 4.1.38 to put forward his own positive thesis: every positive entity is not nothing or nonbeing, because entities have their own identity, their own being or own nature, own reality. Anticipating Nāgārjuna's famous, soteriologically motivated view that things are not void, but only devoid of any essence, the nihilist contends that the so-called positive things do not possess any being because they exist only relatively or dependently. Because of relative and dependent nature (*āpekšikatva*), there is no proof of own-being of entities. The thesis of universal non-being boils down to the relativity of all things.

Gautama answers this objection in 4.1.40. The main points of that reply are: first, that even in case of relational or relative properties such as "short" or "long," no comparison is possible without an objective standard. If a cat is smaller than a tiger only relatively, then the tiger's size cannot again reciprocally depend upon the cat's size. Second, it is our knowledge of smallness and bigness, etc., which is relative and mutually dependent upon context, not the actual size of things. For example, the cat will not grow in size if instead of comparing it to a tiger we compare it to an ant. The skeptic superimposes the relativity of human judgment onto the objective nature and existence of things judged. Third, not all properties are subject to such relativity, even if shortness and largeness are. That a cat is a cat does not change if we compare it with a larger cat or a smaller mouse.

Finally, Uddyotakara brings four major charges against any relativism of the above sort:

(A) If anyone tries to give a proof, adducing a source of certain knowledge, of his nihilistic conclusion, then at least he is committed to the existence of that proof. Hence, he cannot claim that nothing exists, for at least the proof has to *be there*.

(B) If the nihilist expects his sentence "All is non-being" to have a meaning, then the being of his own sentence-meaning must be a counter-example to his own claim, unless he is happy to say that his own statements are senseless.

(C) If the nihilist admits the existence of a speaker and a hearer of his assertion, then he is not seriously saying that no entity whatsoever exists.

(D) If the nihilist does not wish to take the stance "Everything is non-existent" and the sentence "Everything is existent" to be synonymous, then the distinction between their meanings exists, in which case "Nothing exists" must be false. If the distinction between their meanings does not exist, then the "None-ist" could very well pass for an "All-ist," and the nihilist ends up agreeing with his radical opponent who says "All things are real."

Mind the gap: from essencelessness and positionlessness to emptiness of emptiness

In a famous set of verses in MMK[8] chapter 15, Nāgārjuna invites us to consider what makes something an intrinsic nature. Burning, we say, is the nature of fire. When water is heated, we call its hotness extrinsic because this foreign property is borrowed from fire. But even the hotness of fire is caused by the fuel. "Genuine" "intrinsic" and other variants of "essentially own" and "real" nature of things thus crumble into other-dependent, description-dependent, and framework-relative properties that we arbitrarily divide into own and not-own properties. That does not mean that, like the ancient nihilists did, we should call everything "other than itself." Everything is neither essentially real, nor essentially unreal, and they cannot be essentially both real and unreal, nor can they be essentially neither real nor unreal.

But this four-fold negation itself should not be treated as "the correct view" of things. Even the middle way should not be fixed into an ontological permanent address:

> "Exists" is one edge, "doesn't exist" is another edge. Purity and impurity are both extreme edges. Therefore avoiding both edges, the wise ones do not even place themselves in the middle ... by engaging in disputes suffering does not ameliorate; suffering is cured when one attains non-dispute.[9]

I would like to conclude by hinting at the deep significance of the feeling of an absent feeling for jettisoning the dispute between self-ism and no-self-ism. The self cannot be reduced to a flow of feelings, since we seem to be able to catch it as a locus of absence of a feeling. If, for example, one day I find that my passion for something is simply gone; through the window of that experience I seem to have an encounter with my bare self. But then, digging deeper, I may find that even this introspector self can be thrown out as a philosophical or grammatical construct. Nevertheless, there would still not be complete hollowness, but a rich impersonal ownerless consciousness of subjectivity without a subject.

Following the meditation-recipe of emptying one's mind of all sensory or intellectual impressions and ideas, which we find in both the *Bhagavad-Gītā* and in Descartes' *Meditations*, Henri Bergson describes a contemplative Yoga-like thought experiment, ending up with the following conclusion:

> *The representation of the void is always a representation which is full* and which resolves itself on analysis into two positive elements: the idea, distinct or confused, of a substitution, and the feeling, experienced, or imagined, of a desire or regret.[10] (emphasis mine).

So the idea of absolute nought is a self-destructive pseudo-idea, "a mere word." Emptying the mind may reach its climax with eradication of even this idea of this last desire or regret: the desire to get rid of all thoughts, or the regret that one has not quite been able to get to the empty heart of things. Overcoming this desire or regret has been achieved, it seems, by Nāgārjuna: after rejecting even the *position* of essencelessness reached by the reasoned refutation of all logically contradictory positions. Such mutual cancelling out gets us to the middle way. The *Mahābhārata* similarly instructs: "Give up both dharma and adharma, truth and falsehood, and then give up that by which you give up."[11]

In the end, the world of ordinary objects and conventional truth is left un-denied as an object of non-attached double-denial, when one denies the denial of the world of ordinary experience. One lives with a wonderful lightness, without any interest in world-affirmation or world-denial. Abhinavagupta instructs us, "Don't renounce anything, don't grasp anything, just stay as you are and enjoy." But such throwing away of the ladder of logic befits only those who have painstakingly argued their analytic way, rung by rung, up and down, ascending and descending to that depth of fullness that is at the heart of the seductive void we cannot avoid as thinking, feeling beings.

Notes

Introduction

1 *Critique of Pure Reason*, by Immanuel Kant, trans. Werner S. Pluhar (Indianapolis: Hackett Publishing, 1996), B.274.

2 See Index entry "Object" in The Path of Purification (Visuddhimagga) translated from Pali by Bhikkhu Nyanmoli, Buddhist Publication Society, Candy, Sri Lanka. 1975.

3 An excellent resource for early Buddhist realist concepts of an object of sense-perception, is A.K. Warder's paper "Objects" in *Journal of Indian Philosophy*, 3, 1975.

4 Michael Dummett, *The Nature and Future of Philosophy* (New York: Columbia University Press 2010). Also the last chapter of M. Dummett, *Thought and Reality* (Lines of thought) (Oxford and New York: Clarendon Press; Oxford University Press, 2006).

5 See Chapter 1 of P. F. Strawson, *Individuals* (London: Routledge, 1959).

Chapter 01

1 The central idea of this paper comes from an insight—recognizably Kantian—found both in ancient Nyāya and Vaiśeṣika root-texts, enshrined in remarks like "Like a viewer standing behind many windows there must be someone the same who sees both" which we find in Praśastapāda's *Padârthadharmasaṃgraha*, Chapter on the self as a substance which unifies the manifold of multimodal sense-experience. See: G. Jha and Sridhara, *Padārthadharmasaṅgraha of Praśastapāda: With the Nyāyakandalī of Śrīdhara* (Chaukhambha oriental studies; 4) (Varanasi: Chaukhambha Orientalia, 1982).

2 Derek Parfit, *Reasons and Persons* (Part III) (Oxford: Oxford University Press, 1986).

3 Georg Christian Lichtenberg (late 1780s), "We Should Say 'It Thinks' Or 'There Is Thinking Going On' Rather Than 'I Think.'" See *The Wastebooks*, trans. R. J. Holligdale (New York: Review of Books, 2000, anon).

4 The basic Jaina methodological framework is one of non-skeptical and non-agnostic alternation. Among conflicting theories of reality t1, t2, t3, etc., Jaina philosophy recommends a reconciliation roughly in the following form: "Either t1 (from point-of-view v1) or t2 (from point-of-view v2) or t3 (from point-of-view v,), etc." There is no picture of any exclusive ultimate reality inaccessible to and beyond all these alternations. Hence, my phrase "disjunctive metaphysics." The disjunction is not due to epistemic limitations but lies at the very heart of reality which is non-one-faced (*anekānta*).

5 Udayanācārya. Vindhyeśvarīprasāda Dvivedī and Lakṣmaṇaśāstri Drāviḍa (ed.), *Ātmatattvaviveka: With the Commentaries of Śaṅkara Miśra, Bhagīratha Thakkura, and Raghunātha Tārkikaśiromaṇī* (Calcutta: Asiatic Society, 1986), subsequently

Udayana, 1986. A not too accurate summary of the work is to be found in Karl Potter (ed.), *Encyclopedia of Indian Philosophies* (Princeton), Vol. II (Nyâya Vaiśeṣika), 526–556. I have drawn heavily from especially Chapters 3 and 4 of this vast work entitled, "The dispute about denying the distinction between property and property-possessor" and "The dispute about non- apprehension of the self," respectively.

6 P. T. Geach, *Truth, Love and Immortality* (Los Angeles: University of California Press, 1979).

7 "*darśana-sparśanābhyām ekārtha grahaṇāt*"—Nyāya-Aphorisms, No: 3.1.1. The exact context is the proof that any individual sense-faculty (or their conglomeration) cannot serve as the self. Literally translated, it means, "Because the same object is grasped by both sight and touch."

8 Colin McGinn, *Mental Content* (Oxford: Oxford University Press, 1989).

9 For the most reliable and accessible account of this Buddhist view, see Steven Colins, *Selfless Persons* (Cambridge: Cambridge University Press, 1985).

10 W. James, *Principles of Psychology*. Vol. 1, Chapter X, p. 32 in *The Works of William James* (Cambridge: Harvard University Press, 1981).

11 Vasubandhu, *Abhidharmakoṣa*, Chapter VIII, p. 1217 of the Bauddhabharati Edition. For Theodore Stcherbatsky's translation of this passage, see pp. 52–53 of *The Soul Theory of the Buddhists* (Delhi: Bharatya Vidya Prakasan, 1976).

12 James, *Principles of Psychology*, Vol. 1, 322.

13 Vasubandhu, *Abhidharmakoṣa*, p. 1205. "Therefore, the person is only nominally real, like a 'heap' or a 'stream', etc."

14 One might ask, "Must this ego be a substance?" In Kant the transcendental subject never becomes an object of knowledge, hence is never categorizable as a substance. But I see no reason to feel constrained by such Kantian strictures. All that it takes to be a substance are (a) ability to bear several qualities, (b) persistence across several moments of time, and (c) remaining the same while the qualities change. But is it possible for a self to have a state of consciousness without the fact being known to that self? Aren't all perceptions automatically apperceptive? My arguments from the identities and distinctions on the objective side of a series of perceptual experiences prove all these features for the required subject. Hence, I do not overstate my case.

15 Remark 265, p. 94c of Wittgenstein's *Philosophical Investigations*.

16 See Parfit, D., Oxford University Press, & ProQuest. *Reasons and Persons* (Oxford [Oxfordshire]: Clarendon Press, 1986).

17 See Chapter 13 of this book.

18 I cannot here go into a full defense of the realists' rejection of the doctrine of reflexivity of all cognitive States. One obvious argument is the infinite regress which will set in if every cognition of x has to be a cognition of cognition of x. The other peculiarly Nyâya argument is that at the same point-instant the self can be in touch with only one (simple or compound) object. Finally, memory does not register every cognitive episode that happens to us; hence, not all of them are even internally apperceived. But this is a subtle and demanding topic of controversy.

19 James, *Principles of Psychology*, Chapter X, Vol. L.

20 I had imagined Berkeley to be the exemplar of the position I am attacking by this argument: that external objects are reducible to series of sense-qualities but the self remains substantial. But even Berkeley, I recently noticed, in his consistent moments, goes to the Humean length of asserting: "Mind is a congeries of Perceptions," and denies any real distinction between "that thing which perceives"

and "Perceptions" themselves. See remarks 580 and 581 in his philosophical Commentaries, Notebook A.

21 K. C. Bhattacharyya, "The Subject as Freedom," in *Search for the Absolute in Neo-Vedānta* (Honolulu, University of Hawaii Press, 1976), 93.

22 Udayana, 1986, 738.

23 Udayana, 1986, 739.

24 Ibid., 743.

25 Frege, 1973, 17–38.

Chapter 02

1 See Pranab Kumar Sen's chapter "Strawson on Universals," and P. F. Strawson's reply to it in *Universals, Concepts and Qualities: New Essays in the Meaning of Predicates*, ed. Arindam Chakrabarti and P. F. Strawson (Ashgate: Oxford 2006).

2 P. F. Strawson, *Individuals: An Essay in Descriptive Metaphysics* (London: Methuen, 1959), 227.

3 Ibid., 226.

4 See C. L. Elder's paper, "Realism, Naturalism and Culturally Generated Kinds," *The Philosophical Quarterly* 39, no. 157 (October 1989): 425–444, on realism concerning such properties as parenthood, being a joke, adulthood, etc.

5 P. F. Strawson, "Entity and Identity," in *Contemporary British Philosophy*, ed. H. D. Lewis, Fourth Series (London: George Allen Unwin, 1976), 200.

6 Bimal Krishna Matilal, *Perception: An Essay on Classical Indian Theories of Knowledge* (Oxford: Clarendon Press, 1986), 417.

7 In this chapter, I do *not* claim the converse that if realism concerning universals is true then realism concerning perceived particulars must be true as well. But here is the sketch of an argument which *could* be given to support such a claim. Upon a Berkleyan anti-realism about perceived objects, a wooden table is the same as someone's idea of the wooden table. But the idea of woodenness is only a *part* (and not a *property*) of the idea of a wooden table. Since the part-whole relation is *not* the relation which can bind objective properties with their relevant exemplifiers, to be a Berkleyan anti-realist about material objects is to give up realism about universals. Transpose this, and you obtain the converse of *my* claim. There is a hint of this argument in Frege's essay "Der Gedanke," where he talks about the weight of a heavy shell being a *property* and not a part of a shell, and accuses the idealist of losing sight of this distinction.

8 Crispin Wright, "Realism, Anti-Realism, Irrealism and Quasi-Realism," in *Midwest Studies in Philosophy*, ed. P. A. French, T. E. Uehling, and H. K. Wettstein, Vol. XII, Realism and Antirealism (Minneapolis: University of Minnesota Press, 1988), 25.

9 In *Mathematics, Matter and Method Philosophical Papers*, Vol. I (Cambridge: Cambridge University Press, 1975), Putnam writes, "a consistent realist has to be realistic not only about the existence of material objects, in the customary sense, but also has to be realistic about the objectivity of mathematical necessity … and about entities which are neither material objects nor mathematical objects" (p. viii). He developed a realistic theory of *properties* where he argued that quantification over properties (as distinct from classes) is indispensable for science and ordinary language. Perhaps, like many of his earlier doctrines, this will be rejected by him *now*.

10 P. F. Strawson, "Universals," in *Midwest Studies in Philosophy*, ed. P. A. French, T. E. Uehling, and H. K. Wettstein, Vol. IV, Studies in Metaphysics (Minneapolis: University of Minnesota Press, 1979), 3.
11 Ibid.
12 Strawson, "Entity and Identity," 206.
13 P. F. Strawson, "Kant's New Foundations of Metaphysics," in *Metaphysik nach Kant?* (Klett-Cotta: Stuttgarten Hegelkongress, 1987, 1988), 158.
14 Citation needed.
15 Matilal, *Perception*, 344. See, especially, his "principle P2" and his "exception clause E1."
16 Strawson, "Universals," 6.
17 P. K. Sen, "Universals and Concepts," in *Logical Form, Prediction, and Ontology*, ed. P. K. Sen, Jadavpur Studies No. IV (New Delhi: Macmillan India, 1982).
18 Ibid., 260.
19 See P. F. Strawson, "Concepts and Properties or Predication and Copulation," *The Philosophical Quarterly* 37, no. 149 (October 1987): 405.
20 Citation needed.
21 Udayana, *Ātmatattvaviveka*, text and Hindi translation by K. N. Tripathi, Benares, 1983, 229.
22 P. K. Mukhopadhyay, *Indian Realism: A Rigorous Descriptive Metaphysics* (Calcutta: K. P. Bagchi, 1984). See discussion of universal-blockers in this work as well as in Shastri (*Critique of Indian Realism* [Agra: Agra University, 1964], 319–327).
23 This criterion actually coincides with the Nyāya test of *tulyatva* (equi-extensiveness) because each of those tests is applied only to *simple* properties, that is, after a putative universal has passed the test of simplicity.
24 See D. M. Armstrong, *A Theory of Universals*, Vol. II of *Universals and Scientific Realism* (Cambridge: Cambridge University Press, 1978), 19–23. Also see David Lewis, "New Work for a Theory of Universals," *Australasian Journal of Philosophy* 61, no. 4 (December 1983): 345, for a list of disqualified properties. Lewis comments: "A distinctive feature of Armstrong's theory is that universals are sparse. There are the universals that there must be to ground the objective resemblances and causal powers of things." The similarity with Nyāya here is quite remarkable!
25 In a passage quoted by Sen ("Universals and Concepts," 253) as part of an unpublished article called "The Existence of Universals" by Strawson.
26 Michael Dummett, "More about Thoughts," *Notre Dame Journal of Formal Logic* 30, no. 1 (Winter 1989): 17, writes, "A dance-step, for example, is an immanent object … It would be unreasonable to deny that the dance-step is an object: two dancers can execute the same step … has objective properties and can be spoken of and thought about."
27 W. V. Quine, in the last line of the paper, "Logic and the Reification of Universals," in *From a Logical Point of View*, 2nd edn., revised (New York: Harper Torchbooks, Harper & Row Publishers, 1961), 129.

Chapter 03

1 In Arindam Chakrabarti, "Against Immaculate Perception: Seven Reasons for Eliminating Nirvikalpaka Perception from Nyāya," *Philosophy East and West* 50, no. 1 (2000): 1–8.

2 Jayanta Bhaṭṭa in *Nyāyamanjarī*, Vol. 2, *ahnika* 5, 30 (Mysore edition, 1983).

3 An otherwise cautious analyst of human experience, Hume oversimplified the problem of concept-formation by assuming that the idea (concept?) of a fruit is simply a fainter copy of the sensory impression of a fruit. Duly dissatisfied with this crude theory of concepts, Kant puzzled over what he called "the secret art" of concept-formation (Critique of Pure Reason, B 180) by means of which, out of our sensory encounter with a small number of particular dogs the general and interpersonally shared concept of a dog arises in our minds. But it has been always taken for granted, both by Hume and by Kant, that at first there is only acquaintance with bare particulars and then at some later point there arises the general concept which captures the universal they all instantiate. This is what I question in this chapter.

4 I am grateful to Simon Blackburn for helping me formulate this point, although he himself has no stake in any metaphysical or epistemological thesis about universals.

5 Replies 571, my emphasis.

6 "A Road Not Taken in Indian Epistemology: Kumārila's Defense of the Perceptibility of Universals" by John Taber, *Indian Epistemology and Metaphysics*, ed. Joerg Tuske (London: Bloomsbury, 2017).

7 J. L. Austin, *Philosophical Papers*, 3 (Oxford: Clarendon Press, 1961), 3.

8 See note 4 above.

9 Pranab Kumar, "Strawson on Universals", 42, fn48.

10 Although even a direct realist Austin makes fun of the doctrine of perceptible universals, when he asks "'Do we taste universals in particulars too?' in a footnote to 'Are There Apriori Concepts?'" in *Philosophical Papers* (Oxford: Clarendon Press, 1961), Aristotle did assert somewhat mysteriously "Although one perceives a particular, perception is of the universal." Aristotle. *Posterior Analytics*. 100a.17.

Chapter 04

1 The question of the relation between sensory experience and deployment of concepts and words which I discuss here, and then again in Chapter 22, has been suggestively and famously raised by Wittgenstein in the following remark: "Describe the aroma of Coffee—Why can't it be done? Do we lack the words?"
Philosophical Investigations, sec. 610.

2 Matilal's Naiyāyika English.

3 What follows is a summary of Matilal's later formulation.

4 B. K. Matilal, *The Word and the World* (Delhi: Oxford University Press, 1990).

5 The definitional *Nyāyasūtra* 1.1.4 also classifies perception into two types—qualificatory and non-qualificatory.

6 B. K. Matilal, *Epistemology, Logic and Grammar in Indian Philosophical Analysis* (The Hague: Mouton, 1971), 25–26. *Perception*, 344–354.

7 See Śaṅkara Miśra's, *Bhedaratnam* and its discussion of *nirvikalpaka pratyakṣa*.

8 B. K. Matilal, *The Logical Basis of Metaphysics* (Cambridge, MA: Harvard University Press, 1991), 93–97.

9 See his paper, "Thought and Perception," in *The Analytic Tradition: Meaning, Thought, and Knowledge*, ed. D. Bell and N. Cooper (Oxford: Blackwell, 1990).

10 Of course, I am not suggesting that the Buddhist's ineffable sensation has any similarity with Dummett's implicit knowledge which is partly an *ability*—a concept Buddhists would find hard to stomach—except that they are both unverbalized.

11 D. Bell and N. Cooper, ed., *The Analytic Tradition: Meaning, Thought, and Knowledge* (Oxford: Blackwell, 1990).

12 B. K. Matilal, *Perception: An Essay on Classical Indian Theory of Knowledge* (Oxford: Oxford University Press, 1986).

13 Michael Dummett, "The Relative Priority of Thought and Language," in *Frege and Other Philosophers* (Oxford: Clarendon Press, 1973).

Chapter 05

1 Donald Davidson, "The Folly of Trying to Define Truth," *Journal of Philosophy* 93, no. 6 (1996): 263–278.

2 Ibid., 276.

3 I shelve the question of whether there remains any viable form in which correspondence theory could be defended in the face of Frege's or Davidson's attacks. It is a question hardly deserving neglect now that Alston and Searle have both made strenuous attempts to rehabilitate the correspondence theory of truth.

4 Roy Perrett, "Is Whatever Exists Knowable and Nameable?" *Philosophy East and West* 49, no. 4 (October 1999).

5 This is why there are limits to our ability to articulate or understand what it is that we are ignorant of—the root of Meno's paradox and also of some basic notions of Advaita Vedānta epistemology.

6 Gottlob Frege, "The Thought: A Logical Inquiry," in *Philosophical Logic*, ed. P. F. Strawson (London: Oxford University Press, 1973), 21.

7 Ibid., 17.

8 Kant, *The Critique of Pure Reason*, B83.

9 Ibid., B83/A59.

10 That is what Tarski did *not* despair of, in spite of the level-conflating, paradox-generating nature of natural languages.

11 Upadhyaya Gaṅgeśa, "Definition of Valid Knowledge," In *Tattvacintamani*, trans. Nandita Bandypadhyaya (Calcutta: Sanskrit Pustak Bhandar, 1989).

12 Ibid. Gaṅgeśa remarks this at the end of the section on the final definition of truth (following rejection of about twenty aborted ones).

13 Roy Perrett, "Is Whatever Exists Knowable and Nameable?" *Philosophy East and West* 49, no. 4 (October 1999).

14 Frege, "The Thought: A Logical Inquiry," 18–19.

15 Michael Dummett, *Frege: The Philosophy of Language* (New York/London: Harper and Row, 1973), 442–470.

16 Nyāya would agree with me that I cannot unparadoxically say I am aware that p but p is false, but it would not concede that my apperception that I have perceived that p amounts to my knowledge or even belief that my perception is correct. For one thing, correctness is known only inferentially in Nyāya.

17 Frege, "The Thought: A Logical Inquiry," 20.

18 Ibid.

19 This is one reason, to anticipate an important point from section 5, a Nyāya awareness cannot be treated like a proposition or a sentence which would be wholly false if it had a false conjunct.
20 The usual example is contact-with-a-monkey, which the tree possesses at the top but does not possess at the roots.
21 Gaṅgeśa, "Definition of Valid Knowledge."
22 Udayanacarya, *Atmatattvaviveka*, ed. Vindhyesvariprasada Dvivedin and Lakshmana Sastri Dravida (Calcutta: Asiatic Society, 1986).
23 This is not a direct quotation but the gist of the beginning of Chapter 5 of *Problems of Philosophy*. Bertrand Russell (London; New York: Oxford University Press, 1959).
24 Russell supported this kind of scientific realism.
25 This reductio argument was originally given by Fitch and revived several times by W. D. Hart, Dorothy Edgington, and Tim Williamson.
26 This position was recently christened "Gödelian Optimism" by Neil Tennant in *Taming of the True* (Oxford: Clarendon Press, 1997).
27 "Astitva Jñeyatva Abhidheyatva." Karl H. Potter. *Festschrift Fūr Erich Frawuwaller, Wiener Zeitschrift fur die Kunde Sud— und Ostasiens*, XII-XIII (Vienna, 1868), 275–280.
28 This is why Karl Potter in one place calls the Nyāya God an un-liberated soul!
29 It is a rather sketchy omniscience that we all have when we wield the concept of "everything." These "things" are such that if you have seen one of them you have seen them all, but of course this will be like seeing one thousand ants and claiming to have seen all thousand.
30 Nyāya has a similar view about numbers that are causally but not recognitionally knowledge-dependent.
31 Udayanacarya, *Atmatattvaviveka*.

Chapter 06

1 Donald Davidson, *Inquiries into Truth and Interpretation* (New York: Clarendon Press; Oxford University Press, 1984), 198. "Of course truth of sentences remains relative to language, but that is as objective as can be."
2 Hilary Putnam, *Representation and Reality* (Cambridge, MA: MIT Press, 1988), 108.
3 Davidson, *Inquiries into Truth and Interpretation,* 225.
4 Davidson and Putnam both started off as anti-idealists and anti-relativists. But Davidson's final position (in spite of his insistence on Truth-condition theory of meaning which is a hallmark of realism) comes to be branded as "anti-realism" by radical metaphysical realists like Michael Devitt (see his *Realism and Truth*, p. 180) because he jettisons the idea of confronting our beliefs with reality and gravitates toward a coherence theory of truth. Putnam is more clearly perceived as an idealist who rejects metaphysical realism and subjective idealism by a single stroke of argument (see his *Reason, Truth and History*, p. 143). Curtis Brown ("Internal Realism: Transcendental Idealism" in *Midwest Studies in Philosophy*, Vol. XII (1988) brands Putnam as an idealist refuter of idealism.
5 See Śaṅkara's *Brāhmasūtras* 2/2/28–30. See any standard translation or the summary in Karl Potter (ed.), *Encyclopedia of Indian Philosophies*, Vol. II (Princeton, NJ: Princeton University Press, 1981).

6 See *Critique of Pure Reason*. A368–A380 and B274–B279.
7 See, for the Buddhist Idealist position and arguments, "Proofs of Idealism in Buddhist Epistemology" Ch. 5 of *Indian Epistemology and Metaphysics,* edited by Joerg Tuske, Bloomsbury 2017. See Stanford Encyclopedia article on George Berkeley and its Bibliography for editions of his *A Treatise Concerning the Principles of Human Knowledge.*
8 This particular formulation of the idealistic argument I owe to Diṅnāga's Alambanaparikṣa.
9 This argument of Śaṅkara anticipates Ryle's famous point about counterfeit coins: some of our ascriptions of externality could not be fake unless some others (indeed, most) were genuine.
10 This point is urged against *Moore's Refutations of Idealism*, by A. J. Ayer in his *Philosophy in the Twentieth Century*.
11 See Śaṅkara's commentary on *Prasnopaniṣad* VI, 2.
12 See Karl Potter, *Encyclopedia of Indian Philosophies*, 95. Also the somewhat scholarly discussions by Daniel Ingalls in "Śaṅkara's Arguments against the Buddhists," *Philosophy East and West* 3, no. 4 (1954).
13 C. Thomas Powell (in "Kant's Fourth Paralogism," *Philosophy and Phenomenological Research* [1988]) finds the expression "objects outside us" triply ambiguous. It could be used to mean: (a) Things in themselves. (b) Things within experience or appearance which we actually perceive in space. (c) Parts of appearance which we do not actually perceive but which we inter as existing in space. Recognition of this third category brings out Kant's empirical realism at its sharpest.
14 *Prolegomena*, section S49.
15 *Critique of Pure Reason*, A369.
16 Kant says that Berkeley has no criterion of truth.
17 "Real, for both philosophers, is not what can exist independently of the mind, but what stands in connection with a perception in accordance with the laws of empirical advance." (*Critique*: A493, *Principles*: S35) See Eckart Forster, "Kant's Refutation of Idealism," in *Philosophy, Its History and Historiography*, ed. A. J. Holland (New York: Springer Publishing, 1985).
18 C. M. Turbayne suggests this in his "Kant's Relation to Berkeley," in *Kant Studies Today*, ed. Beck (Chicago: Open Court Publishing Company, 1969). Also see the following two pieces for two opposed interpretations of the Refutation: Molt K. Gram in "What Kant Really Did to Idealism" (in *Essays on Kant's Critique of Pure Reason*, edited by Mohanty and Shanan [Oklahoma, 1982]) maintains that Kant proved the qualified mind-independence of phenomenal objects in space. Paul Guyer in *Kant and the Claims of Knowledge* (Cambridge, 1987), 279–329, proves with elaborate evidence from *Kant's Posthumous Manuscripts* that Kant actually sought to prove the absolute mind-independence of noumenal things in themselves. That Kant did not misunderstand or distort Berkeley's position has been proved by many and most recently by R. C. S. Walker, "Idealism: Kant and Berkeley", in *Essays on Berkeley: A Tercentennial Celebration*, ed. John L. Foster and Howard Robinson (London: Oxford University Press, 1985).
19 Berkeley locates this source in God and Kant in things in themselves.
20 Although in some strange way it exists and also causes our intuitions! Kant's awkward position in this respect is too well-known.
21 *Critique of Pure Reason*, B277, note: a.
22 See Strawson, *Bounds of Sense*, pp. 56–57.

23 As Allison argues convincingly, Kant's inner sense does not yield even an appearance of myself to myself. Very much like Hume's frustrated self-search it simply yields knowledge of my fleeting states.
24 See Edward G. Lawry, "Did Kant Refute Idealisms?" in *Idealistic Studies* (1980), on this point.
25 *Critique of Pure Reason*, B276.
26 Is the idea then something like this: I look at myself at t1 and find that I am in a nasty mood and then after an hour I introspect again and find that I have cheered up. In order to understand this change in me, I look at the wall or the table in front of me to notice how across t1 and t2 the wall or the table has remained unchanged?
27 *Critique of Pure Reason*, A358.
28 The best account of Indian realisms remains this old volume: *Critique of Indian realism: A Study of the Conflict between the Nyāya-Vaiśesika & the Buddhist Dignāga School*, ed. D.N. Shastri (Agra: Agra University, 1964).
29 This is what Buddhism has ultimately done.

Chapter 07

1 Gottlob Frege, "The Thought: A Logical Inquiry," in *Philosophical Logic*, ed. P. F. Strawson (London: Oxford University Press, 1973), 17–38.
2 See Manoratha's commentary on PV p. 173, Pratyakṣa Chapter, verse 354: "Even though the awareness in itself is undivided, to those whose vision erroneously sees division, the unitary grasped-grasper-awareness appears as if it has a difference or duality," in *Pramāṇa Vārttika with Manoratha commentary*, ed. Swami Dvarikadas Shastri (Varanasi: Baudhha Bharati, 1994). More recently this idea of an intrinsically objectless but self-luminous awareness that is taken to be transitively directed to an external object, albeit erroneously, has been beautifully analytically spelled out by Birgit Kellner in "Proofs of Idealism in Buddhist Epistemology: Dharmakīrti's Refutation of External Objects," in *Indian Epistemology and Metaphysics*, ed. Joerg Tuske (London/New York: Bloomsbury Publishing Plc, 2017), 103–128.
3 Of course, the Buddhist nominalist deems this as ridiculous, a multiplication of entities beyond necessity as Indian realists would find Frege's positing two additional "external" objects called truth-values the True and the False.
4 See Internet url: selfpace.uconn.edu/class/ana/MooreProof.pdf.
5 *(kastarhi nāsti? ityāha: bāhyo nīlādir arthah* kevalam *nāsti, tat-sādhakatvenabhimatasya adhyakṣasya asāmarthyāt*—PV p. 169).
6 *A Blue Hand: The Tragicomic, Mind-Altering Odyssey of Allen Ginsberg, a Holy Fool, a Lost Muse, a Dharma Bum, and His Prickly Bride in India*, by Deb Baker.
7 See "Realism" in *Truth and Other Enigmas* (1982) and Chapter 11 of *Seas of Language* (1996).
8 *Logic, Language and Reality*, Motilal Banarsidass Delhi, 1985, p. 276.
9 In the second book of the fourth chapter of *Nyāyasūtra*.
10 NS, IV, 2. 3–17.
11 One who holds that when an effect emerges out of its own material cause, something new begins to exist, *ārambhavādin*.
12 Frege, "The Thought: A Logical Inquiry."

13 "That blue etc.—all kinds of objects—are manifested in perception is impossible to deny. If you say 'That much even we, Buddhists, accept' that is like trying to keep the cow which you have sold off. For, think about it: what exactly is this 'manifested/ illuminated-ness?' which does not fade away even when all properties of an (external or internal) object of awareness have been deconstructed as incoherent? How can you keep saying that the very concept of object of awareness is incoherent and yet admit that objects are manifested in perception?" This and previous extracts from Udayana's work all refer to *Ātmatattvaviveka: With the Commentaries of Śaṅkara Miśra, Bhagīratha Thakkura, and Raghunātha Tārkikaśiromaṇī*, ed. Vindhyeśvarīprasāda Dvivedī and Drāviḍa Lakṣmaṇaśāstri (Calcutta: The Asiatic Society, 1986).

14 For the connection between realism and the formlessness thesis about cognitions, see Matilal, *Perception.*

Chapter 08

1 Theaetetus 158 b–c. J. McDowell, *Theaetetus*, Clarendon Plato series (Oxford: Clarendon Press, 1973).

2 Chinmayananda and Gauḍapāda Ācārya, *Discourses on Mandukya Upaniṣad with Gaudapada's Karika* (Madras: Chinmaya Publication Trust).

3 Wāsudeva Paṇsīkar and Laxmaṇa Śāstrī, eds., *The Yogavāsiṣṭha of Vālmīki: With the Commentary vāsiṣṭhamahārāmāyaṇatātpāryaprakāśa*, Vol. II (Bombay: Munshiram Manoharlal, 1981). Nirvāṇa 2. Ch. 105.

4 Paṇsīkar, ed. *Yogavāsiṣṭha*, Vol. II. Ch. 105 v. 18.

5 Paṇsīkar, ed. *Yogavāsiṣṭha*, Vol. II. Ch. 105.

6 Ibid.

7 Sri Anandatīrtha, *Viṣṇutattvavinirṇaya*, trans. K. T. Pandurangi (Bangalore: Dvaita Vedanta Studies and Research Foundation, 1991), 31 [Sanskrit text].

8 Vallabha, *Nyāyalīlāvatī* (Varanasi: Chowkhamba Sanskrit Series, 1991), NL, 454–457.

9 N. Dreaming Malcolm, *Studies in Philosophical Psychology* (London, New York: Routledge & Paul; Humanities Press, 1962) Passim.

10 Śaṅkarācārya, *Brahmaśaṅkarabhāṣyasūtram*, Vol. II (Vārāṇasī: Ṣaḍdarśanaprakāśana pratiṣṭhānam, 1982) 2.2.28–30. 716–736.

11 Vallabha, *Nyāyalīlāvatī*, 454–457.

12 Theaetetus 158 b–c. McDowell, *Theaetetus.*

13 Vallabha, *Nyāyalīlāvatī*, 454–457.

14 Ibid.

15 Madhusūdana: Chapter 1. Section on refutation of the relation between seeing and seen. *Advaitasiddhiḥ (ed)* Anantakrishna Sastri, N., Balabhadra, Viṭthaleśopādhyāya, & Brahmānandasarasvatī. (Dillī: Parimala Pablications, 1982). 453–454.

16 In his Editor's Introduction to *Advaita Siddhi*, a partial English translation by Karuna Bhattacharya, ICPR. (1991).

Chapter 09

1 For an introduction to Bhartṛhari's thought, see B. K. Matilal, *The Word and the World* (Delhi: Oxford India Paperbacks, 2015).

2 *VP III.7.101–124.*
3 *VP III.7.101–102.*
4 Prayoga-mātre nyagbhāvaṃ svātantryād eva niḥśritaḥ *(VP III.7.123).*
5 Ayaṃ svātantryavādaḥ pronmīlitaḥ *(IPVV, Vol. 1, p. 9).*
6 In an insightful footnote (12) to page 150 of his exemplary translation of Utpala's Vṛtti on IPK.
7 From a lost text.
8 Though I share the standard scholarly scruples about translating *kāraka* as "case".
9 Starting from Vyāsatīrtha and Madhusūdana Sarasvatî, the many-tiered, centuries-old, commentarial disputation between Nyāyāmṛta and Advaitasiddhi.
10 Dṛgdṛśyasambandhānupapattibhaṅga *(N.1.33).*
11 With a pun on *māyin*, meaning both: those who propose that the world is *māyā* or illusion, and cheating tricksters.
12 *viṣayaviṣayabhāvasya ca adviṣṭatvena asambandhatvāt.*
13 Jñāna/kriyājanyaphalāśrayatvam.
14 (1.4.49).
15 Beginningism and transformationism are the competing causal theories of Vais' eṣika and Sāṃkhya respectively.
16 *VP III.7.51.*
17 *VP III.7.80.*
18 *On Pāṇini 1.4.50.*
19 *VP III.7.64.*
20 Sṛṣṭidharācārya, in his commentary on Puruṣottama's Bhāṣā-Vṛtti on Aṣṭādhyāyî.
21 PI: pt. II.
22 *VP IH.7.78.*
23 As in cognate objects in English as in "I ran a good run" or in Sanskrit when the word karma meaning action assumes the accusative place: *niyataṃ kuru karma tvam.*
24 What Kierkegaard exactly says in Either/Or, Part 1, p. 32, is this: "What philosophers say about actuality is often just as disappointing as it is when one reads a sign in a secondhand shop: Pressing Done Here. If a person were to bring his clothes to be pressed, he would be duped, for the sign is merely for sale."
25 One can read Gadādhara Bhaṭṭācārya's Viṣayatāvāda (translated by and commented upon by Sibajiban Bhattacharya) or Tyler Burge on objects of thought for that.
26 *PI: II, xi, page 222 e.*

Chapter 10

1 Ludwig Wittgenstein, *The Blue and Brown Books: Preliminary Studies for the 'Philosophical Investigations'* (New York: Harper Torchbooks, 1960), 67.
2 Whatever mistake one can make in giving introspective reports falls on the predicate side. One can think that one is depressed when one is actually agitated; one can think that one is having a headache because of nervous tension when one is actually having the headache due to bad posture. But no one can make a mistake the correction of which takes the following form: "I had thought that it is I who was having a headache, but actually it was my wife."
3 Elizabeth Anscombe, "The First Person," in *Mind & Language: Wolfson College Lectures 1974* (Oxford: Clarendon Press, 1975) 59.

4 See P. F. Strawson, *Individuals: An Essay in Descriptive Metaphysics*, chapter 3: Persons (London: Routledge, 1991).
5 P. F. Strawson, "Reply to John McDowell," In *The Philosophy of P. F. Strawson*, ed. Lewis Edwin Hahn (Chicago/Lasalle: Open Court, 1998), 147.
6 Frege (1973), 33.
7 Frege (1973), 25–26.
8 In *Śaktivāda*, Part II, on the meaning of special words.
9 *uccārayitrtāvacchedakatvarūpa-anugatadharamopalaksita Caitrātmatvādikam eva pravrtti-nimittam ityapi asangatam, sāmānyatah (uccārayitrtvasya) anugamakatve padāntaroccarayituhmaitrādeḥ pratīti-prasango durvārah).*
10 Jonardon Ganeri, *Semantic Powers: Meaning and the Means of Knowing in Classical Indian Philosophy* (Oxford: Clarendon Press, 1999) 240. See also Jonardon Ganeri, *The Self: Naturalism, Consciousness, & the First-Person Stance* (London: Oxford University Press, 2012) 302.
11 Para Trimsika Vivarani (PTV), translation, pages 70–71.
12 PTV page 27, text.
13 IPV 1.5.13, Vol. 1. page 252.

Chapter 11

1 More or less following Udayana's scheme for setting up his opposition in the book *Ātma-tattva-viveka*, alternatively titled *Down with the Buddhists (Bauddha-dhikkāra).*
2 Jayanta, *Nyāyamañjarī*, Chapter 7,ed. Varadacarya, Oriental Research Institute series (Mysore: University of Mysore. Oriental Research Institute, 1970).
3 Abhinavagupta. *Īśvara-Pratyabhijñā Vimarśinī*, 1. VII. 2–5.
4 Jayanta, *Nyāyamañjarī*.
5 From the *Nyāyamañjarī,* Chapter 7.
6 Including illusory experience, significantly for a Buddhist critic.
7 Jayanta, *Nyāyamañjarī*, Vol. II, 334.
8 *Nyāyamañjarī,* Chapter 8.
9 The clearest philosophical reconstruction of Jayanta's arguments for the existence of a permanent self in response to the strongest Buddhist No-Self-ist arguments is to be found in Alex Watson's chapter 12 "Self or No-Self? The Atman Debate in Classical Indian Philosophy" in *Indian Epistemology and Metaphysics* edited by Joerg Tuske, Bloomsbury 2007.
10 An argument against the Yogācāra Buddhist.
11 Gottlob Frege, "The Thought: A Logical Inquiry," *Mind* 65, no. 259 (July, 1956): 289–311, also in *Philosophical Logic*, edited by P. F. Strawson, Oxford Readings in Philosophy, OUP, 1968.
12 This is somewhat like recognition in Jayanta Bhaṭṭa.
13 IPK 1,VII,verse 6.
14 IPV, Vol. 1, 75-76.
15 In IPVV, Vol. 1,105.
16 IPK 1, I, 4.
17 *atra aṃśe indriya-vayaparaṇam api asti… tataśca sākṣātkāram upalakṣayati "ūhaḥ"*—IPVV, Vol.1, 101.

18 *sā ca samvit para-śarīrādi-sāhityena avagatā svam svabhāvam jñānātmakam avagamayati, na ca jñānam idantayā bhāti… bhāti ca yat tadeva aham ityasya vapuḥ iti para-jñānam svātmā eva.*

Chapter 12

1 This feeling is at odds with the view aired by some philosophers that knowledge determines or constructs its own subject-matter/object rather than being structured and determined by it.

2 Sydney Shoemaker, *The First-Person perspective and Other Essays* (Cambridge: Cambridge University Press, 1996), 254–255.

3 Bertrand Russell, *Theory of Knowledge: The 1913 Manuscript* (New York: Routledge, 1992), 36–40.

4 "avedyatve sati apaorokṣa-vyavahāra-yogyatvam"—the final definition of "self-luminousity" on page 16 of Citsukha, *Tattvapradīpikā*, ed. Swami Yogīndrānanda (Vārāṇsī: Ṣaḍḍarśana-prakāśanapratiṣṭhānam, 1974).

5 Of course, the observation model of self-knowledge has lost its popularity after the work of Wittgenstein and Shoemaker. There are also some interesting incompatibilist accounts of self-knowledge in Indian Epistemology.

6 *Brahadarnayaka Upaniṣads:* IV.3.7.

7 Perhaps that is why Śaṅkara, who was so obsessed with the incompatibility of the subjective and the objective, also reminds us, "The self is not altogether a non-object."

8 It is also the organ whose quieting is the goal of much of religious practice in the Indian tradition.

Chapter 13

1 Long before one was aware of the "dangerous liaisons" of international academic politics (where colonialism still rules under the garb of post-colonialism) not just one's thought and talk, but even one's everyday sensibilities had become incorrigibly "comparative."

2 Aristotle, *De Anima*, 425a–426b.

3 An objection originally raised by Michael McGhee.

4 Thus, one type of ego-causing mental function is called "the sick (*kliṣṭa) manovijjñāna*"! Here I do not discuss this complicated Buddhist theory of *manas*.

5 *Bṛhadāraṇayaka Upaniṣad* (I. 5. 3).

6 The direct relevance of this keen observation to the proof of the existence of *manas* may be unclear. Nonetheless, it surely reminds us of the work of Merleau-Ponty and more recently Mark Johnson (*The Body in the Mind*) who talk about our processing external sensory data through an internalized body schema.

7 Śaṅkara's commentary on *Bṛhadāraṇayaka Upaniṣad* (I. 5. 3): *yadi viveka-kṛn mano nāma nāsti, tarhi tvañ mātreṇa kuto viveka pratipattiḥ syāt? yat tad viveka-pratipatti kāraṇam tan manaḥ.*

8 A famous example given by Vyomaśiva and Jayanta Bhaṭṭa which takes care of this challenge.

9 In the first edition of CPR.

10 *vipacyamāna karmāśaya sahita ātmanā saṃyogo jīvanam iti vadanti–Nyāyamañjarī.*

11 *sukhādi pratîtir indriya-jā; sâkṣâtkâri-pratîtitvat, rûpadi-pratîti-vat/na ca satadyakaro jñânâtma eva iti vâcyam, nīlādi-bodhe 'pi tathâbhâva-prasaṅgât*—Nyâyalīlāvatī, p. 326.

12 *Aniyataviṣayaka* also helps us feel bodily sensations such as thirst and excitment which are not specific objects of any one of the five external sense organs.

13 Encyclopedia, Vol.II n, p. 94.

14 As in synaesthesia.

15 De Anima 425^{b}15 in J. Barnes, *The Complete Works of Aristotle: The Revised Oxford Translation* (Bollingen series; 71:2) (Princeton, NJ: Princeton University Press, 1984).

16 Cognitive inner events such as seeings or hearings.

17 According to Richard Sorabji, Aristotle does believe in a "common faculty" residing in the heart, and asserts this in his short work *On Sleep*.

18 Kaṭha Upaniṣad 2.1.1.

19 Mahābhārata. XII.255.9. *dhairyopapattî vyaktiś ca visargaḥ kalpanâ kṣamâ sad asad câśuta caiva manaso nava vai guṇâḥ.*

20 From: *Abalupta Chaturtha Charan* (Obliterated Fourth Stanza), a book of poems in Bengali by Sisir Kumar Das Kolkata, 1986).

21 The assignment of intent to the *manas* is at least as old as the *Yajurveda*.

22 Yajurveda, 34/1, Śivasankalpa Sūktam.

23 *Bṛhadāraṇyaka Upaniṣad*, 1.5.3.

24 As the *Yogabhāṣya* comments, "The river of *citta* flows both ways, it flows towards evil, it flows towards the good also."

25 Which, the *Bhagavad Gītā* reminds us, is the mother of desire: "*saṃkalpaprabhavān kāmān.*"

26 This will not be approved by the Nyāya where desire is the property of the self, but in Sāṃkhya the self is pure consciousness which cannot have desire or even knowledge of objects, all of that being done by evolutes of *prakṛti*.

27 Potter, Encyclopedia II, p. 217.

28 In this context, the words of the *Maitrāyaṇi Upaniṣad* clearly bring out the value-orientation of most traditional Indian theories of the inner sense: "*Manas* is of two kinds: pure and impure. The impure *manas* is filled with resolves to get what is desired. The pure *manas* is content, it has no desire. When, being made waveless without wants and distractions, the *manas* is well-fixed, then it ceases to be a *manas*—and that is the ultimate state to be in. The *manas* has to be held fast in the heart only as long as it is still there. This knowledge is *mokṣa*, all the rest is proliferation of theories and books. The *manas* that has washed away all its dirt with *samādhi* enjoys a bliss which cannot be described in words, only the inner organ can feel it (just as it is about to disappear). Just as water cannot be separated from water, fire cannot be seen apart in fire, sky cannot be distinguished from the sky, an inwardized *citta* vanishes from the sight of the self. It is the *manas* which is the cause of bondage as well as of liberation for human beings. A *manas* addicted to worldly objects makes for bondage and a *manas* that is objectless leads to liberation."

29 Averroes, *Middle Commentary on Aristotle's* De Anima, ed. Alfred R. Ivry (Provo: Brigham Young University Press, 2002), 99.

30 Stephen Chak Tornay, "Averroes' Doctrine of the Mind," *Philosophical Review* 52, no. 3 (May, 1942): 270–288.

Chapter 14

1 *prāmāṇyam svata eva, anyathā anavasthānāt* (Madhvācārya in *Viṣṇutattvavinirṇaya*).
2 *sukham eva sukhatvena anubhavāmi, stambham eva stambhatvena jānāmi iti anubhavā* (*Tarkatāndava,*1. p.46).
3 And it must be distinguished from the issue of knowledge of knowledge, or intrinsicism versus extrinsicism.
4 *aham ghatam jānāmi ityevambhūtaś ca viṣayaprakāśaḥ ghaṭo'yam ityatrāpi hi mayā vedyate iti antaḥ praviṣṭam* (IPVV, v1, p.103).
5 *apratyakṣopalambhaṣya nārthadṛṣṭiḥ prasidhyati.* "The object-disclosing character of an awareness, which itself remains unperceived, can never be established" (my translation). Dharmakīrti, *Pramāṇaviniścaya*, ed. Ernst Steinkellner (Beijing: China Tibetology Publishing House/Vienna: Austrian Academy of Sciences Press, 2007) 154.
6 Especially Citsukha's account.
7 The resulting array of alternative definitions of *svaprakāśatva* are too complex to elucidate in this chapter.
8 Hence I am ascribing myself a different piece of cognition when I am claiming to have seen a blue pot rather than when I am claiming to have seen just a pot.
9 Athough Plato and Jayanta Bhaṭṭa have both talked about pleasures being false (or correct).
10 Jay F. Rosenberg, *Thinking about Knowing*, Chapter 2.
11 Recall the title of Spinoza's small, unfinished book: *Improvement of Understanding.*
12 Notice how Descartes drops all reference to the *object* of experience when he makes the incorrigibility claims: "I certainly seem to see, to hear, to be warmed. This cannot be false."
13 Ayer 1956, pp. 65–66.
14 Hogan and Martin, "Introspective Misidentification: An I for an I," in *Self-Reference and Self-Awareness*, ed. Andrew Brook and Richard DeVidi (Amsterdam/Philadelphia: John Benjamins Publishing, 2001).
15 I am grateful to my friend Mark Siderits for the kindness of reading an earlier version of this chapter and suggesting improvements.

Chapter 15

1 Denied by Yogācāra phenomenalists.
2 M.Siderits, *Buddhism as Philosophy: An Introduction* (Ashgate world philosophies series) (Aldershot, England: Indianapolis, IN: Ashgate; Hackett Pub, 2007).
3 Harty Field (1980), Stephen Yablo (2005).
4 Hans Vaihinger, *The Philosophy of 'As If,'* trans. C.K. Ogden (New York: Barnes & Noble, Inc., 1924/1968), 44.
5 Stcherbatsky was tempted to claim contentious parallels between Kant and Dharmakīrti (1930).
6 Before Vaihinger published his massive work, *The Philosophy of As If*—the first fully developed Fictionalist manifesto—Jeremy Bentham's *Theory of Fictions* stood as the main source of fictionalism among English-speaking philosophers.
7 Vaihinger, *The Philosophy of 'As If'*, 44.

8 See Churchland 1989, pp. 125–127 for a critique.
9 See epigraph from Quine above.
10 Gideon Rosen, "Problems in the History of Fictionalism," in *Fictionalism in Metaphysics*, ed. M. Kalderon (Oxford: Clarendon Press), 14.
11 I have found support for this simpler description in Meg Wallace, 2007. See: Meg Wallace, "Saving Mental Fictionalism from Cognitive Collapse." https://philpapers.org/rec/WALSMF
12 2008, p. 429.
13 As Ted Parent (2012) does in "In the Mental Fiction, Mental Fictionalism Is Fictitious" (internet, with author's permission).
14 For their distinction, see Chakrabarti 1997, pp. 92–97.
15 A version of this argument was concurrently formulated by Parent 2012.
16 I can imagine ways in which all of the refutations above could be rebutted by an advocate of FM. But my hunch is that the different interpretations of FM under which *all* the refutations could be resisted would be mutually incompatible. This shifty character of FM constitutes its main weakness. FM is sometimes a prescriptive claim about how much grain of salt we should take our own folk phenomenological conversation with, and sometimes a descriptive claim about the interpretation of what folk-psychology actually does or does not commit us to. The following references were included at the end of this chapter without corresponding in-text citations. They should be included in the general bibliography of the book.

Chapter 16

1 The *Nyāya* term for *presupposition* in this sense is *Abhyupagama* (cf. Appendix). But sometimes Uddyotakara thinks, like Russell, that "The Self is so and so" not only posits but asserts (says = *abhidhatte)* that *the self exists.* (See Appendix P-3).
2 See *Kusumānjali*, 3rd *Stavaka* and the discussion thereof.
3 See *Ātmatattvaviveka*, 1st Chapter. The relevant portion is translated by B.K. Matilal in his section on *Udayana* in "*Nyāya-Vaiṣeśika*" (*A History of Indian Literature* Series) Otto Harrasowitz, 1977, pp. 97–100.
4 N.V. 3.1.1.
5 See *Fellowship Lectures* (Vol. II) 2nd Edition 1906, by C.K. *Tarkālankāra.*
6 E.g., "My mother was barren."
7 E.g., "I am silent or dumb." Interestingly enough, Hintikka thinks that for Descartes, "I think" is a performatory certainty, because "I am not thinking," perhaps—would be "*svakriyā virodhi*"—if stated consciously. Compare someone's saying "I am absent"—in a roll-call, which is Bernard Williams's illustration of self-refuting statements (Descartes, p. 74) or Prior's illustration of somebody answering a phone call by saying "I'm not here."
8 Thus, Udayana at the beginning of the 3rd Chapter of the *Ātmatattvaviveka: asti tābādiha darśanasparśanābhyāmekārtha pratisandhānam tadidam (a) ekaikaviṣayaṃ (b) vā syāt samudāya viṣayaṃ vā (c) tadatirikta vastu viṣayaṃ vā …*
9 Gautama does not usually speak of the possibility of a direct *perception* of the self. Later, of course, Uddyotakara—through Udayana and after him most Naiyāyikas—admitted the possibility of a direct perception of the self. Apart from the case of a Yogic-meditation, of course, such perception is not an experience of the pure ego as such but is more like a logically presupposed component of our reflective

after-cognition when it takes the form of the knowledge that I have known a jar. The Naiyāyika analyzes it, like Russell (cf. *Problems of Philosophy*, Chapter 5, on acquaintance with the self) as a direct cognition of a complex object "my-cognition-of-a-jar"—where, as an element, the self must also have been an object of cognition. Thus although the general Nyāya strategy is to infer the abiding self as the only explanation of our capacity to *reidentify* objects across the data of different senses (from the fact of *pratisaṃdhāna*, or recognition), Uddyotakara speaks also of a separate *ahamiti vijñānam* which might be something like Kant's notion of the "I think" that accompanies all our representations (Critique of Pure Reason B, 132).

10 See Bernard Williams, *Descartes: The Project of Pure Enquiry* (London: Penguin Books, 1978), 89.
11 Strawson, *Individuals*, 105.
12 See S. V. Keeling, *Descartes* (London: Oxford University Press, 1968), 105.
13 Ibid., 105–106
14 *Icchādayo guṇaḥ, guṇāśca dravyasaṃsthānaḥ, tad yadeṣāṃ sthanam sa ātmā iti* (NSB 1/1/5).
15 The official argument of Descartes admittedly fails the moment "I" is substituted by an non-first-person nominative.
16 cf., *Ātmatattva Viveka*, 3rd controversy.
17 Jayanta Bhaṭṭa, *NyâyaMañjarî*, ed. K. S. Varadacharya (Mysore: Oriental Research Institute, 1969), 15.
18 N. S. 3/2/46–3/2/55. Except that about pleasure and pain the Nyāya view is that they are *objects* of consciousness, not conscious states themselves.
19 Saul Kripke, *Naming, Necessity and Natural Kinds*, p.101.
20 *Bhaṣya* on NS 3/2/53 clearly points this out.
21 The Manas of Nyāya or of Indian philosophy in general.
22 N.S.B. 3/1/1. Here, for the sake of example, we have to provisionally forget the Nyāya notion of the very inseparable relation between parts and their whole. Because the standard Nyāya theory would take the *whole* reality as a completely new and distinct entity.
23 *3. 1.* I.
24 *Aneka gavākṣāntarvartī prekṣavat ubhayadarśī kaścid ekaḥ.*
25 *Na hi bhāvaṃ anādādraṃ paśyāmaḥ ... tato yadādhāro bhāvaḥ sa ātma-* Uddyotakara.
26 *Anumeyasya nitya parokṣatvāt tadeva sāmānyato dṛṣṭam*—Jayanta.
27 *Śarīrādiṣu bāadhakapramāṇopapattau satyam kāryatvāt*—N. Mañjari.
28 *Varnānāṃ śravaṇaṃ kramena samayasmṛtyā tadarthagrahaḥ. Tatsamskārajamantyavarṇa kalanākale tadālocanaṃ. Ākānkṣādi nibandhanānvaya kṛtaṃ vākyārtha saṃpindanaṃ. Jñātraikena vinātidurghaṭamato nityātma siddhir dhruvaṃ. Nyāyamañjarī*, Part II.

Chapter 17

1 Immanuel Kant, *Toward Perpetual Peace and Other Writings on Politics, Peace, and History* (New Haven, CT: Yale University Press, 2006).

2 Immanuel Kant, "Idea for a Universal History with a Cosmopolitan Purpose," In *Kant's political writings*, ed. Hans Reiss (Cambridge: University Press, 1970).
3 Dharmakīrti. *Santānāntarasiddhi.*
4 John Stuart Mill, *An Examination of Sir William Hamilton's Philosophy* (Toronto: University of Toronto Press, Scholarly Publishing Division, 1979).
5 Dharmakīrti. *Santānāntarasiddhi*, verses 7–26, In F.Shcherbatskoĭ, Harish C Gupta and Debiprasad Chattopadhyaya, *Papers of Th. Stcherbatsky* (Soviet Indology series; no. 2) (Calcutta: Indian Studies: Past & Present, 1969), 87–93.
6 P. F. Strawson, "Critical Notice of Wittgenstein's Philosophical Investigations," in *Wittgenstein and the Problem of Other Minds*, ed. Harold Morick (New York: The Humanities Press, 1967).
7 Paul Churchland, "Eliminative Materialism and the Propositional Attitudes," *Journal of Philosophy* 78, no. 2 (1981).
8 Peter Carruthers, *An Integrative Theory of Self-Knowledge* (London: Oxford University Press, 2011).
9 Abhinavagupta, *Iśvarapratyabhijñāvimarśinī*, eds. K. A. Iyer and K. C. Pandey (Delhi: Motilal Banarsidass, 1986), 216.
10 Abhinavagupta, *Īśvarapratyabhijñāvimarśinī*, Vol 1.
11 "*iha anumātuḥ vyāptigrahaṇakāle… vyāpter eva asiddhiḥ*" from *Īśvarapratyabhijñāvimarśinī*, 217–219.
12 Abhinavagupta, *Īśvarapratyabhijñāvimarśinī*, Vol. 1, 75–76.
13 "*sa ca paraśarīrādisāhityena avagataṃ svaṃ svabhāvaṃ jñānātmakaṃ avagamayati, na ca jñānaṃ idantayā bhāti… bhāti ca yat tadeva ahaṃ ityasya vapuḥ iti parajñānaṃ svātmā eva*" in Abhinavagupta's *Īśvarapratyabhijñāvimarśinī.*

Chapter 18

1 R. Gandhi, *Presuppositions of Human Communication* (Delhi: Oxford University Press, 1974).
2 R. Gandhi, *The Availability of Religious Ideas* (Library of philosophy and religion) (New York: Barnes & Noble Books, 1976).
3 "*Gāyatrī*" literally means "that which protects (*trāyate*) when sung (*gāyanāt*)".
4 *The Bhagavad Gita.* Translation by Laurie Patton. (Penguin, 2018), Introduction.
5 *kathaṃ bhīṣmaṃ ahaṃ saṃkhye droṇaṃ ca madhusūdana/iṣubhiḥ pratiyotsyāmi pūjārhāv arisūdana*//BG:2.4.
6 Sargeant, Winthrop, *The Bhagavad Gita: An Interlinear Translation from the Sanskrit, with Word-for-Word Transliteration and Translation, and Complete Grammatical Commentary, As Well As a Readable Prose Translation and Page-by-page Vocabularies* (Garden City, NY: Doubleday, 1979) (751 pages).
7 Barbara Stoler Miller (transl.); Barry Moser (illus.), *The Bhagavad-Gita: Krishna's Counsel in Time of War* (New York: Columbia University Press, 1986).
8 Ibid. Chap 2, verse 4.
9 VP III. Chapter 7/verses: 163–164.
10 Ibid. VP III, pp. 419–420.
11 *sakheti matvā prasabhaṃ yaduktaṃ he kṛṣṇa! he yādava! he sakheti!/ajānatā mahimānaṃ tavemaṃ mayā pramādāt praṇayena vāpi*//BG:11.41.

Chapter 19

1 H. H. Price, *Belief: The Gifford lectures Delivered at the University of Aberdeen in 1960* (New York: The Humanities Press, 1969).
2 Ananthalal Thakur, *Gautamakṛtaṃ Nyāyadarśnam* (Darbhanga: Mithilā Vidyāpītha, 1967) 365–369.
3 John McDowell, "Meaning, Communication, and Knowledge," in *Philosophical Subjects: Essays Presented to P. F. Strawson*, ed. Van Straaten, 135.
4 Vātsyāyana, *Nyāyabhāṣya* 1.1.7. in Thakur (1967).
5 This story is told by the sixteenth-century logician Mathuranātha at the beginning of his gloss on the fourth part of Gaṅgeśa's *Tattvacintāmaṇi*.
6 Kāmākhyānātha Tarkavāgīśa, *Tattvacintāmaṇi with Rahasya of Mathuranātha* (Calcutta: Asiatic Society, 1974), 7–8.
7 Compare this with an account given roughly four hundred years later: "Specifically, when S & H are masters of a common language the following can happen: A belief of S gives rise to an utterance by him, which utterance produces in his audience H a belief with the same content; and all this happens in such a way that if S's belief is knowledge then we may allow that title to H's belief too," Fricker (1987).
8 Austin, *Philosophical Papers*, 81–82.
9 C. A. J. Coady. "Testimony and Observation." *American Philosophical Quarterly* (1973).
10 Of course, it would be rash to conclude that since it is indirect it must be inferential, as Fricker (1987) seems to have done.
11 We are following the Nyāya model of inference where there is a subject of inference, that is, a place, *pakṣa*, for example, a hill, in which a predicated property, the inferable, *sādhya*, for example, a fire, is established, via the presence of a sign, reason, middle term, or mark, *hetu*, for example, smoke, which is known to be connected with the inferable by a relation of pervasion, *vyāpti*, or invariable unconditional concomitance.
12 Again to use Matilal's notation.
13 Gareth Evans, *The Varieties of Reference*, ed. John McDowell (Oxford: New York: Clarendon Press; Oxford University Press, 1982), 123.
14 Elizabeth Fricker, "The Epistemology of Testimony," *Proceedings of the Aristotelian Society, Supplementary Volumes* 61 (1987), 57–106.
15 Davidson, *Inquiries into Truth and Interpretation*, 200.

Chapter 20

1 Wittgenstein, *Philosophical Investigations*, 27–64.
2 Augustine *De Magistro*. Against the Academicians/The Teacher by Augustine of Hippo, Hackett 1995.
3 Michael Dummett, *What Do We Know When We Know a Language in the Seas of Language* (London: Oxford University Press, 1996).
4 Kant, *Critique of Pure Reason*, A133/B172.

Chapter 21

1 *Nāsadīya Sūkta* Ṛgveda X. 129 has the phrase "tama āsīd" (there was darkness) in its third verse. Sāyaṇa packs in the entire Advaita Vedānta metaphysics of

positive ignorance here while commenting upon this occurrence of the word "darkness." Let me translate extracts from his gloss here: "Before creation, at the state of dissolution, matter and the entire material world were concealed in darkness. Just as nocturnal darkness covers all things, so were things. Here, that positive ignorance of which another name is '*māyā*' because it obstructs the true nature of the self is called 'darkness'... When it (the world) comes to light through name and form out of that engulfing darkness, then that is said to be its 'birth.' By this, the view that the effect which is nonexistent in the causal state comes into being—this kind of nonexistent-ism or non-pre-existence *(asatkāryavāda)* of the effect—is rejected... Thus '*tamas*' means the positive unknowing which is the root cause. But how can darkness which is the covering agent and the world which is the covered object, the nominative and the accusative of the act of covering, be essentially of the same nature? This query is answered by the expression '*apraketam*', meaning that which is not clearly knowable. This darkness is inscrutable and the world inside it at that primordial state is not distinguishable by name and form... It is this indistinguishablility which is further emphasized by the analogy of water, because '*salilam*' here means 'like water'. Just as milk mixed with water is impossible to tell apart similarly the world assumes indiscriminablity through darkness." Apart from distinction-effacing "*tamas*," this verse mentions another crucial word—"*tapas*"—which means "austere exertion." How did the One Spirit when immersed in such borderless "gloom of unknowing" manage to exert Itself to uncover the universe? Sāyaṇa's answer is: "Through brooding thought about what is to be investigated by questioning" *(praṣṭavya paryālocanena)* because the *Muṇḍaka Upaniṣad* says about the Ātman-Brahman: "His *tapas is of* the nature of cognition." The total picture of creation is thus very similar to the phenomenology of the birth of a poem or painting which emerges out *of* painful creative fervor in the midst of an undifferentiated darkness of pregnant confusion. Does the artist know what is about to be uncovered? The answer has to be "Neither yes nor no." Creation is thus always a process of manifestation of the unmanifest, murky uknowability being the root of it all.

2 Samuel Todes and Charles Daniels, "Beyond the Doubt of a Shadow," in *Dialogues in Phenomenology. Selected Studies in Phenomenology and Existential Philosophy*, ed. D. Ihde, R. M. Zaner, Vol. 5 (Dordrecht: Springer, 1975), 86–93.
Also see *Seeing Dark Things: The Philosophy of Shadows*, by Roy Sorensen (New York: Oxford University Press, 2011).

3 Michael Baxandall, *Shadows and Enlightenment* (Connecticut, Mass.: Yale University Press, 1995), 2–15.

4 John Gage, *Color in Turner: Poetry and Truth* (New York: Frederick A. Praeger, 1969), 198.

5 Leonardo da Vinci, *Leonardo on Painting*, ed. Martin Kemp, trans. Martin Kemp and Margaret Walker (New Haven/London: Yale University Press 1989), 377.

6 Bertrand Russell, *The Philosophy of Logical Atomism* (Chicago: Open Court Publishing Company, 1998), 211.

7 Baxandall, *Shadows and Enlightenment*, 2.

8 Aristotle, *Opuscula, The Works of Aristotle V6,* trans. and ed. by T. Loveday and E. S. Forster (Oxford: Clarendon Press, 1913), 79.

9 Aristotle, *Opuscula, The Works of Aristotle V6,* trans. and ed. by T. Loveday and E. S. Forster (Oxford: Clarendon Press, 1913), 79. (Emphasis mine).

10 Leonardo Da Vinci, *Notebooks*, eds. Martin Kemp and Irma A. Richter (London: Oxford University Press, 2008), 114.

11 Vyomavati, Chowkhamba edition by Gopinath Kaviraj and Dhundhiraja Shastri, along with *Sūkti* and *Setu* glosses by Jagadīúa and Padmanābha, explains away motion *of* shadows as follows: "In each successive place where the projection of light is obstructed by a screening substance (like an umbrella) we apply the word 'shadow.' The movement in the screening substance is then falsely superimposed upon the visible absence of sun-light, and we get the usage 'shadow moves.'" What is interesting is that a later Jaina text called *Nyāyakuncudacandra* quotes this passage and refutes the erroneous superimposition account proposed by Vyomaśiva by arguing: "Motion of one thing can only be superimposed on another existent thing. If shadows do not exist as positive entities, how can they be the locus of superimposition of the screen's motion?" The language of the reply, however, suggests that the Jaina author is making the common mistake of conflating Vaiśeṣika absences with nonexistent entities. The final argument: shadows must be ultimately real because they are things which have superimposed motion; that whatever has superimposed motion, like the trees on the bank, is ultimately real does not actually refute the absence-theory of shadows of the Nyāya-Vaiśeṣika because absences are ultimately real in that scheme of things.

12 Gage, *Color in Turner: Poetry and Truth,* 176.

13 Da Vinci, *Notebooks,* 90.

14 G. E. Moore, *Commonplace Book* (New York: Macmillan, 1962), 142.

15 Johann Wolfgang von Goethe, *Theory of Colors* (Santa Cruz, CA: BLTC Press, 2008).

16 Aristotle, *De Anima,* The Complete Works of Aristotle: *The Revised Oxford Translation,* trans. J Barnes (Princeton, NJ: Princeton University Press, 1984), $425^{b}15$.

17 Stephen Hawking, "Introduction," *Shadows of Creation: Dark Matter and the Structure of the Universe,* Michael Riordan and David N. Schramm (London: W H Freeman & Co, 1991), viii.

18 Michael Riordan and David N. Schramm, *Shadows of Creation: Dark Matter and the Structure of the Universe* (New York: W H Freeman & Co, 1991), 200.

19 We find at least five well-defended positions in *Classical Indian Philosophy* about the ontological status of shadows: (A) They are general absences of strong light (*pr auḍhaprakāúakatejahsāmānyābhāvaḥ*) according to Nyāya Vaiśeṣika. (B) They are misperceived dark-blue color superimposed from the eyes onto a surface relatively deprived of light according to Śrīdhara in *Nyāyakandalī.* (C) Darkness is a substance,—dense, thin, and intangible, blackish-blue in color and visible without the help of light. It is an evolute of earth or *ākāśa* according to Rāmānuja and Vedāntadeœika. (D) Darkness and shadows form a positive, mobile, independent, and tenth category of substances by destroying which light has to manifest itself and other things hidden by gloom according to Bhāṭṭa Māmāmsā and Advaita Vedānta. (E) Darkness is a substance with color, touch, and healing properties according to Jaina Metaphysics.
The best account of all these views and their polemics is to be found in Vadidevāsuri's *Pramāṇānayatattvālokālaṅkāra,* Chapter 5, 849–858.

20 Baxandall, *Shadows and Enlightenment*, 2.

21 Plato, *Republic,* Bk VII, ch xxv, 514A, 521B.

22 Book V Lesson 22, commentary 1129.

Chapter 22

1 John McDowell, *Mind and World* (Cambridge, Mass.: Harvard University Press, 1996) 10.
2 P. F. Stawson, "Perception and Its Objects," in *Perception and Identity*, ed. G. F. Macdonald (New York: Cornell University Press, 1979), 47.
3 P. F. Strawson, *Freedom and Resentment and Other Essays* (London: Methuen, 1974), 5.
4 P. F. Stawson, "Knowing from Words," in *Knowing from Words: Western and Indian Philosophical Analysis of Understanding and Testimony*, ed. A. Chakrabarti and Bimal K. Matilal (New York: Springer Publishing, 2010), 23–28.
5 Evans, *Varieties of Reference*, Chapter 6.
6 Matilal, *Perception: An Essay on Classical Indian Theories of Knowledge*.
7 Richard Sorabji, *Animal Minds and Human Morals: The Origins of the Western Debate* (New York: Cornell University Press, 1995), 35.
8 *Nyāyasūtra* 1.1.4.
9 Dummett, *The Logical Basis of Metaphysics*, 1.12–13.
10 I have given a number of strong reasons why, I think, the idea of pre predicative perception should be fully dropped and proposition 1 above should be fully embraced by Nyâya philosophers. See my (2000) "Against Immaculate Perception."
11 Strawson, "Knowing from Words," 412.
12 See Kant's remarks on *sinn* and *sinnes* in section 28 "On Imagination" of his *Anthropology*.
13 In Strawson's last book *Analysis and Metaphysics*, 62–63.

Chapter 23

1 See Krishna Chandra Bhattacharyya, "Reality of the Future," in *Studies in Philosophy* (2nd rev. edn.), ed. Gopinath Bhattacharyya (Delhi [India]: Motilal Banarsidass, 1983).
2 Strawson. P.F., Comments and Replies to *The reality of the future* J. J. C. Smart in *Philosophia* 10 (3–4): 141–150 (1981).
3 Wittgenstein, *Philosophical Investigations*, 42.
4 G. P. Baker and P. M. S. Hacker, *Wittgenstein: Understanding and Meaning: Volume 1 of An Analytic Commentary on the* Philosophical Investigations, *Pt. II: Exegesis §§1–184*, 2nd edition (Oxford: Wiley-Blackwell, 2009), 118.
5 A. N. Prior, *Past, Present and Future* (Oxford: Clarendon Press, 1967),142.
6 J. J. C. Smart, "The Reality of the Future," *Philosophia* 10 (1981): 141–150.
7 Bhattacharya, "Reality of the Future" see note 1 above.
8 Professor Anscombe ends her book *Intention* by discerning this issue.
9 See Michael Dummett, *The Seas of Language* (Oxford: Clarendon Press, 1996), 257.
10 See Alexander Miller, "What Is the Manifestation Argument?" *Pacific Philosophical Quarterly* 83, no. 4 (December 2002): 352–383.

Chapter 24

1 See Arindam Chakrabarti, "Idealist Refutations of Idealism," *Idealistic Studies* 22, no. 2 (1992): 93–106.

2 Jenny Keefe, "James Ferrier and the Theory of Ignorance," *The Monist, April 2007.*
3 "To defer" has two senses: to respect and to postpone. Insofar as the unknown realities are taken to be accessible to a supreme knower, one defers or shows Kantian humility about noumena. Insofar as the unknown realities are taken to be knowable in principle at a later stage, like the neurophysiology of those parts of the human cortex which control and enable counterfactual reasoning, the realist, unlike a skeptic, takes possible knowledge of it as future epistemic agenda.
4 See "An Epistemic Existence Argument" in Billy Joe Lucas, which proves that if an epistemically unsurpassable being is possible, then an omniscient being actually exists. Billy Joe Lucas, "The Second Epistemic Way," *International Journal for Philosophy of Religion*, 18, no. 3 (1985): 107–114 Published by Springer.
5 *Mahāyāna-sūtrālamkāra*, according to Paul Giffiths in "Omniscience in the Mahāyānasūtrālankāra and Its Commentaries," *Indo-Iranian Journal* 33, no. 2 (April 1990): 85–120.
6 Maṇḍana here almost anticipates Kant's problematic expression "infinite given magnitude" about space.
7 Dummett, *Thought and Reality* (*Lines of Thought*), 101–102

Chapter 25

1 See "Why Anything? Why This" Derek Parfit, London Review of Books, January 22, 1998, and Jim Holt's, *Why Does the World Exist?* (New York, London: Liveright Publishing Corporation, 2012).
2 Bertrand Russell, *The Philosophy of Logical Atomism* (Routledge Classics) (Volume 24) 1st Edition (London: Routledge, 2009), 287.
3 Birgit Kellner, "Negation—Failure or Success? Remarks on an Allegedly Characteristic Trait of Dharmakīrti's Anupalabdhi-theory," *Journal of Indian Philosophy* 29 (2001): 495–517. See also by Birgit Kellner: Negation in Indian Philosophy: An entry from Gale's *Encyclopedia of Philosophy.*
4 This is not a very plausible example because it is highly unlikely that we would make such a category mistake, but other category mistakes, we shall see soon, are not that uncommon.
5 *vyadhikaraṇa-dharmāvacchinna pratiyogitāka abhāva.*
6 Raghunātha (1477–1547).
7 For more details, see Arindam Chakrabarti's, *Denying Existence* (Dordrecht, Boston, London: Kluwer Academic, 1997), 235–243.
8 *Mūla-madhyamaka-kārikā* http://indica-et-buddhica.org/repositorium.
9 Jan Westerhoff, *The Dispeller of Disputes: Nāgārjunas Vigrahavyavartani* (Oxford: Oxford University Press, 2010).
10 *Creative Evolution*, by Henri Bergson, translated by Arthur Mitchell, The Modern Library New York, 1911, 304.
11 Book XII, chap 329, verse 40.

Bibliography

A

Abhinavagupta. *Īśvarapratyabhijñāvimarśinī*, Edited by. K. A. Iyer and K. C. Pandey. Delhi: Motilal Banarsidass Publishers, 1986.

Abhinavagupta. *Parā-trīśikā-Vivaraṇa: The Secrete of Tantric Mysticism*. Edited by. Bettina Baumer, trans. Jaideva Singh. Delhi: Motilal Banarsidass Publishers, 2000.

Aquinas, Thomas. *Commentary on* De Anima, trans. Robert Pasnau. New Haven and London: Yale University Press, 1999. 426 b7.

Anscombe, G. *Intention*. Oxford: Basil Blackwell, 1958.

Aranya, Swami Hariharananda. *Yoga Philosophy of Patañjali: Containing His Yoga Aphorisms with Vyasa's Commentary in Sanskrit and a Translation with Annotations Including Many Suggestions for the Practice of Yoga*. Trans. P. N. Mukerji. New York: SUNY Press, 1984.

Aristotle. *De Anima*. Trans. C. D. C. Reeve. Indianapolis: Hackett Publishing Company Inc., 2017. 425a–426b.

Aristotle. *De Anima*. In *The Complete Works of Aristotle: The Revised Oxford Translation*, trans. J Barnes. Princeton, NJ: Princeton University Press, 1984. 425^b15.

Aristotle. *Opuscula*. In *The Works of Aristotle V6*, trans. and ed. by T. Loveday and E. S. Forster. Oxford: Clarendon Press, 1913.

Aristotle. *Posterior Analytics*. Cambridge Mass.: Harvard University Press, 1960. 100a.17.

Armstrong, D. M. *A Theory of Universals*, Vol. II of *Universals and Scientific Realism*. Cambridge: Cambridge University Press, 1978. 19–23.

Ātmatattva Viveka (A History of Indian Literature Series). Wiesbaden: Otto Harrasowitz, 1977. 97–100.

Austin, J. L. Footnote to "Are There Apriori Concepts?" In *Philosophical Papers*. Oxford: Clarendon Press, 1961.

Austin, J. L. *Philosophical Papers*. Oxford: Clarendon Press, 1961. 81–82.

Ayer, A. J. "Moore's Refutations of Idealism." In *Philosophy in the Twentieth Century*. Weidenfeld and Nicolson, 1982.

Ayer, A. J. *The Problem of Knowledge*. London: Macmillan, 1956. 65–66.

B

Baker, Deb. *A Blue Hand: The Tragicomic, Mind-Altering Odyssey of Allen Ginsberg, a Holy Fool, a Lost Muse, a Dharma Bum, and His Prickly Bride in India*. Penguin Books, 2009.

Baker, G. P., and P. M. S. Hacker. *Wittgenstein: Understanding and Meaning: Volume 1 of An Analytic Commentary on the* Philosophical Investigations, *Pt. II: Exegesis §§1–184*, 2nd edn. Oxford: Wiley-Blackwell, 2009.

Baxandall. *Shadows and Enlightenment*. Yale University Press, 1997. 2–15.

Bell, D., and N. Cooper (ed.). *The Analytic Tradition: Meaning, Thought, and Knowledge*. Oxford: Blackwell, 1990.

Bentham, J., and C. K. Ogden. *Bentham's Theory of Fictions*. London: K. Paul, Trench, Trubner & Co, 1932.

Bergson, Henri. *Creative Evolution*, trans. Arthur Mitchell. New York: The Modern Library, 1911. 304.

Bhāškarī. A *Commentary on the Iśvarapratyabhijñāvimarśinī of Abhinavagupta*. Eds. K. A. Subramania Iyer and K. C. Pandey. Allahabad: Princess of Wales Sarasvati Bhavana Texts, 1940.

Bhaṣya. *Nyāyadarśanam: With Vātsyāyana's Bhāṣya, Uddyotkara's Vārttika, Vācaspati Miśra's Tātparyaṭīkā & Viśvanātha's Vṛtti*. Edited by Taranatha, Amarendramohan, Taranatha, Tarkatirtha, Amarendramohan, and Vātsyāyana. 2nd ed. New Delhi: Munshiram Manoharlal, 1985.

Bhattacharya, Gopinath. *Essays in Analytical Philosophy*. Kolkata: Sanskrit Pustak Bhandar, 1989.

Bhattacharya, K. C. "Reality of the Future." In *K. C. Bhattacharya: Studiesin Philosophy, Vol. II*. Calcutta: Progressive Publishers. 271–280.

Bhattacharyya, K. C. "The Subject as Freedom." In *Search for the Absolute in Neo-Vedānta*. Honolulu: University of Hawaii Press, 1976.

Bhattacharya, Krishna Chandra. "Reality of the Future." In *Studies in Philosophy*, edited by Gopinath Bhattacharyya. 2nd rev. edn. Delhi [India]: Motilal Banarsidass, 1983.

Bhattacharyya, Sibajiban. "Gadādhara Bhaṭṭācārya's Viṣayatāvāda." *Journal of Indian Philosophy* 14, no. 2 (1986): 109–193; 217–302.

Bhaṭṭa, Jayanta. *Nyāyamañjarī*, Vol. II. Mysore: Oriental Research Institute, 1983. 30.

Bhaṭṭa, Jayanta. *Nyāyamañjarī*. Delhi: Sri Satguru Publications, 1995. 133–145. Book XII, chap. 329, verse 40.

Brahadarnyaka Upanishad: I. 5. 3., IV.3.7.—Madhavananda, & Śaṅkarācārya. *The Bṛhadāraṇyaka Upaniṣad: With the Commentary of Śaṅkarācārya*. 4th edn. Calcutta: Advaita Ashrama, 1965.

Buber, Martin, and Walter Kaufman. *I and Thou*. New York: Scribner, 1970. 59.

C

Carruthers, Peter. *An Integrative Theory of Self-Knowledge*. London: Oxford University Press, 2011.

Caturdaśalakṣaṇī: with Raghunātha's Dīdhiti and with Gādādharī and 2 sub-commentaries. Part 1. Chennai: Adyar Library and Research Centre, 1986.

Coady, C. A. J. "Testimony and Observation." *American Philosophical Quarterly* 10, no. 2 (1973): 149–155.

Colins, Steven. *Selfless Persons*. Cambridge: Cambridge University Press, 1985.

Chakrabarti, Arindam. "Against Immaculate Perception: Seven Reasons for Eliminating nirvikalpaka Perception from Nyāya." *Philosophy East and West* 50, no. 1 (2000): 1–8.

Chakrabarti, Arindam. *Denying Existence*. Dordrecht, Boston, London: Kluwer Academic, 1997. 235–243.

Chakrabarti, Arindam. "Idealist Refutations of Idealism." *Idealistic Studies* 22, no. 2 (1992): 93–106.

Chesterton. G. K. *The Best of Father Brown*. London: Orion Books, 2002, 72.

Chinmayananda, and Gauḍapāda Ācārya. *Discourses on Mandukya Upanishad with Gaudapada's Karika*. Madras: Chinmaya Publication Trust, 1984.

Churchland, Paul M. *A Neurocomputational Perspective: The Nature of Mind and the Structure of Science*. Cambridge, MA: MIT Press, 1989, 1993.

Churchland, Paul. "Eliminative Materialism and the Propositional Attitudes." *Journal of Philosophy* 78, no. 2 (1981): 67–90.

D

Da Vinci, Leonardo. *Notebooks*, eds. Martin Kemp and Irma A. Richter. London: Oxford University Press, 2008. 114.

Das, Sisir Kumar. *Abalupta Chaturtha Charan (Obliterated Fourth Stanza) a book of poems in Bengali*. Kolkata: Kabita Pakshik, 1986.

Davidson, Donald. *Inquiries into Truth and Interpretation*, 2nd edn. Oxford: New York: Clarendon Press; Oxford University Press, 2001.

Davidson, Donald, "The Folly of Trying to Define Truth." *Journal of Philosophy* 93, no. 6 (1996): 263–278.

Demeter, Tamas. "Two Kinds of Mental Realism." *J Gen Philos Sci* 40 (2009): 59–71.

Devitt, Michael. *Realism and Truth*. Oxford: Basil Blackwell, 1984. 180.

Dharmakīrti. *Santānāntarasiddhi*, verses 7–26. In F. Shcherbatskoĭ, Harish C. Gupta, and Debiprasad Chattopadhyaya. *Papers of Th. Stcherbatsky* (Soviet Indology series; no. 2). Calcutta: Indian Studies: Past & Present, 1969. 87–93.

Dharmakīrti, Acharya. *Pramāṇavārttika of Acharya Dharmakīrti with Commentary 'Vritti' of Acharya Manorathanandin*. Edited by. Swami Dwarikadas Shastri. Varanasi: Bauddha Bharati, 1994. Pratyaksa Chapter, verse 354. 173.

Dummett, Michael. *The Logical Basis of Metaphysics*. Harvard University Press, 1993. 1.12–13.

Dummett, Michael. "More about Thoughts." *Notre Dame Journal of Formal Logic* 30, no. 1 (1989): 17.

Dummett, Michael. *The Nature and Future of Philosophy*. New York: Columbia University Press 2010.

Dummett, Michael. "Past, Present and Future." In *The Nature and Future of Philosophy*. New York: Columbia University Press, 2010. 142.

Dummett, Michael. "The Relative Priority of Thought and Language." In *Frege and Other Philosophers*. Oxford: Clarendon Press, 1973.

Dummett, Michael. *The Seas of Language*. Oxford: Clarendon Press, 1996.

Dummett, Michael. "Thought and Perception: The Views of Two Philosophical Innovators." In *The Analytic Tradition: Meaning, Thought, and Knowledge*, edited by D. Bell and N. Cooper. Oxford: Blackwell, 1990.

Dummett, Michael. *Thought and Reality* (Lines of thought). Oxford; New York: Clarendon Press; Oxford University Press, 2006. 101–102.

Dummett, Michael. *Truth and Other Enigmas*. Cambridge, Mass.: Harvard University Press, 1978.

E

Eckart, Forster. "Kant's Refutation of Idealism." In *Philosophy, Its History and Historiography*, edited by A. J. Holland. D. Reidel, 1985.

Evans, Gareth. *Varieties of Reference*. Oxford: Clarendon Press, 1982.

Evans, Gareth, and John McDowell. *The Varieties of Reference*. Oxford: New York: Clarendon Press; Oxford University Press, 1982. 123.

F

Field, Hartry. *Science without Numbers*. Princeton, NJ: Princeton University Press, 1980.
Foucault, Michel. *The Order of Things*. Pantheon Books, 1970. Ch. 9, c V.
Frege: Philosophy of Language, edited by Michael Dummett. New York/London: Harper and Row, 1973. 442–470.
Frege, G. "The Thought: A Logical Inquiry," in *Philosophical Logic*, edited by. P. F. Strawson. London: Oxford University Press, 1973. 17–38.
Fricker, Elizabeth. "The Epistemology of Testimony." *Proceedings of the Aristotelian Society, Supplementary Volumes* 61 (1987): 57–106.

G

Gage. *Color in Turner: Poetry and Truth*. First American Edition, New York: Frederick A. Praeger, 1969. 176, 198.
Gandhi, R. *Presuppositions of Human Communication*. Delhi: Oxford University Press, 1974.
Gandhi, R. *The Availability of Religious Ideas* (Library of philosophy and religion). New York: Barnes & Noble Books, 1976.
Geach, P. T. *Truth, Love and Immortality*. Los Angeles: University of California Press, 1979.
Giffiths, Paul. "Omniscience in the Mahāyānasūtrālankāra and Its Commentaries." *Indo-Iranian Journal* 33, no. 2 (April 1990): 85–120.
Goethe, Johann Wolfgang von. *Theory of Colors*. Santa Cruz, CA: BLTC Press, 2008.
Gram, Molt K. "What Kant Really Did to Idealism." In *Essays on Kant's Critique of Pure Reason*, ed. J. N. Mohanty and Robert W. Shahan. Oklahoma: University of Oklahoma Press, 1982.
Guyer, Paul. *Kant and the Claims of Knowledge*. Cambridge: Cambridge University Press, 1987. 279–329.

H

Hawking, Stephen. "Introduction." In *Shadows of Creation: Dark Matter and the Structure of the Universe*. Michael Riordan and David N. Schramm. London: W H Freeman & Co, 1991. viii.
Hogan, Melinda, and Raymond Martin. "Introspective Misidentification: An I for an I." In *Self-Reference and Self-Awareness*, edited by Andrew Brook and Richard DeVidi. Amsterdam/Philadelphia: John Benjamins Publishing, 2001.

I

Abhinavagupta. *Isvarapratyabhijnavvivr tivimarśinī*. Volumes 1, 2, and 3. New Delhi: AkayBookCorporation, 1987.

J

James, W. "Principles of Psychology." In *The Works of William James*. Cambridge: Harvard University Press, 1981.

Jan, Westerhoff. "The Dispeller of Disputes." In *Nāgārjuna's Vigrahavyavartani*. Oxford: Oxford University Press, 2010.

Jayanta Bhaṭṭa. *Nyāyamañjarī*, edited by Gaurinath Shastri Ma. Ma. Śivakumāraśāstrī-granthamālā; puṣpam 5. Vārāṇasi: Sampūrṇānanda-Saṃskrta Viśvavidyālayaḥ, 1982.

Jha, G., and Sridhara. *Padārthadharmasaṅgraha of Praśastapāda: With the Nyāyakandalī of Śrīdhara* (Chaukhambha oriental studies; 4). Varanasi: Chaukhambha Orientalia, 1982.

Johnson, Mark. *The Body in the Mind: The Bodily Basis of Meaning, Imagination and Reason*. Chicago: University of Chicago Press, 1990.

Jonardon, Ganeri. *The Philosophy of Language in Gadahara's Saktivada*. London: University of Oxford Press, 1993.

Joshi, S. D., J. A. F. Roodbergen, and Sahitya Akademi. *The Aṣṭādhyāyī of Pāṇini with Translation and Explanatory Notes, Vol. 4*. New Delhi: Sahitya Akademi, 1991. 1.4.1-1.4.110.

K

Kant, Immanuel. *Critique of Pure Reason*, trans. Werner S. Pluhar. Indianapolis, IN: Hackett Publishing, 1996. A133/B172, B274.

Kant, Immanuel. *Toward Perpetual Peace and Other Writings on Politics, Peace, and History*. Yale University Press, 2006.

Kant, Immanuel. "Idea for a Universal History with a Cosmopolitan Purpose." In *Kant's Political Writings*, edited by Hans Reiss. Cambridge: Cambridge University Press, 1970.

"Katha Upanishad." *The Upanishads - A New Translation*. Trans. Swami Nikhilananda. https://www.shankaracharya.org/katha_upanishad.php.2.1.1.

Keefe, Jenny. "James Ferrier and the Theory of Ignorance." *The Monist*. April 2007.

Keeling, S. V. *Descartes*. Oxford University Press, 1968. 105.

Kellner, Birgit. "Negation – Failure or Success? Remarks on an Allegedly Characteristic Trait of Dharmakīrti's anupalabdhi-theory." *Journal of Indian Philosophy* 29 (2001): 495–517.

Kellner, Birgit. "Negation in Indian Philosophy." In *Encyclopedia of Philosophy*, ed. D. M. Borchert, London: Macmillan, 2005.

Kemp (ed.). *Leonardo on Painting*, p. 337.

Kemp Smith, Norman. *Immanuel Kant's Critique of Pure Reason*. New York: St. Martin's Press, 1965.

Kierkegaard, Soren. *Either/Or: A Fragment of Life*. Part 1. Penguin Classics, 1992. 32.

Kripke, Saul. *Naming, Necessity and Natural Kinds*, edited by Stephen P. Shwartz. New York: Cornell University Press, 1977. 101.

L

Lawry, Edward G. "Did Kant Refute Idealisms?" *Idealistic Studies* 10, no. 1 (1980): 67–75.

Lewis, David. "New Work for a Theory of Universals." *Australasian Journal of Philosophy* 61, no. 4 (Dec. 1983): 345.

Lichtenberg, George Christian. *The Wastebooks*, trans. R. J. Holligdale. New York Review of Books, 2000.
Lucas, Billy Joel. "An Epistemic Existence Argument." *International Journal for Philosophy of Religion* 18, no. 3 (Springer 1985): 107–114.

M

Madhvāchārya. *Viṣṇutattvavinirṇaya*, v. 2. Bangalore: Vrindavan Printers and Publishers, 785.
Mahābhārata with Commentary by Milakantha. Edited by. Pandit Ramchandrashastri Kinjawadekar. Delhi: Munshilal Manoarlal, 1979. Xll.255.9.
Mathurānātha. *Tattvacintāmaṇi-Rahasya.* 7–8.
Matilal, B. K. *Epistemology, Logic and Grammar in Indian Philosophical Analysis.* Mouton, 1971. 25–26.
Matilal, B. K. *Logic, Language and Reality.* Delhi: Motilal Banarsidass, 1985. 276.
Matilal, B. K. *The Word and the World.* Delhi: Oxford India Paperbacks, 2015.
Matilal, B. K. *Perception: An Essay on Classical Indian Theory of Knowledge.* Oxford: Oxford University Press, 1986.
Matilal, B. K. *The Logical Basis of Metaphysics.* Cambridge, MA: Harvard University Press, 1991. 93–97.
Matilal, B., and Chakrabarti, Arindam. "Knowledge from Hearsay." In *Knowing from Words: Western and Indian Philosophical Analysis of Understanding and Testimony* (Synthese library; v. 230). Dordrecht; Boston: Kluwer Academic, 1994.
Matthaei, and Aach (trans. and ed.). *Geothe's Theory of Colors.* Van Nostrand Reinhold, 1971. 87.
McDowell, John. "Meaning, Communication, and Knowledge." In *Philosophical Subjects: Essays Presented to P. F. Strawson*, edited by Van Straaten (Oxford University Press, 1980). 135.
McDowell. *Mind and World.* Cambridge, MA: Harvard University Press, 1996. 10, 26.
McDowell, John Stuart. *An Examination of Sir William Hamilton's Philosophy.* University of Toronto Press, Scholarly Publishing Division, 1979.
McGinn, Colin. *Mental Content.* Oxford: Oxford University Press, 1989.
Miller, Alexander. "What Is the Manifestation Argument?" *Pacific Philosophical Quarterly* 83, no. 4 (December 2002): 352–383.
Miller, Barbara Stoler, *The Bhagavad-Gita: Krishna's Counsel in Time of War*, trans. Barry Moser (illus.). New York: Columbia University Press, 1986.
Moore, G. E. *Commonplace Book.* New York: Macmillan, 1962.
Mukhopadhyay, P. K. *Indian Realism: A Rigorous Descriptive Metaphysics*, Calcutta: K. P. Bagchi, 1984 (Critique of Indian Realism, Agra University, Agra, 1964). 319–327.

N

Norman, Malcolm. *Dreaming* (Studies in philosophical psychology). London, New York: Routledge & Paul; Humanities Press, 1962 Passim.
Nyanmoli, Bhikkhu. *The Path of Purification (Visuddhimagga).* Candy Srilanka: Buddhist Publication Society, 1975.

O

Ogden, C. K. *Bentham's Theory of Fictions*. Paterson, NJ: Littlefield, Adams & Company, 1959.

P

Paṇsīkar, Wāsudeva Laxmaṇa Śāstrī (ed.). *The Yogavāsiṣṭha of Vālmīki: with the Commentary vāsiṣthamahārāmāyaṇatātpāryaprakāśa*. Vol. II. Bombay Munshiram Manoharlal, 1981. Nirvāṇa 2. Ch. 105.

Parent, Ted. "In the Mental Fiction, Mental Fictionalism Is Fictitious" (internet, with author's permission). (2012).

Parfit, Derek. *Reasons and Persons* (Part III). Oxford: Oxford University Press, 1986.

Parfit, D. *Reasons and Persons*. Oxford (Oxfordshire): Oxford University Press; Clarendon Press & ProQuest, 1986.

Parfit, Derek. "Why Anything? Why This." *London Review of Books*, January 22 (1998).

Patton, Laurie (trans.). *The Bhagavad Gita*. Penguin, 2018.

Perception: An Essay on Classical Indian Theories of Knowledge. Oxford: Clarendon Press, 1986. 344–354.

Perrett, Roy. "Is Whatever Exists Knowable and Nameable?" *Philosophy East and West* 49, no. 4 (October 1999).

Peter F. Strawson (ed.). *Philosophical Logic*. London: Oxford University Press, 1973. 21.

PI: pt. II.

Plato. *Republic*. In *Plato: Complete Works*. Ed. John M. Cooper and D. S. Hutchinson. Indianapolis: Hackett, 1997. Bk. VII, ch xxv, 514A, 521B.

Potter. Encyclopedia II. 95. 217.

Potter, Karl H., and Sibajiban Bhattacharya. *The Encyclopedia of Indian Philosophies, Volume 6: Indian Philosophical Analysis*. Princeton: Princeton University Press, 2004.

Powell, C. Thomas. "Kant's Fourth Paralogism." *Philosophy and Phenomenological Research* 48, no. 3 (1988): 389–414.

Pramāṇa Vārttika with Manoratha commentary, edited by Swami Dvarikadas Shastri, Baudhha Bharati Varanasi (1994).

Pramāṇanayatattvālokālaṅkāraḥ: Tadvyākhyā ca Syādvādaratnākaraḥ. Delhi: Bhāratīya Vidyā Book Corporation, 1988).

Price, H. H. *Belief*. Routledge, 1969.

Prolegomena, section S49.

Putnam. "Mathematics, Matter and Method." In *Philosophical Papers*, Vol. I. Cambridge University Press, Cambridge, 1975.

Putnam, Hilary. *Representations and Reality*. M. I. T., 1988. 108.

PV. p.169.

Q

Quine, W. V. "Logic and the Reification of Universals." *From a Logical Point of View*, 2nd edn., revised. New York: Harper Torchbooks, Harper & Row Publishers, 1961. 129.

Quine, W. V. O. *Word and Object*. Cambridge, MA: MIT Press, 1964.

R

Riordan, Michael and David N. Schramm. *Shadows of Creation: Dark Matter and the Structure of the Universe*. London: W H Freeman & Co, 1991. 200.

Rosen, Gideon. "Problems in the History of Fictionalism." In *Fictionalism in Metaphysics*, edited by M. Kalderon. Oxford: Clarendon Press, 2005.

Rosenberg, Jay F. *Thinking about Knowing*. Clarendon Press, 2003. Chapter 2.

Russell, *Theory of Knowledge*, Routledge, 1992. 36–40.

Russell, Bertrand. *An Inquiry into Meaning and Truth*. London: Routledge, 1997.

Russell, Bertrand. *The Philosophy of Logical Atomism* (Routledge Classics) (Volume 24) 1st ed. London: Routledge, 2009. 211, 287.

Rushd, Ibn. *Middle Commentary on Aristotle's De Anima*, edited by Brigham Young University Press, 2002. 99.

Ryle, Gilbert. *Dilemmas*. Cambridge: Cambridge University Press, 1954.

S

Śaṅkara's *Brāhmasūtras* 2/2/28-30. See any standard translation or the summary in Karl Potter (ed.). *Encyclopedia of Indian Philosophies*, Vol. II. Princeton University Press, 1981.

Śaṅkarācārya. *Brahmaśaṅkarabhāṣyasūtram*. Vol. II Vārāṇasī: Ṣaḍdarśanaprakāśanapratiṣṭ hānam. (1982) 2.2.28-30. pp. 716–736.

Śaṅkara Miśra. "The Jewel of Difference." In *Bhedaratnam*. Varanasi: Samparnanand Sanskrit University, 2003.

Śaṅkara's commentary on *Prasnopaniṣad* VI, 2.

Śaktivāda, Part II, on the meaning of special words.

SB/B.U IV.3.7.

Sen, Pranab Kumar. "Strawson on Universals." In *Universals, Concepts and Qualities: New Essays on Meaning of Predicates and Abstract Entities*, edited by Strawson and Chakrabarti. Abingdon: Routledge, 2005.

Sen, Pranab Kumar. "Strawson on Universals." In *Universals, Concepts and Qualities: New Essays on the Meaning of Predicates*, edited by PF Strawson and Arindam Chakrabarti. Ashgate, 2006. 42, fn48.

Sen, P. K. "Universals and Concepts." In *Logical Form, Prediction, and Ontology*, edited by P. K. Sen, Jadavpur Studies No. IV. New Delhi: Macmillan, 1982.

Shastri, D. N. *Critique of Indian Realism: A Study of the Conflict between the Nyāya-Vaiśesika & the Buddhist Dignāga School*. Agra: Agra University, 1964.

Shoemaker, Sydney. *The First-Person Perspective and Other Essays*. Cambridge, Cambridge University Press, 1996.

Siderits, Mark. "Is Reductionism Expressible?" In *Pointing at the Moon: Buddhism, Logic, Analytic Philosophy*, edited by M. D'Amato, J. Garfield, and T. Tillemans, Oxford: Oxford University Press, 2009.

Smart, J. J. C. "The Reality of the Future," *Philosophia* 10, no. 3–4 (1981): 141–150.

Smart, J. J. C. *Problems of Space and Time*. New York: Macmillan, 1964.

Sorabji, Richard. *Animals, Minds, and Human Morals: The Origins of the Western Debate*. New York: Cornell University Press, 1995. 35.

Sorabji, Richard. *Emotion and Peace of Mind: From Stoic Agitation to Christian Tempation*. Oxford University Press: 2002.

Spinoza, B. *On the Improvement of the Understanding, the Ethics, Correspondence*. New York: Dover Publications, 1955.

Sṛṣṭidharācārya, in his commentary on Puruṣottama's Bhāṣā-Vṛtti on Aṣṭādhyāyî.

Stcherbatsky. *Buddhist Logic: In Two Volumes. Vol. II Containing a Translation of the Short Treatise of Logic by Dharmakīrti, and of Its Commentary by Dharmottara, with Notes Appendices and Indices*. Indo-Iranian Reprints 26. Leningrad: Izdatel'stvo Akademii Nauk SSSR, 1930.

Stcherbatsky, T. H. *Buddhist Logic*, 2 vols. Delhi: Motilal Banarsidass, 2008.

Strawson. *Analysis and Metaphysics*. London: Oxford University Press, 1992. 62–63.

Strawson, *Bounds of Sense*. Routledge, 1975. 56–57.

Strawson. P. F., Comments and Replies to *The Reality of the Future*.

Strawson, P. F. "Concepts and Properties or Predication and Copulation." *The Philosophical Quarterly* 37, no. 149 (October 1987): 405.

Strawson, P. F. "Critical Notice of Wittgenstein's Philosophical Investigations." In *Wittgenstein and the Problem of Other Minds*, edited by Harold Morick. Humanities Press, 1967.

Strawson, P. F. "Entity and Identity." In *Contemporary British Philosophy*, edited by H. D. Lewis. Fourth Series. London: George Allen Unwin, 1976. 200.

Strawson. *Freedom and Resentment and Other Essays*. Routledge, 2008. 5.

Strawson, P. F. *Individuals: An Essay in Descriptive Metaphysics*. London: Methuen, 1959.

Strawson, P. F. "Kant's New Foundations of Metaphysics." In *Metaphysik nach Kant?* Klett-Cotta: Stuttgarten Hegelkongress, 1987, 1988. 158.

Strawson. "Knowing from Words." In *Knowing from Words*, edited by Arindam Chakrabarti and B. K. Matilal, Kluwer Academic, 1994. 23–28.

Strawson, "Perception and Its Objects." In *Perception and Identity: Essays Presented to A.J. Ayer, with His Replies to Then*, edited by G. F. Macdonald. Macmillan Publishers Limited, 1979. 47.

Strawson, P. F. "Reply to John McDowell." In *The Philosophy of P. F. Strawson*, ed. Lewis Edwin Hahn. Chicago/Lasalle: Open Court, 1998. 147.

Strawson, P. F. *Universals, Concepts and Qualities: New Essays in the Meaning of Predicates*, edited by Arindam Chakrabarti and P. F. Strawson (Oxford: Ashgate, 2006).

Strawson, P. F. "Universals." In *Midwest Studies in Philosophy*, edited by P. A. French, T. E. Uehling, and H. K. Wettstein, Vol. IV, Studies in Metaphysics. Minneapolis: University of Minnesota Press, 1979). 3.

Tyāgīśānanda, Swāmi. *Śvetāśvatara Upaniṣad*. Mylapore: Sri Ramkrishna Math: 1949. 5/4/3, 10/8/17-27.

T

Taber, John. "A Road Not Taken in Indian Epistemology: Kumārila's Defense of the Perceptibility of Universals." In *Indian Epistemology and Metaphysics*, edited by Joerg Tuske, London: Bloomsbury, 2017.

Tarkālankāra, C.K. *Fellowship Lectures* (Vol. II) 2nd edn. (1906). *Tarkatāndava*, 1. 46.

Tennant, Neil. *Taming of the True*. Oxford: Clarendon Press, 1997.

Theaetetus 158 b–c. McDowell, J. *Theaetetus* (Clarendon Plato series). Oxford: Clarendon Press, 1973.

Todes, Samuel, and Daniels, Charles. "Beyond the Doubt of a Shadow." In *Dialogues in Phenomenology. Selected Studies in Phenomenology and Existential Philosophy*, edited by D. Ihde, R. M. Zaner, Vol 5. Dordrecht: Springer, 1975. 86–93. Also see *Seeing Dark Things: The Philosophy of Shadows*, edited by Roy Sorensen. New York: Oxford University Press, 2011.

Tornay, Stephen Chak. "Averroes' Doctrine of the Mind," *Philosophical Review* 52, no. 3 (May, 1942): 270–288.

Turbayne, C. M., suggests this in his "Kant's Relation to Berkeley." In *Kant Studies Today*, edited by Beck. Open Court, 1969.

Tuske, Joerg. "Proofs of Idealism in Buddhist Epistemology" Ch 5 of *Indian Epistemology and Metaphysics*. Bloomsbury, 2017.

U

Udayana. *Ātmatallvaviveka*, text and Hindi translation by K. N. Tripathi, Benares (1983): 229.

Udayanacarya. *Atmatattvaviveka*, edited by. Vindhyesvariprasada Dvivedin and Lakshmana Sastri Dravida. Calcutta: Asiatic Society, 1986.

Udayanācārya. *Ātmatattvaviveka: With the Commentaries of Śaṅkara Miśra, Bhagīratha Thakkura, and Raghunātha Tārkikaśiromaṇī*. Calcutta: Asiatic Society, 1986.

Udayanācārya. *Kusumānjali*, 3rd Stavaka, in *Nyayakusumanjali*. Trans. N. S. Dravid. Dheli: Indian Council of Philosophical Research, 1996.

Udayana- āch ārya. *Op. cit. Encyclopedia of Indian Philosophies*, edited by Karl Potter. Vol. II (Nyāya Vaiśeṣika). Princeton, NJ. 526–556.

Uddyotakara, Bharadvaj. *Nyāyabhāṣyavārttika of Bharadvaj Uddyotakara*. Ed. Anantalal Thakur. New Dheli: Indian Council of Philosophical Research, 1997. 3.1.1.

Upadhyaya, Gaṅgeśa. *Tattvacintāmaṇi*. Edited by. Kamakhyanath Tarkaratna. Calcutta: Asiatic Society, 1884. Vol. 1, 401.

Upadhyaya, Gaṅgeśa. *Tattvacintāmaṇi*. Trans. Nandita Bandypadhyaya. Calcutta: Sanskrit Pustak Bhandar, 1989.

Utpaladeva. *Isvarapratyabhijnakarika of Utpaladeva: Critical Edition and Annotated Translation*, edited and translated by Rafaelle Torella. Motial Banarsidass, 2002.

Úvetúāvatara Upaniṣad 5/4/3. 10/8/17-27.

V

Vaihinger, Hans. *The Philosophy of 'As If,'* trans. C.K. Ogden. New York: Barnes & Noble, Inc., 1924/1968. 44.

Vallabha. *Nyāyalīlāvatī*. Varanasi: Chowkhamba Sanskrit Series, 1991. 454–457.

VP III.

Vallabhacarya. *Nyāya Līlāvatī (With the Commentaried of Vardhamanopadhyaya, Sankara Misra and Bhagiratha Thakura)*. New Dheli: Rashtriya Sanskrit Sansthan, 2012. 326.

VaradāCāRya, K. *Nyāyamañjarī*. 1st edn. Oriental Research Institute series. University of Mysore. Oriental Research Institute, 1969. No. 116. 295.

Vasubandhu. *Abhidharmakoṣa*, Chapter VIII, p. 1217 of the Bauddhabharati Edition. For Theodore Stcherbatsky's translation of this passage see pp. 52–53 of *The Soul Theory of the Buddhists*. Delhi: Bharatya Vidya Prakasan, 1976.

Vātsyāyana. *Nyāyabhāṣya* 1.1.7.

W

Wallace, Meg. *A Wrinkle in Time*. Ariel Books, 2007.

Walker, R. C. S. *Idealism: Kant and Berkeley*. In *Essays on Berkeley: A Tercentennial Celebration*, edited by John L. Foster and Howard Robinson. London: Oxford University Press.

Warder, A. K. "Objects." *Journal of Indian Philosophy* 3 (1975).

Winthrop, Sargeant. *The Bhagavad Gita*. Garden City, NY: Doubleday, 1979.

Williams, Bernard. *Descartes: The Project of Pure Enquiry*. Routledge, 197. 89.

Wittgenstein. *Philosophical Investigations*, trans. G.E.M. Anscombe. (A Blackwell paperback). Oxford: Blackwell. 1978.

Wittgenstein. *Philosophical Investigations*. Commentary by P. M. S. Hacker et al. (Wiley-Blackwell, 4 edn., 2009). §42, Remark 265, p. 94c, sec. 610.

Wittgenstein, Ludwig. *The Blue and Brown Books: Preliminary Studies for the "Philosophical Investigation"*. Blackwell Publishing, 1991. 67.

Woodbridge, James A. "Truth as a Pretense." In *Fictionalism in Metaphysics*, ed. Mark Kalderon. London: Oxford University Press, 2005. 134–177.

Wright, Crispin. "Realism, Anti-Realism, Irrealism and Quasi-Realism." In *Midwest Studies in Philosophy*, edited by P. A. French, T. E. Uehling, and H. K. Wettstein. Vol. XII, Realism and Antirealism. University of Minnesota Press, Minneapolis, 1988. 25.

Y

Yablo, Stephen. "Go Figure: A Path through Fictionalism." *Midwest Studies in Philosophy* 25 (2001): 72–102.

Yablo, Stephen. "The Myth of the Seven." In *Fictionalism in Metaphysics*, edited by M. Kalderon. Oxford: Clarendon Press, 2005.

Index

Abhidharma psychology 147
Abhinavagupta 102, 114, 124, 128, 131, 132, 133, 134, 135, 155, 160, 201, 202, 205, 292, 304, 310, 316, 317, 319
aboutness 22, 46
absence 8, 18, 40, 57, 81, 84, 103, 131, 132, 135, 147, 153, 179, 185, 191, 199, 231, 233, 235, 236, 237, 238, 239, 240, 241, 243, 244, 245, 246, 262, 263, 269, 284, 285, 286, 287, 288, 289, 290, 292, 313
absence of light 235, 237, 238, 239, 243, 245
absentee 103, 237, 238, 240, 245, 269, 285, 286, 287, 288, 289, 290
accusative 7, 42, 66, 69, 98, 101, 102, 103, 104, 106, 107, 108, 109, 123, 141, 161, 162, 207, 216, 273, 303, 312
action 7, 18, 21, 56, 60, 81, 86, 101, 103, 104, 105, 107, 109, 134, 137, 141, 143, 146, 147, 148, 175, 179, 189, 190, 192, 198, 201, 203, 208, 214, 215, 216, 265, 286, 303
Adams, Bob 261
addressing 5, 119, 123, 124, 197, 203, 205, 206, 207, 208, 209, 215, 216, 292
Advaita Vedānta 97, 98, 99, 100, 105, 120, 121, 122, 140, 152, 163, 164, 165, 175, 233, 245, 246, 276, 280, 298, 311, 313
affect 15, 120, 157, 172, 179, 180, 203
agency 101, 102, 106, 109, 120, 121, 123, 137, 138, 139, 140, 141, 144, 146, 147, 194, 209, 215, 216, 263, 265, 286
agent-instrument-object model of action 146, 147
agnosticism 24, 70, 74
aham 114, 118, 120, 121, 124, 127
ahaṃkāra 114, 120, 121, 146
aloneness 197, 281
analogical inference 134, 199, 201, 202
Anscombe, G. E. M. 113, 115, 123, 142, 303, 314
anti-Buddhist 128, 176
anti-idealist idealists 70, 74, 75
anti-nominalist 78
anti-perceptualist 36
anti-realism 3, 6, 9, 16, 17, 18, 27, 36, 49, 70, 78, 79, 80, 86, 89, 99, 176, 177, 178, 180, 181, 183, 258, 265, 266, 267, 268, 270, 271, 274, 275, 276, 277, 279, 282, 283, 295, 299, 326
anti-reflexivist objection 140, 161
anumeya 193
apoha-theory 82, 290
Aquinas, Thomas 145, 245, 279, 316
arguments against the existence of the self 114, 121, 122
Arindam Chakrabarti 295, 296, 314, 315, 323, 324
Aristotle 43, 57, 86, 117, 145, 150, 151, 154, 188, 243, 245, 249, 267, 297, 305, 306, 311, 312, 313, 316, 319, 323
Arjuna 104, 124, 206, 207, 208
Armstrong, David 30, 142, 144, 296
art 225, 312
artha 3, 4, 185
Āryadeva 121, 122, 135, 304
A-series time 129, 282
assertions 22, 24, 53, 54, 59, 116, 117, 131, 132, 134, 165, 171, 177, 178, 179, 180, 183, 185, 187, 205, 207, 208, 213, 215, 216, 217, 220, 222, 223, 262, 266, 268, 277, 289, 291
āstika schools 147
ātman 14, 145, 151, 186, 189, 192
attention 3, 6, 30, 37, 57, 58, 124, 138, 144, 145, 146, 148, 149, 150, 152, 153, 154, 172, 206, 208, 209, 239
Augustine 226, 227, 228, 229, 311
avācya 50
awareness 6, 7, 11, 14, 16, 17, 18, 22, 25, 38, 40, 44, 45, 46, 47, 48, 50, 51, 52, 55, 56, 57, 58, 60, 62, 63, 66, 67, 69, 71, 74,

75, 77, 78, 79, 80, 81, 82, 83, 84, 85, 90, 94, 96, 97, 98, 99, 100, 101, 102, 105, 108, 109, 115, 117, 121, 128, 129, 130, 131, 132, 133, 134, 135, 136, 137, 138, 139, 140, 141, 142, 143, 144, 145, 148, 149, 150, 152, 157, 158, 160, 161, 162, 163, 164, 165, 166, 167, 171, 198, 202, 212, 214, 215, 216, 217, 219, 220, 221, 222, 229, 230, 240, 246, 249, 250, 274, 275, 276, 280, 281, 282, 287, 289, 290, 298, 299, 301, 302, 307
awareness of cognition 50, 145, 150, 157, 160, 165

bare experience 27
bare locus theory 288
beginningism 87, 103, 303
belief 14, 16, 17, 22, 24, 27, 31, 32, 35, 36, 43, 52, 53, 54, 55, 57, 58, 59, 63, 65, 66, 75, 94, 97, 120, 127, 130, 137, 139, 143, 157, 158, 159, 160, 162, 166, 167, 175, 176, 177, 178, 179, 180, 181, 182, 183, 189, 198, 199, 201, 205, 211, 212, 214, 216, 217, 218, 219, 220, 221, 222, 223, 225, 226, 228, 230, 244, 247, 249, 252, 253, 255, 260, 265, 266, 267, 268, 269, 272, 277, 278, 282, 287, 298, 299, 306, 311
belief in external 272
Bergson, Henri 292, 315, 317
Berkeley, George 9, 36, 58, 66, 68, 70, 71, 74, 80, 82, 273, 275, 294, 295, 300, 325, 326
Bhagavad-Gītā 208, 292, 306, 310, 321, 322, 326
Bhartṛhari 45, 46, 48, 49, 50, 101, 102, 103, 105, 106, 107, 108, 109, 145, 207, 208, 225, 226, 231, 249, 251, 302
Bhaṭṭa, Jayanta 38, 39, 81, 128, 129, 130, 133, 135, 141, 188, 194, 250, 251, 297, 304, 306, 307, 309, 317
Bhaṭṭācārya, Gadādhara 22, 99, 114, 118, 119, 120, 303, 317
Bhattacharya, Gopinath 3, 21, 313, 314
Bhattacharya, K. C. 3, 17, 18, 268, 269, 304, 314, 317
Bhattacharya, Sibajiban 100, 303
Bhāṭṭa Mīmāṃsa 104, 105, 286, 313
bhāvas 193, 290
body 7, 86, 120, 146, 151, 152, 153, 186, 189, 190, 191, 194, 201, 305, 320
Bradley, F. H. 279, 288
brain-mind identity theory 134
breathing 15, 40, 123, 151, 153
Broad, C. D. 256, 257, 258, 262
Buddha 7, 12, 127, 183, 278, 279, 280, 281, 284
Buddhism 3, 4, 9, 10, 11, 12, 17, 21, 36, 38, 46, 47, 49, 66, 67, 68, 69, 70, 74, 75, 77, 78, 81, 82, 83, 84, 85, 86, 89, 90, 95, 97, 102, 114, 117, 121, 123, 127, 128, 129, 130, 131, 132, 133, 140, 147, 162, 163, 173, 175, 176, 182, 183, 185, 187, 193, 199, 257, 258, 275, 276, 278, 279, 280, 286, 290, 293, 294, 298, 300, 301, 302, 304, 305, 307
Buddhist anti-realism 49, 70, 176, 276
Buddhist arguments for non-existence of the self 17, 121, 123, 127
Buddhist idealism 12, 67, 68, 69, 74, 300
Buddhist meditational psychology 147
Buddhist nominalism 38, 290, 301
Buddhist pan-illusionist 78

Cartesian 81, 115, 153, 160, 186, 187, 190, 201, 202
Cartesian reflexivism 160
Cārvāka school 218
case 12, 101, 102, 103, 104, 105, 106, 107, 108, 109, 137, 146, 203, 207, 209, 219, 303
causal efficacy 244, 258
causal efficacy 244, 258
causation 33, 35, 100, 103, 258, 269
central-state identity theory 191
choosing to ignore 81, 105, 145, 172, 197
classical Indian thought 4, 10, 51, 67, 93, 103, 146, 161, 176, 211, 212, 215, 218, 225, 228, 236, 279, 295, 298, 304, 313, 314, 321, 322
Coady, C. A. J. 217, 311
cognition 5, 40, 48, 50, 54, 55, 56, 57, 58, 62, 66, 67, 77, 80, 81, 82, 83, 84, 85, 89, 90, 91, 94, 97, 98, 99, 101, 103, 105, 108, 124, 129, 130, 133, 139, 140, 141, 143, 148, 149, 150, 151, 155, 157, 158, 159, 160, 161, 162, 163, 164, 166, 167,

168, 170, 186, 188, 190, 192, 193, 194, 198, 199, 203, 212, 215, 219, 220, 247, 249, 273, 275, 290, 294, 302, 307, 309, 312
cognitive content 118, 137, 167, 215
cognitive science 200
cognitive states 12, 16, 17, 22, 42, 49, 60, 67, 69, 70, 81, 82, 98, 131, 132, 133, 140, 143, 144, 160, 161, 163, 164, 165, 166, 172, 193, 294
cognizer-self 77, 141
coherence definition of truth 51, 299
color 11, 12, 13, 15, 16, 17, 19, 30, 31, 41, 43, 45, 57, 66, 80, 83, 85, 86, 89, 141, 149, 150, 151, 162, 190, 191, 193, 219, 227, 234, 235, 236, 238, 239, 240, 241, 242, 243, 276, 286, 287, 288, 289, 312, 313, 319, 321
command 208, 213, 214, 215, 216, 249
commonsense realism 9, 21, 26, 59, 80, 180, 286
communicative intent 213, 218
compassion 279
concentration 154, 280
concept, nature of 6, 7, 11, 27, 29, 32, 37, 42, 43, 44, 45, 47, 48, 49, 51, 108, 230, 231, 246, 247, 248, 249, 251, 252, 253, 258, 283, 285, 286, 297
concept of an object 3, 4, 5, 7, 101, 102, 108
concept of a subject 102, 137
concept possession 45, 247, 249, 251
conceptualism about perceptual content 25, 28, 32, 45, 46, 50, 67, 130, 148, 248, 251
conditions of cognition 15, 49, 55, 57, 84, 103, 114, 142, 147, 149, 155, 157, 168, 181, 192, 201, 216, 219, 237, 243, 261, 265
consciousness 3, 5, 6, 9, 10, 11, 17, 18, 44, 46, 48, 63, 66, 67, 68, 69, 70, 74, 75, 79, 80, 81, 82, 83, 85, 90, 92, 97, 98, 99, 100, 114, 117, 120, 121, 124, 125, 128, 130, 131, 132, 133, 134, 135, 136, 139, 140, 141, 146, 147, 149, 151, 160, 161, 164, 165, 175, 177, 180, 181, 182, 187, 188, 189, 190, 191, 192, 193, 198, 199, 200, 201, 202, 203, 205, 233, 251, 252, 263, 274, 276, 280, 281, 283, 292, 294, 304, 306, 309
consciousness and the body 80, 114, 117, 120, 125, 134, 135, 146, 147, 149, 165, 188, 190, 191, 193, 198
consciousness of other knowers 5, 6, 11, 97, 114, 134, 135, 136, 175, 177, 180, 198, 199, 200, 201, 202, 203, 205, 233, 283, 292
consciousness-only and inherence 88
constant co-cognition 11, 63, 67, 82, 83, 275
constructivisms 105
contact 17, 23, 44, 45, 66, 85, 87, 88, 103, 144, 149, 150, 153, 155, 192, 218, 239, 251, 279, 299
contact and memory 218
conventional truth 292
correspondence theory of truth 51, 52, 54, 55, 298
creativity 124, 133, 202, 229

darkness 143, 151, 213, 231, 234, 235, 236, 237, 238, 239, 240, 241, 242, 243, 244, 246, 263, 311, 312, 313
Davidson, Donald 27, 51, 139, 218, 276, 277, 278, 279, 282, 298, 299, 311
death 92, 164, 177, 190, 240, 258, 260, 263
definite knowledge 263
definition (Nyāya) 47, 52
deflationist definition of truth 51
Demos 288
Derrida, Jacques 287
Descartes, René 9, 70, 115, 125, 187, 190, 292, 307, 308, 309, 320, 326
descriptive epistemic content 141
descriptive metaphysics 21, 30, 180, 295, 296, 304
descriptivist theory of proper names 261
desire 60, 81, 102, 103, 104, 105, 108, 127, 145, 146, 149, 152, 153, 154, 155, 159, 175, 177, 178, 187, 188, 189, 192, 193, 194, 197, 198, 199, 201, 202, 207, 214, 215, 216, 269, 280, 286, 292, 306
desired objects 103, 104, 105, 155
determinism 260, 265, 266, 269
dharma 147, 292
Dharmakīrti 80, 131, 145, 198, 199, 201, 275, 279, 280, 288, 301, 307, 310, 315

difference 5, 7, 8, 16, 46, 77, 78, 79, 82, 90, 100, 103, 105, 124, 130, 133, 134, 154, 168, 231, 235, 236, 250, 301
Diñnāga 45, 46, 47, 300, 301
direct acquaintance 17, 36, 134, 139, 151
direct perception 17, 32, 43, 57, 70, 199, 203, 246, 280, 308
direct realism 17, 40, 75, 175, 180, 247, 297
disillusionment 99, 100
disinterest 281
doubt 7, 17, 70, 73, 95, 144, 145, 152, 154, 159, 160, 165, 169, 178, 186, 190, 218, 246, 270, 274
draṣṭā (seer) 192
dreaming 62, 67, 68, 91, 92, 93, 94, 95, 96, 97, 98, 99, 100, 236, 245, 274
dualism 9, 10, 47, 74, 81, 86, 98, 102, 120, 121, 183, 192, 200, 275, 301
Dummet's manifestation argument 271, 272, 314
Dummett, Michael 6, 33, 45, 49, 50, 178, 179, 213, 216, 230, 251, 252, 263, 270, 271, 272, 282, 293, 296, 298, 311, 314, 315
Dvaita Vedānta 158, 302

ego 9, 10, 14, 18, 69, 71, 72, 73, 74, 75, 77, 78, 113, 114, 115, 120, 121, 122, 123, 131, 132, 146, 197, 198, 199, 201, 275, 280, 294, 305, 308
egoism 10, 120, 121, 123, 125, 135, 155, 159
El Greco 3, 4
eliminative reductionism 9, 80, 89, 176, 177, 178, 179, 180, 181, 189, 310
embodied self 72, 81, 115, 145, 146, 147
emotional states 72, 144, 172, 197
emotions 72, 134, 175, 179, 186, 198, 199, 323
empathy 124, 134, 141, 203
empiricism 9, 27, 106, 108, 200, 225
emptiness 92, 116, 121, 176, 183, 185, 197, 211, 250, 258, 286, 291, 292
entity-realism 26
episteme 230
epistemology 11, 12, 14, 21, 27, 33, 35, 46, 47, 49, 50, 52, 53, 72, 75, 82, 88, 89, 98, 102, 113, 117, 129, 131, 138, 139, 151, 157, 158, 159, 161, 166, 167, 183, 198, 211, 212, 214, 215, 217, 220, 222, 228, 240, 246, 247, 260, 279, 298, 300, 301, 304, 305
error 16, 24, 46, 47, 49, 52, 78, 81, 93, 95, 100, 113, 115, 116, 117, 123, 133, 140, 141, 142, 154, 157, 158, 160, 164, 165, 166, 167, 168, 169, 170, 171, 172, 173, 177, 178, 179, 182, 208, 214, 221, 245, 252, 277, 288, 289, 290
error about mental states 157, 167
errors about mental states 16, 93, 95, 100, 113, 115, 116, 117, 133, 140, 141, 142, 154, 157, 158, 160, 164, 165, 166, 167, 168, 169, 170, 171, 172, 173, 177, 182, 277
error-theory 78, 131, 133, 173, 177, 180, 275
essencelessness 280, 291, 292
Evans, Gareth 45, 102, 222, 311, 314
everything 7, 27, 49, 50, 52, 59, 60, 62, 75, 81, 88, 105, 125, 255, 258, 267, 275, 276, 277, 279, 280, 285, 289, 290, 291, 299
excluded middle 266
exclusion 58, 81, 82, 289, 290
exemplification 13, 18, 19, 21, 23, 25, 27, 28, 30, 31, 36, 41, 44, 46, 48, 82, 89, 105, 252, 275, 279, 295
exhibition 22, 211, 226, 227
existential quantification 61, 122, 255
experience of universals 28
extension 42, 43, 52, 57, 83, 247, 260
externalism 16, 47, 55, 56, 58, 78, 91, 105, 138, 157, 159, 162, 167, 169, 170, 269
externality 77, 78, 89, 94, 100, 273, 275, 300
external object 19, 24, 35, 52, 63, 69, 70, 77, 80, 81, 82, 88, 89, 90, 93, 94, 106, 131, 140, 144, 155, 162, 168, 193, 272, 274, 275, 283, 294, 301
external sense organ 147, 149, 153, 191, 306
external world 10, 14, 15, 16, 35, 36, 47, 52, 56, 63, 65, 66, 70, 71, 75, 77, 79, 80, 81, 82, 85, 89, 91, 92, 93, 97, 98, 100, 146, 165, 167, 180, 185, 189, 252, 272, 273, 274, 276, 284

external-world realists 9, 127
extra-mentality 70, 74

fallibilism 47, 52, 159, 167
fear 105, 116, 152, 169, 171, 197, 208, 255, 267, 268
feeling 5, 6, 11, 13, 15, 18, 37, 38, 50, 68, 84, 87, 93, 97, 100, 113, 114, 115, 116, 117, 118, 123, 124, 131, 132, 134, 135, 137, 138, 139, 141, 142, 143, 144, 148, 151, 155, 157, 158, 164, 165, 166, 167, 169, 170, 171, 172, 173, 181, 182, 189, 191, 192, 194, 197, 198, 199, 200, 201, 203, 218, 236, 242, 246, 278, 280, 286, 288, 292, 305, 306
fictionalism 9, 35, 127, 175, 176, 177, 178, 179, 180, 181, 182, 183, 307, 308
first-person singular pronoun 120
freedom 101, 102, 106, 124, 125, 137, 138, 139, 154, 165, 170, 180, 181, 255, 266, 280, 282, 295, 304, 314
Frege, Gottlob 5, 7, 10, 15, 16, 17, 18, 22, 29, 31, 41, 42, 45, 46, 49, 51, 52, 53, 54, 55, 56, 57, 58, 61, 77, 80, 88, 89, 113, 117, 118, 123, 131, 207, 212, 222, 248, 252, 257, 258, 274, 275, 283, 295, 298, 301, 304
Fregean objects 29
Fregean ontology 10, 58
Fregean truth 51, 52, 53, 54, 55, 56
freshness of the content of knowledge 105, 221
Fricker, Elizabeth 222, 223, 311
the future 37, 129, 153, 240, 253, 255, 256, 257, 258, 259, 260, 261, 262, 263, 264, 265, 266, 267, 268, 269, 270, 271, 281, 282, 314, 317, 323, 324
future items 259, 260, 261, 262, 265
future tense 257, 265, 266, 267, 268, 269, 270, 271

Gandhi, Ramchandra 124, 205
Gaṅgeśa 51, 52, 55, 56, 57, 58, 159, 216, 217, 220, 221, 290, 298, 299, 311, 325
gaps 14, 36, 39, 40, 59, 65, 115, 157, 236, 244, 277, 286, 287, 291
Gautama 10, 22, 45, 86, 186, 187, 192, 194, 256, 290, 291, 308
general definitions 52, 54, 55, 250
generality of properties 275, 279
genuine universals 22, 23, 30
Gītā 124, 157, 206, 208, 209, 229, 306
God 5, 6, 8, 36, 60, 62, 66, 68, 69, 70, 103, 123, 135, 154, 155, 179, 185, 209, 221, 267, 272, 273, 276, 278, 279, 280, 281, 282, 283, 284, 299, 300
God's existence 6, 185, 282, 284
Gödel, Kurt 43, 299
God's knowledge 267, 281, 282
God's omniscience 272, 282
grammar 7, 10, 26, 46, 78, 102, 103, 106, 107, 108, 109, 113, 115, 137, 138, 146, 203, 205, 206, 207, 209, 214, 221, 223, 255, 292, 297, 310
the grammatical first person 59, 109, 113, 114, 115, 116, 119, 120, 122, 123, 124, 125, 127, 128, 137, 138, 148, 157, 159, 160, 161, 164, 165, 166, 167, 169, 170, 171, 176, 181, 197, 198, 199, 200, 202, 265, 271, 303, 304, 305
the hand 80, 142, 147
the hearer 208, 213, 218, 220, 221, 222, 227, 257

hearer's belief 222
higher-order perception 138, 140, 158, 160, 162, 165
Hobbes, Thomas 187
hue 234, 235, 238
human freedom 101, 282
Hume, David 3, 17, 28, 114, 117, 123, 131, 132, 139, 142, 187, 217, 230, 294, 297, 301
Husserl, Edmund 45, 49, 102
hypocrisy 28, 68

idealism 3, 4, 9, 10, 12, 16, 18, 36, 46, 62, 63, 65, 66, 67, 68, 69, 70, 71, 73, 74, 75, 77, 79, 81, 82, 83, 88, 89, 90, 91, 93, 94, 95, 96, 98, 162, 176, 180, 248, 274, 275, 276, 277, 295, 299, 300, 301
idealisms 9, 65, 69, 70, 74, 301
identificatory error 115, 116, 117, 142
ignorance 24, 52, 58, 59, 71, 74, 79, 81, 97, 105, 108, 113, 141, 145, 157, 166, 172, 197, 213, 231, 233, 244, 245, 246, 266, 276, 277, 280, 282, 284, 312, 315

ignorance-tolerance 273, 283
illumination 46, 69, 98, 140, 143, 144, 160, 161, 162, 235, 236, 238, 240, 243, 246, 249, 302
illusions 5, 12, 29, 67, 68, 69, 71, 74, 77, 80, 85, 91, 93, 97, 98, 99, 107, 115, 127, 131, 133, 135, 140, 148, 159, 165, 168, 169, 192, 222, 233, 239, 240, 244, 275, 276, 303, 304
imaginary events 256
imagination 12, 13, 36, 37, 42, 65, 67, 78, 79, 89, 90, 92, 97, 101, 107, 108, 114, 124, 125, 130, 143, 144, 145, 146, 148, 149, 151, 152, 154, 155, 182, 183, 197, 201, 202, 228, 241, 243, 248, 256, 259, 267, 276, 285, 286, 287, 288, 292
immanence 6, 33, 43, 296
immunity to error 113, 115, 116, 170
imperative sentences 208, 215, 216
impermanence 92, 122, 280
impersonal subjectivity 74, 75, 100, 292
Indian logic 60, 198, 230, 258, 263, 289
Indian realism 52, 75, 274, 276, 296, 301
indirect knowledge 277
individuals 6, 7, 11, 17, 21, 22, 23, 24, 25, 26, 27, 28, 29, 30, 31, 38, 39, 49, 58, 66, 78, 88, 121, 133, 149, 155, 181, 186, 205, 209, 213, 217, 223, 249, 252, 260, 261, 264, 265, 273, 274, 276
individuation 11, 15, 16, 17, 28, 81, 86, 88, 287
indriya 146, 147, 187
I-ness 114, 124, 197, 202
infallibility of apperception 139, 165, 166, 167, 168, 169, 170, 181, 278
inference 32, 38, 43, 46, 51, 56, 57, 62, 70, 73, 79, 84, 93, 95, 105, 116, 120, 132, 134, 135, 144, 151, 160, 161, 162, 186, 187, 188, 191, 193, 194, 198, 199, 201, 202, 211, 212, 215, 217, 218, 220, 221, 222, 223, 230, 246, 268, 276, 279, 289, 298, 309, 311
inferential view of cognition 162
infinitude 18, 66, 135, 263, 273, 279, 281, 282, 284, 315
inherence 15, 16, 23, 31, 32, 33, 41, 43, 44, 46, 57, 75, 77, 78, 81, 82, 85, 86, 87, 88, 89, 90, 103, 163, 187, 189, 190, 191, 219, 252, 275, 289
inner perception 138, 149, 152, 158, 183
inner sense 14, 56, 57, 71, 72, 73, 74, 75, 130, 138, 141, 143, 144, 145, 146, 147, 148, 149, 150, 152, 153, 154, 155, 157, 161, 163, 177, 191, 192, 193, 236, 301, 306
inner sense organ 147, 148, 150, 153, 155
instantiability of properties 89, 275
instrumentality 101, 102, 144, 177, 178, 192, 194, 207
intensional 42, 43, 207
intentionality 6, 12, 42, 46, 69, 77, 79, 80, 89, 90, 97, 98, 99, 100, 102, 103, 106, 108, 123, 132, 138, 140, 153, 161, 163, 166, 177, 180, 191, 212, 216, 220, 221, 269, 276, 286
intentional qualification 216
intentions 3, 7, 29, 42, 66, 104, 107, 108, 152, 153, 166, 193, 208, 212, 213, 214, 218, 223, 262, 265, 266, 268, 270, 306, 314
internalism 46, 77, 90, 140, 167, 169
internal sense organ 17, 139, 144, 146, 149, 150, 152, 192
interpretation 75, 100, 104, 135, 198, 200, 216, 223, 225, 265, 276, 277, 278
introspection 14, 17, 18, 32, 37, 56, 57, 69, 71, 114, 115, 117, 123, 129, 132, 138, 139, 141, 142, 144, 145, 146, 148, 149, 151, 153, 157, 159, 160, 162, 163, 165, 166, 167, 168, 169, 170, 171, 172, 173, 176, 179, 187, 192, 193, 198, 199, 200, 201, 214, 217, 218, 236, 246, 271, 286, 292, 301, 303
introspective awareness 18, 141, 160, 165, 166
introspective cognition 166, 192
introspective misidentification 139, 167, 170
introspective use of "I" 115
intuition 41, 44, 48, 71, 72, 74, 75, 77, 134, 142, 148, 151, 155, 187, 192, 218, 231, 233, 246, 252, 280, 300
irreflexivism 138, 160, 161, 164

Jaina ontology 243, 280
Jaina philosophy 293
Jaina realists 82
Jayarāśi 51
justification 167, 179, 198, 201, 226, 228, 282, 283

Kaṇāda 153, 189
Kant, Immanuel 3, 14, 17, 18, 27, 35, 42, 52, 54, 55, 56, 57, 65, 68, 69, 70, 71, 72, 73, 74, 93, 145, 148, 149, 153, 155, 177, 180, 186, 193, 197, 231, 248, 274, 276, 277, 289, 293, 294, 296, 297, 298, 300, 301, 307, 309, 310, 311, 314, 315
Kant's anti-idealism 70
Kant's idealism 70, 74
Kant's refutation of idealism 3, 65, 71, 72, 300
Kant's transcendental deduction of categories 148
kāraka 102, 103, 207, 303
karmic body 149
Kashmir Shaivism 69, 131
Kaṭha Upaniṣad 162, 306
knowability 11, 17, 28, 49, 50, 52, 58, 59, 60, 61, 62, 63, 70, 75, 81, 177, 215, 276, 277, 289, 298, 312, 315
knower 57, 58, 68, 128, 129, 133, 134, 135, 136, 138, 139, 140, 141, 161, 192, 194, 202, 228, 315
knower-illusion 140
knowing a truth 61
knowing from words 211, 219, 223
knowing-how 49, 229, 230
knowing-that 49, 229
knowing-what 230
knowledge by testimony 152, 217, 218
knowledge-immanent 62
knowledge-independence 23, 24, 25, 52, 53, 62, 63, 78, 79, 81, 97, 283, 284
knowledge of a language 45, 49, 227, 230, 247, 251
knowledge of meaning 222, 225, 226, 227, 228, 271
knowledge of mental states 4, 134, 157, 162, 169, 203
knownness 5, 62, 63, 105
known-unknown 97, 276
Kripke, Saul 190, 205, 262, 309, 320
Kumārila 43, 162, 281, 282, 297, 324

language 4, 12, 22, 30, 45, 46, 49, 50, 56, 65, 94, 101, 107, 113, 114, 115, 121, 122, 123, 169, 177, 180, 182, 185, 194, 200, 202, 203, 209, 211, 212, 213, 217, 218, 222, 223, 227, 228, 230, 246, 247, 248, 249, 250, 251, 252, 259, 265, 271, 274, 276, 277, 278, 285, 286, 287, 288, 295, 299, 311
language and thought 50, 276, 298
language game 94, 222, 259, 261
language-independent concept possession 249, 251
language learning 218, 247, 250
languageless experience 50
language use 121, 249, 265, 271
learning 36, 37, 38, 47, 100, 116, 118, 169, 171, 197, 200, 202, 209, 211, 213, 214, 215, 218, 223, 225, 226, 227, 228, 247, 249, 250, 251, 253
liberation 10, 46, 60, 81, 97, 100, 127, 145, 147, 153, 154, 190, 244, 245, 276, 281, 306
light 3, 4, 7, 11, 140, 143, 144, 146, 152, 161, 162, 213, 226, 228, 231, 233, 234, 235, 236, 237, 238, 239, 240, 241, 242, 243, 244, 245, 246, 312, 313
linguistic structure of awareness 46
Locke, John 17, 35, 225, 230, 267
logic 3, 6, 7, 9, 10, 16, 18, 24, 29, 32, 44, 49, 51, 52, 54, 55, 58, 60, 65, 70, 72, 77, 81, 83, 85, 89, 92, 94, 106, 121, 131, 135, 137, 138, 141, 148, 155, 182, 189, 190, 193, 194, 197, 198, 199, 201, 205, 209, 226, 228, 229, 230, 237, 239, 255, 257, 258, 260, 261, 263, 264, 265, 275, 276, 277, 279, 282, 285, 286, 288, 289, 290, 292, 293, 295, 296, 297, 298, 299, 300, 301, 302, 304, 308, 309, 310, 311, 312, 313, 314
logic of inherence 77, 87, 89, 90

madhusūdana 98, 114, 120, 123, 207, 302, 303, 310
Mahābhārata 152, 292, 306, 321
Mahāyāna Buddhism 280
manas 14, 144, 145, 146, 147, 148, 149, 150, 151, 152, 153, 154, 155, 163, 186, 187, 188, 189, 191, 192, 193, 305, 306, 309
Maṇḍana Miśra 281, 315
mantā (minder) 192
materialism 81, 146, 180, 190, 191, 310
Mathurānātha 214, 311

Matilal, B. K. 21, 22, 45, 47, 48, 49, 50, 216, 249, 295, 296, 297, 298, 302, 308, 311, 314
matter 7, 9, 54, 69, 74, 75, 243, 295, 312, 313
McDowell, John 213, 248, 251, 252, 302, 304, 311, 314
McTaggart, J. M. E. 129, 258, 282
meaning 3, 18, 29, 31, 41, 49, 118, 119, 128, 151, 152, 162, 170, 179, 181, 194, 202, 205, 206, 207, 208, 212, 213, 214, 216, 217, 218, 219, 222, 225, 226, 227, 228, 229, 230, 250, 251, 252, 259, 260, 264, 265, 266, 271, 273, 282, 283, 285, 290, 291, 299, 304
meanings of sentences 118, 151, 214, 219, 222, 230, 271
meanings of words 114, 120, 128, 162, 194, 225, 226, 227, 250, 251, 260, 304, 323
medieval Indian philosophy 114, 211, 217, 242, 249, 274
meditational practice 92, 135, 147, 155, 182, 292
memory 11, 12, 14, 15, 17, 37, 39, 40, 43, 44, 45, 68, 72, 79, 93, 121, 125, 128, 129, 130, 145, 147, 151, 152, 170, 179, 211, 212, 214, 217, 218, 219, 230, 249, 250, 268, 294
mentalese 230
mental states 3, 5, 7, 10, 11, 12, 13, 14, 15, 16, 17, 18, 21, 31, 63, 70, 72, 73, 74, 78, 79, 81, 82, 97, 103, 108, 116, 117, 127, 131, 133, 135, 140, 141, 143, 144, 151, 157, 160, 164, 165, 166, 167, 169, 170, 171, 172, 175, 177, 178, 179, 181, 189, 190, 191, 199, 200, 201, 220, 227, 284
mereological 27, 85, 86, 90, 127, 142, 176, 273
mereological reductionism 127
Merleau-Ponty, Maurice 305
metacognition 150, 157, 158, 160, 161, 162, 164
meta-knowledge 158, 159, 160
meta-metaphysical 176
metaphysics 4, 8, 9, 11, 13, 17, 18, 21, 23, 27, 30, 65, 66, 68, 69, 70, 75, 85, 100, 102, 103, 113, 117, 123, 129, 133, 135, 136, 138, 140, 146, 147, 149, 154, 175, 176, 178, 179, 180, 183, 186, 209, 236, 239, 243, 244, 246, 253, 256, 258, 259, 260, 263, 264, 265, 266, 267, 268, 269, 276, 278, 280, 282, 284, 286, 287, 293, 295, 296, 297, 299, 300, 301, 304, 308, 311, 313, 314
metaphysics of the future 268
Mill, John Stuart 29, 198, 205, 206, 310
Miller, Alexander 314
Miller, Barbara Stoler 207, 310, 321
Mīmāṃsā 39, 43, 78, 82, 93, 104, 105, 128, 140, 158, 161, 162, 242, 246, 278, 282, 286
mind 4, 7, 8, 10, 12, 14, 16, 18, 19, 23, 31, 35, 36, 65, 66, 67, 69, 70, 71, 74, 75, 77, 78, 79, 81, 82, 86, 89, 91, 94, 98, 99, 101, 103, 106, 117, 122, 127, 134, 141, 144, 145, 146, 147, 153, 154, 160, 163, 166, 167, 169, 175, 176, 178, 180, 182, 191, 192, 198, 199, 200, 201, 202, 208, 209, 226, 244, 246, 252, 267, 271, 273, 274, 275, 276, 283, 284, 288, 291, 292, 294, 297, 300, 301, 303, 304, 305, 306, 310, 314
mind-independence 4, 12, 14, 16, 18, 19, 23, 31, 35, 36, 66, 70, 71, 74, 77, 81, 89, 180, 244, 267, 273, 274, 275, 300
mind-only Buddhism 66, 67, 86
minimalist definitions of truth 51
mirror-like consciousness 280
misidentification 113, 115, 116, 170, 171, 172, 307, 319
mistakes 12, 14, 16, 17, 18, 24, 35, 67, 71, 94, 95, 115, 116, 123, 127, 130, 131, 133, 142, 144, 155, 157, 160, 164, 165, 166, 167, 168, 169, 170, 171, 172, 178, 181, 187, 208, 213, 221, 223, 244, 267, 277, 278, 282, 287, 303
momentariness 18, 68, 77, 86, 92, 127, 129, 131, 132, 133, 140, 176, 186, 193, 257, 275
Moore, G. E. 67, 79, 80, 91, 93, 143, 159, 241, 300, 301, 313, 316, 321
multiplicity of objects 233
multiply exemplifiable individuals 23
mysticism 10, 68, 74, 75, 91, 209

Nāgārjuna 51, 121, 145, 175, 258, 290, 291, 292, 315
Nāgeśa 106

naïve-realism 44, 75, 273
nameability 25, 31, 52, 58, 59, 263, 289, 298
Nativism 48
Naturalism 218, 295, 304
natural kinds 4, 39, 48, 57, 309, 320
negation 13, 26, 88, 122, 129, 143, 277, 285, 287, 288, 290, 292, 315
negative facts 56, 237, 285, 286, 287, 288, 289
negative things 236, 244, 285, 286
nervous system 151, 191
neutralism 256, 268, 269, 270
nihilism 227, 290, 291
Nirvāṇa 280, 302
nobody 284
nominalism 28, 35, 38, 39, 81, 82, 176, 290, 301
nominative 102, 106, 137, 207, 209, 309, 312
non-conceptual experience 4, 37, 38, 48, 49, 139, 247, 248, 249, 286, 289
non-conceptualism about perceptual content 44
non-dualism 5, 63, 69, 98, 99, 100, 102, 103, 107, 124, 138, 209, 233, 280
non-dual pure consciousness 233
non-ego 198
nonentities 68, 87, 264, 286, 290
non-erroneous perception 47, 50
non-existence 7, 17, 50, 91, 103, 122, 127, 130, 132, 193, 199, 234, 237, 258, 259, 262, 263, 285, 286, 287, 290, 291, 312, 313
non-momentary self 133
non-Parfitian self 117
non-particular individuals 7, 21, 22, 23, 24, 25, 26, 27, 29, 31
non-predicative perception 38, 49, 139
non-presentism 256
non-reductive anti-realism 267
non-reductive realism 25, 266
non-reflexivity 162
non-simultaneity of awareness 148
no-self views 21, 81, 114, 130, 140, 292, 304
no-soulism 9, 12, 193
nothing 8, 60, 79, 82, 257, 284, 285, 286, 287, 290, 291
numerical identity 82, 197
Nyāya epistemology 14, 33, 35, 46, 50, 138, 151, 157, 279
Nyāya externalism 56
Nyāya logic 10, 60, 83
Nyāya metaphysics 18, 133, 138, 280
Nyāya pro-soul argument from recognition 129
Nyāya realism 30, 32, 52, 55, 62, 80, 90, 130
Nyāyasūtra 51, 86, 250, 256, 290, 297, 301, 314
Nyāya-Vaiśeṣika psychology 150

object-directed intentionality 100, 276
object-directedness 50, 58, 74, 97, 98, 100, 132, 140, 276
object of awareness 55, 66, 102, 136, 138, 274, 302
object of experience 3, 21, 43, 138, 307
object of ignorance 16, 52, 97, 105, 172, 276
object of imagination 42, 107
object of inner sense 72, 75, 143, 177, 183
object of introspection 141, 142, 144
object of knowledge 7, 17, 52, 72, 105, 108, 113, 137, 141, 172, 294
object of perception 3, 16, 18, 19, 24, 33, 35, 38, 41, 42, 52, 84, 90, 106, 109, 138, 140, 144, 176, 178, 193, 273, 283
object of reference 113, 121, 123
object of thought 7, 117
objects of cognition 89, 104, 275
objects to verbs 101, 102, 106
observer 138, 144, 244
olfactory sense organ 44, 56, 57, 146
omnipresent self 154
omniscience 5, 60, 75, 103, 272, 274, 276, 277, 278, 279, 280, 281, 282, 284, 299, 315
omniscient interpreter 75, 276, 277, 278
optative sentences 212, 215
organ 36, 44, 56, 57, 88, 121, 129, 130, 139, 144, 145, 146, 147, 148, 149, 150, 151, 152, 153, 155, 163, 165, 192, 236, 244, 305, 306
orthodox Indian philosophers 147, 278
ostension 115, 226, 227, 250, 260
the other 39, 124, 125, 129, 134, 194, 197, 198, 202, 205, 206
other bodies 127, 134, 141, 202

otherness 5, 58, 134, 135, 136, 202, 240, 286, 287, 290
ownership 3, 9, 10, 11, 12, 13, 131, 133, 137, 138, 139, 140, 189, 192, 233, 234, 245, 292

pain 5, 15, 17, 18, 30, 60, 78, 79, 84, 85, 97, 100, 113, 116, 117, 120, 131, 132, 134, 135, 141, 149, 153, 163, 170, 179, 187, 188, 189, 191, 194, 199, 227, 249, 258, 279, 286, 309
pan-mentalism 77, 79, 80, 81, 82, 85, 88, 89, 275
paradox 29, 30, 58, 59, 121, 137, 143, 158, 159, 164, 233, 281, 282, 298
paradox of omniscience 281, 282
past 37, 39, 79, 81, 100, 104, 128, 129, 130, 132, 134, 152, 153, 175, 200, 202, 208, 217, 219, 240, 245, 248, 255, 256, 257, 258, 259, 260, 262, 263, 264, 265, 266, 267, 268, 269, 273, 279, 280, 281, 282, 283
past beliefs 53
past events 79, 104, 257
past experience 132, 217, 219
past objects 129, 130, 262
Patañjali 209, 276, 279, 280, 316
perceiving properties 35, 40, 41, 56, 252
perceiving universals 33, 36, 38, 43, 297, 324
perception-ascription 45
perception of absences 18, 57, 131, 244
perception of general features 27, 38, 248
perceptual awareness 16, 50, 58, 80, 83, 139, 149, 161, 162
perceptual cognition 84, 90, 160, 247
perceptual contact 15, 44, 66, 169, 219, 279
perceptual error 133, 169
perceptual experiences 16, 32, 40, 41, 50, 109, 133, 219, 236, 248, 274, 294
perceptual knowledge 32, 33, 46, 56, 70, 167, 211, 219, 281
perceptual recognition 32, 39
perceptual reduction 219
perfect being 279
performance 36, 146, 153, 206, 208, 209, 214, 215, 216, 217, 222, 265, 308
permanence 3, 11, 18, 68, 70, 71, 72, 73, 74, 81, 86, 127, 129, 133, 139, 140, 175, 275, 292, 304
permanent self 11, 70, 73, 81, 127, 133, 140, 175, 275, 304
phenomenalist argument 79, 80, 84, 127, 189
phenomenology 9, 15, 41, 66, 67, 85, 92, 93, 100, 102, 105, 123, 132, 137, 141, 142, 146, 147, 149, 162, 163, 218, 239, 242, 246, 290, 300, 308
philosophy of language 212, 222, 298, 319, 320
philosophy of mind 8, 101, 144, 167, 176, 178, 192, 200, 246
Plato 30, 33, 51, 57, 145, 185, 225, 233, 244, 245, 246, 302, 307, 313
Platonism 28, 32, 33, 41, 43, 228, 252
positionlessness 291
positive entities 239, 285, 290, 313
positive ignorance 74, 105, 245, 276, 312
Prābhākara Mīmāṃsā 39, 40, 140, 143, 161, 162, 286, 288
Pragmatism 51, 57, 180, 279
pragmatist definition of truth 51
pratyakṣa 45, 141, 280, 297, 301
prayer 123, 205, 209
pre-conceptual perception 25, 38, 246, 247, 250, 252
predicate of a judgment 13, 137
predication 5, 6, 13, 15, 23, 25, 26, 27, 28, 29, 30, 31, 32, 33, 35, 41, 42, 44, 46, 47, 48, 49, 50, 51, 53, 54, 56, 61, 86, 99, 116, 129, 130, 137, 138, 142, 144, 158, 171, 172, 185, 189, 190, 199, 200, 212, 216, 221, 226, 247, 248, 249, 250, 262, 263, 265, 279, 289, 295, 296, 303, 311, 314
predicative perception 47, 48, 49, 50, 56, 130, 247, 248, 249, 250
predicative structure of perception 46, 47
pre-predicative perception 46, 49, 139, 247, 250, 314
presence 39, 55, 72, 132, 143, 155, 181, 182, 186, 191, 199, 202, 227, 233, 237, 241, 243, 260, 285, 287, 288, 289, 290, 311
the present 37, 129, 130, 134, 144, 153, 256, 257, 258, 259, 263, 264, 268, 269, 270
present entities 17, 37, 128, 129, 144, 256, 257, 258, 259, 262, 264, 266, 267, 268, 269, 270, 281, 289

presentism 256, 258
prior awareness of particulars 47, 48
privacy 5, 7, 10, 69, 78, 113, 114, 115, 116, 118, 141, 155, 189, 191, 200, 209, 230, 251, 271
privacy of mental states 78, 141
private knowledge 209
private language 115, 200, 230
problematic idealism 70, 274
problem of agency 102
problem of induction 280
promising 255, 265, 266, 268
the pronoun "I" 17, 109, 121, 122, 142, 186
proof of the existence of 115, 185, 186
propertied particulars 247
properties 3, 5, 6, 12, 13, 14, 15, 16, 18, 19, 22, 23, 25, 26, 27, 28, 29, 30, 31, 32, 35, 36, 37, 38, 39, 40, 41, 42, 43, 44, 46, 47, 48, 51, 53, 54, 55, 56, 57, 58, 62, 63, 75, 77, 78, 80, 81, 83, 84, 86, 88, 89, 90, 96, 98, 99, 103, 105, 119, 133, 134, 137, 138, 157, 162, 165, 171, 176, 179, 187, 190, 197, 198, 212, 214, 216, 221, 236, 238, 240, 247, 249, 250, 252, 255, 258, 263, 269, 270, 273, 274, 275, 276, 280, 287, 288, 289, 290, 291, 294, 295, 302, 306, 311, 313
propositional content 222, 223
propositional knowledge 49
public language 114, 122, 123, 228, 249, 283
pure consciousness 63, 66, 69, 121, 151, 233, 281, 306
pure particulars 247

qualia 140, 164, 172, 176, 182
qualification 27, 28, 32, 47, 48, 49, 53, 55, 57, 58, 130, 138, 142, 158, 159, 160, 163, 164, 209, 212, 216, 219, 220, 235, 249, 250
qualitative identity 82, 97, 197
quantification 6, 27, 61, 122, 166, 179, 185, 212, 255, 257, 262, 263, 279, 290, 295
Quine, W. V. O. 22, 26, 28, 145, 170, 175, 185, 207, 218, 226, 251, 255, 263, 264, 287, 296, 308

Raghunātha 50, 83, 293, 302, 315
rationalism 225
Ratnakīrti 198, 199
realism about external objects 3, 10, 12, 13, 14, 16, 19, 21, 24, 25, 35, 52, 89, 247, 275
realism about inherence 75, 77
realism about perceived particulars 25, 26, 295
realism about the external world 77, 80, 81, 272, 274, 284
realism about the future 265, 266, 268, 271
realism about the past 273, 283
realism about the self 9, 14, 16, 19, 70, 81
realism about universals 3, 21, 27, 30, 32, 33, 35, 36, 40, 44, 81, 295
realism-links 9, 25, 26, 272, 282, 284
realisms 3, 4, 6, 8, 9, 10, 21, 25, 31, 40, 65, 81, 90, 284, 301
realist compatibilist position 141
realist-indeterminism 267
reality 5, 6, 7, 24, 26, 27, 52, 55, 62, 63, 65, 67, 68, 71, 74, 75, 81, 85, 94, 99, 100, 105, 136, 176, 177, 181, 183, 222, 236, 237, 251, 252, 256, 257, 262, 263, 265, 267, 268, 276, 279, 280, 282, 284, 289, 290, 293, 299, 309
reality of a philosophical problem 10
reasoning about universals 27, 36
recognitional capacities 43, 130, 253, 267, 283
recognition of absences 236, 237, 290
recognition of particulars 13, 21, 24, 26, 28, 38, 43, 44, 55, 128, 129, 130, 131, 132, 148, 247, 249, 250
recognition of truth 51, 52, 55, 56, 57, 62, 63, 80, 182, 265, 274
recognition of universals 28, 32, 38, 40, 41, 43, 44, 55, 150, 248, 249, 250, 252
reductio-arguments 56, 59, 72, 84, 131, 271, 299
reduction 3, 9, 10, 16, 25, 27, 46, 65, 79, 80, 86, 88, 89, 127, 131, 140, 149, 176, 177, 190, 217, 218, 219, 220, 236, 256, 265, 266, 267, 268, 269, 270, 275, 288
reductive anti-realism 3, 9, 16, 267, 268, 270
reference 5, 16, 27, 29, 31, 41, 42, 49, 54, 56, 62, 65, 67, 69, 72, 104, 109, 113, 114, 115, 116, 117, 118, 119, 120, 121, 122, 123, 125, 133, 139, 140, 142, 168, 171, 178, 179, 180, 182, 185, 186, 189, 198, 203, 205, 207, 209, 220, 226, 255,

256, 259, 260, 261, 262, 263, 265, 269, 270, 307
reference-theoretic sense 259, 264, 265
referent of "i" 113, 114, 118, 120, 123, 139, 142, 186
reflective judgment 145
reflexivism 160, 161, 162, 163, 164
reflexivity 12, 56, 60, 66, 77, 130, 131, 139, 140, 143, 144, 145, 146, 275, 294
refutations of idealism 3, 4, 18, 65, 68, 71, 75, 77, 81, 88, 274, 276, 300, 301, 314
relations 5, 7, 12, 15, 16, 18, 19, 23, 25, 26, 27, 31, 33, 42, 43, 44, 46, 50, 57, 63, 75, 77, 79, 80, 81, 83, 85, 86, 87, 88, 89, 90, 98, 99, 100, 102, 103, 108, 128, 130, 133, 135, 144, 179, 185, 189, 193, 197, 203, 212, 214, 218, 219, 220, 236, 273, 275, 288, 291, 295
relativism 45, 65, 105, 291
remembering 12, 14, 15, 39, 44, 60, 67, 79, 83, 104, 121, 128, 131, 132, 134, 135, 148, 149, 151, 180, 192, 193, 219, 237, 246, 250, 289
representation 17, 39, 48, 72, 73, 74, 133, 148, 155, 164, 177, 178, 188, 287, 292, 299, 309, 322
robust realism 24, 52, 79, 222, 237
Rushd, Ibn 154
Russell, Bertrand 31, 36, 50, 59, 93, 139, 142, 185, 186, 237, 268, 277, 288, 299, 305, 308, 309, 312, 315
Ryle, Gilbert 191, 192, 262, 300

sādhya 193, 194, 311
samavāya 77, 87, 89, 90
saṃkalpa 152
Sāṃkhya-Vedānta metaphysics 145, 146, 147, 152, 153, 154, 172, 269, 303, 306
Sāṃkhya-Yoga 152
Śaṅkara (Śaṅkarācārya) 65, 66, 67, 68, 69, 70, 71, 72, 74, 94, 141, 142, 143, 148, 155, 209, 244, 276, 297, 299, 300, 302, 305
Sanskrit 3, 4, 8, 22, 45, 102, 104, 108, 114, 120, 122, 127, 144, 145, 146, 147, 206, 207, 208, 209, 212, 213, 230, 231, 236, 285, 298, 302, 303, 310, 316, 317, 323, 325
Śāntarakṣita 279
second person 5, 116, 124, 175, 176, 194, 197, 200
seeing 3, 4, 11, 14, 17, 24, 28, 32, 35, 36, 37, 38, 39, 40, 41, 43, 45, 47, 68, 73, 79, 80, 82, 84, 85, 88, 100, 106, 107, 109, 125, 130, 132, 133, 134, 141, 144, 146, 147, 150, 151, 157, 158, 160, 161, 162, 163, 165, 166, 168, 169, 172, 183, 191, 192, 193, 198, 199, 215, 218, 219, 231, 234, 236, 237, 240, 241, 242, 243, 244, 245, 246, 247, 248, 249, 250, 252, 263, 281, 287, 299, 306, 307
the self 3, 4, 5, 9, 10, 11, 13, 14, 15, 16, 17, 18, 60, 68, 69, 72, 73, 77, 81, 86, 109, 113, 114, 115, 116, 117, 119, 120, 121, 122, 123, 124, 125, 127, 132, 136, 137, 138, 139, 140, 141, 142, 143, 144, 147, 149, 150, 151, 153, 154, 158, 161, 162, 165, 167, 168, 183, 185, 186, 187, 189, 190, 191, 192, 193, 194, 197, 202, 208, 280, 292, 293, 294, 304, 305, 306, 308, 309, 312
self-ascription of cognitive states 5, 117, 135, 157, 165, 167, 170, 171, 186, 200, 281
self-body identity 190
self-consciousness 5, 15, 69, 70, 115, 124, 125, 129, 135, 160, 168
self-illumination theory 40, 155, 161, 162, 163
self-intimation theory 14, 69, 139, 140, 143, 160, 161, 162, 164, 169
self-knowledge 13, 60, 72, 73, 117, 139, 141, 144, 167, 171, 172, 305
self-luminosity 66, 69, 121, 139, 140, 143, 151, 160, 161, 167, 301, 305
self-objectification 99, 142, 143, 144
self-perception 138, 142, 150, 162, 169
Sen, Pranab Kumar 29, 30, 31, 33, 35, 42, 44, 229, 296, 323
sensation 4, 11, 12, 13, 15, 16, 18, 46, 49, 68, 72, 78, 79, 88, 89, 106, 127, 134, 138, 140, 148, 149, 150, 151, 168, 175, 191, 192, 193, 227, 239, 248, 275, 298, 306
sense experience 15, 32, 35, 38, 138, 169, 170, 193, 247, 249, 293
sense-object contact 44, 45
sense of ego 120, 123

sense organ 17, 36, 44, 56, 57, 88, 129, 130, 134, 139, 141, 144, 145, 146, 147, 148, 149, 150, 151, 152, 153, 155, 165, 191, 192, 218, 236, 244, 280, 306
sense-perception 43, 45, 47, 79, 80, 141, 246, 293
sense-reference 118
sentence-awareness 107
sentence-forming 208
sentence-frame 171
sentence-holism 211
sentence-meaning 120, 128, 194, 207, 208, 229, 230, 291
sentences 5, 18, 29, 31, 42, 43, 49, 51, 53, 54, 59, 104, 106, 107, 113, 114, 117, 118, 119, 120, 128, 137, 138, 148, 152, 176, 178, 180, 192, 207, 208, 209, 212, 214, 215, 216, 218, 219, 220, 221, 222, 223, 225, 228, 229, 230, 251, 257, 260, 265, 266, 267, 268, 269, 270, 271, 277, 279, 288, 291, 299
sentence-token 113, 114
sentence-type 113
shade 41, 86, 234, 235, 236, 240, 241, 244, 245
shadows 6, 8, 231, 233, 234, 235, 236, 237, 238, 239, 240, 241, 242, 243, 244, 245, 246, 270, 276, 290, 312, 313
shared beliefs 277, 278
sheer darkness 235
Shoemaker, Sydney 115, 138, 139, 142, 160, 305
signs 105, 114, 125, 132, 187, 198, 199, 202, 226, 259, 276, 303, 311
simple universals 48
simulation theory 200, 201
sincerity 127, 176, 211, 236, 260, 265, 268, 269
singular names 206
singular referring 121
skepticism 51, 75, 91, 92, 95, 96, 99, 130, 144, 159, 183, 199, 200, 218, 223, 251, 278, 290
sleep 68, 91, 92, 93, 95, 107, 121, 131, 151, 181, 207, 236, 246, 306
Smart, J. J. C. 255, 257, 263, 314
smell 5, 11, 13, 30, 38, 44, 51, 56, 57, 146, 148, 149, 150, 151, 157, 218, 248
Socrates 29, 30, 32, 33, 47, 51, 54, 91, 95, 192, 260
solipsism 189, 197, 199, 223
space 5, 6, 17, 32, 33, 40, 41, 65, 70, 71, 72, 74, 81, 82, 84, 85, 87, 116, 125, 149, 166, 186, 188, 193, 238, 239, 245, 263, 273, 274, 276, 282, 300, 315
the speaker 5, 29, 103, 104, 107, 108, 113, 115, 119, 120, 124, 179, 203, 208, 212, 213, 214, 216, 218, 219, 220, 221, 222, 223, 228, 230
speaker intention 107, 208, 212, 214
speech-acts 205, 209, 222, 256, 268
speech-generated awareness 212
spiritual exercise 93
spiritual sciences 279, 280
Śrīdhara 293, 313
Śrīharṣa 51
statement-realism 26, 179
Strawson, Peter F. 5, 6, 15, 21, 22, 26, 27, 28, 29, 30, 31, 32, 33, 35, 40, 44, 115, 116, 118, 125, 180, 189, 199, 200, 247, 248, 249, 251, 252, 257, 293, 295, 296, 297, 298, 300, 301, 304, 309, 310, 311, 314
subject-center 140
subjecthood 123, 135, 139, 209
subjectifying 203, 205
subjective failure 289
subjective feel 15, 164
subjectivity 66, 69, 74, 75, 97, 100, 114, 124, 134, 135, 136, 183, 194, 197, 202, 205, 292
subject-matter 6, 55, 137, 305
subject of experience 3, 5, 13, 115, 138
subjects 3, 4, 5, 7, 11, 13, 14, 15, 17, 21, 28, 37, 42, 47, 57, 72, 73, 74, 75, 77, 86, 94, 99, 102, 106, 109, 111, 113, 115, 116, 120, 123, 124, 130, 131, 134, 135, 136, 137, 138, 139, 140, 141, 142, 144, 147, 149, 153, 158, 160, 161, 162, 167, 168, 169, 171, 172, 186, 191, 192, 193, 194, 195, 197, 198, 203, 209, 212, 216, 219, 221, 230, 275, 279, 284, 291, 292, 294
subject-terms 6, 101, 142, 185, 211
substance 6, 7, 13, 15, 18, 31, 32, 42, 44, 51, 57, 60, 69, 73, 75, 77, 79, 80, 84, 85, 86, 87, 89, 149, 152, 186, 187, 188, 189,

190, 191, 192, 193, 194, 218, 233, 239, 242, 243, 246, 287, 293, 294, 313
substances 3, 6, 30, 32, 44, 57, 77, 81, 86, 87, 88, 186, 189, 190, 191, 214, 218, 239, 242, 243, 313
substantial self 9, 10, 13, 14, 27, 42, 56, 66, 86, 88, 123, 127, 131, 140, 176, 192, 294
suffering 5, 18, 45, 81, 97, 106, 119, 120, 135, 149, 183, 197, 206, 246, 255, 261, 279, 280, 292
the supreme person 114, 121

Tarski, Alfred 43, 279, 298
taste 3, 9, 11, 13, 19, 30, 38, 43, 44, 48, 86, 130, 141, 148, 149, 150, 151, 155, 217, 218, 236, 248, 281, 297
tasting universals 297
techne 230
telling 38, 93, 118, 124, 138, 165, 171, 172, 173, 183, 200, 209, 213, 217, 219, 223, 228, 229, 250
testimonial knowledge 57, 152, 211, 215, 216, 217, 218, 219, 220, 221, 222, 223, 228, 249, 311, 314
theism 272, 278
theories of objecthood 103, 105, 106, 107
Theory-Theory 200, 201
thought 6, 7, 9, 10, 11, 12, 18, 27, 28, 33, 36, 37, 40, 41, 42, 49, 50, 51, 52, 54, 55, 56, 57, 65, 72, 73, 74, 75, 77, 78, 82, 99, 100, 102, 104, 117, 118, 120, 137, 148, 169, 170, 187, 189, 193, 203, 211, 222, 226, 237, 246, 247, 251, 252, 257, 258, 267, 276, 283, 284, 288
thought-experiments 92, 171, 172
time 5, 6, 9, 12, 13, 14, 15, 16, 22, 23, 33, 37, 39, 40, 41, 50, 57, 58, 60, 61, 71, 72, 73, 82, 89, 91, 100, 101, 127, 128, 129, 130, 131, 133, 134, 135, 148, 153, 167, 176, 186, 188, 193, 208, 253, 255, 256, 258, 260, 263, 264, 265, 266, 270, 280, 282, 294
touch 3, 9, 11, 12, 13, 17, 23, 30, 38, 42, 56, 65, 85, 97, 101, 123, 141, 146, 147, 148, 149, 151, 161, 162, 163, 169, 192, 193, 218, 242, 248, 276, 294, 313
Tractatus Logico-Philosophicus 25, 80, 81, 85, 114, 222, 284
tranquility 154
transcendental arguments 44, 131, 132, 133, 203
transcendental deduction 148, 193
transcendental subject 72, 73, 120, 294
translation 42, 113, 176, 182, 198, 203, 206, 207, 208, 209, 216, 230, 257, 266, 267, 270, 271
trust 73, 146, 152, 158, 159, 191, 211, 212, 213, 215, 217, 218, 221, 277
truth and belief 31, 53, 54, 55, 57, 58, 59, 97, 159, 166, 175, 228, 277, 278, 282, 299
truth-bearers 18, 31, 52, 62
truth-conditions 49, 179, 265, 271, 274, 283, 285, 299
truth-telling 213, 228
Turner, J. M. W. 235, 312, 313

Udayana 10, 11, 16, 17, 30, 45, 49, 50, 55, 58, 59, 62, 77, 78, 81, 82, 84, 85, 89, 90, 95, 97, 99, 100, 145, 186, 275, 282, 294, 295, 296, 302, 304, 308
Uddyotakara 97, 185, 186, 187, 188, 189, 291, 308, 309
understanding 5, 13, 18, 33, 43, 48, 99, 104, 113, 118, 128, 171, 176, 177, 180, 194, 197, 201, 211, 212, 213, 214, 215, 216, 218, 219, 221, 222, 223, 225, 226, 227, 228, 229, 230, 231, 246, 249, 250, 251, 253, 260, 265, 266, 267, 268, 271, 274, 277, 278, 282, 283, 298, 301, 307
unimaginable 65, 276, 285
uniqueness 38, 39, 44, 48, 86, 87, 88, 107, 113, 123, 124, 135, 142, 146, 149, 194, 197, 212, 230, 260, 261, 262
universal 6, 18, 19, 21, 22, 23, 28, 30, 31, 32, 33, 36, 37, 38, 39, 40, 41, 42, 43, 44, 48, 51, 52, 54, 55, 57, 58, 59, 60, 61, 62, 68, 69, 71, 77, 86, 99, 101, 122, 125, 127, 135, 198, 199, 202, 242, 251, 258, 279, 280, 281, 285, 287, 289, 290, 291, 296, 297, 310
universal-blockers 30, 57, 296
universal concomitance 198, 199, 202
universal knowability thesis 52, 59, 60, 61, 62
universal quantification 61, 122, 279, 290
universals 3, 10, 21, 22, 23, 25, 26, 27, 28, 29, 30, 31, 32, 33, 35, 36, 38, 40, 41, 43,

44, 48, 49, 52, 57, 58, 75, 78, 81, 88, 176, 189, 214, 242, 250, 251, 252, 284, 287, 295, 296, 297, 316
universals, language-independent 35
universals, mind-independent 23, 31, 35, 36
universal subject 135
universal unreality 290
universe 6, 135, 233, 243, 257, 263, 268, 279, 280, 281, 285, 312
unknowability 17, 24, 27, 52, 53, 62, 63, 71, 79, 81, 277, 284
unsayability 25, 48, 50
unteachable understanding 225, 227
untrustworthy inference 73
unverbalizable 44, 45, 47, 49, 50, 250
upādhi 23, 58
Upaniṣads 121, 139, 145, 152, 162, 197, 302, 305, 306, 312
utterance 5, 22, 48, 58, 59, 103, 113, 114, 118, 119, 120, 121, 125, 128, 148, 166, 176, 201, 202, 211, 212, 213, 214, 215, 216, 217, 218, 219, 220, 221, 222, 223, 227, 228, 230, 260, 267, 269, 270, 278, 311

Vācaspati 97, 187, 188, 250
Vaiśeṣika 57, 60, 84, 85, 86, 87, 88, 95, 147, 153, 186, 189, 243, 293, 294, 313
Vallabha 94, 95, 96, 97, 302
Vasubandhu 12, 84, 85, 91, 294
Vātsyāyana 45, 47, 86, 128, 187, 192, 193, 213, 250, 311
veil of ignorance 197, 233, 245
verb 7, 59, 101, 102, 103, 104, 105, 106, 107, 108, 115, 127, 137, 152, 162, 179, 207, 208, 209, 213, 214, 215, 216, 227, 229, 250
veridical awareness 52, 55, 158, 246, 287
virtue 42, 51, 157, 177, 281
viṣaya (object of knowledge) 4, 108
visual illusions 240
visual objects 235
visual perception 39, 41, 84, 148, 162, 242, 243
void 251, 284, 286, 287, 290, 292
volition 15, 146, 186, 188, 215
Vyāsatīrtha 91, 98, 99, 102, 103, 120, 121, 158, 159, 303

Western analytic tradition 94, 215, 277
Western psychology 154
will 86, 107, 145, 181, 198, 201, 266, 280
witness-consciousness 69, 105, 163
Wittgenstein, Ludwig 7, 14, 25, 27, 80, 85, 102, 107, 108, 113, 114, 115, 116, 117, 123, 135, 141, 142, 144, 145, 171, 222, 227, 235, 249, 259, 261, 278, 294, 297, 303, 305, 310, 311, 314
word-generated knowledge 211, 212, 217, 221, 223
the world 4, 5, 6, 7, 8, 16, 27, 37, 63, 66, 70, 72, 74, 75, 78, 79, 80, 81, 89, 93, 97, 98, 99, 100, 147, 159, 170, 179, 197, 203, 209, 218, 222, 223, 228, 248, 249, 250, 251, 252, 256, 257, 273, 277, 278, 279, 280, 283, 284, 287, 288, 289, 292, 297, 302, 303, 312, 315

yoga 135, 153, 276, 278, 280, 292, 308, 316
Yogācāra 18, 36, 69, 77, 78, 81, 82, 84, 89, 102, 117, 140, 162, 163, 176, 198, 199, 275, 276, 304, 307
Yogavāsiṣṭha 91, 92, 93, 302
you 3, 4, 5, 6, 11, 13, 107, 109, 114, 116, 123, 124, 125, 136, 171, 194, 197, 198, 199, 200, 201, 202, 205, 208, 209, 212
Yuktidīpikā 152